The

Genogram Journey

Also by Monica McGoldrick

Genograms: Assessment and Intervention, Third Edition
with Randy Gerson and Sueli Petry

Women in Families: A Framework for Family Therapy
with Carol Anderson and Froma Walsh

Living Beyond Loss, Second Edition
with Froma Walsh

The
Genogram Journey

Reconnecting
with Your Family

Monica McGoldrick

W. W. Norton & Company
New York • London

For information about permission to reproduce
selections from this book,
write to Permissions, W. W. Norton & Company, Inc.
500 Fifth Avenue, New York, NY 10110

For information about special discounts for bulk
purchases, please contact
W. W. Norton Special Sales at
specialsales@wwnorton.com or 800-233-4830.

Composition and book design by Molly Heron
Manufacturing by Quad Graphics Fairfield
Production Manager: Leeann Graham

Library of Congress Cataloging-in-Publication Data

McGoldrick, Monica.
The genogram journey : reconnecting with your
family /
Monica McGoldrick. – Rev. ed.
p. cm.

Previously published under title: *You Can Go Home
Again.*
Includes bibliographical references and index.
ISBN 978-0-393-70627-7 (pbk.)
1. Families–Psychological aspects. 2. Family
assessment.
3. Genealogy. I. Title.

HQ518.M38 2011
306.87--dc22
2010027653

ISBN: 978-0-393-70627-7 (pbk.)
W. W. Norton & Company, Inc.,
500 Fifth Avenue, New York, N.Y. 10110
www.wwnorton.com
W. W. Norton & Company Ltd.,
15 Carlisle Street, London W1D 3BS

2 3 4 5 6 7 8 9 0

All the genograms for this book were drawn with the software GenoPro. While they have been modified here to maximize their visibility, the GenoPro software allows readers to reproduce these genograms with virtually all their features, including the insertion of pictures.

I am extremely grateful to Dan Morin for the efforts he put in over the past several years to make GenoPro, originally a genealogy charting system, conform to the format for genograms that has been developed over the past three decades through a collaboration of family therapists, family physicians, and others interested in this extremely useful tool.

Because GenoPro stores genograms in XML, an open database format, researchers will soon be able to examine data from multiple genograms, making it possible to track family patterns over generations and across families and cultures.

In the future, GenoPro plans to release a "collaboration module" enabling multiple users to edit the same genogram. Although this collaboration module is designed for geographically distant family members to work together via the Internet to create a common shared database of their family tree, it will be equally useful for family therapists who want to share genograms with each other and with their clients, allowing them, for example, to complete their genograms at home before a session.

All readers are welcome to download GenoPro from www.genopro.com/genogramformat. This version of GenoPro has specialized settings to display the genogram symbols used in this book. This version is being offered for free for the first six months, after which the user is welcome to purchase GenoPro for a one-time fee ($49.00 as of this book's printing).

Please note: All technical questions regarding the software should be directed to www.genopro.com

FOR MY MOTHER

who taught me that it is possible to repair a cutoff and come to love someone with whom you have had profound conflicts. I believe that it is not so much our mothers who have let us down as it is the yardsticks by which we have measured them. I dedicate this book to her for her courage as a woman and for her willingness to keep growing until her last breath. She lives in my heart every day.

AND FOR BETTY CARTER

my mentor, soul mate, and sister, with whom I thought through so many of the issues discussed here about how to reconnect with your family. I dedicate this book to her in gratitude for her love, humor, and brilliance in systems thinking, and for the blessing of over 30 years of collaboration with her.

Contents

Acknowledgments

Thanks are due to many people for their support on the material in this book. This book is dedicated to my mother, Helen McGoldrick, for her belief in me and her encouragement through the decade I was developing the original edition of this book.

This book is also dedicated to my friend Betty Carter, who was like my second mother, my mentor, friend, and closest collaborator for 30 years. The ideas in this book evolved out of many conversations with her over the years about theory, about teaching, about clients, about our families, and about our lives. No words can express my appreciation for her generosity and creativity in helping me think about how to help people change their family relationships. No one has had a better mentor or friend than I have had in her.

My husband has been a crucial part of my sense of "home" since we first met in 1968. I am very grateful to him for his support and for our many years together. Our wonderful son John went from birth to young manhood as the book evolved. I have been so blessed to have him in my life over these past 25 years and he has "grown me up" as I helped him grow up. It has been the greatest joy of my life.

I am also grateful to my sisters, Neale and Morna, for all they have meant to me in my life and for their role in my sense of home. My nephews, Guy and Hugh, though far away are also deeply part of my sense of rootedness and belonging. Guy has been my graphics consultant for many years and I thank him specifically for his suggestions on photos, genograms, and stories for this book. He has been a great resource.

My formal and informal godchildren have also been a major inspiration: Natalie, Ariane, and Stephan Baer; Irini Syrcos; Maria Anderson; Claire Whitney; Patti, Gina, Ryan, Terry, and Christiana Thanos; and Irene and Gabe Berkowitz. This book is also for them as the next generation.

Many dear friends and colleagues offered direct and indirect support throughout the years of writing and rewriting this book. Carol Anderson, Froma Walsh, Nydia Garcia Preto, Paulette Hines, Nollaig and Henry Byrne, Imelda McCarthy, Ken Hardy, John Folwarski, Jayne Mahboubi, Michael Rohrbaugh, Kalli Adamides, Fernanda Fihlo, Robert Jay Green, Charlotte

Fremon Danielson, Nancy Boyd and A. J. Franklin, Elaine Pinderhughes, Barbara Petkov, Sueli Petry, Roberto Font, Fernando Colon, Glenn Wolf, Salome Raheim, Vanessa Jackson, and Vanessa Mahmoud were all important resources for me, though they may not have realized the role they were playing. Randy Gerson was a collaborator in developing the concept of genograms, and for his amazing creativity in creating computerized genograms and his enthusiasm for the concept I will always be grateful. My trainees and clients have been a wellspring of insights and have inspired me by their courage in dealing with the hard issues in their families.

Dan Morin, the developer of Genopro (www.genopro.com), has become a trusted friend in the course of writing the second edition. The genograms in this book conform to his Genopro program, which not only draws genograms but also creates a database, and has the potential to help us study patterns in multiple families over generations. Creation of such a program to develop a database to study genogram patterns has been a dream of mine since 1980, when I first discovered that Randy Gerson had developed a computerized genogram graphic. Randy and I sought support for years to develop a computerized genogram database with which we could research families. Dan's program is the start of such a system, which will hopefully be fully developed over the next few years for this exact purpose. I am very grateful for his efforts to make his program conform to the conventions that have been worked out and for his creativity in improving his system for the use of clinicians. Dan was a real trooper as this book came to fruition, working day and night to make his program conform to the genogram standards and thinking creatively how to develop a user friendly product to help us all map out family patterns. I owe him a great debt for his dedication to the development of this amazing tool. Fran Snyder and Agi Sanchez kept our office going, which left me free to focus on this project, and for their support I am very grateful. Ben Forest, our enthusiastic computer consultant, spent many hours helping us figure out and coordinate the genograms and the text for this book. His support has also been essential for this project. Thanks also to Leeann Graham and Adrian Kitzinger of Norton for their work on the genograms that appear in the book.

Anna DePalma came into my life at just the right time to help with the photo editing, and with her wonderful eye and great organizational skill she helped me tremendously with the complex organization of pictures. And Tracey Laszloffy, a respected colleague for many years, has become in the last months of editing a trusted friend and a wonderful collaborator on the manuscript. I am deeply grateful for her brilliance, writing skill, enthusiasm for this book, and collaboration, especially on Chapter 9. I am especially grateful to Gary Jaffe who came in at the last minute to work on the genograms and worked with me tirelessly for weeks on end to get the photos and genograms into shape. This book owes a great deal to his care, hard work, good eye, and I owe him many thanks. My deep thanks also to my friend and lawyer, Brian Fleisig, who has helped me steer through many difficult shoals in publishing for years. He has been a wonderful mentor and kept me sane through some very difficult struggles as this book developed. Having good counsel is indeed a great gift.

Finally, the Norton editorial board and especially my editors, Andrea Costella and Deborah Malmud, have believed in this book and have been an incredible support for this second edition and all my Norton projects. Libby Burton was extremely generous in her efforts with picture permissions, which could have been a real nightmare. Her work on permissions has made a tremendous difference in the ability of this book to convey the stories of its participants. To my copyeditor, Casey Ruble, I owe a special debt of gratitude for caring so much about the writing—the ideas and the genograms themselves. And to Vani Kannan, who has overseen the last stages of birthing this book, I am also tremendously grateful. No one can know how much the editorial efforts on a book mean to its author, and I have been blessed indeed with Norton's support. I am extremely grateful for Norton's interest in the project and the enormous help and support they have given me in bringing this book to fruition.

Preface

In his novel *Roots*, Alex Haley tells of Omoro Kinte talking to his son, Kunta Kinte, about the death of his beloved grandmother, Yaisa. Omoro explains that every community has three different sets of people: those whom Yaisa had just jointed in eternity; those among whom Omoro and Kunta walked in their daily life; and those who are the people of the future, waiting to be born, who will replace them both, first the father and then the son, when they join the grandmother in eternity, sooner than they might realize (Haley, 1976).

I published the first edition of this book in 1995. I felt the need to update it now—15 years later—thanks to new information about some of the families previously described, information that helps to illustrate the key issues of the book. In the intervening years I have also had new thoughts that have made me even more powerfully motivated to encourage people to pay attention to those to whom we belong. We are at risk of losing our center if we do not appreciate how much we are all linked in our journey through life and how much we need to find ways to hold on to our connections. As James Baldwin once said, in a quote I have remembered all my life: "The moment we cease to hold each other, the sea engulfs us and the light goes out" (1976, p. 706).

This book is meant for family therapists and other clinicians, their clients, and anyone who wants to understand his or her family and change problematic, conflictual, or cut-off relationships. The book grew out of my own efforts to "go home again"—efforts that began more than 30 years ago when I first learned of Murray Bowen's ideas about family systems and began to try to change my role in my own family. Through exploring my family history, I came to love my powerful and vulnerable mother more deeply. I came to acknowledge my sweet, brilliant, funny father's limitations in ways that did not make me love him less, but did enable me to love my mother more.

I spent many years doing genealogical research on my family as well as tracking down relatives from Wyoming to "the Glen" near Ballybofey, in County Donegal in Ireland, and Leap, near Skibbereen. My personal journey made me realize that I am a part of all that came before, and that all generations must pay attention to the legacy we leave to our children and our children's children.

For four decades I have been teaching family therapy and trying to enrich others with the power of systems theory, which has made so much difference in my own life. My earlier book, *Genograms: Assessment and Intervention*, now in its third edition, explains the principles and practice behind building a family genogram. I have become so enamored of genograms that I can never read a book without doing the genogram of the characters. I hope you will be as fascinated and inspired as I have been by the stories of the famous families described here and will feel empowered to work on transforming your own life through a systemic understanding of your role in your family and the families of your clients.

I believe that we should do the genograms of our heroes, our governmental leaders, and the theorists whose teachings we follow to better understand their strengths and limitations, just as we would benefit from examining the genograms of the authors of the *Diagnostic and Statistical Manual of Mental Disorders* (DSM), who have described the supposed characteristics of mental illness.

So that you have some idea of the person who is talking to you here, I want to say a bit about my own history. I am the middle of three sisters, a fourth-generation Irish American. Born in Brooklyn in 1943 (raised on the Brooklyn Dodgers), I grew up from age 6 on a farm in Solebury, Pennsylvania. My mother was one of the most interesting women I have ever known, and I struggled with her for all the years of my childhood, adolescence, and young adulthood. She graduated from Barnard, class of '34. She gave up a successful career in public relations to marry my father, whom she adored for all of their 37 years together. My father, a well-known reform politician in New York City, was also a lawyer and a professor of political science. In fact, I come from a family of teachers (including both my sisters, all the in-laws, and all but one of the members of my parents' generation). My adored caretaker, Margaret Pfeiffer Bush—an African American from Asheville, North Carolina, who, because of racism, did not learn how to read until after I did—ran the family along with my mother and was the person to whom I was closest throughout childhood although she was the "servant" in the pernicious racial arrangement of privileged families in the U.S. My father was a beloved visiting dignitary on weekends.

My great Aunt Mamie was our "Santa Claus." And Uncle Raymond shared with me his enjoyment of music and of the Russian language, and was thrilled that I brought another physicist into the family (my husband).

I also had a wonderful informal family, including Elliot Mottram, my uncle's high-school friend, and his wife, Marie, who convinced my father to buy the farm next to theirs in Solebury. They were lifelong friends of my parents, and godparents to all of us.

In terms of our extended family, we were close only to my Aunt Mamie. My mother's mother could charm us with her piano rendition of the "Golliwog Cakewalk," but it was not until later that I was able to make connections with our other extended family, including my dear cousin Hughie and the other McGoldricks in Donegal, Ireland. From Hughie I learned several important family secrets, which helped me understand my family and myself more deeply. All the McGoldricks from the Glen now live in my heart, as do Patsy and Curley Cahalane, Tadg Wholley and all the other Cahalanes from Cork, with whom I reconnected, once I found them in 1975. With a background in Russian studies in college and graduate school—my theses were on Dostoevsky and Pushkin—I fell in love with counseling and therapy and switched to social work (my thesis was on children's humor in psychotherapy). With the advent of the mental-health-center movement in the late 1960s, I began family therapy. My areas of special interest have included culture, class, gender, race, couples, the life cycle, schizophrenia, remarried families, sibling relationships, intermarriage, family therapy with one person, and the impact of loss on families. For many years I taught at the Robert Wood Johnson Medical School in the Psychiatry Department and at their Community Mental Health Center, before becoming director of the Multicultural Family Institute in central New Jersey in 1991.

In my excitement about genograms as a way to understand family systems, I came to the idea of using the stories of famous families to convey systems ideas in an understandable way. Hopefully this second edition will engage therapists, counselors, clients, and a general audience in learning to understand themselves and their families, in finding a sense of "home," and in transforming their own role in their family system wherever it is not working for them.

MONICA McGOLDRICK
August 2010

The
Genogram Journey

1 Why Go Home Again?

To go home may be impossible, but it is often a driving necessity, or at least a compelling dream. . . . Home is a concept, not a place; it is a state of mind where self-definition starts; it is origins—the mix of time and place and smell and weather wherein one first realizes one is an original. . . . Home . . . remains in the mind as a place where reunion, if it were ever to occur, would happen. . . . It is about restoration of the right relations among things— and going home is where that restoration occurs, because that is where it matters most.

Take Time for Paradise
—A. BARTLETT GIAMATTI

Our family is, except in rare circumstances, the most important emotional system to which most of us ever belong; it shapes the course and outcome of our lives. Relationships and functioning (physical, social, emotional, and spiritual) are interdependent, and a change in one part of the system is followed by compensatory change in other parts of the system. This, of course, makes the family our greatest potential resource as well as our greatest potential source of stress. This book's aim is to show that at the deepest level we are all a part of all that our families have been and that keeping our connections matters. Becoming a "researcher" on family patterns and history is the best way to start the process of understanding relationships that may have been frustrating, boring, tense, or painful. This book will help you embark on a lifelong undertaking to understand your own family in a new way and will help therapists learn the skills to help their clients do the same. This involves learning or relearning family stories so that you can judge the so-called villains and victims for yourself. The research starts by examining the basic facts about your family—the details of births, deaths, relationships, moves, weddings, lawsuits, and wills—the nitty-gritty of life. The charged emotional experiences of family history are hidden in these events. By collecting the material that forms your family tree and understanding your genogram, you can survey the family over multiple generations. As you consider further details about relationships and events, you can clarify the chronology of the family's history. Mapping a family in this way can be the start of a fascinating and profoundly rewarding journey.

Because family patterns, once established, tend to be perpetuated by everyone involved in them, not all family members have equal power or influence on family processes. Given the reciprocal aspect of all relationships, each person's individual participation in any system is all he or she can change. Cause-and-effect thinking—which asks "why?"—tends to blame someone for the problem, however unwittingly, and does not seem as useful as identifying patterns and tracing their flow.

When a person changes his or her predictable emotional input in a family, reactions also change, interrupting the previous flow of interactions in the family. Other family members are likely to be jarred out of their patterned responses, and to react by trying to get the disrupter back into place again. In two-person subsystems, such as married couples or parent-child relationships, the element of reciprocity of emotional functioning can be striking, as in enduring marriages of the sinner and the saint, the dreamer and the doer, or the optimist and the pessimist, or in relationships such as the nagging parent and dawdling child. This is not to say that the power of both partners to change a relationship or resolve the problem is equal. For example, women and children have decidedly less power to influence the social structure than do men; the poor, people of color, and those in the lesbian/gay/bisexual/transgender (LGBT) community are highly disadvantaged in their freedom to change existing social structures; and those whose spiritual perspective is not part of the mainstream are disadvantaged within the larger social system. But this does not mean that relationships are not reciprocal. Rather, one must factor in the dimension of power in order to think clearly about how to change them.

Failure to acknowledge the disparities of opportunity and power that exist within our society mystifies those who are in an oppressive, inequitable situation and are not on an even playing field. Women have long been expected to put the needs of others before their own. Even to define their own values, wishes, or opinions has generally been seen as selfishness. People of color are raised to be deferential to whites and to tolerate the privileges that whites have in this society. They must fight harder for any opportunities they get and work hard not to be derailed by the prejudice and slights they experience on an everyday basis. Gays and lesbians are told by official U.S. policy and by social attitudes and laws that their relationships are not legitimate. Heterosexual white males who try to define themselves will generally be responded to with respect; women, people of color, gays, lesbians, bisexuals, and those who are not of the dominant religious groups who try to define themselves may be penalized, ostracized, or even harmed by the family or community. Thus, our assessment of a person's development must include assessment of social obstacles to accomplishing the tasks that lead to maturity.

Emotional maturity is a measure of the extent to which individuals are able to follow their own values and self-directed life course within their particular social context, while being emotionally present with others, rather than living reactively by the cues of those close to them. They do not spend their life energy on winning approval, attacking others, intellectualizing, keeping themselves emotionally walled off, or maneuvering in relationships to obtain control or emotional comfort. They can move freely from emotional closeness in person-to-person relationships to work on their personal life goals. They can calmly state their beliefs or feelings (or, when appropriate, refrain from stating their feelings or beliefs)—without having to attack others or defend themselves. In their personal relationships they can relate warmly and openly without needing to focus on others or on activities or impersonal things in order to find common ground.

In cultures that focus on family or community functioning rather than on the individual, expressions of individuality will look different than in Anglo-European contexts. Ignoring such cultural differences leads to errors, such as an Anglo therapist thinking that daily phone calls in a Latino or Jewish family indicate fusion in the same way they might in an Anglo family. A client from a younger generation who is angrily and defiantly adopting mainstream American norms over the objections of immigrant parents may be undermining important cultural values for harmony. A therapist/coach may need to help the client understand where the parents are coming from and find more culturally congruent, respectful ways of disagreeing, if at all possible.

This book is about helping people explore their most important connections in life: the ties to family, to those people who gave them their first concept of "home." It is based on the principle that the more we know about our families, the more we can know about ourselves, and the more freedom we have to determine how we want to live.

Such self-understanding is essential for clinicians and educators, so that we can offer our wisdom, creativity, and resilience, and not replay in our work problems we have failed to understand from our own histories. Even the worst and most painful family experiences—alcoholism, sexual abuse, suicide—are part of our accumulated identity. Only by understanding what led to those behaviors can we begin to understand the dark side of ourselves and learn to relate more fully to others.

And only by learning about our families and their history—getting to know, over several generations, what made them tick, how they related, what secrets they kept, and where they got stuck—can we really understand our own role, not simply as victim or reactor to our experiences but as an active player in interactions that repeat themselves over and over in our family dramas. Learning about our family heritage can free us to change the part we play and thus change our future.

The notion of "family" is deeply tied to the sense of who we are in the world. We resemble other members of our family. Their quirks and gestures are similar to ours. Our family members have been there (or we believe they *should* have been there) at all the important occasions of our lives—births, marriages, graduations, illness, deaths.

However, we often feel that if our families cannot acknowledge us, love us, and support us, no one else will. No matter how old we are, no matter how distant emotionally or physically, family still seems to matter. These relationships are our most important in life, yet we often fail to connect with family members; we cannot find the door that opens up communication. Some may say that it does not matter if we never loved our parents or siblings or they us, but it does matter. However far we travel in miles or achievements, our family belongs to us and we belong to them. Indeed, our experiences in our first families are often repeated with our marriage partners and children, sometimes in strange and eerie ways.

Family will inevitably come back to haunt us—in our relationships with our spouses, our children, our friends, and even at work. Beneath each family's particular idiosyncrasies lie patterns that cut across cultural and time differences. And though the specifics of family structure and roles are changing rapidly and dramatically, the basic ways that families relate are universal.

More than a hundred years ago, Abraham Lincoln (see page 234 for genogram), who did so much to create the right relations among people, refused to be in contact with his dying father, whom he had not visited in 20 years, saying: "If we could meet now, it is doubtful whether it would not be more painful than pleasant" (Oates, 1977, p. 103). Lincoln's frank hopelessness about changing his relationship with his father, who had apparently been abusive to him in childhood, is familiar to many adults today. In spite of Lincoln's brilliance and clarity on so many issues affecting our nation as a whole, his pessimism about his father led him to miss the possibility that in that final encounter something different might have happened. It is not much different today, when many outwardly successful people seem incapable of relating to members of their own families, unable to look into their fathers' hearts, so they do not die as strangers. In *The Prince of Tides*, Pat Conroy described the complex power of family connections in a meeting of the narrator's sister and their abusive father:

There was something I . . . felt as they ran to each other. . . . in the deepest part of me, an untouched place that trembled with something instinctual and rooted in the provenance of the species. . . . It was not [my sister's] tears or my father's tears that caused this resonance, this fierce interior music of blood and wildness and identity. It was the beauty and fear of kinship, the ineffable ties of family, that sounded a blazing terror and an awestruck love inside of me. (1988, p. 660)

What is it that makes approaching our families so hard? Why are we obsessed with how we are doing with our marriages and our children, while we tend to ignore our parents and siblings? Why is it that so many people seem locked into boring or painful routines with their families or running away from home?

Most people recognize the emotional price they pay for maintaining a "non-relationship" with important family members. Not to be in contact with your family is an intense experience, because deep down you cannot help longing for something more gratifying. If two sisters do not speak for 40 years, each experiences a profound loss. They may resemble each other, have the same voice and mannerisms, and have a shared history that belongs only to them. Anyone who happens to suggest that they both appear at the same family event will realize the intensity of feeling behind their apparent lack of connection.

Throughout this book famous people and their families are presented, often with their family tree or genograms to illustrate family patterns and to offer suggestions about how to change them. The particular families were chosen because of the patterns they illustrate and because biographical material was available over several generations. The stories here are incomplete, mainly because I am only showing certain facets of the family to make a point. In truth, remarkably few biographers recognize the relevance of family context for their subjects, and it was difficult to find famous people for whom family material was available. I regret any inaccuracies in my information, but as we know, family histories are always incomplete and information is always skewed by the misremembering, distortion or fantasy, and elaboration of family members, and we must do the best we can with whatever we can learn.

Although each family is unique in its particular history, all families are similar in their underlying patterns. Famous families are undoubtedly influenced by their notoriety, but all families have basic ways of dealing with love, pain, and conflict, making sense of life, and bridging time, class, and cultural barriers. All families must find ways of dealing with loss and of integrating new members. Thus, in terms of emotional process, famous families are as "ordinary" or "unique" as any other.

Many people would prefer to downplay family history. Sigmund Freud (see page 172 for genogram), who has probably influenced our thinking about human behavior more than anyone else, focused almost exclusively on the importance of childhood fantasies about parents, ignoring the realities of parents' lives, the role of siblings, and the importance of the extended family. Were there secrets in the Freud family that he dared not talk about? Recent research suggests that there were, but it is interesting that so many of Freud's biographers have gone along with his blind spot about exploring the family. One would assume, for example, that, given Freud's own theories, his biographers would be interested in his mother, who lived to be 95 years of age. But little attention has ever been paid to her role in their family. We know nothing of her relationships with her parents, her siblings, or her early life. Why not? Did Freud never ask her? As might be expected, Freud's theories seem to have been shaped by his own personal family history, in which there was much he wanted to ignore, keep secret, or forget. He wrote about himself that he felt like the heir of "all the passions of our ancestors, when they defended their temple" (Freud, 1975, p. 202) and he did his best to be sure that his own family history would be told the way he intended—with the stories he himself could not handle erased. He destroyed many personal and family records, embarrassed, as so many are, by the mental illness and criminal acts of various family members. At least one of his secrets, his affair with his sister-in-law, Minna, was kept secret for almost 100 years and only confirmed recently by serendipitous findings.

But in truth, it is not possible to destroy our history. It lives on inside us, probably the more powerful for our attempts to bury it. We and our families are likely to pay a high price in the present for trying to block out the past. Attempts to cover up family history tend to fester, influencing others born long after the original painful experiences and relationships. Freud's biographers have had to struggle to uncover the intriguing private mysteries he left behind. We, too, will have to search for underlying patterns that can make our family histories so full of mystery; often we must choose indirect methods to piece the puzzle together.

Fortunately, in recent years, there has been more interest in the extended family. The impact of Alex Haley's exploration of his own African-American history in *Roots,* which traces his family back to Africa, was immense. Haley's powerful description of his search alerted our entire nation to the value of understanding family origins. In part through Haley's persistence in the endeavor, genealogy became one of the most popular avocations in America.

From a family systems point of view, all family members are equally important—the renegades, the black sheep, the villains and the heroes. We can learn as much from the "sinners," the skinflints, and the hypochondriacs as we can from the saints, the martyrs, and the Horatio Algers. Those who became drunkards or addicts must be viewed in relation to their illustrious brothers who became U.S. presidents, as in the case of George Washington (see page 221 for genogram), John Quincy Adams (see page 70 for genogram), Theodore Roosevelt (see page 96 for genogram), Jimmy Carter, Bill Clinton, and others. Sometimes the ne'er-do-wells make the heroes look more heroic. In our own families, the failures can provide lessons about the cracks in our family's relationship system. We need to know about everyone, because without the whole it is impossible to understand the individual parts. Those who have not had a voice because they were poor or because they were women or for whatever reason may be equally important in a family's psychological reality, even if they lacked visibility within or outside the family.

Problems in our families of origin are often repeated in the families we create ourselves, however much we may wish it were not so. Even people with remarkable abilities in other areas can be blinded to new ways of perceiving their families and may lose all objectivity when they return to their childhood homes. It is especially difficult to see how our own thinking and behavior can perpetuate problems that already have a long history.

Queen Victoria: Fusion and Cutoff

Queen Victoria's relationships to her husband and children were set up in her own childhood experiences (Genogram 1.1). Raised as an only child, Victoria experienced the death of her adoring father when she was only 8 months old. From that time on she slept with her mother every night until she was 18, sharing everything with her. Victoria was almost completely isolated from other close relationships, as her German mother had immigrated alone to England to marry, and after the very early death of her husband, her British relatives had little connection to her, leaving her isolated in a foreign land.

As Victoria matured, she began to feel smothered by the demands of her exiled and isolated mother, and at 18, when she acceded to the throne, she turned her back on her. The earlier intense mother-daughter bond was replaced almost immediately with a passionate and turbulent relationship with her first cousin and husband, Prince Albert.

When her mother died 24 years later, Victoria went into paroxysms of grief, experiencing deep guilt and remorse over their long estrangement. As she sorted her mother's papers, her emotions gave way entirely; she found that her mother had saved every scrap of Victoria's childhood memorabilia. Realizing too late how deeply her mother had loved her, she felt intense

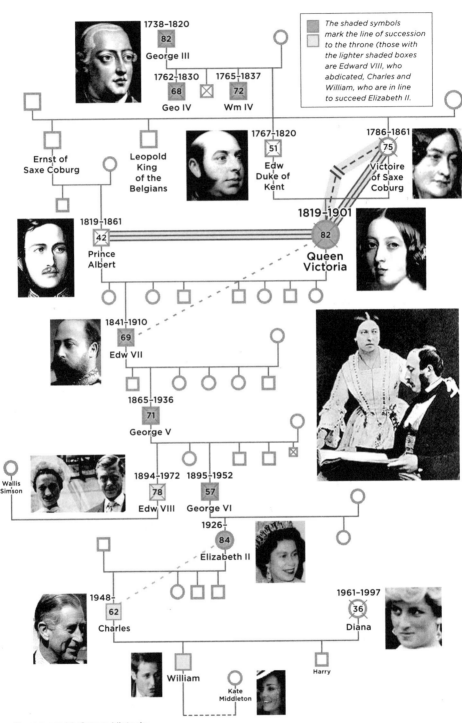

The shaded symbols mark the line of succession to the throne (those with the lighter shaded boxes are Edward VIII, who abdicated, Charles and William, who are in line to succeed Elizabeth II.

1738–1820
82
George III

1762–1830
68
Geo IV

1765–1837
72
Wm IV

Ernst of
Saxe Coburg

Leopold
King
of the
Belgians

1767–1820
51
Edw
Duke of
Kent

1786–1861
75
Victoire
of Saxe
Coburg

1819–1861
42
Prince
Albert

1819–1901
82
Queen
Victoria

1841–1910
69
Edw VII

1865–1936
71
George V

Wallis
Simson

1894–1972
78
Edw VIII

1895–1952
57
George VI

1926–
84
Elizabeth II

1948–
62
Charles

1961–1997
36
Diana

William

Kate
Middleton

Harry

Genogram 1.1. Queen Victoria.

regret. In a typical response to such pain, she now blamed outsiders, especially her governess and her mother's advisor, for the cutoff she had effected herself: "Her love for me. It is too touching: I have found little books with the accounts of my babyhood, and they show such unbounded tenderness! I am wretched to think how for a time two people estranged us. . . . To miss a Mother's friendship, not to be able to have her to confide in when a girl most needs it . . . drives me wild now" (cited in Woodham-Smith, 1972, p. 412).

Victoria, though already in middle age, described herself here as a "girl," elsewhere calling herself a "poor orphan child" who felt as if she were no longer cared for after her mother's death. She seemed, as one observer noted, "determined to cherish her grief and not be consoled" (Weintraub, 1987, p. 290). For weeks she took all her meals alone, considering her children "a disturbance," and leaving all the business of government to her husband, who was himself already terminally ill.

When Albert died a few months afterward, Victoria was overwhelmed completely. She had made Albert into the centerpiece of her life; every other relationship had become secondary. She did not attend his funeral, yet for years slept with his nightshirt in her arms. She made his room into a "sacred room" to be kept exactly as it had been when he was alive. Every day for the rest of her long life she had his linens changed, his clothes laid out afresh, and water prepared for his shaving. To every bed in which she slept, Victoria attached a photograph of Albert as he lay dead. And for the next 40 years she wore mourning dress in the style of the year he died. Years before, Victoria had written, "How one loves to cling to grief" (Benson, 1987, p. 96), and now she certainly did. She developed an obsession with cataloguing everything, so that nothing would be changed. She surrounded herself with mementos of the past and gave orders that nothing ever be thrown away. There were to be no further changes or losses, and as long as she lived, these orders were obeyed (Strachey, 1921).

Victoria's reactions, however constricted and rigid they may appear to us, are understandable human reactions to distress. It is as if time stops. Families may close down, attempting to control those aspects of their world over which they still have some power, because in the one area that really matters— human relationships—they have lost a sense of control.

Queen Victoria was a great and remarkable woman whose personality dominated the 19th century and in many ways continued through the 20th. Ruler of England for two thirds of a century, she wrote more than any monarch in history (her total production would equal 700 volumes!). She was by all accounts a woman of many paradoxes—difficult, demanding, and capricious, but also gentle, passionate, humble, and scrupulously honest. On the other hand, she suffered, as many people do, from the deep-seated effects of family problems. The problems of her isolated childhood seemed to limit her relationships with her own children, with whom she said she never felt at ease. She had grown up quite alone, always with adults and never with other children.

One can only speculate, with the benefit of our current psychological wisdom, about how Victoria's children must have viewed their own child-hoods. We know that Victoria refused to make any accommodation to her oldest son's need to learn how to rule, treating him like a child until her last breath, when he was 50. A hundred years later, Prince Charles is in a simi-larly ambiguous position. He has entered his 60s without the opportunity to engage in the career he has been anticipating throughout his life. At no level does his mother (great-great-granddaughter of Queen Victoria) seem to have allowed him a share of power to prepare him for succession.

Most people avoid confronting family issues because they can't see a way to change the relationships they find frustrating. This leads them, as it did Queen Victoria, to seek new relationships in which they attempt to make up for what-ever has gone wrong earlier. And if these new relationships don't bring ful-fillment, the general bitterness and pain is likely to increase. In fact, running away from home (emotionally or physically) typically traps people in the past; it does not resolve current problems with children and spouses or eliminate lingering regrets about being a virtual stranger to your original family. As the saying goes, the thread to your past is the ladder to your future.

Benjamin Franklin: The Most Famous Runaway in U.S. History

Perhaps the most famous runaway in American history was Benjamin Franklin, who in 1724, at the age of 17, left his family in Boston and moved to Philadelphia, telling no one of his whereabouts. He was bitter about fam-ily conflicts, especially with an older brother, James, to whom he had been apprenticed as a printer at 12. This brother had beaten and humiliated him whenever he did not toe the line. Having actually run the press while his brother was in prison for his writings, Franklin could not stand to be under his brother's thumb when the brother returned and reasserted his role. Nor could he tolerate, apparently, the lack of his parents' support.

Eventually a brother-in-law tracked Franklin down in Philadelphia and persuaded him to contact his family. Franklin returned to Boston to do so, and, more important, to ask for some money. He was unsuccessful on both counts, and remained estranged. Although his parents lived for 25 more years, Franklin rarely communicated with them and appears never to have repaired his relationships with them in any but a superficial way. In all his prodigious writings he hardly mentioned them. In the next generation, Franklin had an out-of-wedlock son, William, to whom in early days he was very attached. William became his companion and collaborator for many years. But that relationship, too, ended in a bitter and forever unreconciled split.

Even when you try to do the opposite of what your parents did, you may unwittingly repeat the same pattern. In an almost uncanny way, Franklin's son William ended up with a cutoff from his own son. Like his father, William had a son out of wedlock, and like his father, he tried to fashion his son into a companion. But William and his son also ended up bitterly estranged. Franklin's grandson then fathered two children out of wedlock, from whom he, too, became cut off. Another multigenerational pattern repetition accompanied these cutoffs in the Franklin family: After cutting off his son, Franklin doted on his son's child, Temple; in the next generation, William doted on *his* grandchild to such an extent that he pretended she was his own.

Whatever has happened in your family shapes you. Events that occurred long before your birth, never mentioned in your family during your lifetime, may influence you in powerful, hidden ways. When, for example, a child dies before another's birth, the "replacement" child may manage until he or she tries to leave home, at which point the family may go into a crisis triggered by the original loss, though no one may link the upheaval to the first child's death years earlier.

Every fact of your family's biography is part of the many-layered pattern that becomes your identity. If your aunt commits suicide, for example, it affects most immediately her husband and children (your uncle and cousins), who are left with a legacy of pain, anger, guilt, and social stigma. However, it also affects her parents (your grandparents), who will forever wonder where they went wrong. It will affect her aunts and uncles and her siblings (including your parents), who will share the most intense family pain, wondering what they might have done differently to keep her from killing herself. But those are only the obvious people affected. Your aunt's suicide will also affect her nieces and nephews (you, your siblings, and cousins), who will have to wonder whether your parents might ever, like their sister, decide on such a course of action. And it will affect your aunt's grandchildren, who will be influenced by their parents' pain over the experience as well as by their own fears about the meaning of their grandmother's death. Your own children will probably have similar doubts about whether suicide runs in your family and how it might again come into their lives. In addition, each family member will have to respond to the reactions of the others. Inevitably, the impact of such an experience will ripple throughout the whole family, and for a long time to come.

To understand family patterns, we need to develop a perspective on this shared multigenerational life-cycle evolution. The "family" comprises the entire emotional system of at least three, and increasingly four, generations who move through life together, even though they often live in different places. As a family we share a common past and an anticipated future. The patterns of the current family life cycle are changing rapidly; there is less continuity than ever before between the demands on current families and the patterns of past generations. Thus it is easy to lose all sense of connection with what has come before in the family, and this can be a serious loss. With advances in audio, video, and Internet technology, we now have, for the first time in history, new capabilities for transmission of the culture from one generation to the next, yet current families often fail to share the cultural and family stories that have long been a primary wellspring of social and personal identity.

We are living a great deal longer than human beings ever lived before, so we have much more potential for connecting with previous generations. At the same time, as a culture we have become so mobile that we suffer from disconnection. On average, Americans move once every 4 years. And the divorce rate is approaching 50%, making the separations among family members even more serious.

Our image of a family with a working father, a homemaker mother, and several children now describes less than 6% of the population. Although women of some ethnic backgrounds have always worked outside the home, the majority of women of all backgrounds are now employed regularly throughout their adult lives. We thus require very different patterns of caretaking for children and for other family members—the elderly, for instance—who were traditionally taken care of by women in the home.

From a life-cycle perspective, it is important to track family patterns over time, noting especially those transitions at which families tend to be more vulnerable because of the necessary readjustments in relationships. A life-cycle orientation frames problems within the course that families have moved along in their past, the tasks they are presently trying to master, and the future toward which they are moving. Any family is more than the sum of its parts. The individual life cycle from birth to death takes place within the family life cycle. Problems are most likely to appear when there is an interruption or dislocation in the family life cycle, whether because of an untimely death, a chronic illness, a divorce or migration that forces family members to separate, or because the family is unable to launch a child or tolerate the entry of a new in-law, grandchild, or grandparent into the family home.

It makes sense to consider problems and relationships within the entire three- or four-generational family as it moves through time. Relationships with parents, brothers and sisters, children, and grandparents go through stages as we move along the family life cycle, just as parent-child and couple relationships do.

Issues that are not resolved at one point in the life cycle tend to linger for resolution at the next phase, even though some players in the drama may have been replaced. We also tend to evaluate our experiences differently at different points in the life cycle, depending on what else is happening in our lives.

Usually people take on certain roles in families—hero, villain, jokester, victim. These characterizations reinforce basic family messages by indicating who the "good guys" and "bad guys" are. As we become aware of a family's stories and the messages embedded in them we can evaluate whether to maintain these "labels" or not. It is not unusual for people to feel acute embarrassment, shame, or even despair about certain details of family history. They worry that negative traits are inherited or that they are doomed to repeat family mistakes. Family skeletons may remain in the closet because some people don't want to know the truth and because others don't want to tell. Avoidance of painful memories distorts family relationships, causing more problems than the original behavior itself. When families keep secrets, their relationships become dishonest and insecure.

At times the coincidence of events in families, even over several generations, may seem mystical. How does it happen that patterns repeat without the participants' knowledge of the earlier experience? In one family, the 13-year-old daughter ran away from home and was killed while hitchhiking. The parents kept her ashes on the mantel but never spoke of the event. They moved to a different city and had another daughter, who also ran away when she was 13. Fortunately, the parents were able to find this daughter and at that point opened up discussion of family relationships for the first time. The secret of the dead sister was revealed and the family finally dealt with this earlier loss. It turned out that the mother had had a twin sister who had also died at age 13, a loss she had found too painful to speak about, even to her husband. How families transmit such secrets is surely a mystery, but the more we can learn about our family's history, the more perspective we will gain on the present.

Failing to connect with family leaves a person alone in profound ways that lovers, children, friends, and work cannot replace. If we are estranged from our family, a part of our spirit remains buried deep within. And the ghosts can haunt us—voices in our head sounding disapproval, threats of further abandonment, or loss of self. These ghosts can stand between you and all that you cherish in life, or they can taint an otherwise productive and satisfying life with sadness. By remaining unaware of family ghosts, a family can be locked forever in these formative experiences, unable to move beyond them.

Our culture tends to focus on the individual, or at most on couples and children, downplaying the importance of extended families, though their role is enormous in shaping our lives. And the idea of "moving on" whenever problems arise has been a time-honored concept in our society. If you don't get along with your parents or if they don't like your choice of mate or way of life, just move to California and see the family once or twice a year. After all, almost anyone can get through family visits at that frequency. This book's aim is to show another way, to help you understand that at the deepest level we are a part of all that we have been and a part of all that our families have been.

2 Family Trees: The Past as Prologue

We ourselves are the embodied continuance
Of those who did not live into our time.
And others will be and are our immortality on earth.

—JORGE LUIS BORGES

To make sense of what we experience in the present—to understand our symptoms, conflicts, cutoffs, and even the multiple characterizations of different family members—we must understand our family's history. We use the genogram—a kind of annotated family tree—as a tool in learning about families. Because families are so complex (most have more than 50 family members), we use genograms to keep track of the basic facts of an entire family's history. Genograms not only remind us about what parts of the family story we know already but also alert us to what we don't yet know. The main symbols employed in a genogram appear on the inside cover of this book and are fully explained in the book *Genograms: Assessment and Intervention*, which I coauthored with Randy Gerson and Sueli Petry (McGoldrick, Gerson, & Petry, 2008).

Genograms map out the basic biological and legal structure of the family—who was married to whom, the names of their children, and so on. Just as important, they can show key facts about individuals and the relationships of family members. For example, one can note the highest educational level completed, a serious childhood illness, or an overly close or distant relationship. The facts symbolized on the genogram offer clues about the family's secrets and mythology, as families tend to obscure what is painful or embarrassing in their history.

A genogram includes multiple types of family information: the basic facts (who is in the family, the dates of their births, marriages, moves, illnesses, deaths), information regarding the primary characteristics and level of functioning of different family members (education, occupation, psychological and physical health, outstanding attributes, talents, successes, and failures), and relationship patterns in the family (closeness, conflict, or cutoff). Once the primary family information is indicated on the genogram, it is possible to examine it from the multiple perspectives of all family members. One genogram might emphasize the relationship patterns in a family; another might highlight the artistic patterns; another, the patterns of illness; and so forth. A genogram is generally drawn from the point of view of a key person or nuclear family, going back in time at least two generations and forward to the children and grandchildren of the key person or people. Other genograms may be drawn to show in detail various branches of the family or aspects of their functioning and relationship.

Studying the patterns of family conflict and alliance on a genogram can help you to see the automatic responses people often have to family events, even when they think they are being objective. For instance, repeated gossip between a mother and her daughters about the "superficial, materialistic, and selfish" daughter-in-law may seem an objective response to her clearly observed personality traits. Only when we realize that the "scapegoating" of the daughter-in-law has been a theme in the family for three generations can we step back and rethink the relationships. Perhaps the negative attitude toward daughters-in-law is based more on the family's view of males as "family heroes"—so no woman would be good enough, especially if they think she is stealing their son or brother away. Furthermore, the "hero" brother may be the counterpart to another brother who is "the loser"—the former playing out the family dreams and aspirations, the latter the family fears. Often when family members become polarized around an issue, it is not the issue itself that is the problem but the emotional alliances in the family that determine who takes which side. Therapists often need to help clients take a broader view of their lives, and genograms are an ideal tool for this because they let the family history speak for itself.

Let us look again at Benjamin Franklin in terms of his own relationships and those that may have been precursors for his patterns (Genogram 2.1).

One biographer wrote of Benjamin Franklin that he was less a single personality than a whole committee: "a harmonious human multitude" (Van Doren, 1991, p. 782). Probably all of us are less single personalities than committees. We play different roles in each relationship, and we are perceived differently depending on the context and on whom we are relating to. Revising the part we play in our families begins with an exploration of the time-honored opinions we have held about the "good guys" and the "bad guys" in our families. Each person in a family typically views his or her perspective as the correct, just, and objective one, and yet, as we know, every story is like *Rashomon,* made up of as many points of view as there are participants.

The comments of Benjamin Franklin's supporters and critics in their various biographies provide intriguing examples. One biographer concluded that Franklin was the best-integrated man she had ever studied, an "admirable, beguiling character, diversified brilliance balanced by talent for happiness" (Bowen, 1974, p. xii). D. H. Lawrence said the opposite: "He made himself a list of virtues, which he trotted inside like a grey nag in a paddock. . . . Middle sized, sturdy, snuff-colored Doctor Franklin . . . I cannot stand him [because] he tries to take away my wholeness and . . . my freedom" (cited in Wright, 1990, p. 2). Mark Twain joked about his accomplishments: "Full of animosity toward boys, [Franklin had] a malevolence which is without parallel in history . . . he had a fashion of living wholly on bread and water, and studying astronomy at mealtime—a thing which has brought affliction to millions of boys since, whose fathers had read Franklin's pernicious biography" (cited in Middlekauf, 1996, p. xvii). Melville criticized him as full of platitudes, obtrusive advice and mock friendliness, possessed of a bookkeeper's mind (Wright, 1986, p. 2). John Adams wrote of him: "I have no friendship for Franklin. . . . I am incapable of having any with a man of his moral sentiments" (McCullough, 2001, p. 277). A Federalist contemporary, William Cobbett, wrote that he was "a crafty and lecherous old hypocrite . . . whose very statue seems to gloat on the wenches as they walk in the State yard" (cited in Wright, 1990, p. 2).

Although we have no written comments from Franklin's own relatives—his devoted wife, whom he abandoned for years at a time, even when she was dying, while expecting her to handle the family business by herself; his daughter, whom he admonished for being frivolous in wanting nice clothes, while he flirted in Paris with women in fancy dress; his son, whom he cut off at the time of the Revolution and refused to reconnect with even years later—their perspectives on him would surely be just as diverse. Where we stand in the family plays a crucial role in determining how we view things. Each family member has a different relationship with parents, siblings, spouses or partners, children, grandparents, uncles, and so on. Each individual relationship influences that person's opinions and interpretation of the actions and choices of everyone else. And our behavior in any family situation depends on the relationship we have with the others involved.

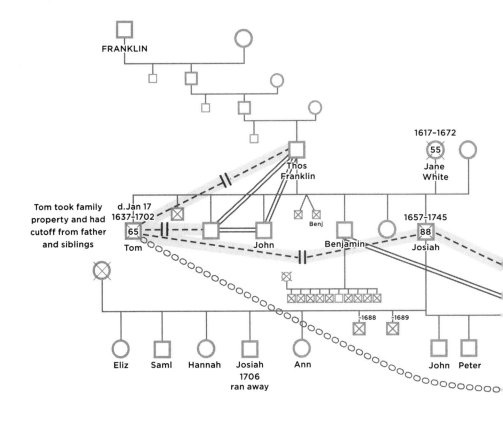

FRANKLIN

1617–1672
55
Jane
White

Thos
Franklin

Benj

1657–1745
88
Josiah

Tom took family
property and had
cutoff from father
and siblings

d. Jan 17
1637–1702
65
Tom

John

Benjamin

1688   1689

Eliz   Saml   Hannah   Josiah
1706
ran away

Ann

John   Peter

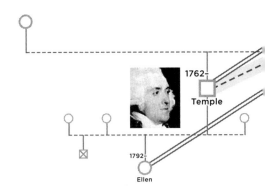

1762–
Temple

1792–
Ellen

Genogram 2.1. Benjamin Franklin.

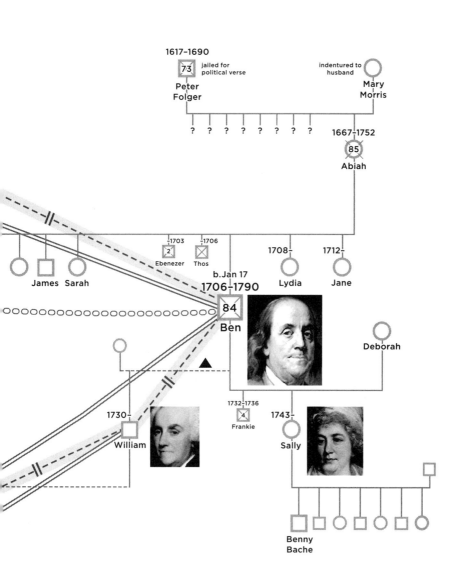

1617–1690

73 — jailed for political verse

Peter Folger

indentured to husband

Mary Morris

? ? ? ? ? ? ? ?

1667–1752

85

Abiah

1703
2
Ebenezer

1706
Thos

1708
Lydia

1712
Jane

James Sarah

b. Jan 17
1706–1790

84
Ben

Deborah

1730
William

1732–1736
4
Frankie

1743
Sally

Benny Bache

Although the contradictory impressions of Benjamin Franklin relate to the particular position of each observer, each view also reflects Franklin's different behavior in different relationships. His multifaceted personality seems rooted in the special position he had in his family. Early on his father, Josiah, proclaimed Ben to be the most special of all his children. He vowed that this tenth son would be the "tithe of his loins"—his offering to God in return for all the blessings the family had received since coming to America. He said he would see to it that Benjamin studied at Harvard and became a minister. He later reneged on this promise, not allowing him even a minimum education, although Ben's gifts as a scholar were evident from childhood. Josiah withheld so much of what he had promised to give that we have to suspect he had deep-rooted ambivalence toward this son.

The question is why? Who was Benjamin Franklin to his family? Whose shoes was he supposed to fill? Was his life course a reflection of roles and patterns laid out by the generations that preceded him?

Franklin was the youngest son of a youngest son for five generations back. He knew that fact, but apparently not its family implications: His father identified with him in a special way. We all tend to identify with a child who is in our sibling position, just as we may identify with the child who most resembles us physically. If this pattern is repeated for many generations, there is a special legacy—an even greater intensity about our wish for this child to fit our image of him or her. Josiah's decision that Benjamin would be "the tithe of his loins" makes sense in terms of this special position.

Franklin was also a "replacement child" for no fewer than three other sons who were lost around the time of his birth. The first, Ebenezer, had drowned unattended in the bath at age 2. The next, Thomas, named for the paternal grandfather, died a few months after Benjamin was born. During the same period, his 21-year-old half brother, Josiah, the father's namesake, ran away to sea—returning only once briefly 9 years later before disappearing forever. It is very likely that the Franklin family blamed themselves for these losses, especially for the accidental death of Ebenezer. They probably hoped that their last son Benjamin would accomplish enough for four sons (which he did!). Yet they may also have feared becoming too attached to him because of their previous losses.

Any child's death has a tremendous effect on the entire family, often for generations afterward. Families frequently misremember miscarriages, stillbirths, and childhood deaths because of the trauma involved. Children born later may not even be told about the dead child. The fact that Franklin's birth was near in time to the deaths of two baby brothers would have added to his special place in the family.

We also know from Franklin's autobiography that he dreamed of following his lost half brother, Josiah Jr., to sea. Did the family convey to him an expectation that he should replace this brother? Had there been conflicts with Josiah that led to his leaving the family? Were conflicts with his parents part of a legacy that Ben inherited once Josiah left? We cannot be sure, but we do know that Franklin remembered all his life the one brief last visit Josiah made to the family years later. Josiah Jr.'s loss apparently made a deep impression on all of them.

Looking at the timing of Franklin's birth on his genogram also shows that he was born 4 years to the day after the death of his father's oldest brother, Tom. Anniversary dates are generally important in families, and very much worth tracking. Families often obscure the emotional connections such coincidences can create, setting up almost mystical connections between events or people. Franklin himself wrote to his son in his autobiography about the resemblance between his uncle Uncle Tom and himself:

> [Tom] died in 1702, on the 6th of January, four years to the day before I was born. The recital which some elderly persons made to us of his character, I remember, struck you as something extraordinary, from its similarity to what you knew of me. "Had he died," said you, "four years later, on the same day, one might have supposed a transmigration." (Franklin, 1968, pp. 47–48)

This Uncle Tom—whose death without heir ended five generations of Franklins in their home community of Ecton, England—was a very learned man, an ingenious inventor, trained as a smith but qualified also as a lawyer. He became an important man in his community, and "the chief mover of all public-spirited enterprises" for his county. Indeed, this does sound remarkably like Benjamin, founder of one of the first newspapers in America, the first public library, the first volunteer fire company, the first hospital, the postal service, and the University of Pennsylvania, one the first universities. What is more, he was president of the Pennsylvania Society for the Abolition of Slavery, ambassador to England and France, and, of course, a major force in the fashioning of our Declaration of Independence and Constitution.

It turns out that Franklin's identification with his Uncle Tom probably elicited mixed feelings in his father. Just as there was a bitter split in Ben Franklin's generation involving Ben, his brother James, and his parents, there had been a bitter split over religious differences in the father's generation. Ben's father and two of his brothers, John and Benjamin (Franklin's godfather and namesake), became estranged from this Uncle Tom (Franklin's uncle), who kept the family homestead while they were all forced to move away. The family was never united again.

Dates may have other idiosyncratic meanings for a family and are worth inquiry. For example, in the Franklin family the fact that Franklin's birth took place on a Sunday implied that the parents had had sex on a Sunday, which was considered a sin. This made Franklin a child of the Devil—not a small consideration for Franklin's staunchly religious father, who was "the keeper of the morals" of their church community! The family dealt with this "sin" by maintaining strict secrecy about the exact date of his birth. A birth that takes place on Friday the 13th, or on the same day that an important family member left or died, or on a day that has some other significance, may also gain special meaning for the family.

A similar example of the power of coincidental events occurred in the family of Mahatma Gandhi (Genogram 2.2). When Gandhi was 13, his father and uncle were both elderly and worrying about getting their sons married before they died. So a triple wedding was arranged for Gandhi, his next older brother, and a cousin. Unfortunately the father suffered an accident just before the wedding and his health declined from that point forward. Gandhi and his mother became the father's primary caretakers. He described in his autobiography: "I was devoted to my father, but no less was I devoted to the passions that the flesh is heir to. I had yet to learn that all happiness and pleasure should be sacrificed in devoted service to my parents. And yet, as though by way of punishment for my desire for pleasures, an incident happened which has ever since rankled in my mind" (Gandhi, 2008, p. 9). Gandhi's wife was pregnant, which he said was "a circumstance which, as I can see today, meant a double shame for me. For one thing I did not restrain myself, as I should have done . . . and this carnal desire just got the better of what I regarded as my duty to study and of what was even a greater duty, my devotion to my parents" (p. 27). His father died while Gandhi was having sex with his wife that night and he never forgave himself. He described the son who was born soon after: "The poor mite that was born to my wife scarcely breathed for three or four days. Nothing else could be expected. Let all those who are married be warned by my example" (p. 29). Could it be that the very difficult relationship Gandhi had with his oldest surviving son, Harilal—born 2 years after this trauma, who was always rebellious and apologetic for his rebellion, and died a homeless alcoholic—was bound up in the conflicts of this experience? Gandhi himself was preoccupied the rest of his life with guilt for not having been present when his father died, and it seems to have powerfully influenced his belief that one should never give in to human impulses for pleasure. His son's refusal to conform to his ideas was perhaps the biggest disappointment of Gandhi's life.

Yet another possibly controversial decision arising at the birth of a child is the choice of a name. From a systems perspective, the answer to Shakespeare's question, "What's in a name?" is: "A lot!" Names in a family can tell you a great deal about the role that different children were meant to play—who they were to be like. Some cultures have prescribed rules for naming. In Greek culture, children are named for particular grandparents, depending on their birth order. In Jewish culture children are generally named for the dead, not the living. When families do not follow the typical patterns of their culture, one needs to ask why. John Quincy Adams (see page 70 for genogram), for example, changed a four-generational family pattern of naming the oldest son John by naming his oldest son for George Washington, to the distress of his parents. He may thus have compounded family conflicts about the expected or desired role of this oldest son, whose life ended in suicide, as we will discuss later.

In the Freud family (see page 172 for genogram), Sigmund was named for his paternal grandfather, a rabbi who died shortly before his birth, and he grew up to feel that there is much in a name—"perhaps even a piece of the soul." He, the "golden Sigi," as his mother called him, was given the honor of naming his younger brother; he chose Alexander, after his hero Alexander the Great. In the next generation Freud alone named all six of his children, including his four daughters, for his male heroes, teachers, or friends, or for their female relatives. In other words, Freud's power to name the members of his family continued in his adult life, reflecting how his special position as his mother's golden son lasted throughout his life. We do not know why his younger brother Julius, who died in infancy, was named for an uncle who was still alive (though he was dying at the time), as this was against the Jewish custom of the era. Perhaps it reflected an emotional process in the family that was stronger than the cultural rule.

The name chosen for a child may tell a lot about a family's "program" or dreams for a child. In Franklin's case, he himself thought it significant that he was named for his father's favorite brother, who was also Franklin's godfather. This uncle, like so many others in the Franklin family, was an ingenious man, who lived with the family for several years while Ben was growing up. But what did the connection between these two Benjamins mean to the family? And what did it mean that this second father figure, who had lost his wife and nine of his ten children, moved into their home? Apparently a great deal. Franklin's father soon became locked in conflict with his brother over the younger Benjamin's future, and not only retracted his early promises about

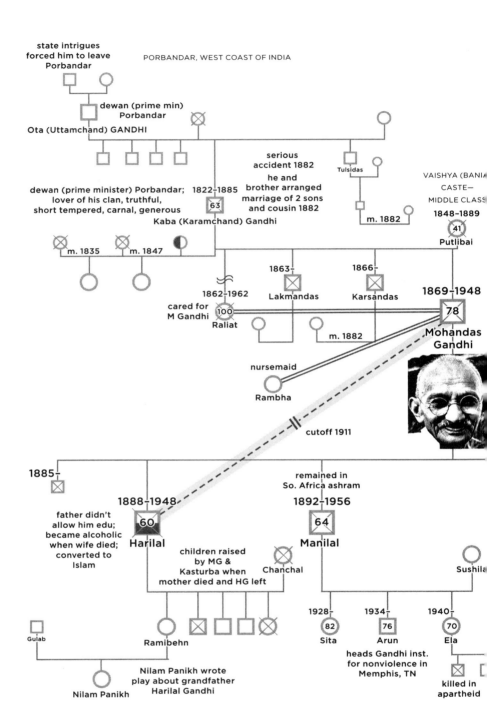

state intrigues
forced him to leave
Porbandar

PORBANDAR, WEST COAST OF INDIA

dewan (prime min)
Porbandar

Ota (Uttamchand) GANDHI

serious
accident 1882
he and
brother arranged
marriage of 2 sons
and cousin 1882

Tulsidas

VAISHYA (BANIA
CASTE—
MIDDLE CLASS

dewan (prime minister) Porbandar;
lover of his clan, truthful,
short tempered, carnal, generous

1822–1885

63

Kaba (Karamchand) Gandhi

m. 1882

1848–1889

41

Putlibai

m. 1835   m. 1847

1863–

Lakmandas

1866–

Karsandas

1869–1948

78

Mohandas
Gandhi

1862–1962
cared for
M Gandhi

100

Raliat

m. 1882

nursemaid

Rambha

cutoff 1911

1885–

remained in
So. Africa ashram

1888–1948

father didn't
allow him edu;
became alcoholic
when wife died;
converted to
Islam

60

Harilal

children raised
by MG &
Kasturba when
mother died and HG left

Chanchal

1892–1956

64

Manilal

Sushila

Gulab

Ramibehn

1928–

82

Sita

1934–

76

Arun

heads Gandhi inst.
for nonviolence in
Memphis, TN

1940–

70

Ela

killed in
apartheid

Nilam Panikh wrote
play about grandfather
Harilal Gandhi

Nilam Panikh

Genogram 2.2. Mahatma Gandhi.

1869–1944

⊘ 75

Kasturba

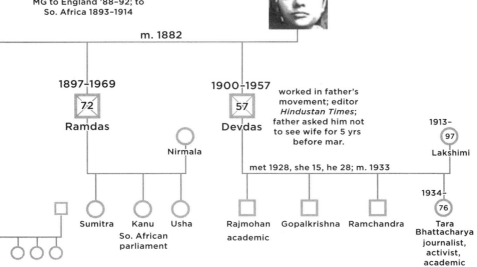

Gandhi was having sex with
wife when father died; in guilt
stopped having sex and viewed
sons as expression of his guilt

MG to England '88–92; to
So. Africa 1893–1914

m. 1882

1897–1969

☐ 72

Ramdas

Nirmala

1900–1957

☐ 57

Devdas

worked in father's
movement; editor
Hindustan Times;
father asked him not
to see wife for 5 yrs
before mar.

1913–

⊘ 97

Lakshimi

met 1928, she 15, he 28; m. 1933

Sumitra   Kanu   Usha

So. African
parliament

Rajmohan   Gopalkrishna   Ramchandra

academic

1934–

⊘ 76

Tara
Bhattacharya
journalist,
activist,
academic

his son's education but also repeatedly stood in the way of his advancement. Such triangles are common when a particular child becomes the favorite of a grandparent, aunt, uncle, or godparent and then triggers the resentment of the parent or perhaps activates old conflicts. Whenever a parent is especially negatively focused on one child in particular, it is worth exploring the possibility that this is part of a triangle with another parental figure who views this child as special.

Thinking About Family Relationships

When you see a pattern in which insiders move out, such as Franklin's half brother Josiah running away to sea or Ben disappearing at 17, or when you see outsiders moving into the family, such as Uncle Ben coming to live with the Franklins, a natural inquiry arises about conflicts and alliances that may have divided the family's loyalties. Within the Franklin family there is a repeated pattern of intense closeness, conflict, distance, and cutoff, with attempts at closeness seeming to complement the cutoffs, all of which led to further predictable cutoffs. For example, it is predictable that as the estrangement developed between Franklin and his son William, he reached for closeness with William's son, Temple; tension then developed between Temple and his father William. This was repeated in the triangle between William, Temple, and Temple's daughter Ellen.

The central triangle in the Franklin family while Ben was growing up involved Ben, his father, and his uncle Benjamin, who had come from England to live with the family when young Ben was 6. As mentioned earlier, this uncle had lost his wife and all but one of his 10 children. He stayed with the Franklin family for the next 4 years, during which time he and Josiah began a long tug-of-war for young Ben's allegiance.

Father and uncle had not seen each other for 30 years. They were opposites in personality. Josiah was pragmatic, business minded, a mechanical genius, and a fanatical Puritan. Uncle Benjamin was a bit fantastic in personality, a freethinker, a great talker, a dreamer, and a poet given to endless philosophizing, reading, and perpetual rhyming. He was also an inventor, but always hard up for money, while he concentrated on his poetry. As Uncle Benjamin began to inspire his young nephew in the direction of humorous, iconoclastic writing, Josiah became increasingly hostile toward both of them. As Franklin later wrote: "Our father . . . used to say nothing was more common than for those who loved one another at a distance to find many causes of dislike when they came together. I saw proof of it in the disgusts between him and his brother Benjamin" (Randall, 1984, p. 32).

The more Uncle Benjamin agreed that young Ben should get the best education possible and go into the ministry, the less enthusiasm Josiah had for his old promise, and finally—although Franklin was a brilliant student—Josiah withdrew him from school and humiliated him by insisting he take a trade. Yet like uncle, like nephew: The more his father resisted his education, the more Ben loved learning. Although his father terminated Ben's formal schooling by the time he was 8, he eventually received honorary degrees not only from Harvard but also from Yale, St. Andrews, and Oxford. Perhaps in the end Josiah feared being outstripped by this replica of his own brother more than he wished his favorite son to be "the tithe of his loins."

Questions and Stories: Keys to Understanding

Getting to know your family in a different way, or, if you are a therapist, helping your clients to get to know their families differently, requires becoming expert at asking questions. It's strange how often we do not ask the relevant questions in our families. Some questions occur to us but we don't ask them because we sense they would make others upset—we may be wrong in these perceptions, but we can be right, too. Other questions never even come to mind because unspoken family rules forbid broaching them. Family wisdom may have it that "Uncle Charlie isn't worth talking to because he's a lazy, pompous fool" or that "Cousin Betty is an inveterate liar and remembers nothing anyway." In all families there are rules, assumptions, and stories that members are expected to take at face value. It often takes close scrutiny to divest oneself of family assumptions. A person may have been told his Aunt Charlotte "can't handle stress, so don't discuss anything personal with her." She is never asked to help out when problems arise, and no one ever thinks of asking her opinion. This person may need to be coached to wonder *who* decided Charlotte couldn't handle stress and on what basis. It is best to question each assumption about a person's family, to ask who came to each conclusion and how. You may be amazed once you begin this line of questioning, at times becoming intrigued about the family myths you have absorbed without challenge. This can be the beginning of a journey of self-discovery and empowerment, where the key stance to take is for curiosity to overtake the sense of victimization or passivity about family dynamics.

Questions about the facts of birth and death in a family—who, when, where, how?—may uncover emotionally charged events such as suicide, alcoholism, pregnancy outside of marriage, stillbirths, miscarriages, abortions, or affairs. A person may have forgotten that his grandfather had a twin whose death at age 10 left a legacy that is still affecting the family two generations later. A daughter may not have noted that her parents' separation occurred the same year as her grandmother's heart attack. The family may not mention, unless one digs for the facts, that a grandmother was actually married once before. The excuse given may be that it didn't really count because it "never took"; her first husband was a scoundrel and left her after 2 months.

Once the person is aware what questions he or she might want to ask the family, the next phase is to figure out how and when to approach different family members for possible answers. I will discuss this complex strategic issue in greater depth in later chapters. The important thing is to develop a questioning attitude and a healthy skepticism, never being too sure that anyone's point of view is "the truth." With the concept of a genogram as guideline, you can begin to explore how each family member would have experienced the relationships and events of the family's history.

You may become like a detective, looking to make connections—between important dates, between the kind of relationship patterns of grandparents and parents, between current patterns and the way parents were at the same life-cycle phase. There may be intense anxiety around weddings, stemming from the fact that a grandfather died 3 days before the mother's wedding. A father may have feared ending up a failure like his father. A mother and her sisters may be anxious that they will be deserted just as their grandmother with five small children was. Unacknowledged, such information may wreak havoc by generating unexplained anxiety throughout the family. Known, such information can create understanding and strengthen bonds.

From this perspective, information is power—a person tries to learn whatever he or she can wherever possible, because you never know when a certain piece of information will help make a connection. Any detail may turn out to be significant. If you want to understand your mother as more than a "dragon lady" whose domineering intrusiveness overwhelms you even at age 40, you will need to try to see her as a daughter, a niece, a sister, a friend, a coworker, a granddaughter, a lover, and a cousin. Furthermore, learning more about your mother's mother in each of those roles will give you clues about *your* mother. For this reason it is worth asking each relative for the facts as well as the myths and stories heard in childhood. It is also useful to ask family members about the reactions of others to a given family experience. For example, how did the father's brother react when the grandfather cut the father off? How did his sister and his aunt, the grandfather's sister, react? Who actually knew about the conflict that led to the cutoff? How did they handle holidays and family get-togethers after that?

Respect for the family's resistance to change is crucial to any effort to understand family patterns. One must respect families' reluctance to expose secrets or change the way they relate, however harmful these ways may have been. Families often feel, as the saying goes, that "the devil you know is better than the devil you don't know." There is a great security in what is familiar. Change is stressful because of the uncertainty it brings. The fear is: "If I mention my father's suicide, things might get worse." If you are a therapist, it is best to proceed with clients gently, encouraging them to open things up cautiously and respectfully, and only when they are ready to handle the fallout and reactivity that may arise. When it comes to opening up really difficult secrets or patterns, it is best that clients only raise the question if they themselves have decided it matters. Two common errors are to go bluntly after information, disrespecting the pain that such secrecy reflects for the family, or, on the other hand, fearing to raise relevant issues at one's own expense. Thus, learning to understand your family becomes a journey of self-discovery that also involves realizing that we and our families are all in it together and are all impaired by secrecy that prevents us from realizing where we really are in our lives and where we are going.

An important assumption behind all family questioning is that people are always doing the best they can, given the limitations of their particular perspective. Typically people tend to think of themselves as the reactors in their family drama, viewing parents as the actors who determined their fate. We need to shift this perspective to realize that we are all actors and reactors. The father who abused his child was probably himself abused in his childhood; statistics tell us that abuse tends to beget abuse. This does not justify current behavior, of course; it only provides insight into its curse. This is a complex concept and a bit paradoxical. At the same time that you need to take responsibility for your own behavior, it is essential that you develop empathy for the "programmed" behavior of others. Understanding how we have all been "programmed" allows us the chance to eliminate behaviors of our own that adversely affect our relationships. You may have decided, for example, that your father never "gives" anything. It may take some thinking to realize that in your frustration you have stopped asking or expecting him to "give" and that this behavior perpetuates your father's distance and doesn't offer him the opportunity to change. Of course, being ready to open yourself to possible disappointment requires clarity about who you are—that is, realizing that if your father cannot be generous and giving it is about him and not about you. So your generosity in being open to him takes nothing away from you, even if he is never able to be generous back.

Before you begin asking questions, you need to be sure of your intentions. If the goal is self-justification or to prove others in the family wrong, others will probably sense it immediately. If you want to understand your cold and distant father who was abused by his own father, it will probably not help to ask him: "If your father was so abusive, how come you didn't tell someone or get out of there?" Such a question would probably make your father defensive. It would make more sense to convey empathy for his experience in the question: "It must have been scary never to know when your father would go into a rage. Did you ever have warning signs?"

If you believe that your parents should have "known" your feelings and owe you their approval, you are not ready for engaging a problematic parent. You would be likely to get a defensive and angry reaction and then react to it. But if you can get yourself to the point where you can express a genuine and noncombative interest in what happened, family members might actually welcome the opportunity to tell their versions of the story.

The ability to maintain one's sense of self without becoming defensive, regardless of others' perceptions, is essential to this process. It requires the ability to be the sole judge of your own worth, and not depend on the approval of others. This means not needing others to feel worthwhile, and judging the rightness of your own values and behavior for yourself, whatever misperceptions others may have of you.

It is important that you not begin asking questions until you are prepared to handle the answers. If a person asks his mother about her overall experience with him as a child, he needs to be ready to hear how frustrating she may have found him, without launching into a tirade about all *her* motherly inadequacies. The person needs to realize that becoming defensive or attacking in reaction to a family member's response to questions won't produce anything fruitful. The goal is to ask questions because one is interested in understanding the other's experience in order to learn about one's history. The person will then assess all information for him- or herself. All reactions from others, however hostile or rejecting, are "information." One must be prepared to hear negative feelings and observations—that an adored father was perceived by his brothers as a patsy or as a shylock in business, or that the family views him as arrogant, spoiled, selfish, or succeeding by luck. One then needs to consider for him- or herself whether there is any truth in what has been said and, if not, how this perception came to be. How has this perception affected the behavior of each family member?

The stories people tell about themselves and their family histories must be listened to carefully—both for what they reveal and for what they omit. As an example, let's look again at Benjamin Franklin, who left us a remarkable source in his autobiography. The first part was addressed "Dear Son" to William, who was then governor of New Jersey. The moral of his cautionary tale is clearly to inspire William with the story of his father's frugal, industrious rise from poverty and obscurity to affluence and reputation:

Having emerged from the poverty and obscurity in which I was born and bred, to a state of affluence and some degree of reputation in the world, and having gone so far through life with a considerable share of felicity, the conducing means I made use of . . . may . . . therefore be fit to be imitated. (Franklin, 1968, p. 43)

Franklin admitted many of his youthful follies or "errata," as he refers to them, quite directly—including mistreating his fiancée by leaving her, failing to write after promising to marry her, and attempting to seduce his best friend's girlfriend. On the other hand, he passes over the biggest secret in his history: who William's mother was, and exactly when he was born. This indicates that a key rule in the Franklin family was not to mention this subject.

Franklin's wife, Deborah, who apparently raised William from infancy, was not his mother. She and Franklin were never formally married in a church and maintained some secrecy about their marriage, though the date of it, September 30, 1730, is given in the autobiography. Their silence about their marriage was apparently because Deborah, having been abandoned by Franklin when he left for England, had eventually married another man, who had disappeared but wasn't known to have died. But this does not explain the secrecy about William's birth, which was a matter of concern to him through his adult life, when rumors that he was illegitimate began to have an impact on his political career. Because there was such an obvious need for clarification, Benjamin's silence on the matter is remarkable.

The family tradition of secrecy continued in the next generation. Franklin seems to have made a point of missing William's marriage, which was kept secret, as was the birth and parentage of his son Temple. The story was apparently put out that Temple was the son of a "poor relation." Temple was often sent greetings by family and friends in their correspondence, but Deborah never once mentioned him in her letters. This may have reflected resentment on her part of the second generation fathering a child out of wedlock, but it is more likely that Deborah was never informed about Temple, as Franklin made not the slightest allusion to him in any of his letters to her, though he continuously gossiped about all other members of the family. Years later a family friend referred with amusement to the game the whole family played in pretending they had not guessed the nature of Temple's relationship to the family (Lopez & Herbert, 1975).

Again in the fourth generation there was secrecy regarding Temple's illegitimate children. Indeed, after the cutoff between William and Temple, William even tried to make people believe that Temple's daughter, Ellen, was his own child.

The repetition of illegitimacy for three generations in the Franklin family seems almost uncanny. What was the connection between the generations in repeating this so-called secret? A pattern of secrecy in a family tends to breed more secrecy and distortion. It teaches family members that the truth cannot be handled and that some experiences can never be integrated.

Franklin's biographers commented on the conspicuous omissions in Franklin's writing. One said:

> Here is a man who talks to us apparently so frankly about himself while increasingly obscuring himself behind the public images, that at intervals we do not know what is fact and what is fiction. (Wright, 1988, p. 9)

Another biography about the "private" Franklin maintained that:

> His present family is practically nonexistent in the Autobiography: his daughter not mentioned a single time, his son alluded to quite casually, his wife brought into the picture mainly in the days when they were not yet married—and then not as a personality but as the illustration of a wrong set to right. The focus is exclusively on himself, or rather on a portion of himself. No soul-searching here. (Lopez & Herbert, 1975, p. 2–3)

If William knew about the negative relationship Franklin had with his own father, he may have resented his father's presentation of the family stories in such a positive light, especially when Franklin was pressuring him to conform to his political views.

Franklin's autobiography reflects his complex ambivalence toward his own father, which he never really worked out. In many of the references to his father, we cannot help but see the implied criticism behind the compliment. He said, for example, that his father focused so much on having educational conversation at mealtime that he taught Franklin to have a perfect inattention to food and a total indifference to what meals were placed before him. Franklin said this lesson served him well in traveling because he was never bothered by the lack of suitable food. In fact, Franklin was, if anything, an epicure who cared a great deal what he ate. Clearly he thought there was something missing in his father's rigorous inattention to good dining, which makes his remark seem ironic.

Franklin went on to describe how his father withdrew him from school because he had decided he could not afford to pay for college education and thought those who were educated ended up making only a meager living anyway. Franklin himself would hardly have accepted these excuses. Scholarships were available at the time and the ministry, for which he was to have prepared, did provide a good living. We can sense also Franklin's covert resentment toward his father for squashing his poetic writing. He said that at about age 13 he began writing poetry, some of which sold "wonderfully," but that "my father discouraged me, by ridiculing my performances and telling me verse-makers were generally beggars; so I escaped being a poet, most probably a very bad one" (Franklin, 1968, p. 24–25). Again, his tone about his father's criticism seems ironic. As we know, he went on to prove his father wrong, and we have all been absorbing Poor Richard's witticisms for over 200 years.

When Franklin wrote his autobiography he had already begun to disapprove of the direction of William's life, although they were still close. He was trying to tell his son to listen to his father's wisdom, which he himself had rarely done. In Franklin's version of his family story he suggested that, although he often did not agree with his father, his father tended to be right. Yet in Franklin's story of his adult life he spoke as if the family he came from did not matter at all. He seems to be reflecting his disappointment in his own family experience and may have been passing along an ambivalent message about the value of family life that played itself out in three generations of parent-child cutoffs.

The details of Franklin's genogram suggest interesting questions about him and his family: Why did he feel he could not survive within the confines of his family? Did he feel forced to escape the pressure of their dreams, ambitions, or fears about his performance? Were Franklin and his older brother James replaying a multigenerational family drama in which the younger brother excels, is forced into submission, and is finally exiled, as seemed to play out between Josiah and his brother Ben?

For a more complete understanding of Franklin and his family, it would be essential to learn about other members of the family. Whom were the other brothers named for? Did anyone else's birth coincide with family losses or important family anniversaries? Were there losses in the parental families that constricted the parents' functioning and pressured them into molding an infant into the role of replacement child?

To understand the family that Franklin himself created, we would have to ask many other questions. In choosing to marry a simple woman with little education, was Franklin repeating the experience not only of his parents but also of his maternal grandparents? We know that his maternal grandfather was a poet, author, and remarkable public figure who married his servant. In later years Franklin himself lived more closely with much more educated women and their families rather than with his own. Was this a departure from the traditional Franklin pattern or was there a history of developing intense connections outside the family?

If we look at Franklin from a family systems perspective his personal accomplishments and idiosyncrasies take on a different meaning. To begin with, he was gifted genetically with a remarkable intellect, physical constitution, and temperament. In addition to this inheritance he seems to have taken on many of the best qualities of various members of his family: He was a mechanical genius like his father, a writer and iconoclast, poet, philosopher, inventor, statesman, diplomat, humorist, and freethinker like his uncles and grandfathers. Perhaps these personal characteristics derived from a special identification with so many family members—his father by birth order, his Uncle Tom by date of birth, his paternal grandfather because this grandfather's namesake (Ben's brother Thomas) died just after Franklin's birth, his uncle Benjamin by name, godparenting, and by this uncle's move into the Franklin home after the loss of his own wife and children.

All too often people are not aware of the traits—whether positive or negative—they have absorbed from their families. They may feel contempt for their family's pretentiousness, unaware that they have absorbed some of the same mannerisms. Awareness of the trait could easily lead to its amelioration. Similarly, a positive awareness of connectedness to family can give a person a sense of belonging and a feeling of continuity that can strengthen his or her own sense of identity.

Gender is, of course, another major factor in establishing identity. To better understand themselves and their families, people need to ask themselves and others what the rules have been for men and women in their families and to what extent they conform to the society of the time. Culture also influences families' rules for gender arrangements.

Gender role constrictions on both men and women in families have played a powerful role over the centuries. This is a fascinating area to explore. One of the most interesting things to look at is how members of your family have responded to these constrictions. Did they sometimes break out of the stringent gender roles of their times? If so, how was this received by others inside and outside the family? It helps to focus especially on family members who did not completely conform to the gender norms of the society—the women who were assertive and daring, who did things on their own and were not cowed, and the men who were sweet and nurturing or who did not play "the good provider" role for whatever reason. You can learn a great deal about yourself and your family by exploring gender roles and how your family reacted over the generations to those who didn't conform to them.

In some ways, of course, family gender norms may not have changed all that much, despite recent dramatic changes for women. The content of what gets said about women may change, yet overall family attitudes toward them may remain remarkably constant. Perhaps a grandmother was viewed as a saint because she cooked, cleaned, and took care of everyone but still was considered "a bit daffy." In this generation, a mother may be described as "a remarkable woman," very successful in her computer business, able to handle a hundred things at once, "but still quite flaky, you know!" It is important to look beyond the family descriptions to the underlying patterns that repeat in spite of changed details. In Franklin's case, he had very little to say about his mother. Like so many of our other founding fathers, who seem to have had problematic relationships with their mothers, he left almost no information about her, in spite of voluminous correspondence on so many other subjects. Jefferson, Lincoln, and Washington also said almost nothing about their mothers, and John Adams was not very positive about his. Perhaps some of the dedication these men had to the concept of a nation was compensation for a perception of their families as unprotective or unfulfilling.

Informal and Extended Kin Who Belong to Us

Society conventionally views family as limited to the biological family of parents, siblings, and children. But most of us have had an informal family system, which is also crucial for our formative development. I myself had a nanny, who played a central role in my family life, and a grand-aunt Mamie, my grandfather's unmarried sister, who was like Santa Claus to us and to many others for five generations of our family. There were also friends of our family who were informal godparents, aunts, uncles, and grandparents. The parents of several of my friends played an important role in my childhood and provided a second home base for me, just as my family provided a home base for others. Every family, of course, includes anyone who belongs, whether biologically linked or not; this includes anyone who was part of the family as they grew up—caretakers, teachers, ministers, friends, neighbors—whoever played a role in the family history. These people are often the unsung heroes and "sheroes" of our families. Maya Angelou has often described her Uncle Willie, a severely disabled man, as having had a powerful influence on her education and values, teaching her her multiplication tables so well that she can still say them in the middle of the night. Angelou discovered when she went home for Uncle Willie's funeral in her tiny hometown of Stamps, Arkansas, that he had had a profound mentoring impact not only her and other relatives but on many others as well. A poem she wrote about him serves as a message to us all about listening to the unsung voices who have influenced us and may be, as Angelou has said, "present in the songs that our children sing." Their lives may not make it into history books, or even to greatness in our own families, but their private and personal influence is tremendous nonetheless.

Uncle Willie played a major mentoring role in Angelou's life, as did her older brother (Genogram 2.3). They were raised mostly by their grandmother and Uncle Willie, returning to their mother only in their teens after many traumatic experiences, the most significant being Angelou's rape by the mother's boyfriend, followed by his murder, probably by a family member, which contributed to Angelou's refusing to speak for several years. Some therapy models would say that by not having her mother's protection, Angelou's mental health was jeopardized, but many years later she described her mother thus:

> My mother is 72. We visit often. I have to see about her and she thinks she has to see about me. But it's a curious thing, because I was taken from my Mom to be raised by my grandmother when I was 3 and except for a disastrous bitter visit when I was 7, I didn't see her again until I was 13. I'm often asked how I got over that without holding a grudge. I see her as one of the greatest human beings I've ever met. She's funny and quite outrageous really. (Oliver, 1989, p. 136)

This seems an amazing reflection of the possibilities of creating workable relationships and reminds us that no rules for relationships are written in stone. No matter what has happened at one point in the life cycle, change in relationships is possible as families grow along with each other.

Another powerful example of the importance of the informal kinship system is the family of the Mexican artist Diego Rivera (Genogram 2.4). Diego was 2 when his twin brother, Carlos, died, causing his mother to become so distraught that she spent all her time at the cemetery and was unable to care for him. She had already had three stillbirths before the twins were born, and by the time Carlos died, Diego had become sickly himself. Though the mother's sister and an older aunt lived in the household, Diego's father gave him to a caretaker, Antonia, who lived in the mountains. Diego spent the next 2 years living with her. He wrote in his autobiography that from that time he loved Antonia more than he loved his own mother. Indeed, many years later, after spending 3 years in Europe, Diego made a surprise return visit to his family at age 24. That same week, his Native Mexican foster mother had had a dream about him and walked for 8 days from the mountains to see him. Diego's mother was shocked: "I am certain you dreamed this news about him. I know you possess him because I never have. That is why I have

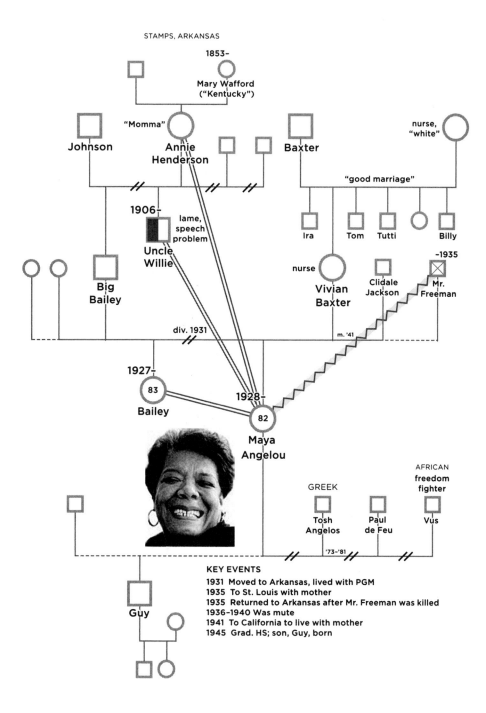

STAMPS, ARKANSAS

1853–
Mary Wafford
("Kentucky")

"Momma"
Johnson
Annie
Henderson

Baxter

nurse,
"white"

"good marriage"

Ira   Tom   Tutti   Billy

1906–
lame,
speech
problem
Uncle
Willie

nurse
Vivian
Baxter

Clidale
Jackson

–1935
Mr.
Freeman

Big
Bailey

div. 1931

m. '41

1927–
83
Bailey

1928–
82
Maya
Angelou

AFRICAN
freedom
fighter

GREEK

Tosh
Angelos

Paul
de Feu

Vus

'73–'81

Guy

KEY EVENTS
1931 Moved to Arkansas, lived with PGM
1935 To St. Louis with mother
1935 Returned to Arkansas after Mr. Freeman was killed
1936–1940 Was mute
1941 To California to live with mother
1945 Grad. HS; son, Guy, born

Genogram 2.3. Maya Angelou.

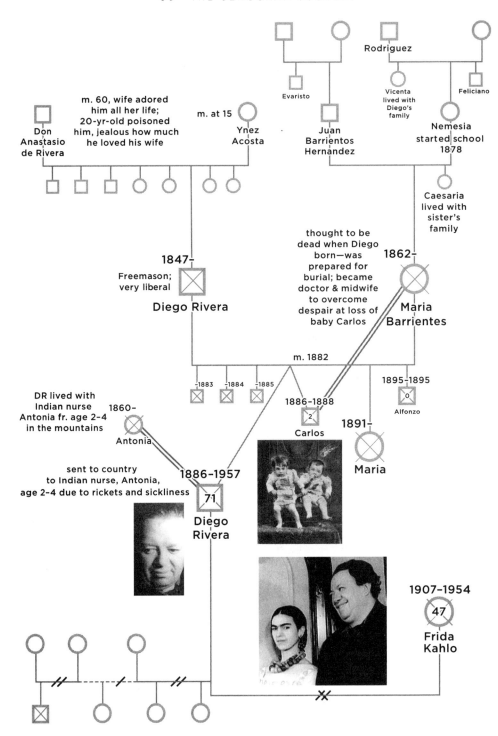

Rodriguez

Evaristo

Vicenta
lived with
Diego's
family

Feliciano

Don
Anastasio
de Rivera

m. 60, wife adored
him all her life;
20-yr-old poisoned
him, jealous how much
he loved his wife

m. at 15

Ynez
Acosta

Juan
Barrientos
Hernandez

Nemesia
started school
1878

Caesaria
lived with
sister's
family

1847–

Freemason;
very liberal

Diego Rivera

thought to be
dead when Diego
born—was
prepared for
burial; became
doctor & midwife
to overcome
despair at loss of
baby Carlos

1862–

**Maria
Barrientes**

m. 1882

–1883   –1884   –1885

1886–1888

2

Carlos

1895–1895

0

Alfonzo

DR lived with
Indian nurse
Antonia fr. age 2–4
in the mountains

1860–

Antonia

1891–

Maria

sent to country
to Indian nurse, Antonia,
age 2–4 due to rickets and sickliness

1886–1957

71

**Diego
Rivera**

1907–1954

47

**Frida
Kahlo**

Genogram 2.4. Diego Rivera.

been so sick and unhappy. If it is only because I gave birth to him from my own body, you shall never be able to claim him truly as yours." The foster mother replied: "You gave birth to him, but if it were not for me, he would not be alive. You were not able to keep his life going. I was. That is why he is more mine than yours. Were you able to see him when he was far away and count your steps so that you could meet him the moment he arrived?" . . . At that her voice broke and the mother took her in her arms. They both began to cry. Watching them, Diego said he felt small and insignificant compared to their 'stupendous expression of love.' He then began to laugh and they all hugged each other" (Rivera, 1991, pp. 42–43).

It was as if they all connected, realizing their love was not a competition. This is how it often is in families and it is important to help families include all those who are important in their concept of "home" and belonging. Surely, no genogram for Rivera would be complete without Antonia, whom he frequently depicted in his art. He, in fact, quoted her as saying she would be with him no matter how far away he went in life: "As long as the sun shines, I will be with you always" (Rivera, 1991, p. 44).

Jostling Your View of Your Family

A good way to jostle rigid views of your family is to go through the exercise of telling the family history from each person's point of view. If negative feelings about a certain person overwhelm you, try to expand your perspective to include how that person was seen by his or her favorite relative or friend. If you think of your father as an arch villain because of the awful way he treated you, it may help to explore his early life and think about how his parents, siblings, and grandparents viewed him as a little boy. It may also help to imagine what it would be like to take the opposite position—to think of your rigid, domineering mother, for example, as a positive influence, perhaps because she taught you self-discipline and was a hard worker.

How might your mother's older sister have viewed her when she was 3 and her sister was 9? How might she have felt when she was 5 and her father deserted the family? How did her best friend feel about her in high school? How did your father feel about her when he was courting her? It may be especially helpful to think of how she felt about her own mother and her childhood, as a way to put the history of the women in your family in perspective.

In severely troubled families there is a tendency for some members to be the caretakers of others, whom they may regard in a patronizing way. Even in less troubled families, members are often "protective" of one another in ways that constrict their relationships. Before you say, "Oh, I can't bring up that issue, my mother's too old and feeble and it would kill her to try to break through her denial now," try to be very clear as to whose denial you are worried about. Work on the assumption that all people do the best they can. Given the benefit of the doubt, people often respond to a sincere request to learn about the family—even if they have spent a lifetime acting crazy, rejecting, hostile, intrusive, oblivious, or inept in other ways.

Even in-laws (so often viewed as crass, materialistic, haughty, dippy, or "lower class") can be astonishing sources of information about family stories. They have, of course, spent years observing the patterns of the family, and by now they are probably experts. Another good source is family friends, or even former family friends. They, like in-laws, might tell the stories that everyone else avoids because they are not as bound as the insiders by rules about "family secrets."

Here are a few questions that may help you get started on your family journey:

- How do family members think about each other? What characteristics are mentioned? Is someone considered the loudmouth? the spendthrift? the soft touch? the dead hero? the all-knowing matriarch? What are the roles and labels in the family? Does someone play the "goody two shoes" and somebody else the "bad seed"? Is one the villain and another the hero? Is one "weak, boring, and slow" and another "brilliant, domineering, and manipulative"? List the different ways family members are described, noting especially the opposites in role or label.

- Who was named for whom in the family and why? Do names reveal the roles people have played? Who chose the names? Why were they chosen? If names have no apparent rhyme or reason, could there be hidden meanings? Was someone named for a mother's lost sweetheart? If members are named for the dead, have they taken on their characteristics? What were the naming patterns in the family and are they reflected in the structure or have they influenced the psychological patterns of family members?

- Were there coincidences between the births of family members and moves or migration? illness or death? changes in family finances? How did migration influence children's family experience? How did financial changes influence the lives of children? How did illness and death influence them at different ages?

- How much did your family conform to the gender stereotypes of your culture and era? Which family members did not conform to these expected gender roles and how were they viewed by others? What can you learn about your family's flexibility or inflexibility from its history of allowable gender roles?

3 Family Stories, Myths, and Secrets

Storytelling is fundamental to the human search for meaning . . .
each of us is involved in inventing a new kind of story.

Composing a Life
—MARY CATHERINE BATESON

Remember, what you are told is really threefold: Shaped by the teller,
reshaped by the listener, and concealed from them both by the deadman
of the tale.

The Real Life of Sebastian Knight
—VLADIMIR NABOKOV

All history, including the histories of our families, is part of us, such that
when we hear any secret revealed, a secret about a grandfather or an uncle,
or a secret about the battle of Dresden in 1945, our lives are made suddenly
clearer to us, as the unnatural heaviness of unspoken truth is dispersed.
For perhaps we are like stone—our own history and the history of the
world embedded in us.

A Chorus of Stones
—SUSAN GRIFFIN

We are born not just into our family, but also into our family's stories, which
both nourish—and sometimes cripple—us. And when we die, the story of our
lives becomes part of our family's web of meaning (Kotre & Hall, 1990). Family
stories tend to be told to remind members of the cherished beliefs of the family. We sing the heroes and even the villains whose daring the family admires.
Taping or writing down the stories of older family members can bring a richness to people's search for perspective on family that cannot be achieved in any
other way. Technology now allows us to convey the sound and visual reality of
family stories better than at any other time in human history.

The passage of time shears away some details and highlights others, yielding
a subjective, continuously reedited overview of memories and stories that strive
for a meaningful narrative. When a disjunctive experience is introduced—

one that doesn't jibe with a family's story or the culture's dominant narrative—we may be left challenged and bewildered. Everything that gets said in a family crosses the intersection of the said and the unsaid. Traumatic family experiences can create myths and superstitions about the dangers of the outside world that flow down the generations, influencing descendants who have no conscious awareness of the origins of the beliefs. Nor do they understand how family stories develop around the facts to reassure, to explain, or to limit the pain of certain family experiences. Family stories and myths are worth analyzing for the signals they contain about the family's covert values and rules. Families transmit messages that seem to prescribe behavior for generations to come. They embed in the narratives the sense they make of their lives, as well as rules for relationships and behavior.

One family's stories may revolve around the courage of family members against great odds, another's about their humorous comeback after humiliation. In families characterized by pessimism, stories may carry a message that "you never win." Usually people have stereotyped roles in family stories— hero, villain, jokester, victim—roles that, by identifying the "good guys" and "bad guys," reveal the values in the family. Becoming aware of family messages allows people to consciously decide whether or not to maintain these roles and beliefs.

Family myths are transmitted both explicitly and—more often—implicitly, which increases their power to influence the next generation, as these beliefs are generally accepted as reality. People may need to be exposed to values different from those of their own families before they can question or become fully aware of their family's rules. Families communicate in numerous subtle verbal and nonverbal ways. All families develop private jokes, routines, and references, which are transmitted from one generation to another.

My mother used to say, "Never trust a short woman." She was 5 foot 9; her mother-in-law was about 4 foot 6; we can guess the implications of her imperative. Other messages, such as putting a plate under the orange juice when certain guests visited, conveyed important class messages about where she felt we stood in relation to others. We had other communication rules about never mentioning a person's race or cultural background, which conveyed messages about our place in the social setup. Children learn early what can and cannot be discussed. All families convey messages about gender, social class, race, and ethnicity, which can be valuable to examine.

Children may be drawn into a family myth or expectation to carry out missions left incomplete by another member's death, or they may be constrained by parental fear of repeating a painful experience in the past. Whether family experiences lead parents to compensate by neglecting or overfocusing on a child, the legacy can become a burden for the next generation.

The Bronte Family

The Bronte family (Genogram 3.1) seems to have developed the belief that leaving home was dangerous, and in the end no one could leave at all. The belief probably originated in early family experiences of illness and death, but the myth itself influenced later reactions when family members did leave. Charlotte, the oldest to survive to adulthood, once wrote an epitaph for one of her heroines, which also seems apt for her family: "The orb of your life is not to be so rounded; for you the crescent-phase must suffice" (Bronte, 2004, p. 340).

Much information is missing about the earlier generations of this extraordinary family, which produced two of the greatest novelists the world has known: Emily Bronte, author of *Wuthering Heights*, and Charlotte Bronte, author of *Jane Eyre*. Probably there was a legacy of emotional conflicts in the family of the Bronte father, Patrick, as his father, Hugh Bronte, and grandfather, Welsh Bronte, were both apparently adopted and then mistreated in their adoptive families in a story extremely reminiscent of *Wuthering Heights*. The Bronte mother, Maria Branwell Bronte, came from a family in which four children died in infancy or childhood, including the three closest to her in age. And there were many more losses, including the loss of both parents, before Maria married Patrick in a double wedding with Maria's first cousin and Patrick's best friend; on the same day Maria's younger sister, Charlotte, married another cousin of theirs, Joseph Branwell, in a different town.

If we take a systemic view of the coincidence of events, concurrent events in a family often represent more than random happenings. The fact that four members of the same family were married on the same day may suggest some fusion in the Bronte family, which often results from loss. In fact, the family had just suffered a series of pivotal losses: As mentioned, both parents had died—Maria's father, Thomas Branwell, in 1808, and her mother in 1809. The family business had then been taken over by Thomas's older brother, Richard, and Richard's son, Thomas, but then Thomas died tragically in December 1811 and Richard died the following year. This final death precipitated the breakup of the family. Richard's other son, Joseph, married Charlotte, Maria's younger sister, and Maria married Patrick Bronte, while her cousin Jane (daughter of Richard's only sister) married Patrick's best friend.

There followed in the family of Patrick and Maria Bronte a further series of tragic losses, which seem to have influenced the future behavior of family members profoundly, limiting their ability to leave and turning them inward on themselves and on one another. Patrick came to see himself as "a stranger in a strange land," and seems to have conveyed to his children this sense of alienation and need to protect oneself from the outside world. The six Bronte

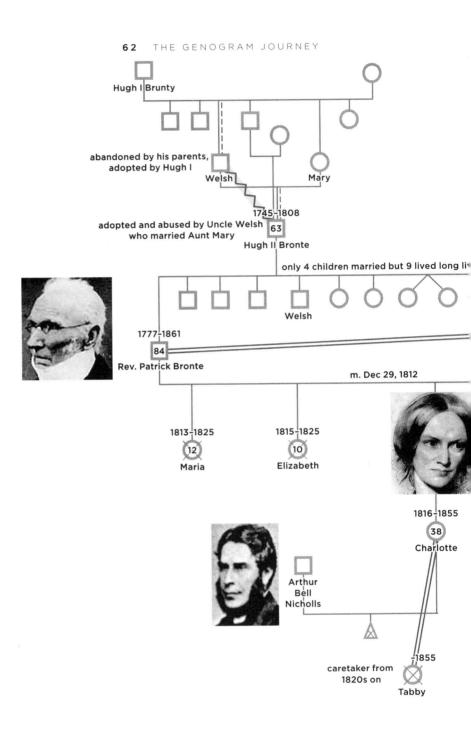

• An "X" appears in cases of untimely, recent, or significant death.

Genogram 3.1. The Bronte Family.

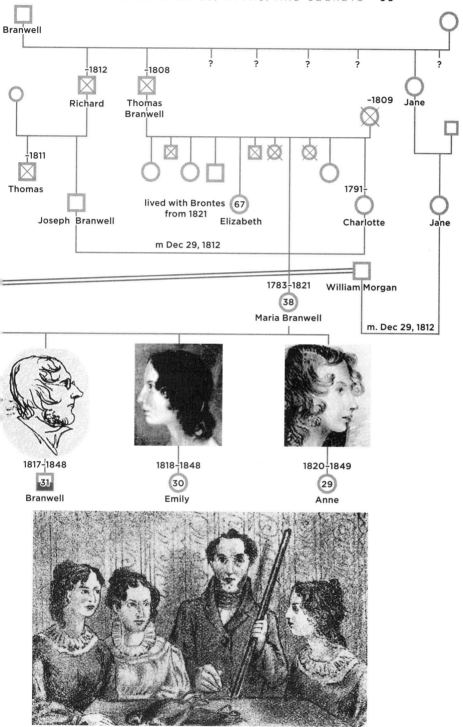

Branwell

-1812
Richard

-1808
Thomas
Branwell

? ? ? ? ?

-1809
Jane

-1811
Thomas

Joseph Branwell

lived with Brontes
from 1821

67
Elizabeth

1791-
Charlotte

Jane

m Dec 29, 1812

1783-1821
38
Maria Branwell

William Morgan

m. Dec 29, 1812

1817-1848
31
Branwell

1818-1848
30
Emily

1820-1849
29
Anne

children were born in a 7-year period; soon after the youngest was born, Maria developed a serious blood disorder. During her painful illness, all six children developed scarlet fever, which must have intensified the family's sense of fragility and trauma. Maria died an excruciatingly painful death a year later, having rarely seen the children in the final year because of her suffering. The oldest daughter was only 9 and the youngest was not yet 2. Following her death, the father, Patrick, found his children's presence a painful reminder of his wife rather than a comfort: "Oppressive grief sometimes lay heavy on me . . . when I missed her at every corner, and when her memory was hourly revived by the innocent, yet distressing prattle of my children" (Frazer, 1988, p. 28).

Patrick withdrew into himself and began dining alone, which he continued to do for the rest of his life. His daughter Charlotte later said that "he did not like children . . . and the noise made him shut himself up and want no companionship—nay, to be positively annoyed by it" (Frazer, 1988, p. 28). He appeared to outsiders eccentric, carrying a loaded pistol at all times, even during prayers. From the time of Maria's death, nothing in the Bronte home was changed—no furniture was moved, added, or eliminated—and very few people visited. Such rigidity is a common response in families beset by trauma.

Maria's unmarried sister, Elizabeth, moved in and remained there for the rest of her life. Four years later a family caretaker, Tabby, was added. She also stayed for the rest of her life, dying within a few weeks of the death of the last surviving Bronte child, Charlotte. Throughout their childhood the six children were left very much on their own and, while the externals in their lives remained constricted, they developed a most extraordinary inner life of imagination and fantasy.

When the oldest daughter was 12, she and her sisters were sent to a local boarding school, but further tragedy followed this attempt to leave home. The two oldest sisters developed tuberculosis at the school and died within a few months. The death of the oldest, Maria, named for her mother, was especially tragic, because the school authorities were extremely abusive to her in her last days. The other sisters were witness to the torment of their favorite sister, who had become their mother's replacement. The morbidity of it all was exaggerated by the fact that the cemetery where mother and sisters lay buried surrounded the family house on two sides. There was no getting away from the eerie sense of death. Probably the stories about children mistreated in school situations and misunderstood by parent substitutes in the writings of the Brontes reflect attempts to work through these painful childhood memories.

Such early losses must have reinforced the developing Bronte "story" or belief that life in the outside world was dangerous. After the oldest daughter's death, the other children were withdrawn from school, and from that point on, whenever the remaining four children tried to leave home, they were forced to return because they or another member became ill or needy. The only son, Branwell, on whom the greatest hopes were placed, was accepted at the Royal College of Art in London and left home to attend, but he never actually enrolled, returning home addicted to drugs and alcohol. Thereafter he periodically left home for jobs, which he never managed to keep. The real deterioration of Branwell coincided in reciprocal fashion with his three sisters' initial publishing success, which they accomplished under male pseudonyms, telling neither their father nor their brother what they were doing. As Charlotte said: "My unhappy brother . . . was not aware that . . . [we] had published a line. We could not tell him of our efforts for fear of causing him too deep a pang of remorse for his own time misspent and talents misapplied. Now he will never know. I cannot dwell longer on the subject at present—it is too painful" (Frazer, 1988, p. 315). By the time Branwell died, 3 years later, the sisters were renowned under their own names. Branwell painted their portrait, painting himself out of the image (Figure 3.1). Of the three surviving

Figure 3.1. Portrait by Branwell Bronte of himself and his sisters in which he has obliterated himself.

sisters, Charlotte was the most successful at leaving home, managing at one point to stay away at a school for 2 years; she was the only one able to develop friendships outside the family, but she too always returned home.

There was something eccentric as well as extraordinary about the Brontë family. Patrick Brontë rarely spent time with his family, though he could not tolerate their leaving him. The children, deprived of outside stimulation, created an amazing fantasy world of shared stories, invented and written jointly in minuscule, almost indecipherable handwriting and put together in about 800 tiny manuscript books, about 400 of which still survive. It is almost as if they were fusing in the private world of their imagination; their minds roamed free in fantasy, creating historical sagas with imaginary characters, as well as historical personages they had heard about. As Charlotte later wrote, they "wove a web in childhood" (Fraser, 1988, p. 99). As an adult she feared their childhood dreams "withered the sod."

Charlotte, even in her youth, looked somehow like a little old woman, but described herself as "undeveloped." Even as a woman in her mid-thirties, she wore children's chemises. Charlotte's fantasy world remained her "secret joy," and when she was forced to work as a teacher, she found it difficult to stay at her task, longing for the fantasy life on which she had become extremely dependent and which she used as an escape from her mundane existence: "I carefully avoid any appearance of preoccupation and eccentricity which might lead those I live amongst to suspect the nature of my pursuits" (Fraser, 1988, p. 111). Whenever she was away, Charlotte tended to have an "indefinite fear" about those at home, a legacy, as her biographer Rebecca Frazer called it, of "her overcast youth," worrying unceasingly about her father, as he himself always exaggerated fears about his own health. When she was away, she experienced a variety of symptoms, from a hysterical form of blindness to chronic and severe headaches, anxiety, and depression. She wrote: "At home . . . I talk with ease and am never shy—never weighed down by that miserable 'mauvaise honte' which torments and constrains me elsewhere" (p. 128). A friend warned her that staying home would "ruin her," but she gave up encouraging her to leave when she saw Charlotte's response, though she could never "think without gloomy anger of Charlotte's sacrifices to the selfish old man" (Fraser, 1988, pp. 221–222). Charlotte herself wrote of her life: "I feel as if we were all buried here—I long to travel—to work, to live a life of action but saw these as my fruitless wishes" (p. 224). To another friend she wrote: "Whenever I consult my Conscience it affirms that I am doing right in staying at home—and bitter are its upbraidings when I yield to an eager desire for release" (p. 183).

The other Brontë siblings were even more unable to leave the family. Emily, after a few unsuccessful forays, gave up completely. She became ill at the time of Branwell's funeral and died 3 months later. Anne became ill at this time as well and died 5 months after Emily, leaving only Charlotte of the six siblings. Charlotte feared that the shadow of her brother and sisters' last days would now linger forever. Her description of her reactions at the time are an excellent expression of ways the legacy of trauma can shut a family down, locking them into myth, secrecy, and avoidance of any experience that reminds them of what they cannot bear to face: "I must not look forwards, nor must I look backwards. Too often I feel like one crossing an abyss on a narrow plank—a glance round might quite unnerve" (Fraser, 1988, p. 320). She buried herself in her work, clinging to her faculty of imagination to save her from sinking.

Several years later a most persistent suitor, her father's curate, Arthur Nicholls, persuaded her to marry him. Her father went into a rage and fired him. A year later, unable to put up with Nicholls's replacement, Patrick relented and agreed that Nicholls could marry Charlotte, if they would both agree never to leave him. They agreed. Charlotte was not really in love with Nicholls, as we know from her letters to her two close friends, but shortly after the marriage she accompanied him to his home in Ireland and there she began to see him in a different light. She saw his humor and found him more interesting in the context of his family. She began to fall in love with him. She became pregnant. She returned from her travels, however, out of anxiety about her father's health, which soon improved. Hers, however, began to deteriorate and she soon died, losing the baby as well.

The cause of Charlotte's death is unclear. Many have speculated on a possible psychological component. Her beloved caretaker, Tabby, had died just before she did. Charlotte died at age 38, the same age her mother had been at death. Only Patrick lived on, dying at the ripe age of 86.

Thus ended a most creative family. One might almost think they were "doomed" psychologically by the narratives they had created in response to their many losses, even while the narratives they created in their writings will last as long as our culture.

The Adams Family

The Adams family story (Genogram 3.2) involves a belief in high achievement, which meant that for four generations they were a family of spectacular highs and lows—amazing successes and abysmal failures. They seemed to accept a myth that there were only two options: You were either a great success or a great failure. Charles Frances Adams, the most successful member of the third generation, observed: "The history of my family is not a pleasant one to remember. It is one of great triumphs in the world but of deep groans within, one of extraordinary brilliancy and deep corroding mortification" (Nagel, 1983, p. 3). The public accomplishments of many members of the Adams family are astonishing, as are the catastrophic failures of others. As their biographer Paul Nagel has pointed out, "No Adams, success or failure, made a comfortable accommodation to life" (p. 6).

In this family across four generations, there were two U.S. presidents, a famous diplomat, accomplished essayists, historians, and wealthy businessmen. There were also illiterates, alcoholics and ne'er-do-wells, failed marriages, and suicides. In fact, even the most successful family members were often depressed, full of self-doubt and rarely satisfied with their efforts.

The Adams family had a sense of being different from the common crowd. This is not surprising, given their accomplishments. They saw themselves as having a unique independence of mind, devotion to public service, and freedom from impulses of greed or political ambition. Along with this sense of specialness and expectation of greatness came self-criticism. They were hard on others in their demands but even harder on themselves, holding themselves up to impossible standards.

John Adams, the second president, was his own greatest critic, extremely sensitive to the criticism of others, full of self-doubt, and questioning of his own motives. He was equally quick to criticize his children in the hope that they might avoid succumbing to weak nature. As Abigail once said to her husband: "Sometimes, you know, I think you too severe. You do not make so many allowances as Human Nature requires" (Nagel, 1983, p. 21).

John's letters to Abigail are marked by self-criticism that continued to characterize the Adams family. Despite his extreme diligence as a lawyer and patriot, he repeatedly castigated himself as a lazy wastrel. The family intolerance for human frailty joined their pessimistic view of human nature that led them to expect it. Like his own father, a deacon, John believed in dedication to family, self-reliance, and service to others. The father of his wife, Abigail Smith, was an independent-minded minister who resisted the religious hysteria of his day. Both families were steeped in a Puritanism that emphasized original sin and human fallibility. Like many families living in times of great change, the Adams developed a strong sense of family identity that brought the parents and children together in common cause against adversity. As the family grew in eminence they developed a sense of mission as the moral conscience of the nation.

Once he became involved in politics, John spent more and more time away from his New England home, leaving Abigail to run the farm and rear the children. She had nurtured the hope that out of the American Revolution would come greater equality for women and recognition of their rights. She was sorely disappointed, as even her husband did not take her cause seriously. To justify her deprivations and disappointments, she tried to focus on her husband's goals and ideals. She commiserated with John that his efforts and sacrifices for his country were never sufficiently appreciated, that he alone was not stooping to partisan politics and knew what was best for the country. His project was to start a nation, and hers to produce a new generation that would lead that nation. John, too, was interested in raising the children correctly, but he often had to be satisfied with giving advice and admonitions by mail.

Both parents were demanding of their children. Perhaps because Abigail's brother's dissipation had devastated her family of origin, to the point they would not speak his name, she was obsessed with her children's good behavior and achievement. Indeed, her dissipated brother's own son died of alcoholism at the same age as his father, and the multigenerational pattern was evident in the family. Abigail said, "God grant that we may never mourn a similar situation" (Nagel, 1983, p. 33). She pondered the sins of her brother, knowing that, despite the most earnest parental efforts, vice and viciousness could take early root and, as she put it, "tho often crop'd, will spring again" (Nagel, 1983, p. 28). She told her oldest son, John Quincy, when he was only 10: "I had much rather you should have found your Grave in the ocean you have crossed, or any untimely death crop you in your infant years than see you an immoral profligate or a Graceless child" (Nagel, 1983, p. 30).

As much as they tried to get their children on the right track, John and Abigail's entire lives were marred by problems with their children. They never realized that their anxiety, high standards, harsh criticism, pessimistic expectations, and the suffocating togetherness of the family might contribute to their children's difficulties. To a considerable extent their worst parental fears were fulfilled. Their oldest daughter, Abigail (Nabby), partly in response to her parents' intrusions, ended up marrying an uncaring, irresponsible husband who eventually went to prison for fraud and debt. Charles Adams became alcoholic, lost the family investments, and became cut off from his parents and family. Thomas, also alcoholic and a failed lawyer, was described negatively by everyone as an embittered and difficult bully; he too made a disaster of his and his family's lives. Thomas was apparently reminded through his life that he was responsible for his maternal grandmother becoming ill and dying while caring for him when he had cholera at 3. John and Abigail ended up having to support Charles's and Thomas's wives and raise their children.

The one exception seemed to be the eldest son, John Quincy. At the age of 14 he accompanied his father to Europe on a diplomatic mission. He returned

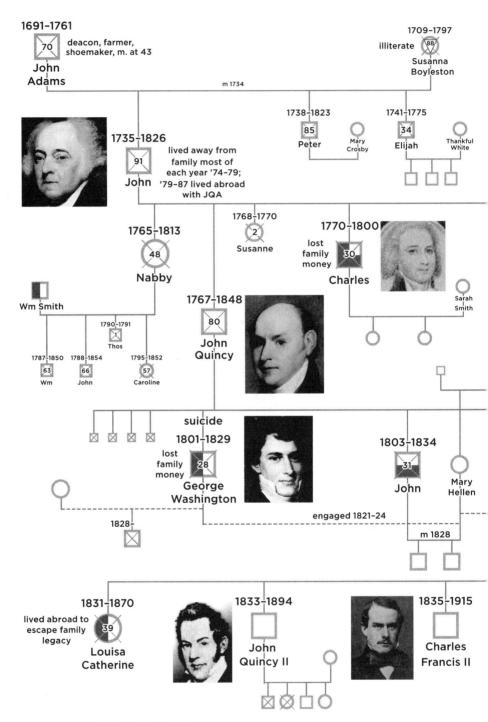

1691–1761

70   deacon, farmer, shoemaker, m. at 43

John Adams

m 1734

1709–1797

illiterate   88

Susanna Boyleston

1738–1823

85

Peter

Mary Crosby

1741–1775

34

Elijah

Thankful White

1735–1826

91

John   lived away from family most of each year '74–79; '79–87 lived abroad with JQA

1765–1813

48

Nabby

1768–1770

2

Susanne

1770–1800

lost family money   30

Charles

Sarah Smith

Wm Smith

1790–1791

1

Thos

1767–1848

80

John Quincy

1787–1850

63

Wm

1788–1854

66

John

1795–1852

57

Caroline

suicide

1801–1829

lost family money   28

George Washington

1803–1834

31

John

Mary Hellen

1828

engaged 1821–24

m 1828

1831–1870

lived abroad to escape family legacy   39

Louisa Catherine

1833–1894

John Quincy II

1835–1915

Charles Francis II

Genogram 3.2. The Adams Family.

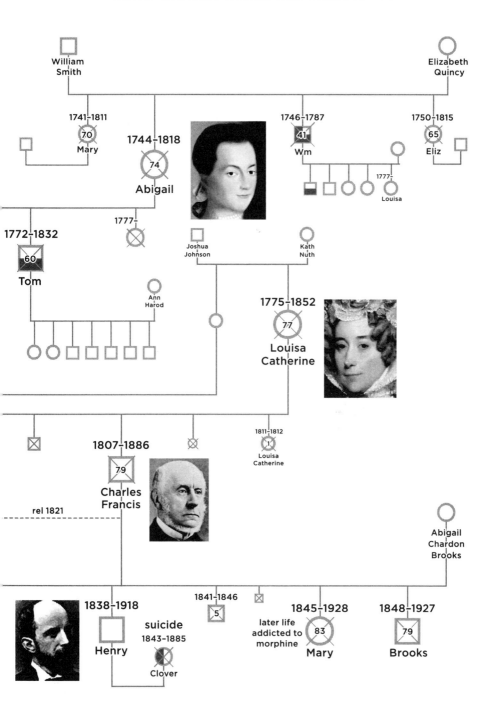

to go to Harvard and eventually start his own law practice. At the age of 27, he was sent to his own diplomatic post in Holland and began a career in public service. Eventually he became the sixth president of the United States. John Quincy shared not only his father's dedication as a statesman but also his outlook on life, taking it even further in harshness and severity. The expectations for him had been great. His father had said to him: "You come into life with advantages, which will disgrace you if your success is mediocre. And if you do not rise to the head not only of your Profession, but of your country, it will be owing to your own Laziness, Slovenliness, and Obstinacy" (Nagel, 1997, p. 76). Unlike his brothers, John Quincy was partly able to fulfill these expectations, but at great personal cost. Despite his achievements, his life was even more overshadowed by self-doubt and depression than his father's was. He never felt that he was living up to the standards handed down to him by his parents. Like his father, he was defeated after a single term as president and saw the world of politics as crass, devoid of ideals, and unappreciative of what the Adams family had done for the nation. It was not until years later, when he returned to Washington as a congressman and became the major spokesman for the antislavery movement, that he developed some sense of accomplishment.

John Quincy's marriage was a difficult one. His wife, Louisa Catherine Johnson, an extraordinarily capable woman, was a joyous and affection-craving spirit. She wondered in later life whether, if she had been more mature, she might have recognized that her husband's "unnecessary harshness and severity of character" would make the marriage a perpetual trial. Not surprisingly, she had problems with the outlook of the Adams family, which took itself so seriously and saw the world as prone to such evil. Her father's bankruptcy at the time of her marriage humiliated her and left her painfully dependent on her critical and distant husband, who ignored her as he attended to his career or withdrew in bouts of depression. Often left alone, she became depressed herself. Her husband could not or would not respond to her emotional needs. She had four miscarriages before she had a child who survived. Many more losses followed. In all she bore 10 children, only three of whom lived to adulthood.

John Quincy took up the family escutcheon of public service, family greatness, and intense anxiety about childrearing and passed it on to the next generation. He taught his children that much was expected of an Adams in the constant struggle against an unappreciative world. He once wrote to his son:

> Your father and grandfather have fought their way through the world
> against hosts of adversaries, open and close, disguised and masked . . .
> and more than one or two perfidious friends. The world is and will

continue to be prolific with such characters. Live in peace with them; never upbraid, never trust them. But—"don't give up the ship!" Fortify your mind against disappointments. (Shepherd, 1975, p. xxi)

He also taught that the family must stay together and recognize its special place in history. However, long separations again had their impact on the next generation. Because of his diplomatic duties, John Quincy and Louisa spent many years abroad, leaving the older children behind with their grandparents. Their oldest son, George Washington Adams, later felt that his parents' absence during those formative years left him unprepared for life. George was the oldest son of the oldest son of John Adams, who was the oldest son of another John Adams. As if this positioning wasn't enough pressure, George's birth followed four miscarriages, which must have intensified the parents' expectations for the first surviving son. A lot was expected of this unfortunate young man, who was born just after his grandfather lost a bitter election for a second term as president. Further conflict was embedded in his very name. Instead of being named for his father, grandfather, and great grandfather, he was named for our first president, which wounded John Adams (McCullough, 2001), who believed that Washington owed his career to Adams himself (Adams, 1976). Surely there must have been conflicted family meaning to this naming.

Sadly, George Washington Adams was ill-equipped to live up to the expectations of the Adams family. He once said he could not remember a day when he didn't think about becoming president. The parents' letters from abroad exhorted him to live up to his legacy. He never could. Just before entering college at 16, he had a dream in which he was showing interest in a young woman when his father appeared, "his eyes fixed upon me" (Nagel, 1983, p. 268). Under his father's gaze, George lost interest. He said he was always trying to escape that gaze.

Years earlier in 1816, his grandfather had written to him: "I fear that too many of my hopes are built upon you" (Musto, 1981, p. 57). George, in fact, was unruly and difficult from childhood on. He did poorly at everything he tried. He blamed his parents' long absences for his difficulties and lack of self-discipline, though he seemed also relieved of the pressure of their presence when his father moved to Washington to become our sixth president. Left behind in Boston to handle family affairs, he made a mess of them and of his own life over the next 4 years. Finally, in 1828, his father was defeated for reelection. George's engagement to a flirtatious first cousin, Mary Catherine Hellen, was broken in February when she married his younger brother, John, which must have been painful for him. (She had also had a romance with the third brother, Charles Francis!) George then impregnated a maid and she gave birth in December.

By the spring of 1829 George's life was in shambles. His parents requested that he come to Washington to accompany them home to Boston. On the boat on the way to meet them, he became very disturbed, and in the middle of the night jumped overboard and drowned, probably in anticipation of having to live again in the shadow of his father. Born at the moment of failure of his grandfather and of the miserable death his dissipated, alcoholic uncle, Charles, who had lost the family savings, George killed himself at a similar moment of failure in his father's life, leaving a painful and humiliating legacy like that left by his uncle.

John Quincy's second son, John, also became an alcoholic failure and died from a mysterious disease at the age of 31. As in the earlier generation, only one son, the third, Charles Francis, survived to carry on the Adams legacy. As a youngest son and probably freer of the family constraints, he was a very different man from his father. Charles Francis was also the only child to accompany his parents on their travels. Perhaps because of her connection to him, Louisa was better able to soften for him the negative aspects of the Adams family legacy. Louisa later warned him: "Go on and do not suffer yourself to be intimidated or brow beaten as your brother was, but pursue your course steadily and respectably" (Musto, 1981, p. 44). Charles Francis was more relaxed, less self-critical, and better able to face differences with his father squarely without letting his father dominate him. He still had the strong sense of the Adams legacy and the family's special place in history. It was he who began editing the family papers, which would demonstrate to the world the uniqueness of his parents and grandparents. At first he did not follow the same path to public duty but rather was content to manage the family finances and be a family man. He even used the pessimistic Adams views about the corruptibility of his countrymen as an argument against entering the dirty business of politics. He did eventually become a congressman at age 56, and later even ambassador to Great Britain (like his father and grandfather before him), where his remarkable diplomatic skill managed to keep England out of the Civil War. His success at this made him the most noted American diplomat of his time. Indeed, Charles Francis found considerable satisfaction in fulfilling the family tradition of public service. But, perhaps luckily for him, when his name was submitted as a candidate for the presidency in 1872, he lost!

Charles Francis married Abby Brooks, the favorite daughter of a wealthy Boston businessman. Abby was not a strong personality in the mold of Abigail and Louisa. She depended on her husband for constant reassurance and allowed him to think for her in all areas except the social. She loved to entertain and successfully resisted the Adams tendency toward social isolation.

It was in the area of childrearing that Charles Francis departed most from the generations before him. Perhaps aware of the fate of his brothers and uncles, he was determined to be an easier, less demanding, and more available father. He considered parenthood the most serious of all his duties. Although he still focused on his children's development, he was determined to raise them differently. He spoke of his mission: "I hardly dare to look at my children with the hope that I can do for them what I ought in order to save them from the dangers which I barely escaped myself without shipwreck" (Nagel, 1983, p. 186). He believed in offering sympathetic encouragement and in nourishing independence, and he recognized the limitations of parental influence. Most of all, he spent a good deal of time with his children when they were young.

Charles Francis partially succeeded in shifting the Adams legacy. Among the sons of the fourth generation, there were no great failures, early deaths, or alcoholics. The only early deaths were the women. The oldest daughter, Louisa Catherine, considered the most brilliant of all the children, was difficult and resentful from an early age, feeling she could have become president if she had been male. The family was indeed dismayed that their first child was a girl (Nagel, 1987). Louisa Catherine rebelled against the family and attempted to escape the legacy by marrying and living in Europe, where, however, she led a hedonistic, almost suicidal existence. She died in an accident at the age of 39. The other tragic woman of this generation was the wife of Henry Adams, Clover, a gifted photographer who committed suicide at the age of 42, having apparently struggled much with the gender constraints of her time. The youngest sister, Mary, was disobedient and stubborn as a child, and the most conventional of the fourth generation as an adult, submitting to family ways, and in later life she became addicted to morphine.

John Quincy II, the oldest son of the fourth generation, felt the burden of the family legacy acutely, considering "John Adams a grievous heavy name to bear" (Nagel, 1983, p. 239). He felt overwhelmed by the expectations others had of him. "What can a man say when he is thus absolutely beaten over the head with ancestry?" His relationship with his father was never easy. It was dominated by the son's self-doubt and the father's encouragement, mixed with impatience. It might have been easier if others had left him alone, but because of his position, the family heaped counsel and then criticism on him. He burned his diary and his letters, believing "the less weight you carry the better" (Nagel, 1983, p. 240). He wanted to be left alone (a dream shared by all the generations of the Adams family), but this could not be. In response to his father's continuous prodding, he replied: "I am afraid you, like most parents, overestimate your children. I am no consequence here under heaven except to my home" (Nagel, 1983, p. 243). John Quincy II blundered in the face of his father's pressure to become a family leader. He viewed himself as his father's errand boy: "I should be grateful once (but I know it is useless) if I might in any one thing be considered as an individual and not a Son or Grandson" (p. 239). As a consequence, John retreated from responsibility, handing over even the management of the family finances to his younger brother. He was put up to run for election several times, as state representative, as governor, and once even as vice president, but he only enjoyed his candidacy when he was sure he would not win. John wanted to lose. He shrank from the unpleasant grind of politics that would come with victory. He once confessed to his father: "Politics, except just at election time, had not much attraction for so lazy a devil as I am" (p. 242). Even in the personal arena John's life was doomed to misery, when two of his beloved children died of diptheria, an experience from which he never recovered. He became a sad, quiet, retiring figure who carefully destroyed all his papers, as if to make sure that the legacy would stop with him.

The three younger sons of the fourth generation all became accomplished in their fields, though they too had their problems. Where John resolved to obliterate all traces of his life, Charles Francis Jr. determined to leave a huge written record about himself (carefully edited, of course). Charles also determined from his earliest years to succeed in areas beyond the traditional Adams role of statesmanship. He became a successful entrepreneur and president of the Union Pacific Railroad, although he eventually lost it to Jay Gould. He said of his failure: "There being nothing more for me to do, I got up to go. . . . My ideas were right, but I did not hold to them. I was weak of will" (Shepherd, 1975, p. 419). Here we see again the underside of the Adams success— their lack of self-assurance, evident even for those who achieved greatness as Charles Francis Jr. did. He was continually disabled from digestive ills and, after losing much of the family fortune in 1893, cut off from his brothers and sister, as the earlier Charles (John Quincy's brother) had lost the family investments and become cut off two generations earlier.

Henry Adams, the most famous of the fourth generation, was an eminent historian, and Brooks, also a historian, was one of America's earliest geopoliticians. There was still a sense of specialness and commitment to public service, but this fourth generation consisted more of thinkers than doers. Rather than entering politics, they wrote about it. These sons were all philosophically interested in the family outlook they had inherited from the earlier generation. They edited the family papers and speculated on the fate of humankind. With them the traditional Adams ability to view the world with derision and pessimism was harsher than ever. Henry and Brooks wrote cynical historical essays with emphasis on the poor prognosis for the social ailments of their times. They saw little hope in modern trends. Brooks was argumentative and misanthropic; Henry, in particular, felt he was being left behind by the Industrial Age.

Family historian David Musto has written a penetrating analysis of the patterns in the Adams family:

> The middle generations of the Adams family had an unusual dispar-
> ity in life-spans between the successful and the less successful. Not all
> the shorter lives can be attributed to failing the family's imperatives,
> but the contrast is suggestive. The successful: John, John Quincy,
> and Charles Francis Adams, lived an average of 80 years, while the
> remainder: Charles, Thomas Boylston, Nabby, George Washington,
> and John 2nd lived an average of 40 years. The fittest survived. The
> imperatives of excellence and achievement which developed in the
> Adams family during the first years of our national life were a burden
> as well as a spur to subsequent generations. (Musto, 1981, p. 57–58)

By the fourth generation, there was no longer the unifying shared family outlook to keep the Adams family together. Rather, each of the Adams
in this generation was strongly individualistic, brilliant, and often eccentric.
Each strove to escape the Adams legacy. Each found his or her own way. On
the other hand, there was little to keep the siblings together, and after the
father died, each went his own way and the estate was eventually divided.
Ironically, Charles Francis's sympathetic encouragement of independence and
individual development did not lead to stronger family ties as he had wished.
Perhaps the anxiety and fear of the world was no longer there to keep the
family together. In any case, the loss was not mourned by the children. As
Brooks, the last member of the fourth generation argued: "It is now full four
generations since John Adams wrote the constitution of Massachusetts. It is
time we perished. The world is tired of us" (Musto, 1981, p. 44).

The high expectations of achievement in the Adams family did not apply
to the daughters. Abigail Smith Adams (wife of the second president) and
her sisters were given a certain latitude to distinguish themselves, perhaps
because their only brother was a failure. In the next generation John Quincy
Adams's older sister, Nabby, took considerable responsibility, particularly
when her father and brother were in Europe, but in terms of achievement,
she was expected only to marry well and be a good wife. Her husband, like
her mother's brother, turned out to be an alcoholic failure, and she ended
up spending time in prison with him for debt. John Quincy's wife, Louisa

Catherine, was a very gifted woman (like her mother-in-law, Abigail) who often lived a life of quiet desperation. In the third generation no daughters survived infancy. Charles Francis's wife, Abby Chardon Brooks, was a light-hearted, spontaneous, and sociable woman. After a few years of marriage into this demanding, self-critical family, however, and with the arrival of babies, public life, and other distresses, she found that "the poetry of life has fallen into prose" (Nagel, 1987, p. 260). However, through the tragedy of the early death of their son, Arthur, Charles collapsed into depression and self-reproach for having punished the boy just before his fatal illness; in Charles's time of trouble, Abby's strength emerged, and over their many years together they evolved a strong closeness and ability to enrich each other.

Family Secrets

Family secrets have far-ranging influences, undermining families for genera-tions, and family stories and myths are profoundly influenced by the secrets families keep. All families have secrets. They remind family members of their boundaries. At times it is the content of the secret itself that is powerful: a suicide, a pregnancy that occurs outside of a marriage, or a sexual liaison. In other cases it is the boundary established by the secret that gives it its power, as when one family member is excluded from knowledge of a certain family experience. A secret may also be a source of power—binding together those who share it, though it may also create shame and guilt because of its rule of silence. Because they create covert bonds and splits in a family, secrets also have a mystifying power. Imagine, for example, the power of a parent naming a child for a secret lover. The spouse may not know the meaning of the child's name. The child, siblings, and the other parent may experience a distance that none of them understand. This could ripple down to that child's experi-ence of being a parent to his own children. Winston Churchill's mother, Jenny Jerome, seems to have been named for her father's lover, Jenny Lind. Jenny named her younger son, John Strange Spencer, for her lover, John Strange Jocelyn. One can only guess at how the secrets in this family may have influ-enced family relationships under the surface.

Secrets usually reveal a family's vulnerabilities. The playwright A. R. Gurney described the legacy of his great grandfather's suicide, never men-tioned in his own lifetime:

> My great-grandfather hung up his clothes one day and walked into the
> Niagara River and no one understood why. He was a distinguished
> man in Buffalo. My father could never mention it, and it affected the
> family well into the fourth generation as a dark and unexplainable

gesture. It made my father and his father desperate to be accepted, to be conventional, and comfortable. It made them commit themselves to an ostensibly easy bourgeois world. They saw it so precariously, but the reason was never mentioned. (Witchel, 1989, p. 103)

Four generations later the pattern set in motion by this death was still operating. Gurney was 48 when he first learned of the suicide from his father-in-law, who was a genealogist. This was at the time when Gurney's own father died, and, in an interesting continuation of the pattern, Gurney himself later refused to talk about his father's death. Without realizing it, we may go for generations following patterns set up by the secrets of earlier generations.

Secrets are especially important in families because of the potential trauma their revelation may cause for those not prepared for the knowledge. When Peter and Jane Fonda's mother committed suicide (Genogram 3.3), the entire community colluded to keep the facts from them. Jane read about the death in a movie magazine 6 months later, surely a horrendous way to learn such a secret; shortly after the death, Henry Fonda remarried. While he was on his honeymoon Peter Fonda "accidentally" shot himself in the stomach. One wonders whether the dreadful secret wasn't already showing its power. For the rest of his long life, Henry Fonda apparently never once discussed his wife's suicide with his children. A further element to the secret is probably the fact that Fonda's new wife, Susan, stepdaughter in the prominent family of Oscar Hammerstein and then only 20, had at just about that time "adopted" a baby, shortly afterwards adopted by Henry. One has to wonder if this wasn't another secret; it would add layers of complexity to the suicide if it coincided time-wise with the baby's birth. Why would Susan, such a young woman from a prominent family and dating a very famous actor, adopt a child? And why would he soon after adopt her child?

Some secrets exist to protect family members, as in this instance; some protect an entire family from shame. Some secrets are kept because of society's disapproval of certain behaviors, as has often been the case with sexual orientation, such as for the lesbian relationships of Margaret Mead, Eleanor Roosevelt, and Katharine Hepburn. But society also plays into distortions and secrecy of various kinds that support the dominant values of the culture. For example, until very recently the media have generally participated in keeping the extramarital affairs of male politicians secret, and our legal system created documents to attest to fictions about adopted children's origins.

Secrecy is often maintained about money—whether to hide wealth or to hide poverty. Men often keep their finances secret from their wives, considering

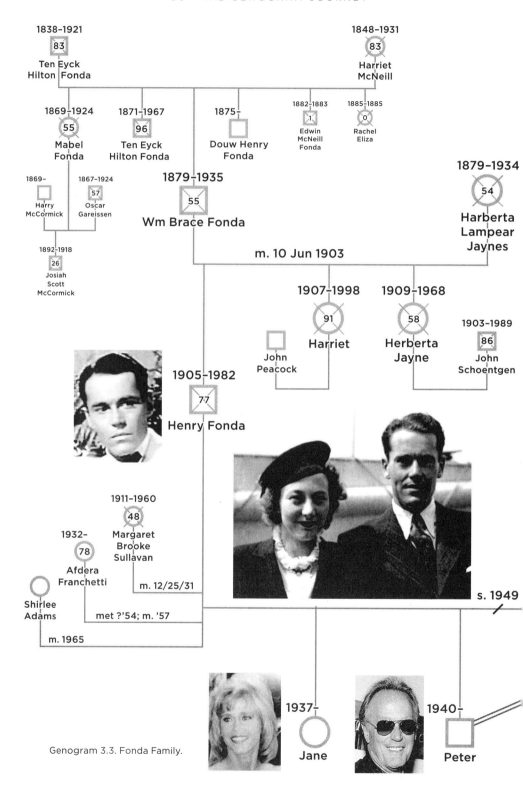

Genogram 3.3. Fonda Family.

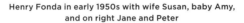
Henry Fonda in early 1950s with wife Susan, baby Amy,
and on right Jane and Peter

Oscar
Hammerstein

killed self on
April 14, 1950,
42nd birthday

1908–1950

Frances
Seymour

1928

Susan
Blanchard
Jacobson

m. 12/50

1949

Amy's birthdate uncertain;
Fonda adopted 1953;
probably biological father

Amy

family at HF's funeral: Jane, Amy, Shirlee, & Peter

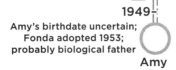

this to be "none of their business." Male power is thus protected, but such secrecy also reflects ways men are valued for their money. Women have their money secrets too. They may hold back a certain amount of the household money in a separate fund, or they may keep secret how much they spend for clothes or presents or how much they give to help a friend or relative for fear of their husband's disapproval. Money secrets obviously have different meanings in different families, but they may vary in meaning for each family member as well. To understand secrets it is important to assess whom the secret protects or excludes.

Women are generally the confidantes of other women as well as of men. They keep secrets to protect men's vulnerabilities, or to keep secret their alliances with other women, which might threaten the men in their lives. They may keep secrets to protect children from their father's rage. They may also keep secrets about their age or appearance, generally a response to the societal values favoring youth and beauty. Men's secrets pertain mostly to their main areas of vulnerability: perceived financial, work, or status incompetence. The culture generally tells men to be strong, all-knowing, and capable of handling anything, so they are pressed to keep secret the fears and attitudes that would give the opposite impression. Most of all, men keep their private selves secret from other men. It is valuable to notice who keeps which secrets from whom in families and how that has influenced relationships.

Secrets tend to beget other secrets. If parents married because the mother was pregnant and this has become a family secret, the entire family history may end up being distorted or avoided out of anxiety about that one secret. The subject of family history may be completely avoided for fear that one question could lead to another and expose the secret. The family story then becomes mystified with an aura of unreality because of one secret that cannot be told. In exploring family history there are a few indicators of deeply embedded family secrets:

- If the subject of the past is entirely avoided
- If there is tension whenever a particular relative or time period in the family history enters the conversation
- If there is more emotion than would seem justified by the "facts" of a particular aspect of the family story

Generally speaking, the greater the family anxiety is about disclosure, the more aspects of family life and history will require distortion to maintain the secret and the greater the power of the secret will be.

Multigenerational Secrecy About Incest in Nathanial Hawthorne's Family

Perhaps no writer has shown more preoccupation with the multigenerational power of secrets than Nathaniel Hawthorne (Genogram 3.4). His stories reflect an obsession with both anguished confession and concealment of potentially ruinous ancestral secrets, along with an eerie, mystifying multigenerational legacy of guilt for the misdeeds of ancestors long dead. This is the overt theme of *The House of Seven Gables*, in which the ghosts of the Salem witch trials, who are responsible for ominous misdeeds, overshadow the lives of those more than a century later. *The Scarlet Letter*, Hawthorne's other most famous novel, is about the damage caused by sins kept secret and the mystification created by secrecy in relationships. Hawthorne's friend, Herman Melville, believed there was a dark secret in Hawthorne's own life, which would, were it known, explain all the mysteries of his career. Others who knew Hawthorne had the same suspicion. Hawthorne's lawyer wrote: "I should fancy from your books you were burdened by secret sorrow; that you had some blue chamber in your soul into which you hardly dared enter yourself" (Young, 1984, p. 99). Hawthorne lived for years as a recluse, rarely leaving his house except at twilight: "I have made a captive of myself and put me into a dungeon and now I cannot find the key to let myself out—and if the door were open, I should be almost afraid to come out" (cited in Cowley, 1983, p. 4). In his preface to *The Scarlet Letter* he alludes to misdeeds in his family generations earlier. He said that his hometown, Salem, Massachusetts possessed a mysterious hold over him and that the figure of his first ancestor had haunted him since childhood; he wondered if his ancestors ever thought to repent "and as pardon for their cruelties" (Hawthorne, 1969, p. 300) which had been written up in various histories he found in the Customs House documents. He continued:

> At all events, I . . . as their representative, hereby take shame upon myself for their sakes, and pray that any curse incurred by them . . . may be now and henceforth removed. . . . Such are the compliments bandied between my great-grandsires and myself across the gulf of time! . . . Strong traits of their nature have intertwined themselves with mine. (Hawthorne, 1969, p. 300)

Hawthorne isolated himself for years, studying the old records of the town of Salem, just like his novel's narrator. He apparently discovered in

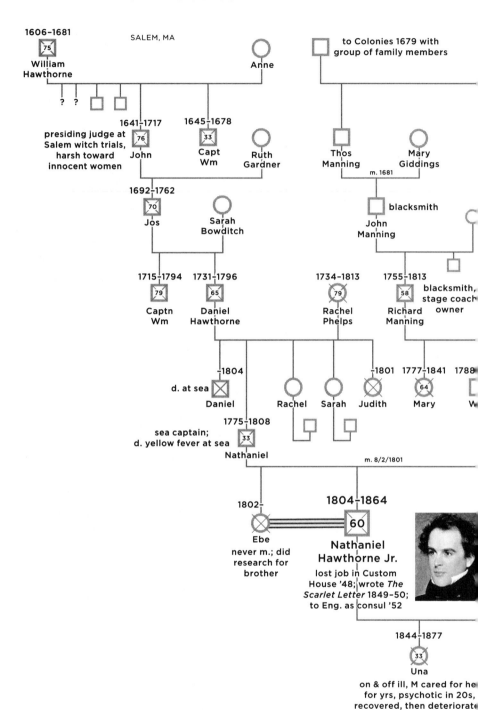

Genogram 3.4. The Hawthorne Family.

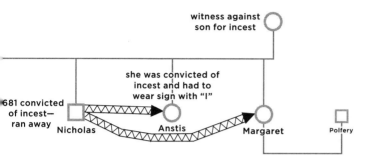

witness against
son for incest

she was convicted of
incest and had to
wear sign with "I"

681 convicted
of incest—
ran away

Nicholas

Anstis

Margaret

Polfery

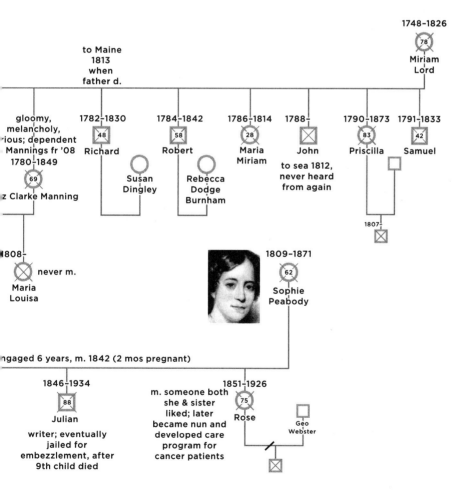

1748–1826

78

Miriam
Lord

to Maine
1813
when
father d.

gloomy,
melancholy,
·ious; dependent
·Mannings fr '08

1780–1849

69

z Clarke Manning

1782–1830

48

Richard

Susan
Dingley

1784–1842

58

Robert

Rebecca
Dodge
Burnham

1786–1814

28

Maria
Miriam

1788–

John

to sea 1812,
never heard
from again

1790–1873

83

Priscilla

1807–

1791–1833

42

Samuel

1808–

never m.

Maria
Louisa

1809–1871

62

Sophie
Peabody

ngaged 6 years, m. 1842 (2 mos pregnant)

1846–1934

88

Julian

writer; eventually
jailed for
embezzlement, after
9th child died

m. someone both
she & sister
liked; later
became nun and
developed care
program for
cancer patients

1851–1926

75

Rose

Geo
Webster

Salem public records the details of the sins of his earliest maternal ancestor, Nicholas Manning, who came to America in 1662 and was brought to trial for incest with two of his sisters. Nicholas's wife and mother testified against him. The judge in the case, William Hawthorne (1606–1681), was also possibly an ancestor of Hawthorne's on his father's side. Hawthorne spoke of revealing secrets in his tales, yet keeping "the inmost Me behind its veil" (Hawthorne, 1969, p. 294).

The theme of sibling incest seemed to preoccupy Hawthorne throughout his life, and there are suggestions that he may have had an incestuous relationship with his sister, Ebe. At his death Hawthorne left two unfinished manuscripts on the theme of incest. He wrote an early story about sibling incest, which he published at his own expense and then tried to retract by destroying the copies. He never mentioned this story again, nor was it included in his collections. Yet, 50 years later his sister Ebe referred to this early hidden story as a good example of her brother's special genius. The story involves a brother and sister in the early days of Salem, who have lived in fervent affection and "lonely sufficiency to each other" since they alone of their family survived an Indian attack. It is through the death of his parents that the brother gains this sister's love. Hers was "the love which had been gathered to me from the many graves of our household" (Hawthorne, quoted in Crews, 1966, p. 51). The story mirrors events of Hawthorne's life. His seafaring father died when he was 4, and the family was forced to live amid "uncongenial" relatives, the mother becoming a recluse, which left Nathaniel alone much of the time with his favorite older sister, Ebe. The third sibling, a younger sister, was much different in appearance and personality and grew up in a different position than Nathaniel and Ebe. Years later when Hawthorne became engaged to marry, Ebe was very opposed and though Ebe lived with the couple for many years she rarely spoke to Hawthorne's wife.

It is crucial to understand how secrets in your family may have worked to distort family processes and may organize relationships even generations later, as appears to have been the case in the Hawthorne family.

Charles Lindbergh's Three Secret Families

Another strange story of secrecy is that of the three secret families of Charles Lindbergh in addition to his well-known family with his writer wife Ann Morrow Lindbergh, with whom he had 6 children, one of whom was notoriously kidnapped as a baby in 1932 (Genogram 3.5). Lindbergh was the first person to complete a solo and nonstop transatlantic flight in 1927 in his plane *The Spirit of St. Louis*. A handsome aviator treated as a national hero, he played a major role in promoting aviation in the U.S. Over time Lindbergh's famous reputation became tarnished through indications of his Nazi sympathies. In later years he promoted conservation of natural resources. He died in 1974.

His youngest daughter, Reeve, described finding out about his three secret families decades after his death:

> Thirty years after my father's death and about two and a half years after my mother had passed away, I learned that my father had secret families in Europe: three of them. I had brothers and sisters I had never known about: two girls and five boys, living in several different countries on another continent. . . . During all the years when he was the stern arbiter of moral and ethical conduct in our family he had been leading another life, living according to a whole different set of standards from those he had taught me. . . . I became furiously angry, as angry as I have ever been in my life. I was not angry with my "new," living relatives, no more to blame for the circumstances of their birth than I am, but with my long-dead father. I raged against his duplicitous character, his personal conduct, the years of deception and hypocrisy. . . . What really drove me crazy . . . was that he had once written a chastising letter to my sister when she was at college. It was an angry letter, a searing page of paternal moralizing, telling her that she had too many boyfriends and doing it in a cruel way hinting at her potential "promiscuity," a strange word for a father to use. . . . Ann had saved it for thirty years. And she died before she knew about his own behavior. (Lindbergh, 2003, pp. 201–202)

Reeve was pained to see that her sister had had to absorb over all the years the father's rigid moralistic judgments when his whole life and behavior were characterized by such duplicity. (See also pages 308–309 for discussion of Reeve's reaction to her father's antisemitism.)

Reeve tried to understand what had happened, overwhelmed by the "absolutely Byzantine layers of deception on the part of our shared father, two of whose three mistresses were indeed sisters. The children did not even know who he was. He used a pseudonym with them (to protect them, perhaps? To protect himself, absolutely!)" (Lindbergh, 2003, p. 203). She concluded: "Every intimate human connection my father had during his later years was fractured by secrecy. He could not be completely open with anybody who loved him anywhere on earth . . . what remains with me is a sense of his unutterable loneliness" (Lindbergh, 2003, p. 218).

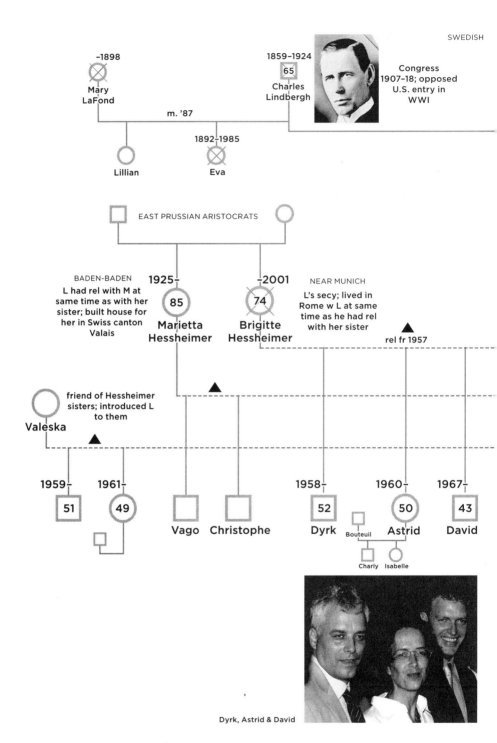

SWEDISH

-1898
Mary
LaFond

m. '87

1859–1924
65
Charles
Lindbergh

Congress
1907-18; opposed
U.S. entry in
WWI

1892–1985
Eva

Lillian

EAST PRUSSIAN ARISTOCRATS

BADEN-BADEN

L had rel with M at
same time as with her
sister; built house for
her in Swiss canton
Valais

1925-
85
Marietta
Hessheimer

-2001
74
Brigitte
Hessheimer

NEAR MUNICH

L's secy; lived in
Rome w L at same
time as he had rel
with her sister

rel fr 1957

Valeska

friend of Hessheimer
sisters; introduced L
to them

1959-
51

1961-
49

Vago   Christophe

1958-
52
Dyrk

Bouteuil

1960-
50
Astrid

Charly   Isabelle

1967-
43
David

Dyrk, Astrid & David

Genogram 3.5. The Lindbergh Family.

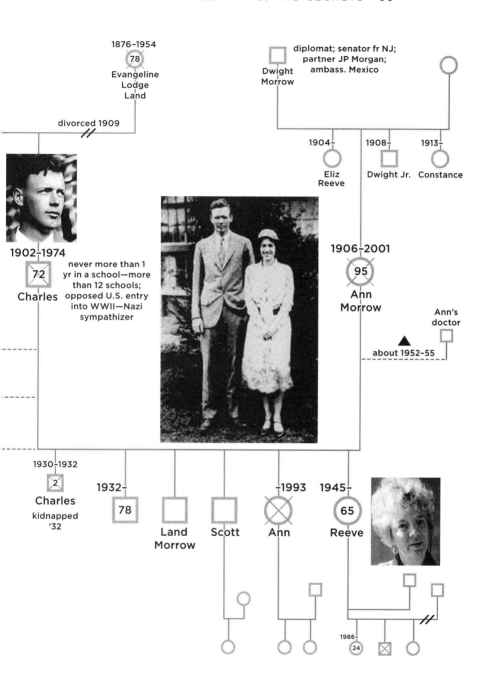

1876–1954
78
Evangeline
Lodge
Land

diplomat; senator fr NJ;
partner JP Morgan;
ambass. Mexico
Dwight
Morrow

divorced 1909

1904–
Eliz
Reeve

1908–
Dwight Jr.

1913–
Constance

1902–1974
72
Charles

never more than 1
yr in a school—more
than 12 schools;
opposed U.S. entry
into WWII—Nazi
sympathizer

1906–2001
95
Ann
Morrow

Ann's
doctor

about 1952-55

1930–1932
2
Charles
kidnapped
'32

1932–
78

Land
Morrow

Scott

–1993
Ann

1945–
65
Reeve

1986–
24

From his deathbed in Hawaii Lindbergh managed to write to all three mistresses pressing them each to keep their segment of the family secret. At some point over the years his daughter Astrid, who had learned to call her father "Careu Kent," saw a picture of Charles Lindbergh and recognized it as the man she knew as her father; she then found his love letters to her mother over many years. It was not until both her own mother and Ann Morrow Lindbergh died in 2001 that she revealed the truth and contacted her siblings in the U.S. Reeve concluded:

> I'm hoping that as I get older I'll get braver, and someday I may even be brave enough to . . . let the family history go, let it be. Gently, so as not to disturb anybody, I may open a door and just walk through it. I may tiptoe away from the closed rooms of the past with all their stories and move quietly into the present I love so well, and then even further out into the open future, forward from here. (Lindbergh, 2003, p. 220)

This passage reflects extremely well the sensibility toward the complexities of the pain of secrets, which are complex to unravel in a family where many lives are implicated in the secret and exposing oneself may mean exposing another who may not have the same readiness for exposure. Care must always be taken for other family members' experience.

Exploring Your Family Stories, Myths and Secrets

Family gatherings, holidays, and times of family transition—weddings, funerals, birthdays—are an excellent time to listen to the stories that get told and think about how each person is characterized. This is a good starting point for the adventure of exploring family stories and myths from a systemic perspective and seeing hidden connections in the family tree. You might think about the following questions:

- Have family members tended to conform to the middle-class American family life-cycle norms? If not, are there other family norms, such as late marriage, not marrying, not having children, living in unconventional groupings, and so on? What values might these patterns reflect?
- Have family members tended to conform to the middle-class American family life-cycle norms? If not, are there other family norms, such as late marriage, not marrying, not having children, living in unconventional groupings, and so on? What values might these patterns reflect?

- Are there "off-time" events on the genogram? "May-December marriages" (in which one partner is significantly older than the other)? families having children very early or very late? marrying very early or very late? leaving home very early or very late?

- Are there coincidences of life-cycle events—births, deaths, marriages, leaving home, onset of illness—that may have intensified the meaning of particular events in the family?

- What kinds of rituals does the family maintain? holiday rituals? dinnertime rituals? leisure-time rituals? vacation rituals? family get-together rituals? What customs do these rituals strengthen? What cultural patterns are minimized?

- What rules are there for celebrating weddings? funerals? births? birthdays? anniversaries? What happens when someone breaks the rules?

- What are the basic rules in the family?

- What are the general stories told in the family? Were there cautionary tales? Do these stories seem to reflect the family's underlying beliefs, myths, and values in any decipherable way?

- What are the stories about particular issues? the migration stories? the death stories? the stories about dealing with the outside world? the education stories? the money stories? the holiday stories? the betrayal stories? the survival stories?

- What seem to be the myths in the family?

- What family legacies were there in the areas of strength, vulnerability, anxiety, success, hope in the face of despair?

- In what areas does the family keep secrets? Are there secrets about money? death? pregnancy? sexual behavior? marriage? affairs? parentage? school or work failure?

- How are secrets in the family maintained? Who conveys the messages and how?

- What impact have secrets had on the relationships in the family?

4 Family Ties and Binds

"Then you should say what you mean," the March Hare went on.

"I do." Alice hastily replied, "at least—at least I mean what I say— that's the same thing, you know."

"Not the same thing a bit!" said the Hatter. "Why, you might just as well say that 'I see what I eat' is the same as 'I eat what I see.'"

"You might just as well say," added the March Hare, "that 'I like what I get' is the same as 'I get what I like'!"

Alice In Wonderland
—LEWIS CARROLL

Families do not communicate optimally and relationships often go awry. In fact, some researchers have suggested that, as in *Alice in Wonderland*, communication is often used more to obscure than to clarify meaning. Some family theorists have actually developed a hypothesis that to the extent family members are dependent on the reactions of others for their sense of well-being, direct communication will be sacrificed in the service of the relationship system. In other words, the more dependent family members are on the approval of others for their self-esteem, the more likely it is that communication will be distorted. To understand a family, you need to explore the way their emotional relationships work: Who communicates what to whom? And, just as important: Who doesn't? In theory, if everything were perfect in a family, members might communicate openly, clearly, empathically, and with tolerance for difference at all times. Family relationships would always be in harmony.

Responses to Stress

As we know, there is no life without change, and no change without disruption, so it is not surprising that family communication and relationships are often stressed by change. And, because all members of a family are connected, they react to one another's distress, often compounding their reactions, so that what upsets one ends up upsetting all.

At times of change, family members may cling to "the way things were," as if they could prevent the pain and disturbance that go with all change. In fact, resistance to change is a natural property of all systems. To a degree, resistance is necessary and healthy. But, beyond a certain point, a family that resists change becomes rigid and unable to adapt. Extreme resistance to change leads to distorted communication that will weaken the family in the end.

Characteristic ways of coping with stress are usually learned. People tend to do things the way their family did them, just as the family probably handled things the way their own families did. When a family is under stress, there is a tendency to fall into certain types of "discommunication": Family members may blame others or themselves for what is going wrong. They may become placaters, denying their own experience in order to adapt to the needs of others; they may become wishy-washy, rigidly authoritarian, illogical, or altogether silent, whether as a "goody two shoes" or as the "space cadet" of the family, in an effort to cope with their own or the family's distress.

Under stress some families pull together, closing the doors to keep outsiders out and insiders in—demanding a sameness in feelings and behavior, which family therapists call "enmeshment." Leaving the family or even disagreeing may be seen as disloyalty. Other families seem to fall apart under stress, defaulting to a mode of "everyone for him- or herself." Such families cannot reorganize themselves to handle problems. Outside regulatory systems such as the police or social-service systems may become overly involved with these families in an attempt to superimpose organization on them.

Sometimes a family's coping patterns seem to reverse themselves over each generation. If the grandfather was an alcoholic and handled his stress by going to the pub, and the grandmother berated him when he came home, the next generation may swear off alcohol and develop rigid rules for censuring others by silence and avoidance of all emotional issues—drink as well as other problems. The third generation, responding to the second generation's rigidity, may again turn to drinking and acting out to deal with stress. If we look more closely at the patterns of relating in such a family, we may find a stable pattern of emotional avoidance and a cycle of shame/guilt/repentance that remains the same right down the generations, although superficially the behavior of each looks different.

Families react to many stresses, both internal and external, as they move through the life cycle. The flow of anxiety through a family can be described as having both a horizontal and a vertical dimension (McGoldrick, Carter, & Garcia Preto, 2010). The "vertical flow" includes patterns of relating and functioning that come down the family tree over historical time. Generational attitudes, myths, taboos, expectations, labels, and the legacy of trauma that come down a family tree (the vertical stressors) all influence how family members will deal with any experience and what kind of relationships they will have. This heritage is the given—the hand you are dealt. What you do with it is up to you. The "horizontal flow" of anxiety comes from the pressures on a family as it moves through time, coping with the inevitable stresses and changes of family development and with the unpredictable stresses—economic reversals, untimely deaths, natural disasters, and so forth.

With enough stress on the horizontal (developmental) axis, any family will break down. Stressors on the vertical (historical) axis may create added problems, so that even a small horizontal stress can have serious repercussions on the system. For example, if a young mother has unresolved issues with her own parents (vertical anxiety), she may have a particularly difficult time dealing with the normal vicissitudes of parenthood (horizontal anxiety), which are hard enough in themselves. By helping a family understand the typical responses to stress, we can help them avoid being automatically caught up in their patterns. This means mapping out current stresses, along with the chronology of previous events and stresses that may have influenced the family's tendency to respond in certain ways in the present.

For example, President Theodore Roosevelt had a difficult time handling the launching of his daughter Alice (Figure 4.1, Genogram 4.1). Launching children usually creates some stress on any family, but a number of concurrent and prior stressors seem to have intensified this particular transition. For one thing, Roosevelt was going through a difficult period as president. Second, his favorite son, Teddy, who had experienced serious physical and emotional problems over the years, was in academic trouble at Harvard. Furthermore, there was a painful history of family losses: Alice's mother (also named Alice), had died at age 22 of complications of childbirth on Valentine's Day, February 14, 1884, the anniversary of the couple's engagement 4 years earlier. On the very night Alice died, Roosevelt's mother, age 49, died upstairs in the same house. Within a year Roosevelt became secretly engaged to Edith Carow, whom he had known since childhood, though he wrote to his sister, who disapproved:

> I utterly disbelieve in second marriages; I have always considered that they argued weakness in a man's character. You could not reproach me one half as bitterly for my inconstancy and unfaithfulness as I reproach myself. Were I sure there were a heaven, my one prayer would be I might never go there, lest I should meet those I love on earth who are dead. (Miller, 1994, p. 281)

Figure 4.1   **Partial Roosevelt Chronology**

1880, Feb 14	TR proposes to Alice Lee.
1884, Feb 12	Alice gives birth to baby, also named Alice.
1884, Feb 14	Alice Lee Roosevelt dies at age 22.
1884, Feb 14	TR's mother, Mittie Bulloch Roosevelt, dies in same house.
1884, Feb 16	Double funeral is held for Alice Lee Roosevelt & Mittie Bulloch Roosevelt.
1884, summer	TR submerges grief in adventures out West and presidential politics.
1905	TR has difficult time dealing with Alice and her wild behavior.
1906	TR has problems as president.
1906, Jan	Favorite son Teddy is failing at Harvard.
1906, Feb 17	Alice, age 22, marries hard-drinking, sexually promiscuous congressman Nicholas Longworth, age 34.
1907	Marriage unhappy, Alice and Nick are mostly apart and she spends more time with TR.
1925, Feb 14	Alice has daughter on Valentine's Day (same day her mother and grandmother had died and that parents had become engaged). The daughter was the child of her lover William Borah and she wanted to name her Deborah but Longworth refused.

This extraordinary letter was, by the way, suppressed by the family for almost a century, an indication of the power of families to keep certain embarrassing information secret. Roosevelt regarded his daughter Alice, who was called "Baby Lee," as a kind of peace offering to his sister, Bamie, who kept Alice from the time of her birth to the age of 3, when Bamie gave her back with great reluctance.

Roosevelt remarried in 1886 and fathered five more children. He never mentioned his first wife's name again and there is not a word in his autobiography to indicate her existence. Alice grew up to bear a remarkable resemblance to her mother, to whom she learned not to refer. Within the family Alice herself also became invisible. Roosevelt hardly counted her among the family members.

Starved for attention, she became increasingly flamboyant in her behavior by late adolescence, in spite of a deep inner shyness. By the time she was 20 she was continuously making it into the news for her outrageous pranks—drinking, smoking, racing cars, betting on horses. One

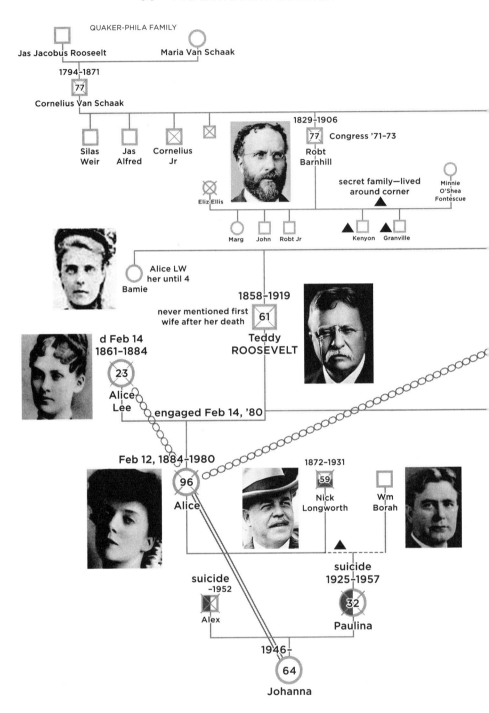

Genogram 4.1. The Roosevelt Family.

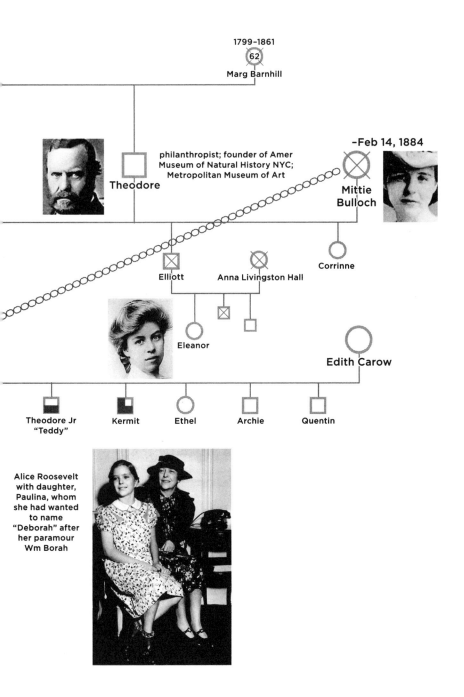

1799–1861
(62)
Marg Barnhill

Theodore

philanthropist; founder of Amer
Museum of Natural History NYC;
Metropolitan Museum of Art

–Feb 14, 1884

Mittie
Bulloch

Elliott

Anna Livingston Hall

Corrinne

Eleanor

Edith Carow

Theodore Jr
"Teddy"

Kermit

Ethel

Archie

Quentin

Alice Roosevelt
with daughter,
Paulina, whom
she had wanted
to name
"Deborah" after
her paramour
Wm Borah

might say that she forced her father to pay attention to her by antics that made the newspaper almost daily. As her younger half-sister later said, she was "a hellion. . . . What wickedry she might commit next was felt almost constantly by almost all the family" (Teichman, 1979, p. 49). On February 17, 1906, at age 22, the same age at which her mother had died, Alice decided to marry and leave home. Both the concurrent stresses in the present and the coincidental experiences of the past undoubtedly contributed to Roosevelt's difficulty in letting his daughter go, and to her difficulty in leaving him.

Alice made a poor choice of husband: a hard-drinking, sexually promiscuous congressman, Nicholas Longworth, 12 years her senior. As she departed, her stepmother is reputed to have said: "I want you to know that I'm glad to see you go. You've never been anything but trouble" (Cordery, 2007, p. 159). The launching was not successful and within a year Alice was spending more time with her father than she was with her husband. This improved relationship with her father was probably what she had been seeking for years.

Alice's one child, born 12 years later on February 14, was apparently fathered by William Borah, a much older married senator with whom Alice had been having an affair. Alice wanted to name her Deborah, but Longworth refused, so Alice named her Paulina after St. Paul. Paulina led a miserable and neglected life, first attempting suicide when she was in college. She then married someone of whom her mother disapproved, who drank heavily and killed himself when their daughter, Johanna, was 6. Paulina, after further depression, suicide attempts, and hospitalizations, finally took her own life when Johanna was 10. At this point Alice, guilt-ridden over her daughter's death, decided to make it up by developing a close relationship with Johanna, which she did. They had a happy relationship until Alice died at age 96 in 1980.

It might seem that Paulina was "doomed" as the stand-in for the stand-in, the second-generation daughter of loss and neglect, whose life was marked by such eerie coincidence of birth, death, and anniversaries—for three generations. Her birth was related not just to unfortunate coincidence but also to the secrets of a failed marriage and affair. In fact, her legal father, Nick Longworth, adored her, but he died when she was 6 just as Johanna's father died when she was 6. Paulina's biological father ignored her completely, though her mother made sure she knew who he was. A most interesting aspect of the story is the loving and generative relationship that resulted between Paulina's neglected daughter, Johanna, and Paulina's neglectful mother, Alice, demonstrating so powerfully that with effort one can turn family dynamics around.

The Marx Family

The immortal Marx brothers (Genogram 4.2), sons of an immigrant German Jewish family that came to New York in 1880, have now charmed three generations with the hilarious antics of their early comic movies. Each brother had a very defined role and characteristics: The wise-cracking Groucho, the "professor" with his glasses, eyebrows, mustache, cigar, and funny walk, was a foil for his look-alike brothers Chico and Harpo, and played off Gummo and Zeppo; Chico had the role and dialect of the uneducated Italian immigrant, playing the piano like a magician; the speechless Harpo, with his harp-playing skills, red clown wig, and the zany, outrageous props that he took out of his huge raincoat, had the role of the not-so-foolish fool; Gummo, the fourth brother, named for his "gum" shoes, played the straightman but couldn't stand the role and went into the retail clothing business, though he later managed the brothers' business; and finally Zeppo, the baby brother (no one knows where he got his name), sang and took over the straightman role from Gummo, until he too couldn't stand having to compete for the limelight. He said he was "sick and tired of being a stooge" (Stables, 1992, p. 47), though, like Gummo, he later rejoined his brothers in a managerial role.

The stage roles of the Marx brothers characterized them from earliest youth: Chico, whose nickname came from always having "chicks," was the oldest surviving child. He was the replacement for his mother's first baby, who had died, and he became her favorite. He was an irresistible charmer, an irrepressible liar, and a perpetual optimist, continuously preoccupied with seducing women. Though he had less than 2 years of education, he was brilliant with numbers, an ability he put to use primarily in compulsive gambling.

Harpo, whose name derived from the harp he played with such brilliance, became the solid man of the family—happily married, generous, friendly, understanding. A tranquil soul, Harpo dreamed his way through life—smiling, watching, never needing to top anyone, practicing his harp in the corner and having the most contented existence of the five brothers. He finished only the first grade and after that wandered the streets, getting his first jobs from his con artist older brother, Chico, who talked his way into so many jobs that he often sent Harpo in his place when he had double-booked himself. Harpo said of himself: "Most people have a conscious and subconscious. Not me. I've always operated on a subconscious and a sub-subconscious" (Adamson, 1973, pp. 21–22). He almost seemed to do just that—to float through life, exuding warmth and contentment.

Groucho, on the other hand, grew up a misanthrope—a pessimist, skinflint, and grouch—hence his nickname. He later wrote that Harpo had inher-

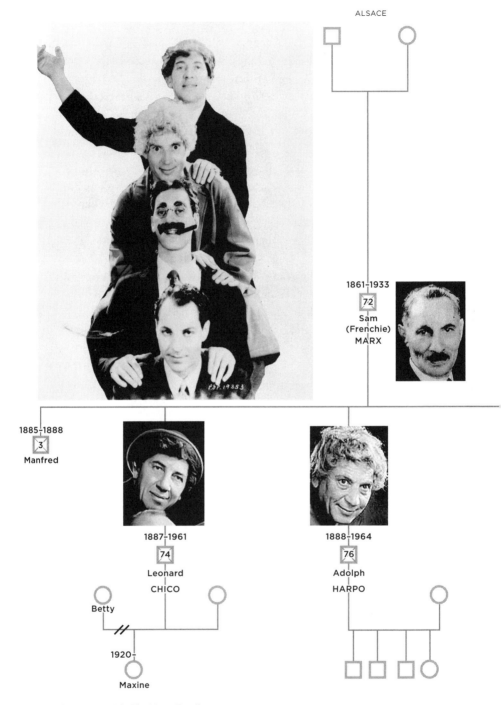

Genogram 4.2. The Marx Family.

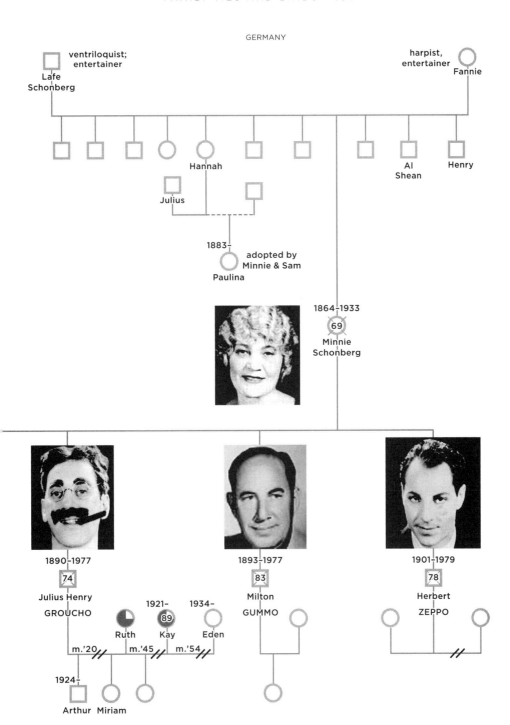

GERMANY

ventriloquist;
entertainer
Lafe
Schonberg

harpist,
entertainer
Fannie

Hannah

Julius

1883–
adopted by
Minnie & Sam
Paulina

Al
Shean

Henry

1864–1933
69
Minnie
Schonberg

1890–1977
74
Julius Henry
GROUCHO

Ruth
m.'20

1921–
89
Kay
m.'45

1934–
Eden
m.'54

1924–
Arthur Miriam

1893–1977
83
Milton
GUMMO

1901–1979
78
Herbert
ZEPPO

ited all their mother's good qualities and he himself got what was left. But he was also the intellectual, publishing many articles and five books in spite of only a seventh-grade education. Groucho never overcame his resentment that Chico was their mother's favorite. Perhaps Harpo, who was born between them, used his silent smile and outrageous antics as a way not to get caught in the middle.

Whereas Chico could talk anyone into anything, Groucho sneered and bullied. Whereas Chico was a spendthrift and a gambler, Groucho was a miser; he was moody, dour, and, unlike all his other brothers, not very sociable. His negative behavior probably intensified the mother's preference for Chico. And Chico's irresponsibility was in part made possible by Groucho's extreme seriousness while at the same time Chico's irresponsibility made Groucho grouchy. In other words, the role each played intensified and exaggerated an opposite role for the other. The more their mother and Chico felt allied against Groucho, the grouchier and more serious he got. His miserliness and seriousness also allowed his brothers to express the carefree, spendthrift side of their personalities; he was always there to protect them financially, as much as he growled about it. Perhaps what Groucho got out of the complementarity was a feeling of moral superiority. What Chico got was the freedom to be irresponsible.

The fourth brother, Gummo, as his shoes suggest, became the prosaic member in the family. Gummo and Zeppo were apparently affable, humorous fellows and decent actors, but that doesn't get you very far when you're trying to share the stage with three great comedians. Actually, Zeppo was considered the funniest of all the brothers off stage. And like most of his brothers except Groucho, he was a gambler. He was also a cold and tough playboy. He had special trouble with Groucho, who hated to share the spotlight.

Lafe, the father of the brothers' mother, Minnie, had been a magician, ventriloquist, and circus strongman who loved to brag to his grandsons about his sexual conquests. His wife, Fannie, was a small, devout, quiet woman whose main outlet was her harp. In Germany the entire family had been ragtag entertainers. In the United States, Lafe became a peddler who repaired umbrellas, while Minnie's younger brother, Al Shean, became one of the all-time great vaudevillians.

Minnie married Simon Marrix (nicknamed "Frenchie" because he came from Alsace), who had immigrated to the United States to avoid conscription. Taking the advice of a cousin who became a tailor and changed his name to Marx, he did the same. He was a marvelous dancer, and Minnie, though warned of his lechery, fell for him anyway.

Minnie ran the family. The title of a Broadway play about the family, *Minnie's Boys*, conveys the centrality of her role. She filled their home with relatives and maneuvered to line up entertainment opportunities for her brother,

her sons, and various relatives. Whether she was a manipulative conniver or a can-do charmer depends, of course, on your point of view.

Frenchie Marx was the kind of person who would laugh at a joke even if he didn't understand it. He was playmate to his sons in their card games, but they seem to have disregarded him in any role other than the family chef. Groucho's stories about his parents are typical of what all the sons felt:

> Whatever visitors came for, they always came to my mother—never to my father. . . . She engineered loans when they needed money. How she did it was always a source of wonder to me, but she invariably came through. She patched up marriages that were foundering and she out-talked the landlord, the grocer, the butcher and anyone else to whom we owed money. Her maneuvers were a triumph of skill, chicanery and imagination. . . . My Pop was a tailor, but he was no ordinary tailor. His record as the most inept tailor that Yorkville ever produced has never been approached. . . . The notion that Pop was a tailor was an opinion that was held only by him. To his customers he was known as "Misfit Sam." He was the only tailor I ever heard of who refused to use a tape measure. (Marx, 1959, pp. 14–15)

Another perspective on Frenchie's tailoring was given years later by Harpo's son, who compared it to his own father's virtuosity with the harp in spite of the fact that he couldn't read a note of music and had no training: "He performed music the way his father, Frenchie, had performed tailoring, with an unerring feel for fabrics and color (harmony), but very little for cutting and fitting (melody and tempo)" (Marx, 1986, p. 2).

In spite of Frenchie's obvious limitations, Groucho and the others attributed to him remarkable strengths as well:

> It's amazing how proficient a man can be in one field and how incompetent in another. My father should have been a chef. He usually cooked dinner for all of us. . . . He could take two eggs, some stale bread, a few assorted vegetables and a hunk of cheap meat and convert this into something fit for the gods, assuming that there are any left. Like most women, my mother hated cooking and would walk miles out of her way to avoid the kitchen. But my father's culinary skill enabled my mother to swing some pretty sharp deals in later years. . . . After eating his food the agents were softened up to the point where Mother could do business with them on her terms. (Marx, 1959, p. 42)

Harpo had a similar view of their father, agreeing that with food he was a true magician, but that his failure as a tailor meant he often had to go off to peddle just to make ends meet, while their mother, with never a complaint, would hit up her brother for a loan. Harpo said that Frenchie never ducked his duty as a breadwinner, though he was the exact opposite of his wife in ambition.

> Frenchie was a loving, gentle man who accepted everything that happened—good luck or tragedy—with the same unchangeable good nature. He had no ambition beyond living and accepting life from day to day. He had only two vices: loyalty to everyone he ever knew (he never had an enemy even amongst the sharpies who fleeced him) and the game of pinochle. I shouldn't knock Frenchie's loyalty. That's what kept our family together. (Marx & Barber, 1985, pp. 21–22)

In the early years, Minnie and the sons formed a coalition that excluded the father. Without this coalition and outlet for her energy, it is possible that the tension between Minnie and her husband might have hit a breaking point. It is also possible that without the various coalitions the Marx brothers themselves formed over the years, they might never have been able to develop their phenomenal comedy team. Having a good common enemy can make you into a strong group. It is not surprising, however, that when the team broke up, it was precipitated by Groucho's resentment of his role as the over-responsible one in the family. The overfunctioner in a relationship system is often under the most pressure and may burn out eventually, becoming resentful even when, as was the case with Groucho, the role was self-assumed. His humor itself (unlike that of Harpo, for example) was always a form of "tri-angling": His jokes involved joining with the audience in ridiculing someone else. It is interesting, though, that he was the only one who managed to continue a career on his own.

The assigned roles in the Marx family played themselves out in the next generation as well. For example, Maxine Marx, the only child of Chico, allied with her father against her mother, Betty, especially after she was sent to live with her grandparents so that her mother could remain with Chico in his itinerant career. As so often happens with children, Maxine ended up blaming her more visible mother and felt drawn to her romanticized, distant father. As tension developed in the couple over the years, Maxine tried to move in directly between her parents:

> Whenever Daddy, Mother, and I went out to dinner, I would scoot into the booth between them. "The two of you are disgusting,"

Mother would say . . . Daddy would just laugh. "Leave her alone. . . . She's just a baby." (Marx, 1986, p. 76)

Later Maxine was able to reflect on what drew her toward her father, illustrating how the facts became subverted in the family emotional process:

> I resented Mother's desperate need to stay close to Chico. I didn't realize that he was being unfaithful to her; I simply thought that she wanted him all to herself. . . . He would lie, cheat on Mother, lose all his savings. . . . He always felt that his charms could get him out of trouble. I knew that he was irresponsible . . . and that he was capable of really hurting me, but somehow it didn't matter. (Marx, 1986, p. 47)

She also became aware of the way she intentionally alienated her mother:

> As I grew older, I resented it when Mother and I would walk down the street and all the men's eyes were on her. I felt totally inadequate, so I began to lord it over her in another area: education . . . I lifted my eyebrow in disdain, when she called from the door, "Maxine, your young swan is here." "Mother," I muttered as I swept out, "It's 'swain,' and nobody uses it today anyway." (Marx, 1986, p. 112)

Maxine also became allied with her grandmother, Minnie, with whom she lived, against her mother. Not surprisingly, Minnie was not close to Betty; she probably felt no wife would be good enough for her favorite son. But Minnie and Betty were also opposites in personality. They had clashed from the time Betty and Chico had married. In fact, all the Marx family had a problem with Betty. She challenged their ways of operating. She had a quick tongue and a frank manner, which seemed to ruffle their seemingly unflappable family. Although the core of the Marx brothers' humor was wild—outrageous breaking up of a situation—the family had its own code of acceptable wildness. Betty was pushed into the role of villain by her mother-in-law, her daughter, and rest of the family, who considered her an outsider. As Maxine said: "From early on, Mother had been made the heavy in my family, and being away from her nitpicking and constant rules I felt a great sense of freedom. Minnie was hardly an authoritarian; she was very much like Chico" (Marx, 1986, p. 42).

Because Minnie had no daughters, it was perhaps natural that she would ally with Maxine, her first grandchild. Minnie took Maxine on as a project, as she had taken on so many relatives before, to make her an entertainer, teaching her to recite German poems before she even knew what she was saying. The more grandmother and granddaughter joined together, the more of an outsider Betty became.

But according to Maxine, Chico's very attraction to Betty was because of the new element she introduced into their family:

> Chico didn't have the antipathy toward Jewish women that his broth- ers Harpo and Groucho showed. Betty was just the type of Jewish girl they shied away from. Bossy and abrasive, she knew exactly what she wanted and wasn't afraid to tell you so. Chico admired her "guts" while his brothers preferred docile *shiksas*. Minnie was manipulative, but never openly bossy, and her sons tended to forget that she was Jewish, too. Not that Betty was shrewish . . . she was just naturally straightforward, whereas the boys were used to Minnie's soft-spoken, devious manner. (Marx, 1986, p. 18)

When Chico brought Betty home, his mother and his four unmarried broth- ers all resented her. As Maxine put it, "Minnie didn't want to share her boys with another woman" (Marx, 1986, p. 22). And not surprisingly, conflicts ensued. For example:

> Minnie was always trying to look very young, with her big blonde wig and chiffon dresses. When the family sat down to eat, she would come sweeping down the stairs in a grand entrance. One evening, Betty, giggling as the grande dame of Grand Boulevard took her seat at the head of the table, whispered a bit too loudly that Minnie looked like the Queen of Sheba. Minnie took this harmless joke well, but the brothers became defensive. (Marx, 1986, p. 20)

Not surprisingly, when two siblings who have been in conflict marry, their spouses tend to get added to the mix. As typically happens with in-law con- flicts, the animosity between the wives of Chico, the ever-careless, irresponsible charmer, and of Groucho, the overresponsible, penny-pinching grouch, primar- ily reflected the issues between the brothers and within each marriage, rather than the differences between the two women themselves. Groucho's wife, Ruth, envied Betty for her jewels and furs because Groucho would begrudge her even a new dress. What Ruth overlooked was that Chico often used his generosity and expensive gifts to buy forgiveness for his gambling and other women. Fur- thermore, Betty's luxuries might have to be hocked any day to pay Chico's gam- bling debts—which Groucho wouldn't have incurred in a million years.

When families have fixed roles and triangles like the Marx family, it is useful to consider the possibilities for increasing flexibility. What if Groucho had worked at letting go of the grouchiness and stinginess and had played instead Harpo's fun-loving role for a while, letting someone else take up the slack about the finances? What if Maxine had become positive toward her mother and challenged Chico, just to see what would happen in the system? Increasing flexibility is often the first step in working toward change in a system.

Communication Regulates Distance

Families generally maintain a stable level of closeness and distance, however much their emotional relationships may seem to fluctuate. This process of distance regulation has to do with who relates to whom and about what. We all know that families may do a lot of talking without becoming intimate. Some families use humor to maintain distance, others use fighting. Some families can appear very warm and friendly to outsiders, but insiders know that it's all "form" and that if you disobey the rules of "appropriate" behavior, you will be shut out.

Families with a high degree of conflict may also have a high degree of intimacy. Some families share an intensely private language, full of obscure jokes and references. Others communicate their connectedness through rituals and patterns passed from generation to generation. Take, for example, James Baldwin's description of a ritual of family storytelling, illustrating the subtlety of what got transmitted down the generations of his family:

> On a Sunday afternoon, say, when the old folks were talking after a big Sunday dinner . . . maybe somebody's got a kid on his lap and is absent-mindedly stroking the kid's head. . . . He hopes that there will never come a time when the old folks won't be sitting around the living room, talking about where they've come from, and what they've seen, and what's happened to them and their kinfolk. But something deep and watchful in the child knows that this is bound to end, is already ending. In a moment someone will get up and turn on the light. Then the old folks will remember the children and they won't talk any more that day. . . . The child knows they won't talk any more because if he knows too much about what's happening to them, he'll know too much too soon to about what's going to happen to him. (Baldwin, 1991, pp. 154–155)

Generally speaking, if something changes the comfortable level of distance established for relationships, the family unit usually will try to bring things back to the familiar pattern. At times it almost seems as if family members are connected by an invisible umbilical cord, operating as one organism even when separated by thousands of miles. Thus if one family member becomes sick, the others may come closer to fill the void or decrease anxiety, or they may begin fighting to preserve the familiar distance and avoid too much intimacy. In times of anxiety and change, families try to stabilize themselves by regulating the distance in their relationships.

The Wright Brothers: Regulating Distance

An amusing example of this process occurred with the Wright brothers, Wilbur and Orville (shown with their sister Katharine in Figure 4.1), when they were trying to design the propeller for the first airplane. Though they seemed like opposites, the brothers were actually described by their father as being as "inseparable as twins." Wilbur once wrote:

> From the time we were little children, my brother Orville and myself lived together, played together, worked together, and in fact, thought together. We usually owned all of our toys in common, talked over our thoughts and aspirations so that nearly everything that was done in our lives has been the result of conversations, suggestions, and discussions between us. (cited in Crouch, 1989, pp. 49–50)

It was said that they were so close they often finished each other's sentences. As their work on inventing the airplane developed, the charge in their already

Figure 4.1. Wilber and Orville Wright with their sister Katharine.

close relationship heated up. For 6 or 7 weeks they worked together day and night, and argued all the way. (Probably the arguing regulated their emotional distance to counterbalance the intensity of their collaboration.) Whenever the brothers were in the same room, the shouting would start, resounding through the house. As their assistant recalled:

> One morning following the worst argument I ever heard, Orv came in and said he guessed he'd been wrong and they ought to do it Will's way. A few minutes later Will came in and said he'd been thinking it over and perhaps Orv was right. The first thing I knew they were arguing it all over again, only this time they had switched ideas. (cited in Walsh, 1975, p. 115)

Switching sides probably was an attempt to stop the escalation of their fighting, which had then gone too far. Yet agreement would have brought them too close, so they quickly moved back to polarized positions, reestablishing a comfortable level of distance.

The brothers' collaboration on the development of the airplane was one of the most productive partnerships in history, a relationship more binding than most marriages, even to the point where each could use their joint bank account without consulting the other. The brothers often began whistling the same tune while at work in their bicycle shop, as if there were a psychic bond between them. And their voices were so alike that listeners could not tell them apart except by seeing them. They attributed this phenomenon to an association of ideas stored in a common memory (Howard, 1987). Though both were mechanically minded and intelligent, it was their combined abilities and efforts that allowed them to succeed at manmade flight. Only together did they experience genius.

The collaboration of these extraordinary brothers created one of the miracles of their time. On the surface this extraordinary "twinship" is somewhat mystifying (Genogram 4.3). Other sibling pairings in the family might have seemed more natural. Consider the fact that Wilbur and Orville were 4 years apart in age, whereas their two older brothers, Reuchlin and Lorin, were only a year apart. Consider also that Orville and their sister Katharine were linked by a shared birthday. I believe the twinship between the brothers was influenced by the hidden connection brought on by the birth and early death of twin siblings, Otis and Ida, born between Orville and Wilbur. The twins' birthday was commemorated by their father for more than a quarter of a century (Crouch, 1989). Though we know nothing of earlier twins in the Wright family, I wonder if the intensity of the Wrights' need for twins doesn't also

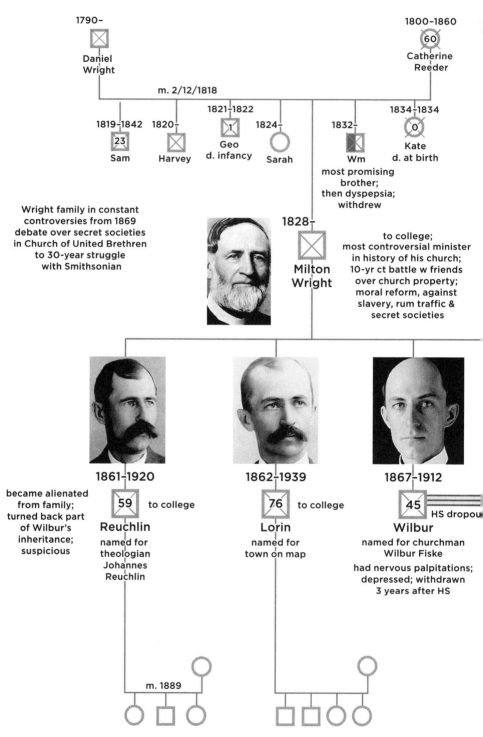

1790–
Daniel
Wright

1800–1860
60
Catherine
Reeder

m. 2/12/1818

1819–1842
23
Sam

1820–
Harvey

1821–1822
1
Geo
d. infancy

1824–
Sarah

1832–
Wm
most promising
brother;
then dyspepsia;
withdrew

1834–1834
0
Kate
d. at birth

Wright family in constant
controversies from 1869
debate over secret societies
in Church of United Brethren
to 30-year struggle
with Smithsonian

1828–
Milton
Wright

to college;
most controversial minister
in history of his church;
10-yr ct battle w friends
over church property;
moral reform, against
slavery, rum traffic &
secret societies

1861–1920
59
Reuchlin   to college

became alienated
from family;
turned back part
of Wilbur's
inheritance;
suspicious

named for
theologian
Johannes
Reuchlin

1862–1939
76
Lorin   to college

named for
town on map

1867–1912
45
Wilbur
HS dropou

named for churchman
Wilbur Fiske

had nervous palpitations;
depressed; withdrawn
3 years after HS

m. 1889

Genogram 4.3. The Wright Family.

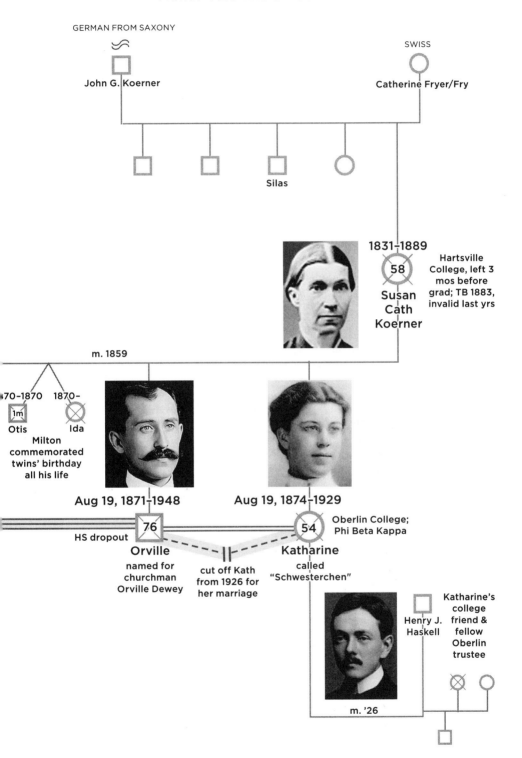

GERMAN FROM SAXONY

John G. Koerner

SWISS

Catherine Fryer/Fry

Silas

1831–1889

58

Susan
Cath
Koerner

Hartsville
College, left 3
mos before
grad; TB 1883,
invalid last yrs

m. 1859

70–1870   1870–

1m

Otis   Ida

Milton
commemorated
twins' birthday
all his life

Aug 19, 1871–1948   Aug 19, 1874–1929

76   54   Oberlin College;
                                        Phi Beta Kappa

HS dropout

Orville   Katharine

named for   cut off Kath   called
churchman   from 1926 for   "Schwesterchen"
Orville Dewey   her marriage

Henry J.   Katharine's
Haskell   college
              friend &
              fellow
              Oberlin
              trustee

m. '26

reflect some earlier traumas involving other twins in previous generations of the family.

As we know, families that lose children often form a special attachment to the surviving children, who become emotional replacements and have difficulty leaving home. Bishop Wright, the father, actually boasted that neither Orville nor Wilbur ever married or left the parental roof. Whereas their two older brothers and their younger sister all left home for college, neither Wilbur nor Orville ever left home or went to college. The reasons for this remain obscure, leaving one to wonder if there was not some covert message for them not to leave, especially as both parents and all their siblings did attend college and had high educational aspirations for all their children.

A possible practical reason for Wilbur's not leaving home was that he sustained a sports injury around the time of finishing high school and withdrew to his home, nursing his mother, who was slowly dying of tuberculosis. The father lost his position as bishop the same year, due to political hassles, which put him in difficult circumstances financially and in his community. However, Wilbur's inability to mobilize himself lasted long after his mother's death and left several family members wondering if he was malingering or depressed. The parental message not to leave may have been intensified not only by the loss of the twins but also by the mother's illness and early death and the father's political problems within the ministry.

Orville and Katharine also had a kind of twin relationship, which intensified after Wilbur died, and they lived together as a pair for many years after his death. One might almost hypothesize that this family "needed" twins. When Orville no longer had Wilbur, he and Katharine became the replacement twins. When Katharine finally decided to marry at the age of 52, having hesitated for over a year to tell Orville of her engagement, he refused to speak to her ever again. As one of the Wright biographers put it: "Katharine violated a sacred pact. In admitting another man into her life, she had rejected her brother. Katharine, of all people, had shaken his faith in the inviolability of the family ties that provided his emotional security" (Crouch, 1989, p. 483). From a family systems perspective this example reflects a common family pattern: Fusion leads to cutoff, and cutoff leads to fusion. In other words, if you cut off feelings about one relationship (say, the twins, who died as infants in the Wright family), you may intensify feelings in another (between Wilbur and Orville), which may get transferred to yet another fusion (between Orville and Katharine) and eventually lead to another cutoff (Orville's cutoff of Katharine for her engagement).

The Wright family demonstrates the power of twins' creativity, but also the deadening effect of the lack of flexibility brought on by traumatic loss that is unresolved. Therapeutic intervention in such families may help them be more proactive in redefining constricting roles set in place by the system failing to adequately acknowledge their traumatic experiences. Once families shut down in response to experiences they feel too overwhelmed to handle, something needs to release the pressure to set the system free again. The act of cutoff is, in this sense, the equivalent of death, and becomes the final act of rigidity in a system that is in trouble.

Handling Family Pain and Conflict

It takes considerable strength and courage to handle conflict, and many families get stuck on this issue. Families that prioritize togetherness tend to avoid discussion of their differences. They cover them up, change the subject, or stifle their own feelings and pretend to agree. Other families repeatedly erupt in response to anxiety. Disagreements may lead to distance, alienation, and unresolved family resentments. Turmoil can be the basic style of relating and such families constantly shift the argument without resolution of the conflict.

When a disagreement reaches a certain level, the family shifts to a different battlefront. For example, a marital conflict may arise over the husband's preoccupation with his job. The wife complains that he is unhelpful and unappreciative, while he feels she is insensitive to his work stress. At a certain point, instead of being able to resolve their conflict, they may switch to a disagreement over the son's behavior. When this conflict becomes too intense, they again shift to another battleground. The husband says the wife "always" interrupts and the wife says the husband "never" listens. The son may then distract the parents by picking a fight with his sister. At this point the parents join together to stop the children's fighting. This continual shifting can keep the anxiety level of the family within certain bounds, but relationships remain the same and conflicts go unresolved. A stable balance may result, though it is quite unsatisfying for the participants.

Sometimes family members, particularly couples, get into a cycle of fighting and making up. There is intense disagreement, maybe even a parting of ways, followed by a loving reconciliation and a renewed avowal of love. Even when not much is resolved, the intensity of the reconciliations may make the conflict almost worthwhile. Sometimes a person even picks a fight to experience the closeness of making up.

Other families live in a "cold war"—no battles, just chronic tension. A cold, contemptuous glance can be the emotional equivalent of a devastating verbal attack. This kind of distancing may not resolve the problems, but it can keep anxiety at a bearable level.

Typically, conflicts between any two family members will affect others in the family. As anxiety rises, conflicts have a ripple effect. Family members become polarized. It is hard to avoid taking sides. Even those who try to remain neutral and above the fray will be seen as having chosen a side by their very silence.

For example, when Kathleen Kennedy (Genogram 5.3, pages 162–163), child of Joseph and Rose Kennedy, married a Protestant in England, against her parents' wishes and their religion, Rose retreated to her room. Joe, torn between his wife and his daughter, had his wife admitted to a hospital to protect her from publicity and, perhaps, from having to commit herself publicly to a reaction; Kathleen had to read about the family's response to the marriage in the newspaper and draw her own conclusions. Joe Jr., the oldest son, finally cabled the parents on Kathleen's behalf: "The power of silence is great" (Kearns Goodwin, 1987, p. 679).

Such responses may temporarily stabilize the family, but they create a situation in which a family will be less equipped to handle future changes and anxiety.

Distortions in Communication

Generally speaking, people communicate most clearly when they are feeling secure. If there is a problem in the family, they usually distort their messages to protect themselves or others. They may not talk at all, they may blame themselves, they may blame someone else, or they may change the conversation by talking about other subjects.

The level of distortion is a good measure of the overall anxiety and rigidity of family relationships. If two family members always agree, this is probably more a reaction to anxiety than because they are soul mates. Conversely, if two family members are always in disagreement, the subjects of their conflict are probably not the real issue. They will end up on opposite sides no matter what the content of their discussion.

Dysfunctional relationship and communication patterns are most likely to develop in times of stress. Consider how often people stop speaking to each other when there is a death in the family or a financial crisis. If many stresses—death, a move, birth, divorce, and remarriage—all occur at the same time, a family will understandably be overwhelmed and probably won't communicate effectively, at least for a time. The legacy of disturbed relationships and communication becomes most serious when the family communication remains distorted over time. Chronically maladaptive ways of relating ripple out and down the system.

Fusion and Cutoff

Under stress, family members may feel pressured to think and act alike—to sacrifice their own identity for the sake of family loyalty. Individuals are forced to give up a part of themselves for the group. Any independent behavior becomes a threat. Such relationships require family members to maintain a strong degree of illusion about one another. Differences must be ignored or minimized. This kind of closeness is called *fusion*. The boundaries of each person are lost and people conform to the needs of others.

There is a profound difference between fusion and a genuinely intimate relationship, which respects and affirms individual differences. Fused families often take a stance of "us against the world," limiting their ability to cope. If family members must always follow the "party line," they have difficulty adjusting to change. Closed to outside influences and ideas, they see others as opponents rather than as potential resources. Too much togetherness can lead to enmeshment and finally to devastating cutoffs when the illusion of total oneness is shattered.

Fusion in the O'Neill Family

Long Day's Journey into Night, Eugene O'Neill's autobiographical play, offers a powerful example of family fusion. O'Neill never really resolved the fusion in his original family (Genogram 4.4). He sought closeness and ran from it at the same time. Only weeks after his first marriage, he fled, totally abdicating his responsibilities for his wife Kathleen and the son she bore (this son, Eugene Jr., first met O'Neill at age 11). Following a tortured affair with the wife of a close friend, O'Neill married again. He was extremely possessive of his second wife, Agnes, wanting her (as he always wanted his partners) to be free of children, family, and friends. When Agnes married O'Neill, she left behind a child from her previous marriage, just as he had left his child. He was intensely jealous whenever he saw Agnes with anyone else, saying: "I want it to be not you and me but us . . . in an aloneness broken by nothing. Not even by children of our own" (Sheaffer, 1968, p. 65).

Even so, the couple did have two children, Shane and Oona. Eugene ignored the children and, when this second marriage ended, he made Agnes the villain. Fusion, when it disintegrates, typically leads to disillusionment and cutoff. In the years after the divorce, O'Neill not only cut off Agnes but his children as well, refusing even to mention their names.

In his third marriage, to Carlotta Monterey, O'Neill's pattern of fusion and cutoff intensified. His first meeting with Carlotta came only a few weeks

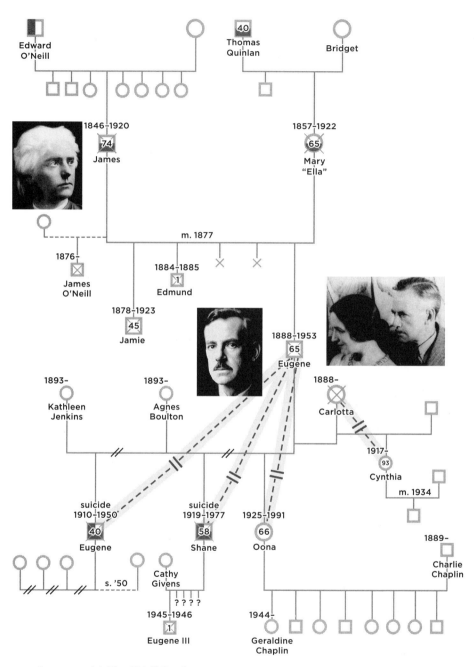

Genogram 4.4. The O'Neill Family.

after the death of his mother in 1922, which probably increased his need for connection. Their relationship began while he was still married to Agnes. Of their first meeting, Carlotta later said:

> He began to talk about his boyhood. He talked and talked, as though he'd known me all his life, but he paid no more attention to me than if I had been a chair. He talked about how he'd had no home, no mother in the real sense, no father in the real sense, and how deprived his childhood had been. Well, that's what got me into trouble with O'Neill; my maternal instinct came out—this man must be looked after, I thought. He broke my heart. I couldn't bear that this child I had adopted should have suffered these things. (Gelb & Gelb, 1987, p. 62)

It is interesting that Carlotta realized their mutual projections so early. She was an "object" to fill his emptiness and he was a "child" she could take care of. Carlotta, like O'Neill himself, had a desperate need to belong. Her previous marriage had foundered because of her husband's continual infidelities.

To justify abandoning his family, O'Neill convinced himself that his second marriage had been a fiasco and that Agnes's resentment of his divorcing her was unjustified. But once he and Carlotta were off by themselves, she having also left behind her daughter, whom she eventually cut off entirely though in later years she lived nearby, Eugene was tormented by guilt over leaving his family. Carlotta became increasingly hostile toward friends who showed sympathy for Agnes, and soon all previous relationships were cut off.

As time went on, O'Neill and Carlotta built a two-against-the world stance. They isolated themselves further by living abroad. Even after they returned to the United States, Carlotta worked to minimize O'Neill's contact with his children. For the next 26 years they developed a romantic legend: the handsome, remote, chateau-dwelling O'Neill, secluded in work and in love with his devoted Carlotta. In later years, because of a Parkinson-like illness, O'Neill was unable to write, and Carlotta's protectiveness intensified. O'Neill, cut off from all three of his children, never saw his grandchildren. Both of his sons eventually committed suicide. O'Neill refused to see his daughter Oona after her marriage at age 25 to the comedian and director Charlie Chaplin, who was O'Neill's contemporary. In the last years both O'Neill and Carlotta were seriously depressed; after he died she went on alone, trying to preserve the legend herself as long as she lived.

Intervention with a family that has become closed down like this one requires acknowledgment of the pain that led them to view fusion and cutoff as a solution rather than the deadly perpetuator of the very losses they were struggling with in the first place. O'Neill, so pained by the sense of loss of his own parents, proceeded to lose all his children and to require his spouses to do the same thing.

The Symptom Bearer

In times of stress one family member may become identified as the patient or symptom bearer. This person, whom therapists often call the IP or "identified patient," may actually serve as a distress signal for the whole family. The symptomatic person provides a focus for the family's emotional energy and distracts them from their anxiety. There may even be an unconsciousness arrangement among family members for one to be symptomatic so the others have someone to care for. Family members may even take turns being the symptom bearer, one person rallying to take care of another. But in rigid families the positions are likely to remain fixed, as in the case of O'Neill and Carlotta. Even when Carlotta herself had to be hospitalized and the roles should have reversed, O'Neill managed to get himself hospitalized in the same hospital, not to be outdone in the role of patient.

Headaches, depression, anxiety attacks, children's school failure or behavior problems—all may provide clues to family problems in which the symptom bearer is peripheral to the primary issue. Often it is the least powerful family members who develop symptoms. When parents are having marital problems, children are likely to become the symptom bearers, particularly if the parents cannot deal with their issues themselves. Women are often the ones who become symptomatic in families, generally having less power to change systems than do men, who are usually socialized not to acknowledge their needs or vulnerability or to ask for help.

In these cases, responding only to the symptom without exploring the overall context in which it occurs may lead to a misunderstanding of what is happening. When a child's stomach aches are responded to only with medication, or school failure only with punishment and remedial help, the response may miss the real issue, which may be the child's distress over family problems.

Symptoms of illness often tell us more about anxiety in the family as a whole than about the sick individual alone. Studies have actually indicated that the time of seeking medical help for a child may have more to do with changes in the parents' anxiety than with changes in the child's state of health.

We can see an example of this in the O'Neill family. Eugene was diagnosed with tuberculosis in 1912; earlier in the same year, miserably alcoholic with no money and no career, he had attempted suicide, after his first humiliating divorce. This was a time of dysfunction for the entire O'Neill family. His mother's morphine addiction was severe, as was his brother Jamie's alcoholism, and his father was profoundly frustrated about the limitations of his own career. The family had become increasingly isolated. Although the tuberculosis obviously had a biological cause, people are, as we know, more vulnerable to illness when their immune system is stressed.

As it turned out, Eugene's TB symptoms led finally to outside attention—he was forced to enter a sanatorium, where he found supports that helped him transform his life. By the time he returned home a few months later, he had developed the goal to become a writer, and soon he was on his way. Within a year his mother had transformed her life as well, entering a convent where she finally overcame her 28-year addiction to morphine. Although such transformations did not extend through the entire O'Neill family, this case shows that new creativity can evolve when a closed system is disturbed enough to be opened up to new outside influence. Such timely infusion of external resources on a system is the very hope of systems therapy.

Triangles

Stress can also prompt the stabilization of triangular relationships, in which two people are joined together against a third. The distance or cutoff in one relationship tends to promote the need for fusion in the other. And the closeness of two people sets up a conflict when a third enters the scene. Such triangles are commonplace—indeed, almost inevitable—in human interaction, though they do cause problems. Molly Haskell, a New York journalist, described the common triangle that developed among her, her mother (who wanted fusion with her), and her husband (with whom her mother developed a deep sense of rivalry). Even though in her head Haskell knew that mother-in-law triangles are so commonplace as to be material for cartoons and jokes, she could not keep herself from getting hooked into the "ferocity" of the triangle:

> It was a tragedy for me that the two people I loved most couldn't get along, yet it was a situation that I, in my own dividedness, had created. Only children . . . expect those they love to love each other, and the child in me persisted long after the adult should have taken over and accepted the inevitable. And yet, beloved of triangles, creators of

triangles by our very birth, how is it possible not to keep re-creating them, and reinserting our mediating and trouble-making selves into their midst? (Haskell, 1990, p. 25)

Haskell described with great clarity how difficult it is to be the third player when two others are alienated—and how hard it is not to get caught up in the pattern yourself:

> Basically their pained looks and noises would pass each other by and hit me, like magnetized arrows, and settle in my stomach. The cocktail hour was our Armageddon, the moment when the demons that had been suppressed by sobriety and the presence of outsiders came to the surface. The first drink would pass in a strained facsimile of civilized decorum, but then Andrew, who was partially deaf anyway and whose voice had a tendency to rise with the least emotion, would unwittingly interrupt Mother. Mother would wince; I would feel her wince and cringe; I would be angry with her for her fastidiousness, angry with Andrew for his boorishness as we turned into a Tennessee Williams parody of ourselves. Andrew the elemental brute; Mother the impossibly refined hostess, and me, rigid with the sense of my two halves breaking apart, feeling vaguely responsible. (Haskell, 1990, p. 25)

When such patterns become fixed, we think of them as "triangles," as they usually involve two people who are "close" and "agree" on things, and a third who is the rejected outsider—the "bad guy" or the "helpless victim" or, as in this case, two people in conflict and a third who feels caught between them and has the role of "helpless victim," unable to let the two deal with their conflict for themselves. The rules of triangles can be laid out in almost mathematical fashion: (A) The friend of my friend is my friend. (B) The friend of my enemy is my enemy. (C) The enemy of my enemy is my friend. Triangles exist any time two people involve a third instead of dealing with their issues directly.

As Haskell described so well, it is exceedingly difficult to be friends with two people who are at war with each other. The sides of the triangle have more to do with the emotional needs of the system than with the characteristics of the players. It was not really Andrew's "boorishness" that was the problem but the threat he represented to Haskell's mother's fantasy of fusion with her daughter. As Haskell described it, Andrew represented the antithesis of what her mother had raised her to be: "the ladylike daughter of the Old Confederacy who would . . . join the garden club and settle down and raise a family nearby. Andrew was my rejection of that dream staring her in the face" (Haskell, 1990, p. 26). The mother probably found it easier to project her negativity onto her son-in-law than to deal directly with her pain that her daughter was not who she wished her to be.

A person caught between two others might indeed become symptomatic, shifting the triangle so that the two "enemies" are forced to join together to care for the symptomatic member. Or, the person in Haskell's role might decide to get out of the way and let the other two individuals figure out how to relate to each other by themselves.

Triangular relationships are a common response of families to stress. Two family members begin to gossip about a third. By validating each other's view about how "obnoxious" or "incompetent" the third person is, the first two shore up their own perceptions, gain a sense of moral righteousness, and probably lower the anxiety they each have in dealing with the third person.

However, when people's close and conflicted or distant relationships are interconnected in triangles, the dysfunctional implications are real. These triangles often reflect problems in the larger system as well, as the example of the Nehru-Gandhi family illustrates (Genogram 4.5).

Jawaharlal Nehru described a triangle in which he felt caught between his parents as he grew up. As a small child he had stolen a pen from his father and the whole family had been involved in searching for it:

> The pen was discovered and my guilt proclaimed to the world. Father was very angry and he gave me a tremendous thrashing. Almost blind with pain and mortification at my disgrace I rushed to my mother and for several days various creams and ointments were applied to my aching and quivering little body. I do not remember bearing any ill-will towards my father because of this punishment. . . . My admiration and affection for him remained as strong as ever, but fear formed a part of them. Not so with my mother. I had no fear of her, for I knew that she would condone everything I did, and because of her excessive and indiscriminating love for me I tried to dominate over her a little. (cited in Ali, date, p. 8)

Despite the brutality of the father's punishment of Nehru, he adored his only son. Nehru's biographer, Tarik Ali, explained the triangle in the Nehru

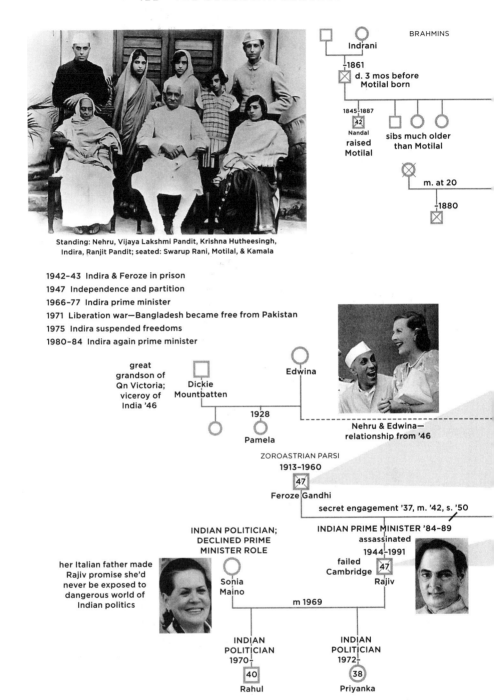

Standing: Nehru, Vijaya Lakshmi Pandit, Krishna Hutheesingh, Indira, Ranjit Pandit; seated: Swarup Rani, Motilal, & Kamala

1942–43 Indira & Feroze in prison
1947 Independence and partition
1966–77 Indira prime minister
1971 Liberation war—Bangladesh became free from Pakistan
1975 Indira suspended freedoms
1980–84 Indira again prime minister

Genogram 4.5. The Nehru Family.

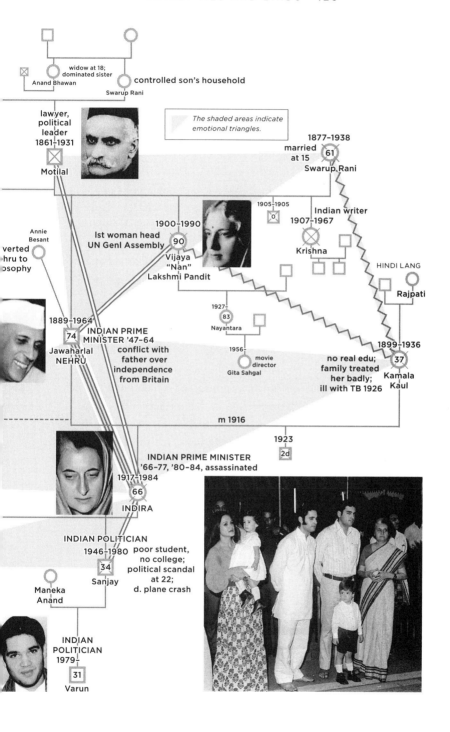

widow at 18; dominated sister
Anand Bhawan

Swarup Rani

controlled son's household

lawyer, political leader
1861–1931

Motilal

The shaded areas indicate emotional triangles.

1877–1938
married at 15

61

Swarup Rani

1905–1905
0

Indian writer
1907–1967

Krishna

1900–1990
1st woman head UN Genl Assembly

90

Vijaya "Nan" Lakshmi Pandit

HINDI LANG

Rajpati

Annie Besant
verted hru to osophy

1889–1964
INDIAN PRIME MINISTER '47–64

74

Jawaharlal NEHRU

conflict with father over independence from Britain

1927–
83
Nayantara

1956–
movie director
Gita Sahgal

1899–1936
37

no real edu; family treated her badly; ill with TB 1926

Kamala Kaul

m 1916

1923
2d

INDIAN PRIME MINISTER
'66–77, '80–84, assassinated
1917–1984

66

INDIRA

INDIAN POLITICIAN
1946–1980

34

Sanjay

poor student, no college; political scandal at 22; d. plane crash

Maneka Anand

INDIAN POLITICIAN
1979–

31

Varun

family in terms of the patriarchal gender arrangements that contributed to the context:

> The violence inflicted on the young boy was . . . part of an older tap-
> estry. The family reproduces in its own unique fashion the relations of
> authority that exist in society as a whole. The subordination of women
> is the most notorious aspect of this process, but there is another,
> equally crucial dimension: the ritual socialization of men. . . . The
> father-son relationship enshrines and symbolizes male domination.
> Violence is always there, lurking in the background, sometimes hid-
> den, sometimes openly practiced. The bruises inflicted are often vis-
> ible. Even when the actual pain has gone, the suppressed anger and
> resentment can stay with the victim for the rest of his life. The effects
> naturally vary from one individual to another. Jawaharlal's attach-
> ment to his father was genuine, but it could not have been free of
> ambiguity. (Ali, 1985, p. 9)

This triangle was played out again in Nehru's relationship with his daughter Indira. As a child, Indira was extremely close to her mother, Kamala,
who was disrespected by Nehru's family and not protected by her husband.
Kamala taught her daughter not to trust men and to become independent.
However, Kamala developed tuberculosis by the time Indira was 11 and died
before Indira reached adulthood, and Indira and Nehru turned to each other
in a closeness that ended only with his death. Indira married Feroze Gandhi,
a Parsi Zooroastrian, against her father's wishes and had two sons, but left her
husband, and soon returned with the sons to live with her father. The husband had always feared his wife would leave him for her famous family, the
pull of family closeness competing with the marital bond. Then in the third
generation, Indira became extremely close to her younger son, Sanjay. She
switched to her older son Rajiv, only after Sanjay's death. In all three generations the couple bond was weak, leaving family members vulnerable to intergenerational triangling for many generations. There were then numerous
triangles with the daughters-in-law, Rajiv's Italian wife Sonia, whose father
had made her husband promise never to involve her in Indian politics. In the
years since her husband was assassinated, Sonia was an extremely influential
member of the Indian Congress. Then there is Sanjay's Sikh wife, Maneka
Anand, whose father's death may even have implicated Sanjay. Beyond that
was the very prominent triangle of Nehru's long affair with a member of the
British royal family, Edwina Mountbatten, wife of Lord Mountbatten, Prince
Philip's uncle.

Family triangles become particularly problematic when they rigidify into stable relationships. Generally, two-person relationships seem to be inherently unstable and under stress tend to reform as triangles. People are likely to feel threatened by anyone who disagrees with them, and then to seek someone else who will validate their view of things. They then see themselves and those who agree with them as the "good guys" in relation to a third person or several people, who get lumped together as bad, sick, or helpless.

Such triangles in families are quite predictable. Parent-child triangles may resolve marital conflict by focusing on the child, who is labeled "sick" or "bad." In other cases children are drawn into closeness with one parent and distance from the other. Marital triangles typically involve a child, an in-law, an affair, a job, or a friend, who becomes the focus of the couple's attention. Three-generational triangles predictably involve grandparent and grandchild siding together, with the parent in the outside position, labeled incompetent, "sick," "mean," "wrong," or "bad." And sibling triangles most often involve "the good seed" and "the bad seed," the star and the loser, or the caretaker and the incompetent in relationship to the parents.

In this process one person seeks support in reaction against another, and each relationship becomes *reactive to* and *dependent on* the other. People can no longer afford to disagree with their ally for fear that she or he might then ally with the "enemy." In this way, triangles become rigid and the real difficulties between people do not get worked out. Triangles occur in all human relationships—in work systems, friendship networks, communities, and, of course, also in international politics. In family relationships triangles can become particularly fierce and painful because members are so dependent on each other for support and self-validation throughout their lives, and because families, unlike other systems, are entered only by birth, marriage, or adoption and can be left only by death, if even then.

The Beethoven Family

The family of composer Ludwig von Beethoven was dominated throughout by triangles (Genogram 4.6). Ludwig's father, Johann, the only surviving son in his family, was held close by his powerful, successful father, also named Ludwig, excluding Johann's mother, Maria, who had been sent to a cloister for her alcoholism. Ludwig's mother Maria had earlier been in an alliance with her mother after the premature death of her father. Maria had an early marriage at 16, but her first husband and an infant son died soon after. Thus, both of Beethoven's parents were tied to their own same-sexed parents; these parents feared losing Johann and Maria and disapproved strenuously of their marriage, on the pretext that their partners were

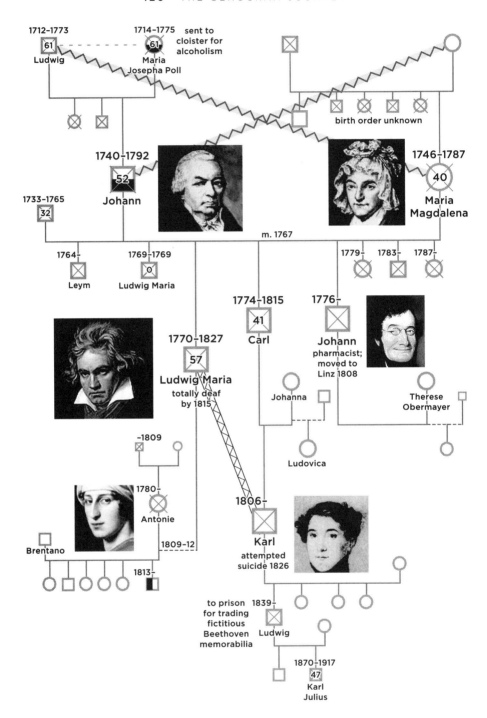

Genogram 4.6. The Beethoven Family.

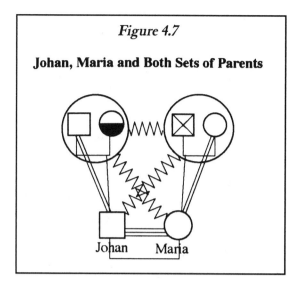

Figure 4.7

Johan, Maria and Both Sets of Parents

unworthy. Their marriage thus occurred in the context of two primary tri-angles with the families of origin (Figure 4.7).

Maria and Johann von Beethoven had seven children, of whom only three survived. The first child, Ludwig Maria, died after 6 days of life in 1769. The second, the famous composer, also named Ludwig Maria von Beethoven, was born on December 16, 1770; he grew up confusing his birth date and that of his dead older brother and namesake. From birth he seems to have been part of a sibling triangle with his parents and dead infant brother, whose name he bore and with whom he felt he could never compare (Figure 4.8).

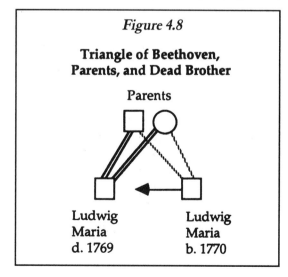

Figure 4.8

**Triangle of Beethoven,
Parents, and Dead Brother**

Parents

Ludwig
Maria
d. 1769

Ludwig
Maria
b. 1770

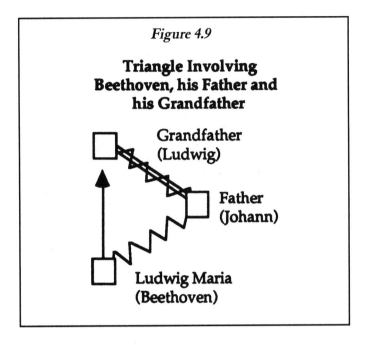

Figure 4.9

Triangle Involving Beethoven, his Father and his Grandfather

Grandfather (Ludwig)

Father (Johann)

Ludwig Maria (Beethoven)

Beethoven was also involved in a three-generational triangle with his father and his paternal grandfather, also named Ludwig (Figure 4.9). The grandfather was a talented singer, choirmaster of Bonn, and a successful wine merchant. Though he died when young Ludwig was only 3, the boy continued to idolize him with something bordering on hero worship. The grandfather, though talented and successful, was also domineering and intrusive toward his only son, Johann, who was amiable and submissive in his youth but lacked talent or initiative which came to irritate his ambitious father. To make matters worse, the grandfather began to broadcast his contemptuous view that Johann would amount to nothing, calling him "Johann the Loafer." Johann fulfilled his father's prophecy by becoming an abusive drunkard, cruel and arbitrary in his demands on young Ludwig to practice, as his father had been demanding of him, and an embarrassment to the whole family.

In the nuclear family, Beethoven, as the oldest surviving child, also ended up in a painful triangle with his parents. Although he defended his father fiercely against outsiders and intervened desperately when the police came to arrest him for drunkenness, he could hardly have avoided being drawn into a triangle with his parents on the side of his sad, gentle, long-suffering mother, a triangle from which he tried to escape as a child by isolating himself. His mother's death from tuberculosis when he was only 17 placed him in charge of the family. The father at this point largely abandoned himself to his

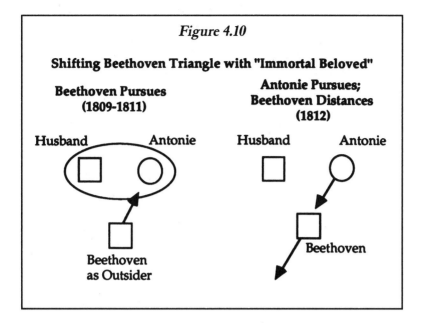

Figure 4.10

Shifting Beethoven Triangle with "Immortal Beloved"

alcoholism. Ludwig became his guardian, even being paid the father's pension, which embarrassed him and greatly humiliated the father. Nowhere in his extensive correspondence does Beethoven refer to his father by name, and when the father was dying, Beethoven left home.

The relationships of Beethoven's adult life were also characterized by triangles. Early on he became involved with a series of unattainable women (either married or otherwise attached), in which not surprisingly he was always the outsider. Sometimes being the outsider in a triangle is preferable, because one can play the role of romantic hero without actually having to make a commitment, and this may have been true for Beethoven.

This pattern continued for years until in 1812 he became involved with Antonie Brentano, his "immortal beloved," a married woman and a mother of four. (Figure 4.10). For Brentano the involvement with Beethoven seems also to have been part of a complex web of triangular relationships, which began in childhood with her deep attachment to a father she rarely saw. When she did fall in love, her father instead arranged for her to marry a wealthy older German businessman and emigrate from Austria to Germany, which she experienced as exile. She returned to Vienna 11 years later, when her adored father died. It was during this nostalgic and painful return to her homeland that she met Beethoven, who was apparently the one person who could draw her out of depression. Having procrastinated as long as she could

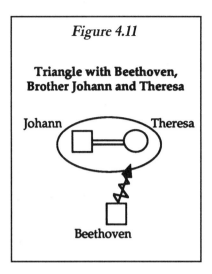

Figure 4.11

Triangle with Beethoven, Brother Johann and Theresa

in returning to Germany, she at last made a desperate proposal to Beethoven that she would give up her family for him. Was Beethoven a replacement for her father or her early love, and thus a part of the interlocking triangles in her family? It seems likely. When Brentano offered to give up everything for him, Beethoven retreated.

From the time Beethoven broke with Brentano he never had another serious involvement with a woman. Instead he turned back to his family of origin and became embroiled in several destructive and intrusive triangular relationships in his brothers' families. His relationships with his two younger brothers had been intense for years, having reached the point of violence more than once, always followed by emotional scenes of reconciliation.

Beethoven almost never referred to his youngest brother, Johann, by name, referring to him usually by leaving a blank space or using an epithet such as "pseudo-brother," "brain-eater," "my ass of a brother," or "brother Cain." Immediately after ending the relationship with Brentano, Beethoven traveled to Linz where Johann was living with Therese Obermayer. Morally outraged, he demanded that Johann break off this relationship. (Figure 4.11). When Johann refused, Beethoven went to the authorities and obtained a police order compelling Therese to leave Linz if the relationship continued. Johann foiled this interference by marrying Therese.

The triangles involving Beethoven and the family of his other brother Carl were even stormier. The marriage between Carl and his wife, Johanna, had been full of strife for years. Ludwig had apparently tried to prevent this marriage also, although at other times he played the role of protector to Johanna against Carl's violence. Like their father, Carl often beat his son,

Karl, to make him obey, and Johanna was not spared either. In 1811 Carl had denounced his wife, charging that she had stolen money from him. She was convicted and sentenced to a month of house arrest, even though any "stolen" money would have been her own because of the large dowry and inheritance she brought into the marriage.

Beethoven would listen to nothing negative about this brother, though some of his friends believed that Carl was taking advantage of him and even being dishonest. When one friend finally took it upon himself to speak directly about the brother's mistreatment of Beethoven, the latter closed his ears and refused to speak to his friend for a decade.

In 1815, the day before Carl died, he wrote a will providing for Johanna and Ludwig to be coguardians for the son, Karl. Beethoven, learning about this, intervened and compelled his brother to change the will, leaving him as sole guardian. Realizing that Ludwig wanted to exclude Johanna from joint guardianship, Carl added another paragraph to his will later that day, which read:

> Having learned that my brother . . . desires after my death to take wholly to himself my son Karl, and wholly to withdraw him from the supervision and training of his mother, and inasmuch as the best of harmony does not exist between my brother and my wife, I have found it necessary to add to my will that I by no means desire that my son be taken from his mother, but that he shall always . . . remain with his mother, to which end his guardianship is to be exercised by her as well as by my brother. (Solomon, 1977, p. 234)

In spite of this, immediately after Carl's death Beethoven moved to attain sole custody of his nephew and to have Johanna declared unfit even for visiting privileges. The struggle went on for years, with the nephew trapped between his loyalty and affection for his mother and his dutiful respect for his strange but famous and seemingly well-meaning uncle. (Figure 4.12). Beethoven was at this time an unkempt, eccentric bachelor of 45, preoccupied with composing though he had alienated most of his patrons by then. He was totally deaf, often in pain, and in very poor health—not the best condition in which to take on responsibility for a 9-year-old. Over the course of various court battles, Johanna won back custody from Beethoven, though he continued his pursuit and retrieved the nephew again. He was intrusive, abusive, inconsistent, and extremely overprotective of his nephew. He used his brother's earlier unjustified accusation of Johanna's embezzlement as justification for obtaining custody. He became convinced that she had destructive powers, saw himself as a divinely authorized and heroic rescuer of his poor, unhappy

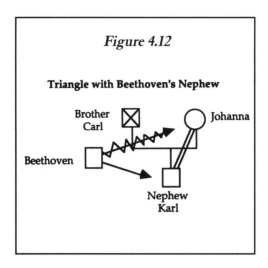

Figure 4.12

Triangle with Beethoven's Nephew

nephew, and applauded his nephew whenever he repudiated his mother. If one did not know the history of triangles in this family, his behavior might have seemed quite mystifying and hard to fathom.

It is interesting and perhaps predictable that, when on several occasions Beethoven moved toward a rapprochement with Johanna, Karl reacted negatively. Such is the nature of triangles that even though they may be hurtful and destructive for all involved, people resist change. Painful as it must have been for Karl to be pulled between his mother and uncle, he was also threatened when they seemed to draw together. In 1822, when she became ill and was unable to pay for her medicines, Beethoven took over a portion of the debt Johanna owed and soon determined to help her financially. Karl, by then 16 years old, vigorously protested this proposed generosity toward his mother and maligned her in an attempt to forestall a rapprochement between her and his uncle. His fear of closeness between them is understandable. As long as they were fighting over him, his role was pivotal. If they joined forces, he might end up the outsider.

Karl and his mother had become estranged after she gave birth out of wedlock in 1820 to a daughter conceived with a well-to-do man (Figure 4.13). The child was named Ludovica, an interesting choice of name! Very possibly the intense hostilities between Ludwig and Johanna reflected a strong underlying attraction. As Beethoven continued to move toward Johanna, Karl's feeling of threat seems to have diminished also, and for some time they seemed to reconnect. The timing of this reconciliation coincided precisely with Beethoven's composing the "Ode to Joy" for his Ninth Symphony. This

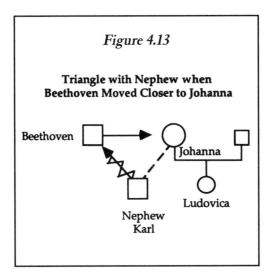

Figure 4.13

**Triangle with Nephew when
Beethoven Moved Closer to Johanna**

Beethoven

Johanna

Ludovica

Nephew
Karl

was the most harmonious period in the relationship between Beethoven and his nephew. Karl worked as his secretary and spent weekends and summers with him.

However, by 1825 Beethoven again became suspicious of Karl and fearful that he had resumed seeing his mother. A number of factors may have intensified the triangle at this particular time. Perhaps their good relationship frightened Beethoven, who seems indeed to have been petrified of closeness, as much as he coveted it. Perhaps Karl's emergence into young adulthood was threatening to Beethoven, or perhaps Beethoven's deafness and heavy drinking were increasing his sense of isolation and powerlessness. Perhaps there were changes in Johanna's life that we do not know about.

The conflicts between uncle and nephew reached a climax when Beethoven began stalking his nephew and withholding money from him. Karl then began sneaking visits to his mother, exacerbating Beethoven's worst fears. He would not leave Karl alone. Finally, at the end of the summer, Karl, despairing of any other solution, tried to shoot himself in the head. He survived but was hospitalized, and his feelings of being tormented by Beethoven were made public. The crisis seems to have relieved pressure from the system. For Beethoven the dream of fusion with Karl—of somehow becoming Karl's father—was broken. The suicide attempt brought in outside influence from doctors, who confronted Beethoven with his nephew's feelings. Though Beethoven sought other explanations for the suicide attempt, Karl's explanation was "weariness of imprisonment." After this Karl became better able to insist on his right to have his own relationship with his mother: "I do not want to hear anything that is derogatory to her; it is not for me to be her judge. . . . In no event shall I treat her with greater coldness than has been the case heretofore. . . . It is self evident that [seeing my mother] will not prevent you and me from seeing each other as often as you wish" (Solomon, 1988, p. 284). Karl decided to enter the military, which he did a few months later, with Beethoven's help. During the last period of his life, Beethoven finally agreed to visit his surviving brother, Johann, from whom he had been cut off because of prior conflicts, and did so with his nephew.

Perhaps anticipating his own mortality, he seems to have put his life in slightly better perspective during the last months. He ended on good terms with Karl, who became his sole inheritor, and also reconciled with Johanna, who, in the end, was the only family member present at his death. Three days before he died, he wrote a codicil to his will, specifying that she would inherit his entire estate if Karl died unmarried, as appeared possible given that he was in the military.

Beethoven's life reflects two classic patterns of triangulation. Prior to 1812 in his romantic relationships he played the role of outsider with women, the "other" lover—a peripheral, safe role that protected him from the responsibility and dangerous power of his childhood triangles. After he gave up the dream of having a family of his own, he intruded aggressively into other people's relationships, as with the families of both his brothers, attempting fusion and creating conflict and cutoff all around him, even though he intended to create a loving family. In the end, possibly through the remedial efforts of Johanna and Karl, he seems to have achieved, for the first time, some sense of connection without fusion or triangling.

Without knowing the history of triangles in the Beethoven family it would be extremely difficult to fathom Karl's suicide attempt or the stormy pattern of Beethoven's relationship to his nephew. Tracking the patterns of communication, fusion, cutoff, and symptom development in a family can open up new perspectives not only on the family but also, hopefully, on each individual's role in family triangles.

Here are questions to explore to understand how the communication and relationships in a family work. As with the questions in other chapters, they are meant to suggest rather than to be exhaustive.

- What were the rules of communication in the family? Who spoke to whom about what?
- What topics were taboo? How were the rules of communication transmitted? Who conveyed them? Were they overt or covert?

- Which family members were extremely close? Which were always in conflict? Who didn't speak to whom? How did others react when two were in conflict or not speaking?

- Who were the most frequent symptom bearers? What symptoms did they show? How did the family respond to symptoms?

- What were the rules for each gender in the family? What did they view as the ideal male and the ideal female? Were there family members who broke out of the traditional gender stereotypes? Were there women or men whose symptoms might have reflected their difficulty accepting gender constraints (e.g., a poetic, gentle man who became alcoholic or a feisty, brilliant women worn down by having no outlet beyond childcare and housekeeping)?

- What were the splits and alliances in the family? Who was in a caretaker/caretakee relationship? a pursuer/distancer relationship? an intense love/hate relationship?

- How did family members react to change? By silence? rigidity? shutting down? trying to hold on to the past? escaping into pipedreams of the future? blaming others? blaming themselves?

- What labels did each family member have: "battle ax," "sad sack," "miser," "weirdo"?

- Were there certain times of great stress and change in the family? Track the family stories of those periods. Who could help to get information about those times?

- How did the family react to stress? Did they draw together? become more separate? Did certain family members have strong reactions such as silence, constant talking, changing the subject, or becoming authoritarian?

- What were the major family triangles? Were there particular types of triangles in the family that repeated over the generations: husband/wife/mother-in-law; husband/wife/affair; father/mother/sick-bad-special child; two close siblings and a third outsider sibling?

5 Death and Other Losses

The single most important thing to know about Americans . . . is that . . . [they] think death is optional.

Brit-Think; Ameri-Think
—JANE WALMSLEY

If I do not connect myself with my own past . . . I will remain adrift from it. Those whom I have loved in the past cannot catch hold of me, for they are dead. It is I who must catch them.

Sister Outsider
—AUDRE LORDE

More than any other human experience, loss puts us in touch with what matters in our lives. Coming to terms with death and other traumatic losses is the most difficult experience we face in life. Sometimes it seems more difficult to lose another than to die ourselves, for without that other, what does our own life mean? When someone important to us dies, it can make us realize how vain some of our pursuits are in comparison to the people in our lives—especially our families. Facing death can be a profoundly life-changing experience, stimulating us to savor our lives more fully and clarify our priorities.

We all hope that death will occur at a point when family members are at peace with each other and when there is a sense of completion about relationships. But we know that frequently this doesn't happen. Untimely deaths are especially difficult to integrate. Regrets about an unfinished relationship can haunt a person throughout a lifetime, and when accounts are left unsettled, a great vacuum may remain. As Robert Anderson's protagonist says in the play *I Never Sang for My Father*: "Death ends a life, but not a relationship, which struggles on in the survivors' minds, seeking some resolution which it may never find" (Anderson, 1968, p. 113).

By examining the multigenerational effects of loss, people can learn a great deal about how families operate, what happens when they get stuck, and possibilities for changing these patterns. Loss may strengthen survivors, bringing out their creativity, spurring them on to accomplishment, or it may leave behind a destructive legacy, all the more powerful if it is not dealt with. People may also follow patterns of loss set up by earlier generations that they know nothing about.

The images people carry with them of funerals and of the dead are an important part of their heritage and identity. How families deal with death is perhaps the best clue about their fundamental values, strengths, and vulnerabilities. We have already seen the pivotal role of deaths in the families of Benjamin Franklin (see page 36 for genogram) and the Wright brothers (see page 112 for genogram). We saw the key impact of early parental death on Queen Victoria (see page 26 for genogram) and, with Franklin, the importance that coincidental deaths had on other family relationships. We saw the triangles that evolved in the Beethoven family (see page 126 for genogram) in the aftermath of loss. This chapter looks at several well-known families—the Freuds, the Kennedys, the Hepburns, and the family of Elizabeth Barrett Browning—to illustrate the legacy of loss across generations.

In a sense all families are marked by their shared losses. At times of loss, family members are generally required to deal with each other in an intimate way at a vulnerable time. This can be particularly difficult for families that are not close. Siblings who have had little to do with each other for years are suddenly forced to share wrenching experiences. This has the potential to bring a family together, but it can also cause old conflicts to resurface. Although a death in the family provides an opportunity to focus on the essential bonds, to reopen relationships that have closed down, to rework old relationships, and to risk saying what has until now been left unsaid, such openings can also intensify old hurts. As with other pivotal family experiences, if things do not get better they will usually get worse.

All change in life requires loss. And death, of course, is not the only loss. Marital separation or divorce, chronic illness, addiction, lack of a job or a house to live in, or becoming handicapped also involve loss—loss of our dreams and expectations as well as real physical and emotional loss. We must give up certain relationships, plans, and possibilities in order to have others. And all losses require mourning, which acknowledges the giving up of the relationship and allows people to move on in life. Mourning is healthy. When families do not adequately mourn their losses, they cannot get on with life. Instead feelings go underground. Family members may blame themselves or each other for a death; they may try to mold others into replacements for the lost person or keep themselves from experiencing closeness again. It is not death itself but the avoidance of the pain of loss that becomes problematic. Families can adapt to even the most traumatic losses, but when they cannot acknowledge the loss and successfully reorganize the system, they become stuck.

Mourning

Our culture's denial of death often means that people do not discuss how they want to die and how they want to be memorialized. A great many people make no will at all, in spite of the extreme hardship this can cause survivors. The quality of dying is often ignored in the service of prolonging life by whatever medical means necessary. The end of life often occurs in a cold, sterile medical setting that allows little consideration for the family's personal experience. And families are often physically separated and thus even more vulnerable to disruption and isolation in the aftermath of loss, which complicates mourning.

Learning the facts about a death can be an important first step in coming to terms with it. If facts about the death have not been admitted, family members are likely to develop their own myths about the death.

Sharing the experience of the loss and finding some way to put it in context are also important. A part of this sharing is joint storytelling about the life and death of the dead person. Such sharing helps families integrate the loss by promoting their sense of familial, cultural, and human connectedness, and empowering them to regain a sense of themselves as moving in time from the past with the lost person through the present and into the future without the person. To develop a sense of control, mastery, and the ability to survive in the face of loss, family members may need to open up relationships with one another and learn more about the family in general—its history, its culture, and the perspectives and stories of different family members. In some African cultures there is a ritual in which each family member reviews her or his history with the dying family member, including their conflicts, as a part of saying good-bye. This seems an excellent way to begin to integrate a loss, because it normalizes the complexity of our intimate relationships, with closeness and conflict acknowledged together.

Sharing memories and stories of the dead can help family members develop more benign, less traumatic perspectives on the role of loss in their lives. It seems important for families to be free to remember as well as to let go of memories. One of the most difficult aspects of denied or unresolved mourning is that it leaves families with no way to make sense of their experience. If events cannot be mentioned or if the family "party line" cannot be expanded upon, the next generation has no models or guidelines for integrating later losses. Family stories are an important facilitator and enhancer of the integration of loss.

Families also need to find ways to reorganize their system without the dead person, a complex and often painful reorientation process. This may entail a shift in caretaking roles or leadership functions, changes in the social network, shifts in family focus (as when an only child dies), or an emotional reorganization of the generational hierarchy (as when the last grandparent dies). Finally, moving beyond loss involves a reinvestment in other relationships and life pursuits. Surviving family members, strengthened by the shared experience of loss, can focus more clearly on what they want to do with the rest of their lives and with their remaining relationships.

Most funeral rituals, incorporating traditions that link previous generations, provide family members with a cushion of belonging as they experience the pain of loss. They provide a special kind of encapsulated time frame, which offers an opportunity for experiencing the overwhelming emotions that death evokes while also containing them. Participating in family funerals, like other rituals of family transition, is also one of the best ways to learn about the family. Rituals allow the person to see family history in the making, as the family stories of the death and other deaths get told and retold. As family members gather from near and far one can see who the key definers of the family's stories are and observe relationships in action that may otherwise be dormant.

Cultures differ greatly in their patterns of mourning—in their rituals and the length of time considered appropriate to "complete" the mourning process. In certain Mediterranean countries, such as Greece and Italy, women have traditionally worn black for the rest of their lives after a husband's death. In Italy it is not uncommon for family members to jump into the grave when the coffin is lowered. In India, until recently, some widows were expected to throw themselves onto the funeral pyre, a sacrifice for their husbands' life after death. At the opposite extreme, some Americans of British ancestry tend to value a "no muss, no fuss," with funerals carried out in a more pragmatic, practical way. They may prefer to have the last illnesses in hospitals, where people are not an "inconvenience" to their families and where their dependence doesn't force emotional obligations. For other ethnic groups, however, a death outside the family's emotional and physical environment is experienced as a double tragedy.

In the U.S. the trend has been increasingly toward minimizing death rituals and expressions of mourning. Through legislation, custom, and public-health and work regulations, considerable social control is exercised over the process. Funeral rituals have been taken over and commercialized by the funeral industry. The allowable leave for bereavement in the workplace (usually 1 to 3 days) severely constrains families from the traditional attitudes and practices of their cultural groups. A failure to carry out death rituals can contribute to a family's experience of unresolved loss, a danger to both personal health and family relationships.

Some people may avoid contacts that remind them of the dead person. Men in particular often develop tension and tightness in trying to keep from "breaking down." If the memories and feelings do finally break through, the pain may be that much more intense. For example, when the Kennedys lost their oldest son, Joe, in World War II, Joe Sr. was the one who handled all the arrangements, "protected" Rose, and kept the family together. Some time later, when he received his son's last letter from the front, his composure disintegrated. Years afterward, Rose said that until the letter came he had been able to block the death from his mind. After that, their roles reversed. As she began to recover from her grief, Joe slipped deeper and deeper into depression. Her religious faith helped her find her way, but his faith was not enough to console him. For months he shut himself away, refusing to read the newspaper, listen to the radio, or talk with friends and family.

The emotional and physical burdens that follow death still seem to be "women's work." Women typically handle the social and emotional tasks of bereavement, from the expression of grief and caretaking of the terminally ill to meeting the needs of surviving family members for support and nurturance, while men arrange for the funeral, choose the coffin, pay the fees, and in general handle the "administrative" tasks of death except for providing the food. Whereas women are free to weep openly, men may deny, withdraw, and avoid their grief, fearing a loss of control. The reactions of each make the other uncomfortable. Men generally take refuge in their work and distance from their wives' open mourning, while women experience their husbands' pulling away as a double loss. This skewed pattern of grieving, which is the norm in our society, breeds isolation for family members, who cannot share their experience of loss and are kept from one of the most important healing resources: each other. As one woman put it, referring to the pain of the loss of one of her three sons: "Through my eyes flow the tears for our whole family." When a family member must grieve alone, the pain is that much worse. Men in our society are often deprived of sharing in the richness of the nodal life experiences that are seen as women's responsibility. Society's denial of male vulnerability and dependency needs, and the sanctions against men's emotional expressiveness, undoubtedly contribute to marital distress after the loss of a family member and to the high rate of serious illness and suicide for men following the death of a spouse.

The different coping strategies of men and women in dealing with loss can increase marital strain, even for couples with strong and stable relationships. When our society allows the full range of human experiences in bereavement as in other areas of family life, we will all surely benefit.

To understand your family, you will need to examine how the family has dealt with loss and how losses have influenced family relationships.

The impact of a death depends on many factors. The untimely death of a child seems to be the most devastating loss a family can experience. It can have a cataclysmic effect on the parents' health and marriage and leave lifelong scars for the siblings. Feelings of guilt tend to be especially strong in the survivors. The deceased child often becomes the receptacle of parents' hopes and dreams, creating an idealized image that is difficult for surviving children to live up to. It has been said that when your parent dies, you have lost your past, but when your child dies, you have lost your future. As Joe Kennedy said about the death of his firstborn son, Joe Jr.: "Now it's all over, because all my plans for my own future were all tied up with young Joe, and that has gone smash. . . . When the young bury the old, time heals the pain and sorrow; but when the process is reversed the sorrow remains forever" (Kearns Goodwin, 1987, p. 693).

The death of a child at any age seems unnatural. However, a death in the "prime of life" also brings special hardships. For the spouse, there is the loss of a helpmate and companion; for the children, there is the loss of a parent, perhaps the breadwinner; for the siblings and friends there is the loss of an age-mate with whom they expected to grow old; for the parents there is the wrenching of the death being "off time."

Not all deaths are equally traumatic. The manner of death also affects the family's response. When we are prepared as much as we can be, when the deceased has lived a long and fruitful life, and when it is an "easy," peaceful death with minimal pain, recriminations, or unfinished business, the family comes more easily to acceptance. Sudden death provides no opportunity to prepare or say good-bye, ripping the person out of the system. A murder, a suicide, or an accident, especially where others feel responsible, may leave even deeper scars on a family. The more sudden, traumatic, or stigmatized the loss, the more widespread its impact is likely to be. Such deaths leave a painful legacy of stigma, guilt, blame, and anguish for the survivors. Suicides are particularly catastrophic. The true circumstances of the death are frequently kept secret, which compounds the emotions families already feel when a life is ended intentionally and isolates the family further.

At the other extreme are the deaths that drain family caretaking resources and require the family to live in a state of prolonged uncertainty. In such cases the family may come to wish the person dead, to see an end to the pain and agony as well as get relief from their burdens. The strain on the caretakers takes energy away from all other relationships and may leave a residue of guilt and ambivalence.

Among the most difficult of all ambiguous losses is when a family member disappears. When there is some hope that the person may still be alive, the psychological presence may remain in the family for years. Fantasies develop about the lost person's survival and return. A similar situation is created in the case of Alzheimer's disease or other catastrophic, degenerative illness or brain injury, where the person may be physically present but psychologically absent for years before death. Such ambiguous losses are extremely difficult to mourn and integrate.

The Context of Loss

The context in which the death occurs, including the state of family relationships at the time of the death and other associated stress factors, will eventually also influence a family's response to loss. When there is family conflict or estrangement at the time of death, a family may be left with a bitter legacy that is hard to undo.

Historical circumstances may also be important. For example, Robert Kennedy's death in 1968 came at a time of great social upheaval and disorganization in our country, especially among the youth. Many of the children in the family were also in their adolescence, a time when their vulnerability to drugs and other reckless behavior put them at much greater risk than was experienced at the time of John Kennedy's death.

When two or more major events occur at the same time, the trauma of the experience is geometrically intensified. For example, the birth of Alice Roosevelt Longworth (see page 96 for genogram), discussed in Chapter 4, coinciding with the death of Roosevelt's wife and mother on the same day surely intensified the meaning of each of those experiences, and was, of course, compounded when Alice Roosevelt's own daughter was born on this anniversary 41 years later.

Sometimes such coincidental anniversary events seem to point up almost mystical connections. Both Thomas Jefferson and John Adams died on the 50th Anniversary of the Declaration of Independence, July 4th, 1826. John Kennedy was shot on the exact day, November 22, that both his paternal great-grandfathers died. Anthropologist Gregory Bateson's middle brother committed suicide on the birthday of the oldest brother, who had died a hero in World War I. Such coincidences intensify the meaning of the death and may perpetuate a legacy of family anxiety around the anniversary date. As individuals, we may also fear that we will die at the same age or same time of year as a parent or sibling with whom we have been identified. If deaths have occurred around Christmas or another important family holiday, they may distort the experience of that day for years to come.

The Impact of Loss

The role and function of the lost person in the family and the resources available to fill in for the dead person will also influence the family's ability to integrate the loss. A person who has been a scapegoat may be hard to mourn. An alcoholic father who dies in a car crash may leave a legacy of guilt and resentment in which the impact of the death is compounded by the painful years that the family lived through with him. It is also difficult for the survivors to compete with the ghost of a dead hero—a supermother, a successful son—or anyone who has been a central figure in the family.

The loss of a parent or primary caretaker presents the most difficult challenge. Central caretaking functions must be assumed by someone else. Single parents must find someone to care for children while they are at work and determine how to manage an economic future with just one salary. Replacing the emotional loss of the parent is still another matter. Sometimes an uncle, aunt, or grandparents can fill in the gap. If practical or emotional resources are unavailable the loss can be greatly compounded.

For example, the death of Robert Kennedy not only came at a more difficult social era of our history but also left a much greater leadership vacuum in the Kennedy family than did the death of his brother John. After John's death, Robert took over the caretaking role for his parents, his sister-in-law and her children, and many others in the family. He even expressed a relief to have the chance to succeed on his own: "Finally I feel that I'm out from under the shadow of my brother. Now at least I feel that I've made it on my own. All these years I never really believed it was me that did it, but Jack" (Collier & Horowitz, 1984, p. 350).

But when Robert himself died 5 years later, Ethel was pregnant with their eleventh child and there was no one who could fill in for him with his children, those of their sister Pat (who had separated from her husband, Peter Lawford, the day John was shot), or the other members of the family who needed support. Ted Kennedy had always been the baby—the "spoiled kid brother." Although he did eventually grow into a family leader, he was not prepared to do so at the time, and the tragedy left a huge vacuum in the entire extended family. Ted knew himself how tenuous his hold was. He told an aide: "I can't let go. If I let go, Ethel will let go, and my mother will let go, and my sisters will let go. . . ." (Collier & Horowitz, 1984, p. 364). It had become a house of cards and he could not manage the family. A nephew later said, "We felt a lot of bitterness toward him. It was probably unfair. There was no real reason for it except that he couldn't fill Uncle Bobby's shoes and didn't try" (p. 371). What followed for the Kennedy family were years of turmoil and problems for the next generation. In the end Teddy Kennedy did transform his role, especially after his remarriage, and became a tremendous resource to his own children, the nieces and nephews, and many of the next generation.

If myth, secrecy, and taboo surround a death and family members cannot talk about the loss, they will become more vulnerable to future losses. When families communicate openly about the death (no matter what the circumstances), and when they participate together in rituals that have meaning for them (e.g., funeral rites and visits to the grave), the loss becomes easier to integrate. Attempts to protect children or "vulnerable" members from the experience are likely to make mourning even more difficult.

The Hepburn Family

The family of Katharine Hepburn Genogram 5.1) is a striking example of a family's ability to develop creative responses to the most stigmatizing of all deaths, suicide, even as the tragedy constricted their functioning. With roots in New England and Virginia, members of her family had founded Corning Glass and Houghton Mifflin Publishers. They were among the most successful and independent-thinking families in New England.

Katharine's older brother Tom hanged himself while he and Kate were visiting close family friends on their Easter vacation. Kate, almost 14 at the time, was the one to find his body. He had torn and braided his bed sheet, making a rope strong enough to hang himself. That morning the father, a successful urologist, told reporters: "My son was normal in mind and body. The taking of his own life can be accounted for only from a medical point, that he was suddenly afflicted with adolescent insanity" (Anderson, 1988, p. 182). Kate was obsessed with absolving her brother and reminded her father of a story he told about a black man who could constrict his neck muscles to avoid dying at the hands of a lynch mob. She recalled that Tom had been intrigued with the story and had tried to hang himself once before, insisting he was trying a stunt. Dr. Hepburn then made a new announcement to reporters, explaining away the suicide as resulting from a foolish schoolboy stunt: "I had entirely forgotten that he considered himself an expert in hanging by the neck in such a way as to look as if he were dying, to the entertainment of his brothers and sisters" (quoted in Anderson, 1988, pp. 185–186). Dr. Hepburn went on to say that his son must have been "rehearsing" for a performance that night, though the death occurred at about 4 a.m., which shows the incredible lengths a family may go to avoid facing a painful reality.

In her autobiography, written 70 years later, Kate maintained that he died "under strange circumstances" and his death had remained unexplained. She admitted that the death must have tortured her parents; her mother never mentioned Tom again, and her father also never once discussed the death with her. Hepburn said death seemed to separate her from the world as she had known it (Hepburn, 1991).

The brother's suicide drew the family into itself. Tom had always been special but also vulnerable. He was the family's great hope. His father had been pressuring him to follow in his footsteps and enter Yale Medical School that fall, and Tom had been hesitant about attending. Since childhood he had suffered various physical and emotional problems, including bouts of confusion and depression.

The parents had withdrawn him from school to protect him, and had withdrawn Katharine as well to be his companion. Though she was younger, this set a pattern for her as caretaker of her older brother. After the suicide, all the siblings were withdrawn from school and tutored at home, turning inward in their pain.

Hepburn didn't mention in her autobiography that Tom's was the fourth suicide in her family, her father's brother having committed suicide 6 years earlier, her maternal grandfather when her mother was 14, and that grandfather's brother 5 years earlier. A fifth suicide, of Katharine's second paternal uncle, Sewell, followed 2 days after Tom's, on April 5, 1921, before they had even had Tom's funeral. This death was again explained away as an accident. It was said that Sewell, who killed himself with carbon monoxide in the middle of the night in the garage, "had a heart attack while working on his car." As with Tom's "stunt," the fact that it was the middle of the night was left out.

From the time Tom died, Katharine began using his birthday as her own, not telling the truth until she wrote her autobiography only a few years before her death. The parents apparently went along with this. Katharine's maternal aunt, Edith, who had always been extremely close to the family, cut off after Tom's suicide because she had deeply objected to her brother-in-law's physical punishment of his children and had felt him overbearing to his son, who was now dead. Edith and her sister, Kit, and their families had spent summers together for many years, both sisters having married men who had gone to Johns Hopkins Medical School with Edith.

The two sisters had been extremely close since childhood; their bond had intensified when they were orphaned through their father's suicide and their mother's death of cancer not long after. Their father, Fred, had shot himself in the head when Kit was 14. Thus, Kit and her daughter Kate experienced

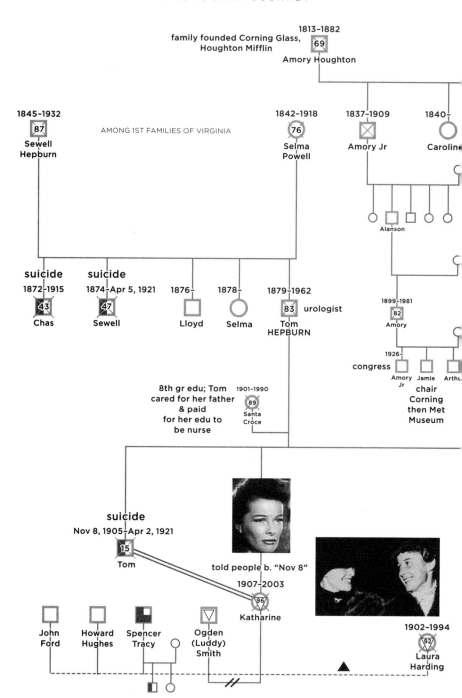

Genogram 5.1. The Hepburn Family.

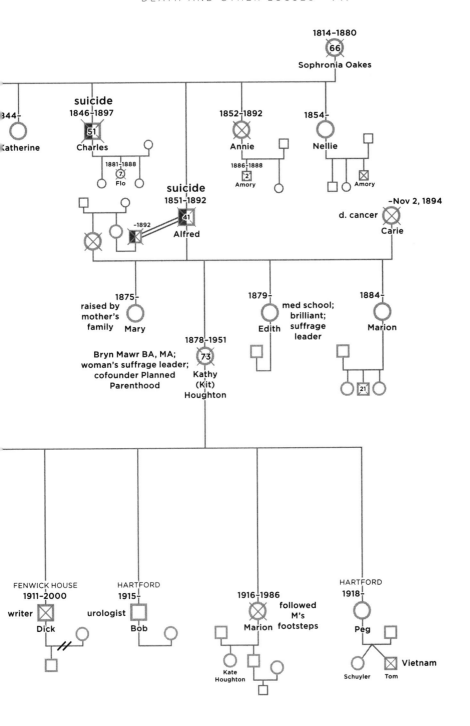

a suicide at about the same age. The grandfather had felt humiliated in the family business by his older brother, Amory, who had inherited the business from their father. Before Kit's mother, Carrie, died of cancer 2 years later, she had been trying to arrange for her three daughters to attend Bryn Mawr, to ensure that they would never be left helpless and dependent as women, as she had been. Kit became the "mother" for both her sisters. Orphaned by the loss of both parents, the sisters were left under the financial control of their uncle Amory, who despised them, especially Kit, and refused to support their education. Kit became a fighter, going to court for the right to control her own money, a lifelong concern of her mother. She won the right to hire a lawyer to be her guardian. At 16 she moved herself and her sisters to Bryn Mawr and went to college while caring for them by herself and in defiance of her uncle. She went on to become a leader in the women's suffrage movement and one of the founders of Planned Parenthood. The uncle's hostility toward Kit is illustrated in a letter he wrote to her when she married Tom Hepburn: "Dear Katherine . . . My opinion of you is the same as it always has been—that you are an extravagant, deceitful, dishonest, worthless person. You have squandered thousands of dollars and left your honest debts unpaid. When you see Tom, please tell him I do not think he could do worse. . . . Disgusted, Your affectionate Uncle, A. Houghton Jr." (Hepburn, 1991, p. 13).

Katherine said that her father's favorite saying was "the truth will make you free." Indeed, the family was viewed with outrage in their neighborhood because the parents were so open about sex, allowing Katharine, for example, to watch the birth of one of her younger siblings. But one topic could never be mentioned: suicide or any of those who had died by suicide.

After Tom's death the other Hepburn children became a self-contained system, with Katharine, now the eldest, taking responsibility for her younger brothers and sisters. She said that her brother's death "threw my mother and father and me very close together, very close" (Anderson, 1988, p. 188). Shortly after the suicide she went through a period of serious behavior problems (vandalism, breaking and entering), symptoms that are not too surprising when we think about the extraordinary ordeal the family had been through and the pressure on her as the oldest surviving child. However, perhaps because of the important legacy of her grandmother, who had elicited a deathbed promise that her daughters go to college, Kate then went off to Bryn Mawr, her mother's alma mater. Here she began to turn her life around. In the end she more than fulfilled her distinguished family's demands for high achievement, at the same time that she seems to have responded (as did her siblings) to the need of the family to remain close together and, in a certain emotional sense, never to leave.

One brother continued to live in the family's summer home. The other followed the father into the practice of urology at Hartford Hospital, living within blocks of the original family home. One sister followed most closely in the mother's footsteps as a nonconformist interested first in politics and eventually becoming a writer of books on Connecticut history. The other, a librarian, remained within 10 minutes of the family home in West Hartford.

Even though Katharine married briefly and lived 3,000 miles away from her family for much of her adult life, she always sent the money she made home to her father, who supported her with an allowance for as long as he lived (Anderson, 1988). One close friend and biographer says that he could not recall a single conversation with Hepburn in which she did not mention her parents and the impact they had on her life. In her autobiography she wrote: "We were a happy family. We are a happy family. Mother and Dad were perfect parents" (Hepburn, 1991, p. 27). Of their impact she said: "The single most important thing anyone needs to know about me is that I am totally, completely the product of two damn fascinating individuals, who happened to be my parents" (Anderson, 1988, p. 14).

Katharine's loyalty to her parents seems to have elicited a price in her personal life. As she said herself, "I never really left home—not really" (Anderson, 1988, p. 25). She kept dolls and stuffed animals on her bed well into adulthood. And even at the age of 80 she spoke of the family home (now owned by her brother) as her home and thought of herself as the dutiful daughter.

There were complex reasons for this, not the least of which may have been another family secret, Katharine's bisexuality. A tomboy from childhood, Katharine shaved her head from age 9 to 13 and called herself "Jimmy" (Anderson, 1988, p. 140). She had relationships short and long throughout her life with both men and women. There were obvious societal reasons for secrecy, which reinforced the family's personal dynamics. Her sudden and brief marriage to Luddy (Ogden) Smith appears to have been a cover for both of them. He took his lover and she took hers, heiress Laura Harding, with them on their honeymoon. Smith remained a close friend of the Hepburn family for the rest of his life.

Hepburn's 25-year relationship with Spencer Tracy seems to have fit well with patterns evolved in her earlier life. He was an alcoholic, 17 years her senior, who already had liver and kidney damage when they met. One might say he was a doomed man, and very moody, reminiscent of her brother. In addition, although separated from his wife for many years, he would never divorce her. His reluctance to divorce was attributed in part to his guilt about abandoning her and their deaf son, and in part to his Irish Catholicism. The combination of Tracy's tough masculinity and his vulnerability seemed irresistible. Hepburn's career took second place to his throughout their relationship, and he always got first billing. Between 1942 and 1950 she made 10 films—four alone and six with Tracy. The four she made alone were compromises to stay close to him. Indeed, he was reported to have frequently been abusive to her, although in private she had certain power over him (Porter, 2004). One senses a repeat of the functional, caring sister, and indeed she was forced to spend a lot of her time caretaking Tracy, who was like a replacement for her brother. The relationship perhaps served several important functions for Kate: She could hold on to her brother; she could have more privacy than is usually available to stars because of the clandestine nature of their relationship; and she could maintain her solitary residence and loyalty to her family of origin, as well as to her other relationships, including that with Laura Harding and others including Claudette Colbert. But the original losses seem never to have been dealt with and left the family in a certain ongoing fantasy world. Hepburn pondered about her brother's death: "Did it push me further into make-believe? Who knows. I would think it must have" (Anderson, 1988, p. 187). The family seems to have had conflicting requests to their children: "Be independent, successful, and fight for what you want" but also "never leave home." In certain ways this would require another rule: "Let's pretend." As often happens with families stressed by tragedy, Katharine and her siblings seem to have found ways to respond to all these directives: Be successful and independent, but don't ever leave. Katharine became one of the most successful American screen actresses of all time, and yet, in a certain sense, she never left home.

Dysfunctional Adaptation to Loss

The process of mourning generally lasts for years, with each new season, holiday, and anniversary reevoking the old sense of loss. Even as this process continues, the family must adjust itself to the absence. Roles and task are reassigned, new attachments formed, and old alliances shifted. Although mourning is never totally over, most families eventually come to terms with their loss and move on. When families cannot mourn, they become locked in time—in dreams of the past, the emotions of the present, or dread of the future. They may become so concerned about potential future losses that they are unable to engage in the relationships they do have, fearing that to love again will mean further loss. Others focus exclusively on their dreams of the future, trying to fill the gap left by the loss with new relationships formed on fantasy and escape from the pain. Usually those who cut short their mourning by rushing into the future find that the pain comes back to haunt them when the dreams give way to the realities of the new relationship.

Problems that families have in other developmental transitions, such as launching their children, marrying, or having children of their own, often reflect this stoppage of time. For example, parents may have difficulty accepting a child's marriage if they have not integrated an earlier loss. Marriages occurring around the time of a death are often influenced by the unresolved loss. Partners may marry primarily out of their sense of isolation or pain after a loss, or in an attempt to replace their loved one or fill in the void. Parents may cling to children born at the time of loss out of their own fear and pain even more than out of love and affection. Unresolved losses even generations before cast their shadow. Denial and escape are also associated with unresolved loss. In some families, the myths, secrets, and expectations that develop around a critical loss may be incorporated and passed down from parents to children. Some families, as we saw with Teddy Roosevelt and as we shall see with the Barretts, stop all mention of the deceased, as if they could thus banish the pain. Families may also make the dead person's room a memorial or mausoleum. The myth-making entailed in such delusional responses binds family members to one another in pathological ways, and may at the same time create great psychological rifts among them. Such myths naturally affect the children, who become replacements for other family members who have died. Often they are totally unaware of this connection—mystified by forces they sense are influencing them.

Many of the rigid patterns we routinely observe in families—drivenness about one's activities, affairs, continuous unresolved conflict, alienation, isolation, fear of outsiders, frequent divorce, depression, workaholism, escapism into sex, TV, sports, or soap operas—may actually be compensations for people's inability to deal with loss.

The Barrett-Browning Family

The romantic story of Elizabeth Barrett Browning (Genogram 5.2), the invalid poet whose love affair with the handsome Robert Browning flourished in poetry before they ever met, and who eloped with him from her sickbed to Italy, took place in the context of a family totally unable to deal with loss. For years Elizabeth had been caught in her family's web of illusion. As the oldest daughter, she was expected to care for her siblings under the dominance of her father Edward Barrett. Elizabeth's only means of individual expression was through her poetry. But even here her father played a pivotal role: He would pay for her poems to be published and she, ever the devoted daughter, would dedicate them to him. She became an invalid, unable leave her bed for days at a time or even to walk, though her illness was never defined. She maintained an extensive correspondence with the great writers of the era, but for years the sickly Elizabeth lived alone in her room, creating some of the world's greatest poetry and becoming quietly addicted to morphine.

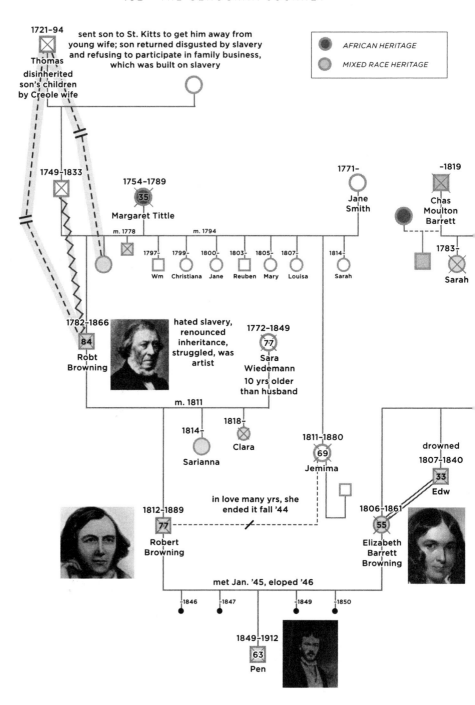

Genogram 5.2. The Barrett-Browning Family.

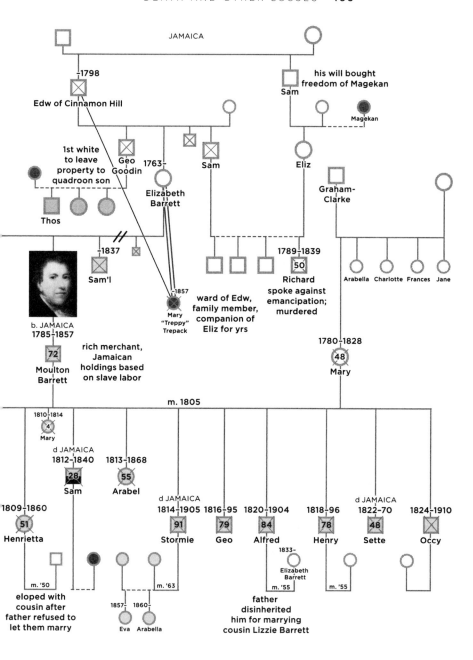

JAMAICA

-1798
Edw of Cinnamon Hill

his will bought
freedom of Magekan
Sam

Magekan

1st white
to leave
property to
quadroon son

Geo
Goodin

1763-

Sam

Eliz

Thos

Elizabeth
Barrett

Graham-
Clarke

-1837

Sam'l

-1857

Mary
"Treppy"
Trepack

ward of Edw,
family member,
companion of
Eliz for yrs

1789-1839
50

Richard
spoke against
emancipation;
murdered

Arabella Charlotte Frances Jane

b. JAMAICA
1785-1857

72

Moulton
Barrett

rich merchant,
Jamaican
holdings based
on slave labor

1780-1828
48

Mary

m. 1805

1810-1814
4
Mary

d JAMAICA
1812-1840

28

Sam

1813-1868
55

Arabel

1809-1860
51

Henrietta

d JAMAICA
1814-1905 1816-95 1820-1904
91   79   84
Stormie   Geo   Alfred

1818-96
78
Henry

d JAMAICA
1822-70
48
Sette

1824-1910
Occy

1833-
Elizabeth
Barrett
m. '55

m. '50

m. '63

m. '55

eloped with
cousin after
father refused to
let them marry

1857- 1860-

Eva   Arabella

father
disinherited
him for marrying
cousin Lizzie Barrett

At 20 her father Edward had married her mother Mary Graham Clarke, who was 25. Together they had 12 children. This family meant everything to Edward. It was an opportunity to make up for the losses of his own early family life. When the fourth child, named Mary for his wife, died at age 4, the family contained its grief, never mentioning her again. Then, when the twelfth child was 3 years old, the wife Mary died. By that time Edward's response was characteristic: As with his daughter's death 14 years earlier, the death of his wife became a forbidden topic; Edward shut up his wife's rooms just as they were, and they were neither entered nor disturbed until the family moved away years later. The Barretts seemed to feel they would be devastated if they faced the loss directly. The family avoided the reality that the mother was gone, just as she had tried to avoid painful realities while she was alive. In all her writings, Elizabeth Barrett Browning wrote only one paragraph about her mother, who died when Elizabeth was 22:

> Scarcely was I a woman when I lost my mother—dearest as she was, and very tender . . . but of a nature harrowed up into some furrows by the pressure of circumstances. . . . We lost more in her than she lost in life, my dearest mother. A sweet gentle nature, which the thunder a little turned from its sweetness—as when it turns milk. One of those women who never can resist; but, in submitting and bowing on themselves, makes a mark, a plait, within—a sign of suffering. Too womanly she was—it was her only fault. Good and dear—and refined too! (Markus, 1995, p. 19)

This powerful, dense, pained assessment suggests a great deal about the family's struggle in dealing with life and death. It is tantalizing to wonder about the mother's submission, which caused inner signs of suffering on her brilliant daughter, who eventually used drugs to avoid her own pain. But we have little information about the mother, whose memory could never be discussed in the Barrett family. "Harrowed" as she was by life's circumstances, the message she seems to have conveyed was that there is no hope of overcoming life's difficulties. Her husband seems to have agreed. Even in the best of times the father had always been a kind of benign dictator with his family. He called their home "Hope End," and it represented, indeed, all the hope left to him. With each loss he turned further inward. Determined to maintain the family, he became a tyrant in his own household. He believed his children should never leave him, and the three who married during his lifetime were immediately disinherited and treated as dead.

Avoidance of loss can create a siege mentality. And although Elizabeth greatly resented her father's hold on her, she herself developed a similar attitude about letting other family members go. When her brothers went away she begged them to come home, complaining that their pleasure for a few days was "disproportionate to the long anxiety of those left at home" (Karlin, 1987, p. 131).

Elizabeth eventually did leave her father's home to marry Robert Browning, a worldly, attractive, admiring poet, 6 years younger than she. Their love began through correspondence months before they ever even met. It was by all appearances the perfect love story.

Their romance began soon after Browning's loss of Jemima, his father's half-sister a year older than he, with whom he had been secretly in love for years. Finally, in the summer of 1844, he went to Italy, hoping to escape the temptation of the incestuous relationship. That December he returned to London to learn that she had become engaged to someone else. Although he destroyed all material evidence of his association with Jemima, his mysterious love poem *Pauline: A Fragment of a Confession* (1833), which he published secretly and anonymously at his own expense, was apparently written about her (Browning, 1979). For decades he went to great lengths to preserve the poem's anonymity. Browning could not forget Jemima. The next month, January 1845, he wrote his first letter to Elizabeth, declaring, without ever having met her, that he was in love with her: "I love your verses with all my heart, dear Miss Barrett. . . . I do, as I say, love these books with all my heart—and I love you too" (Karlin, 1987, p. 47).

Eventually, Browning met with Barrett in her room and nursed her back to health. When she could finally walk again, and appeared to have given up her drug dependence, they eloped to Italy. Even though she was 39 years old, she waited until her father was out on business to make her "escape," and her father never spoke to her again. He could not accept any child who had the audacity to leave him. Elizabeth wrote many pleading and loving letters to him and always kept his picture opposite her bed, but her numerous efforts at reconciliation fell on deaf ears. When she returned home from Italy at the time of her father's death, she found all her letters to him unopened in a packet.

One of Browning's distant relatives, who has researched the family extensively, described their love as fated by the mystical connections of their histories:

> I was overwhelmingly convinced that there was born into both Robert and Elizabeth seeds of a love which had been unable to grow and bear fruit in a past life. I wondered if ancestors of Robert and Eliza-

beth respectively had fallen in love only to be torn apart. This would account for the magnetic attraction of souls, as happened with Robert and Elizabeth. (Browning, 1979, pp. 52–53)

However mystical this seems, the notion that the relationship of Barrett and Browning was influenced by forces far beyond their specific lives is clear, including the hidden factor of the plantations in Jamaica that supported both families. Elizabeth's ancestors had migrated to Jamaica and her father was the first one in his family to be born in Europe in several generations. He was Creole on his father's side. Browning was Creole as well, his paternal grandmother having been of African descent. Although there was much denial about the racial mixtures of slave-holding families, the poet herself felt the need to reveal her heritage to Browning during their courtship: "I would give ten towns in Norfolk (if I had them) to own some purer lineage than that of the blood of the slave!—Cursed we are from generation to generation" (Markus, 1995, p. 106). Elizabeth was deeply opposed to her family's web of involvement in the horrors of slavery, and she wrote about them often, including in a poem written on her honeymoon. Exposing the rape and mixed blood that slavery engendered, in a poem, titled "The Runaway Slave," she depicted an African slave who finally kills her white baby. It seems likely that Elizabeth's father's opposition to her marriage derived at least in part from his fear that the secret of the family's racial heritage would be revealed in mixed-race grandchildren. This was possibly a concern for Elizabeth as well.

The losses that so organized the Barrett family may have been influenced by their denial of who they really were and the unnamable and horrific losses they inflicted on their slaves. Edward Barrett's refusal to allow any loss to be mentioned was something that all the family participated in. It would be interesting to know what role his wife played in this and what she herself thought about it, her own family having also been supported by slavery.

The family pattern of avoiding painful losses can be traced back to Edward Barrett's early life. He came from a family made wealthy by slave-supported businesses in Jamaica. His father left the family early, leaving the mother very much on her own, except for her lifelong companion, Treppy, the daughter of a British planter and a slave. The father further embarrassed the family by having six other children out of wedlock with other women, one African-Jamaican and one Jewish. Interestingly, one of the reasons for Edward's later disapproval of his daughter's relationship with Robert Browning was apparently the suggestion that Browning had African and Jewish blood in his heritage. Browning's grandfather disinherited his children from his Creole wife in favor of those of his second wife, which meant that Browning's family was disinherited. Browning's father himself was so disgusted by a trip to St. Kitts that he refused to benefit in any way from the family's slave money. One cannot help but wonder about the guilt this family felt regarding the source of their wealth, a question to ask about any family whose anscesters benefited from inhumane practices. The emotional trauma in families tends to live on, indirectly when it cannot be acknowledged, seeping into relationships for generations to come.

On the Barrett's side of the family Edward Barrett eventually became the oldest and only surviving son and the only "legitimate" grandson on his mother's side of the family. His family position became even more pivotal when his three maternal uncles all died early, leaving only children born out of wedlock. He was the one to inherit his maternal grandfather's fortune, although some of his out-of-wedlock cousins contested this for years. Edward was expected to carry on the family legacy, and a great deal of pressure was placed on him to succeed in life. He grew up with a sense of responsibility and self-importance that led to rigidity in his relationships. His way was always the right way. Carrying the burden of the family legacy, he probably felt that he could not allow himself to lose control. When losses occurred, he could not afford the luxury of his own grief. His rigidity probably also helped him keep in check any distress he might have felt regarding the inhumanity of the slavery that was the underside of his wealth and success. In fact, his first cousin, Richard Barrett, an upholder of slavery, was murdered in 1839 just after emancipation in Jamaica.

Avoidance and secrecy were a way of life in the Barrett family (Figure 5.1). Although threatened with financial disaster, Edward Barrett kept secret from his wife and family the losses in their plantations in Jamaica. When they did finally lose their home, Hope End, he refused to speak about it until the very last minute. Once they left, no one could ever mention that home again. It is hard not to think that this denial was partially related to their unacknowledged connection to slavery and to the sexual abuse and exploitation that led to mixed-race children as well as to his many losses, which were probably themselves tied to the slave system on which the family rested for several hundred years.

Compounding their difficulty in dealing with loss, several family members who had gone to Jamaica to handle family business died tragically. Edward's only brother, Samuel, died there. Then as mentioned above his cousin, Richard Barrett, a man of distinguished career who took over the handling of family property, was mysteriously murdered in 1839; the body was removed and no stone ever erected for him. Nevertheless, Edward then sent two of his sons to this dangerous locale, because maintaining the family's source of income was crucial to the family remaining together. First he sent the second-oldest son,

Samuel, who died there in 1840. Then he sent the third-oldest son, Stormy. The father was not willing to risk his favorite son, Edward Jr., who was actually the oldest and most qualified to handle the family business.

But keeping him from leaving did not save this son, who drowned the same year close to home at the age of 33 in a freak boating accident. Again, the response to the loss was avoidance and the family pulled even closer together. Neither the drowning nor this son's name was to be mentioned again and the whole family followed its rule of silence.

Figure 5.1   **Key Events in the Barrett Family**

1814	Mary Barrett, Elizabeth's sister, dies at age 4 and is never mentioned again.
1828	Mary Graham Clarke, Elizabeth's mother, dies and is never mentioned again.
1832	Business losses, brought on by coming end of slavery in Jamaica, the source of the family's money, force Edward Barrett to sell his beloved home, Hope End, which could never be mentioned again.
1834	Beginning of emancipation in Jamaica—only those 6 and under freed.
1838	Elizabeth becomes an invalid. Suffers from tuberculosis and other problems.
1839	Edward's cousin Richard Barrett is murdered mysteriously in Jamaica.
1840	Samuel Barrett, the second-oldest son, sent by his father to Jamaica to handle the family business, dies age 28.
1840	Edward Barrett sends his third son, Stormy, to Jamaica to handle the family business.
1840	July: Edward Jr. drowns at age 33, while visiting Elizabeth who begged father to let him come stay with her to keep him from going to Jamaica.
1840	Elizabeth suffers a breakdown.
1844	Dec: Robert Browning's aunt Jemima, his father's half sister, with whom he was in love, becomes engaged.
1845	Jan: Browning writes first letter to Elizabeth, declaring his love without ever having met her.
1845	May: Robert Browning, age 33, meets Elizabeth Barrett, age 39, for the first time.
1846	Couple elopes. Elizabeth's father never speaks to her again.

The death was particularly difficult for Elizabeth, who was only a year older and was very close to this brother. Many years later, she wrote that her brother's death was the one event in her life that never became less bitter but returned to pain her again and again. What had made the loss so difficult to endure was her sense of responsibility and guilt: She had begged her father to let the brother visit her at a seaside retreat where she was recuperating from tuberculosis. No one in the family had ever before dared to disagree openly with the father, who had eventually complied with Elizabeth's wish, with tragic consequences. On a deeper level Elizabeth's guilt about Edward's death may have been a displacement for her father's guilt, as it was he who had tried to protect Edward by not sending him to Jamaica. From this time on the father managed any open disagreement with total estrangement.

The children developed a complicity of silence and secrecy to protect the father from information that would upset him. They kept the details of their behavior from their father, and the father was quite willing to turn the other way. When Elizabeth met daily in her bedroom for over a year with her future husband, Robert Browning, the father chose not to notice. This allowed him to feel self-righteous and betrayed when the two finally eloped, as if he did not know what was going on.

When two of Barrett's other children dared to marry, albeit to cousins so they were not fully leaving the family, they too were cut off. Three of the other children waited to marry until their father had died, by which time they themselves were middle-aged.

Even in Italy Elizabeth was never completely able to leave her family behind. She thought of them constantly and was unable to get over her guilt for the death of her brother and having abandoned her father. Never entirely comfortable in her marital relationship, she always questioned whether she was worthy of her husband:

> I cannot help the pain I feel sometimes in thinking that it would have been better for you if you never had known me. . . . May God turn back the evil of me. . . . If I only knew certainly . . . more certainly than the thing may be known by either me or you;—that nothing in me could have any part in making you unhappy—for everything turns to evil which I touch. (Karlin, 1987, p. 131)

Elizabeth Barrett and Robert Browning had one surviving son, Pen, born when she was 42. She had four miscarriages. She herself died when her son was only 12, having slipped back into her invalidism and drug addiction long before the end, and drawing Pen into her isolation. The product of one of the greatest romances of all time, Pen could not live up to the expectations that his parents and the world had of him. He always remained more a child than a man, unable to commit himself to a way of life, a job, or a wife. His mother had treated him as an extension of herself, dressing him bizarrely in female clothes, against his father's wishes.

Robert Browning also had ritualistic ways of dealing with loss. He would not visit his own family home after his mother died, which was very near the time Pen was born. Later he could not even bear to pass the house where his beloved sister-in-law, Arabel, had died in his arms. Most of all, he could not bear the memories of the home he had enjoyed with Elizabeth in Florence. In all the years of his life he never returned to Florence. He devoted himself to his son, treating him as a reincarnation of his adored wife.

Concern about secrecy continued in the Barrett-Browning family. Many years after Pen's death, the cousins burned Elizabeth's letters to her father, which had never been opened. Burning these letters went very much against Elizabeth's belief that "if the secrets of our daily lives and inner souls may instruct other surviving souls, let them be open to men hereafter, even as they are to God now"(Marks, 1938, p. 608). The pattern of avoiding the pain of loss seems to have continued generation after generation.

The Kennedy Family

Another family in which multigenerational patterns of dealing with untimely loss seem to have had a profound impact is the Kennedy family (Genogram 5.3). No American who was alive in 1963 can forget the image of John Kennedy, Jr., saluting his father's casket on that cold, clear November day. The little boy without a father, 3 years old, born on Thanksgiving Day 2 weeks after his father's election to the presidency, reminded us all of the fragility of our lives. We have images of other Kennedy deaths as well: the Mozart requiem playing at St. Patrick's Cathedral for Robert Kennedy, with his 10 children all in mourning, Ethel still pregnant with the last, Ted's voice cracking in eulogy for yet another brother.

John Kennedy himself had been a stand-in for his older brother, Joe Jr., after the latter's death in World War II. After Robert Kennedy's death, the mantle of leadership was passed to Ted, and we can recall his confused explanation, just a year later, of his role in the death of Mary Jo Kopechne at Chappaquidick. In the next generation there followed the terrible inglorious death of David Kennedy, whose drug overdose seemed so much the fallout of previous losses.

We are fairly familiar with the losses of the Kennedys in our lifetime, just as we tend to be familiar with the losses in our own families within our lifetime. Usually we know less about the losses that have gone before—losses that have very much shaped family myths and attitudes. In fact, the Kennedys' history of tragic loss goes back far beyond the children and grandchildren of Joe and Rose.

Joe Kennedy's father, Patrick Joseph (P.J.), had been the only surviving male in his family. An older brother, John, had died at 1 year of age, and the father, Patrick, died when P.J. was 6 months old. These losses must have left P.J.'s mother with special feelings for her only son and a heightened sense of the fragility of life—especially male life. Having come up the hard way—with no father and as a replacement for his dead brother—P.J. became a hardworking but cautious man. He "married up" to a clever woman, Mary Hickey, from a successful family. He, too, was clever, but his insecurities made it hard for him to say no to anyone. He started a liquor business, and, like so many of the Irish of his time, moved into politics. He was always a caretaker for the families in his ward, serving eight terms in the state legislature. Mary resented his commitment to helping others as the boss of his district because it intruded upon their own family's success. Yet he must have felt the need to do for others because he identified with them, having been raised as a fatherless child in desperate need himself.

The first child of P.J. and Mary was Joseph P. Kennedy, who also became the only surviving son of his parents. His already privileged position of oldest son was strengthened when his younger brother, Francis, died of diphtheria at the age of 2. A granddaughter later said: "The death of the baby was so unexpected and so senseless that [Joe's mother's] only way of coping was to pour even more love onto Joe" (Kearns Goodwin, 1987, p. 227). Though he had two surviving younger sisters, Joe became the focus of attention for the whole family. Perhaps it is this legacy of specialness of the male survivor, intensified by the general cultural bias toward sons, that led Joe to focus his expectations so strongly on his own sons.

Joe grew up to emulate his mother, who believed in putting their family first, and saw his father's support for others as weakness. In the end, P.J. was defeated by the machine politics of Boston (it is very likely that he was double-crossed by his son's future father-in-law, Honey Fitz himself!). Though he accepted his defeat with gentle dignity, underneath he grieved like a child who had been unjustly punished. The lesson his son Joe took from this was that political loyalty and generosity were merely commodities. The decision he then made was to trust no one but himself. He developed a will of steel and a calculating, manipulative approach to dealing with others.

It would seem that Joe felt strong pressure to escape the embarrassing

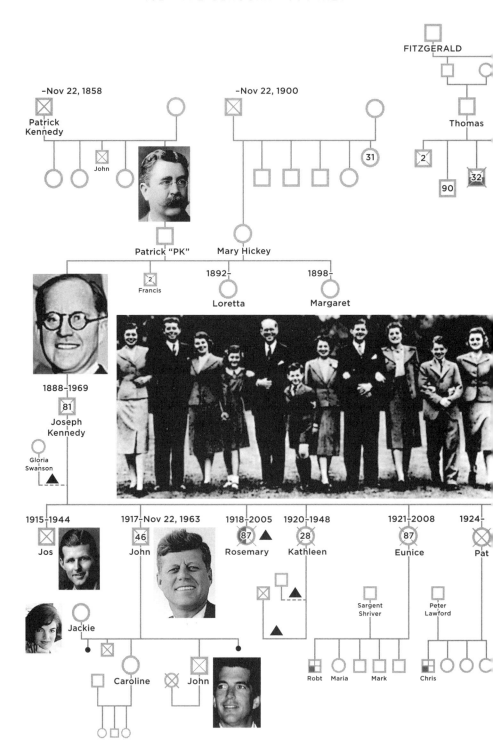

Genogram 5.3. The Kennedy Family.

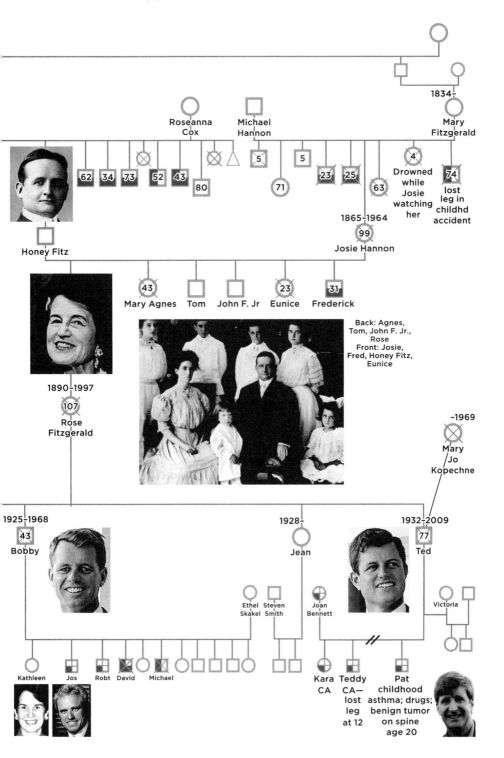

Roseanna
Cox

Michael
Hannon

62 34 73 52 43
80

5

5

71

23 25

63

4
Drowned
while
Josie
watching
her

1834–

Mary
Fitzgerald

74
lost
leg in
childhd
accident

1865–1964
99
Josie Hannon

Honey Fitz

43
Mary Agnes   Tom   John F. Jr   Eunice   Frederick
23   31

Back: Agnes,
Tom, John F. Jr.,
Rose
Front: Josie,
Fred, Honey Fitz,
Eunice

1890–1997
107
Rose
Fitzgerald

–1969
Mary
Jo
Kopechne

1925–1968
43
Bobby

1928–
Jean

1932–2009
77
Ted

Ethel Steven
Skakel Smith

Joan
Bennett

Victoria

Kathleen   Jos   Robt David Michael

Kara   Teddy   Pat
CA   CA—   childhood
       lost   asthma; drugs;
       leg   benign tumor
       at 12 on spine
              age 20

identification with his softhearted father, whose kindness, seemingly based on identifying with others who had experienced loss, was repaid with exploitation and rejection. A clue to Joe's relationship with his father is that, when P.J. died in 1928, Joe did not attend the funeral, instead remaining in California with his paramour, Gloria Swanson. As much as P.J. longed for a close relationship with his son, he did not succeed in achieving it. Just as P.J., having no father at all, had gravitated to his mother, Joe's special closeness was to his mother.

Rose Fitzgerald Kennedy's family also experienced overwhelming traumatic losses at critical times in their history. Her father, John Francis, called "Honey Fitz," was the fourth of 12 children. The only two daughters both died in infancy, as did the oldest son. Three others had lives totally wasted by their alcoholism. Two more, Michael and Edward, had severe alcohol problems as well. The ninth brother, Joseph, had brain damage from malaria and barely functioned. Thus, of the 12 children born in this family, only three, including Honey Fitz, survived in good health. Honey Fitz became the favorite son. After his mother's death, when he was 16, his father developed a special ambition for him to become a doctor, as illness had caused their family such painful losses. However, after a year at Harvard Medical School, the father died and John switched his ambitions to politics, which offered an immediate income and an opportunity to provide jobs for his brothers. When he became mayor of Boston, many said that the whole brotherhood of Fitzgeralds actually ran the government. Honey Fitz considered it his responsibility to provide for his brothers, and he did. Later his grandsons would, of course, do the same.

Honey Fitz met his future wife, Josie Hannon, his painfully shy second cousin, only a few months before the death of his mother. Many said that his bond to her was based on their mutual losses. Josie was the sixth of nine children, only four of whom survived. One brother died of fever at age 6, while the mother was pregnant with Josie. Another had died of inflammation of the lung 4 years earlier. Two other sons died early of alcoholism. The only surviving son had his leg crushed by a train at age 13. But the family's most tragic loss was the littlest sister, who drowned with her best friend while Josie was supposed to be caring for them. The devastating loss any family naturally would feel about the death of a child was compounded by a complex web of guilt and self-reproach that they, and Josie in particular, felt in having failed to protect the children. The family never recovered. Those who knew the three surviving sisters said that sorrow hung over them for the rest of their lives.

It is easy to understand what attracted Josie to the confident, forceful, adventuresome, and enthusiastic Honey Fitz, whose very name reflected his ability to charm others with his words. Honey Fitz's long courtship of Josie was indeed an effort to bring her out of herself with his humor, his magnetism, and his sociability. Like so many generations of the family that followed him, he dealt with loss by mobilizing into frantic activity and trying not to look back. Once the challenge of winning Josie was complete, the difference in their natures was overwhelmingly apparent. Or perhaps the very sadness in Josie that had drawn him to her now became toxic and he fled from it. As the years went by, Honey Fitz expanded outward while Josie turned further inward. It was his beloved firstborn daughter, Rose, who really seemed to replace his mother and sisters. She grew up as his companion in the exciting political arena of his colorful life—she went everywhere with him.

Rose led a charmed life until adolescence, when suddenly it all changed. Her father's main character flaw—self-centered manipulative ambition, the reflection of his early losses—led him to betray her. Perhaps there was also some compulsion to repeat his experience at 16, when he had had to give up his plans for medical school. Rose was a brilliant student, as well as a passionate, untamed spirit. Her dream was to go to Wellesley, where she had been accepted at 16. But Honey Fitz was in trouble: His political wheeling and dealing had led to charges of fraud and to his being ousted as mayor of Boston. Consequently, he made a deal with the leaders of the Catholic Church that sacrificed Rose's dream of attending Wellesley and required her to go instead to a Catholic school.

Rose was abruptly sent to a convent school abroad. She was totally cut off from her family and her exciting social life and put in a rigid environment that demanded silence and denied all spontaneous attachments. Typical of the repressive parochial schools of the era, there was even a rule against girls' forming "particular friendships." Rose's response was one she would manifest repeatedly in her long life: She smothered her feelings of resistance, bowed to her father's will, and forced herself to channel her energies through adherence to prayer, which was the only avenue open to her. A kind of detachment from human relationships was forged in that transition, which was to characterize all her later life. What she lost was a belief in her special relationship with her father, as well as the sense of power to determine her own life. She had to bend to the will of a stronger male. Religion helped her swallow that pill and many other bitter pills to follow.

We are most familiar with the losses of Rose and Joe Kennedy's children by death, but their first loss was not a death. Rosemary, their oldest daughter, suffered mild mental retardation. Such a child represented a loss of dreams, an embarrassment, and a pain that would not go away. Wishing to keep her within the family, they kept her problems a secret for many years and made every effort to maintain her in as normal a fashion as possible. By the time Rosemary was in her early twenties, however, she had developed severe behavior problems. At a certain point Joe decided, while Rose was away, that Rosemary should have a lobotomy. The operation worsened her condition considerably. Apparently, Joe then had her sent to an institution in the Midwest. He never told his wife—not then or afterwards—about the lobotomy. Rose was just told that it would be better if she didn't visit Rosemary for some time.

According to friends and relatives, it wasn't until 20 years later, after Joe's stroke in 1961, that Rose began to piece the story together for herself (Kearns Goodwin, 1987). Why didn't she insist on visiting this daughter to whom she had devoted herself for so many years? How could she never ask? How could it be that others never asked about or questioned the disappearance of one of their members? Did Joe blame himself for what had happened? Did others blame him or themselves for ignoring her for so many years? All we know is that in her memoirs, written 33 years after the operation, Rose maintained that she had participated in the decision for the lobotomy and failed to mention that she had not visited or asked about Rosemary for 20 years.

The Kennedy family never talked about Rosemary's retardation within the family; the first public mention of it wasn't until 1960. We do have a suggestion of the long-range impact of the family's inability to deal openly with this "ghost" in an incident involving David Kennedy, the grandson who eventually died of a drug overdose. One day, in the midst of his troubles, he found a magazine story about lobotomies that included a picture of his aunt Rosemary. He is quoted as saying:

> She had a new pair of white shoes on and she was smiling. The thought crossed my mind that if my grandfather was alive the same thing could have happened to me that happened to her. She was an embarrassment; I am an embarrassment. She was a hindrance; I am a hindrance. As I looked at this picture, I began to hate my grandfather and all of them for having done the thing they had done to her and for the thing they were doing to me. (Collier & Horowitz, 1984, p. 441)

The shame and guilt leading to the secrecy and mystification that surrounded Rosemary's disability, lobotomy, and disappearance give this loss a lingering power. In such circumstances, other family members are left with the feeling that "if she could disappear, I could disappear." And their fantasies fill in the rest of the story with whatever meanings they attach to the pieces of the story they do know.

The ambiguity of Rosemary's loss must have been particularly distressing because it could not be mourned like a death. She remained alive but not physically or mentally present. Rose said in her memoirs that Rosemary was pleased to see them and recognized them, but that she was "perfectly happy in her environment and would be confused and disturbed to be anywhere else" (Kennedy, 1974, p. 286). Yet surely other family members, like David, must have wondered whether this was true and questioned her extrusion from the family.

Unfortunately, Rosemary was only the first of many children lost in the Kennedy family. In each instance there was a similar tendency toward secrecy about any facts that did not fit with a positive image. Joe Jr., the "Golden Boy," programmed by his father to become president, was shot down in an unnecessarily reckless flying mission in June 1944. Only his heroism was mentioned, not his exaggerated risk-taking or the fact that he had received a warning that day from his electronics officer that his plane could not possibly make it (Davis, 1984). The Kennedys also never mentioned that he was living with a married woman, Pat Wilson, at the time of his death. When Wilson wrote a letter of sympathy to Rose, the bereaved mother did not respond.

It is hard to escape the sense that there is a repeated mingling of tragedy, accident, and tempting the fates in the Kennedy family. Joe Kennedy, Jr., had been repeatedly carrying out hazardous bombing missions where he was told his chances of survival were less than 50%. He had already completed his tour of duty but was looking for a mission from which he would return a hero, perhaps because his younger brother, John, had just received a military medal for his performance in the Pacific. (In that instance John had initially been reported missing in action, and a funeral had been held by the surviving crew members. Joe, Sr., was told this news but kept it from his wife and children for a week, after which he learned that John had, in fact, survived.)

In this incident and others to follow there are numerous examples of the Kennedys' avoidant ways of dealing with loss. When Joe, Jr., died, his father announced the fact to the children, warned them all to be "particularly good to your mother," and then retreated to his room, while Rose also retreated to her separate room. Rose said that she and her husband "wept inwardly, silently." At the time Joe said, "We've got to carry on. We must take care of the living. There is a lot of work to be done" (Kennedy, 1974, p. 277–278). Rose turned to religion, repeating the rosary over and over, leaving it up to her husband to handle arrangements and respond to correspondence. She was initially consumed by her grief, whereas he immediately mobilized into action—the usual response of the Kennedy men to loss, and consonant with our culture's gender rules.

The second daughter, Kathleen, who had been cut off by her mother for marrying a British Protestant peer in May of 1944, lost her husband in the war that September. When the news of his death came, she was in the United States with her family, because of her brother Joe's death shortly before. She was out shopping and her sister Eunice went to meet her. Eunice, in typical Kennedy form, complimented her on her purchases and said nothing until they were finished shopping, at which point she suggested that Kathleen call their father before they went to lunch. Joe then gave her the news of her husband's death. That night the family was solicitous of Kathleen, while diligently avoiding any mention of her husband's death! A friend who came to stay with her at the time was appalled by the family's frenetic need to carry on as if nothing had happened (McTaggart, 1983).

Kathleen once told another friend that she had been taught that "Kennedys don't cry." When her brother Joe died and his roommate called her to give condolences, she broke into sobs. Later she wrote him a letter of apology saying: "I'm sorry I broke down tonight. It never makes things easier" (Kearns Goodwin, 1987, p. 690). Following her husband's death, she left her parents' home and returned to England, where she did allow herself to go through months of overt mourning, staying in the home of her parents-in-law for comfort and support.

Four years later Kathleen fell in love with another Protestant, this time a married British peer, Peter Fitzwilliam, who had a reputation for high living, gambling, and affairs. This time Rose Kennedy said that if Kathleen married, she would not only disown her but also see that Joe cut off her allowance. Rose vowed she would leave Joe if he refused. Kathleen decided she could not break off the relationship in spite of her mother's threat. In hopes of appealing to her father, she arranged to meet him while on a weekend trip with Fitzwilliam on the Riviera. In an eerily familiar scenario, Fitzwilliam insisted on flying in a small plane, although weather reports were so bad that all commercial flights had been cancelled and his pilot strongly urged a delay. Their plane crashed in the storm and both Kathleen and Fitzwilliam were killed.

Joe, who had gone to identify the body, said Kathleen looked beautiful and as if asleep, though she had actually been horribly disfigured by the crash. The circumstances of her death with Fitzwilliam were concealed and she was buried as the widow of the first husband. Her father was the only family member to attend her funeral. Even then he took no role in the funeral arrangements, which were handled by her former mother-in-law, who even wrote her epitaph: "Joy she gave, Joy she has found." The Kennedys and the their in-laws joined in a conspiracy of silence about the circumstances of the death.

Friends were appalled that Rose Kennedy sent a mass card with a prayer for those who had not gone to heaven. John and Bobby Kennedy visited Kathleen's housekeeper, drew out all her recollections, and then said: "We will not mention her again." They seem to have kept their word, though Bobby named his oldest daughter for her. Twenty-four years later Rose wrote in her memoirs:

> In 1948 [Kathleen] had taken a spring holiday on the Riviera and was flying in a private plane with a few friends to Paris, where her father was waiting to meet her. On the way—a route threading the edges of the French Alps—the weather went bad, navigation equipment was not adequate, and the plane crashed into a mountainside, killing all on board. Joe was notified and hurried to the scene. He watched as the body of his daughter was brought down the mountainside. We lost our beloved Kathleen on May 13, 1948. (Kennedy, 1974, p. 332)

All reference to the fiancé was eliminated, as if he never existed, along with all reference to the fact that Rose had disowned her daughter.

Since then the Kennedys have sustained many other losses and near losses. Three times John Kennedy was given up for dead and was administered the last rites. Twice Ted almost died, a year after John's death, when he broke his back in a plane crash, and a year after Robert's death, when he almost drowned (and his companion Mary Jo Kopechne did drown) at Chappaquidick. Was it just coincidence that his near-fatal accidents followed so closely the tragic deaths of his brothers, or is this an example of something that has been documented repeatedly in the research on stress: that such experiences increase our vulnerability to emotional upset, illness, and accidents?

What leads a family into such reckless and self-destructive behavior? Many people have seen the reckless risk-taking behavior of Kathleen and Joe, Jr., the extremely promiscuous sexual behavior of Joseph and John Kennedy, and the politically dangerous liaisons of several of the Kennedys (John most of all) as a response to their fear of death—living on the edge and, as it were, "tempting fate" to prove to themselves that they were still alive.

When the news came that John Kennedy had been shot, Rose decided to operate on a principle that she and Joe had adopted years before: Bad news should only be given in the morning, not late in the day, because it would upset your sleep. She therefore arranged for a "conspiracy of kindness" to keep Joe, who had by then suffered a stroke, from learning about the death until the next day. All television sets were unplugged, different stories were told about the relatives and friends who began to appear, and everyone kept up a charade of conversation with him for the whole afternoon and evening. He was told the next morning.

Rose believed that Jackie's composure at the time of John Kennedy's death was an example for the whole world of how to behave. The following week, Rose said, the family "had the Thanksgiving celebration, with everyone of us hiding the grief that gnawed at us and doing our best to make it a day of peace, optimism, and thanks for the blessings that were still left to us" (Kennedy, 1974, p. 448). Rose quoted Jackie's praise for how the Kennedy family dealt with tragedy:

> You can be sitting down to dinner with them and so many sad things have happened to each, and—God—maybe even some sad thing has happened that day, and you can see that each one is aware of the other's suffering. And so they can sit down at the table in a rather sad frame of mind. Then each one will begin to make this conscious effort to be gay or funny or to lift each other's spirits, and you find that it's infectious, that everybody's doing it . . . [they] bounce off each other. They all have a humor. . . . It's a little bit irrelevant, a little bit self-mocking, a little sense of the ridiculous, and in times of sadness of wildly wicked humor of irreverence. . . . They bring out the best. No one sits and wallows in self pity. (Kennedy, 1974, p. 448)

Commenting on the death of her third son, Robert, 5 years after Jack's, Rose said that the grim reality of the second assassination was so incredible that it would seem beyond fiction to imagine. She said others commented on her composure, her bravery, and her self-possession at the funeral, but also that her waving a greeting to others was somehow "inappropriate." Rose responded: "As for my being composed—I had to be. If I had broken down in grief, I would only have added to the misery of the others and possibly could have set off a chain reaction of tearfulness. But, in fact, it was not just I who set an example of fortitude. They all set it for one another" (Kennedy, 1974, p. 477).

Grief is a personal matter. Every family must find its own ways of handling grief. The Kennedys showed many strengths in their handling of an incredible series of tragedies, and they also showed glaring vulnerabilities, particularly in facing up to losses that were embarrassing and not heroic. The remarkable thing about this family is their ability to persevere even after the most devastating losses.

Families like the Kennedys that have experienced so many traumatic, untimely deaths may develop a feeling of being "cursed" and unable to rise above the experience, or they may come to see themselves as survivors who can be struck down but never beaten. For all their difficulties in handling feelings, the Kennedys have shown an amazing life force and courage in overcoming tragedies. It is almost as if their sense of the family mission carries them through. The dignified death of Ted Kennedy and moving as well as honest tributes after his long life may illustrate the transformation he brought about over many years of reassessment of his family's legacy.

The Freud Family

The Freud family (Genogram 5.4) provides another interesting example of pattern repetitions that appear to have been a legacy of loss. Sigmund, the oldest of his mother's eight children, was born in 1856 in Freiburg, Moravia. In addition to being the oldest, he was also the only son for many years. He had an intense relationship with his mother, Amalia, who always referred to him as her "Golden Sigi." By all accounts, he was the center of the household. He was followed by a brother who died, then five sisters, and finally by a brother 10 years younger.

Sigmund's specialness for his father was probably intensified by the death of his paternal grandfather for whom he was named 3 months before his birth. This grandfather was a rabbi, and Sigmund, in his fervency for his new belief system, psychoanalysis, has been compared to a religious leader and thus, in his own way, following in this grandfather's footsteps. Sigmund's father, Jacob, had also lost two children in his first marriage, though we know no details about them. Such losses tend to intensify the meaning of children who come after, particularly the next in line, which in this case would have been Sigmund.

Sigmund's brother Julius, born when he was 17 months old, lived for only 7 months. Sigmund's closeness to his mother may have become even more important after the death of this second son. The loss of the infant would itself have been intensified by the fact that exactly a month before his death, Amalia's youngest brother, also named Julius, died at the age of 20 from pulmonary tuberculosis. Probably she had known that her brother was dying when she named her son for him 7 months earlier, as it is not generally the Jewish custom to name a child for a living family member. In later life Sigmund said that he had greeted this brother with "ill wishes and real infantile jealousy, and his death left the germ of guilt in me" (Krull, 1986, p. 135). In addition, at this time Sigmund's nursemaid was dismissed from the household for stealing and the family moved twice, apparently because of financial difficulties. Freud's nephew, John, and both half brothers immigrated to England shortly afterwards. Furthermore, Sigmund soon had to share his parents' affection with a new sibling, Anna, with whom he was never to get along. Freud's sense

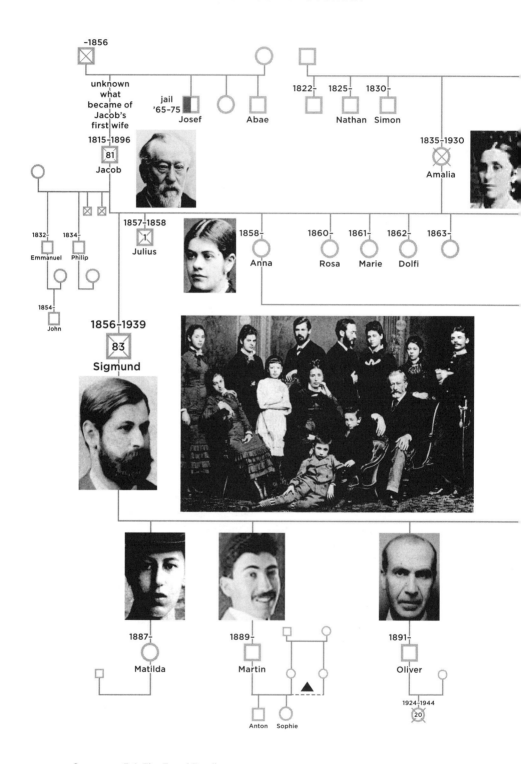

Genogram 5.4. The Freud Family.

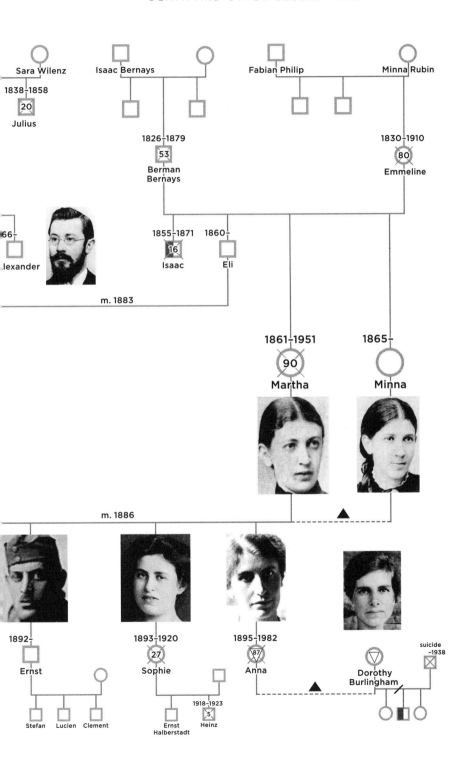

Sara Wilenz
1838–1858
20
Julius

Isaac Bernays

Fabian Philip   Minna Rubin

1826–1879
53
Berman
Bernays

1830–1910
80
Emmeline

66–
lexander

1855–1871
16
Isaac

1860–
Eli

m. 1883

1861–1951
90
Martha

1865–
Minna

m. 1886

1892–
Ernst

1893–1920
27
Sophie

1895–1982
87
Anna

Dorothy
Burlingham

suicide
–1938

Stefan Lucien Clement

1918–1923
5
Ernst   Heinz
Halberstadt

of his own specialness and his religious fervor about his beliefs, as well as the relationships that evolved in the Freud family, were undoubtedly influenced by this pileup of losses near the time of his birth.

Another critical period occurred when Freud was 40 and his father died. This death occurred just after the birth of Freud's last child, Anna, named not for his sister but for the daughter of his high-school Hebrew teacher and mentor, Samuel Hammerschlag (Gay, 1990). Perhaps it is not surprising that this last child, Anna, became his favorite, his primary follower, and by far the most emotionally linked to him of all his children. He also drew closer to his sister-in-law, Minna, who moved into the household at this time. She became his intellectual and emotional companion for many years. In a letter to his then closest friend, Wilhelm Fleiss, Freud described Minna during these years as "otherwise my closest confidante" (Masson, 1985, p. 73). He often traveled alone with her, while his wife stayed with the children, and he soon became sexually involved with her, a pattern that is not uncommon in families following a loss, even though the connection between the death and the affair remains out of awareness. The apparent repetition of this pattern of an affair with a sister-in-law in the next generation—between Freud's oldest son, Martin, and his wife's sister—is interesting as well (Freud, 1988).

Jacob Freud, like his son Sigmund, had been 40 when his father died. Although mere coincidence may be at work here, an exploration of family history often reveals such coincidences. In any case, Freud seems to have had a special identification with his father. He called his father's death "the most important event, the most poignant loss, in a man's life" (cited in Shur, 1972, p. 108). When his father died in 1896, Freud wrote:

> By one of those obscure paths behind official consciousness the death of the old man has affected me profoundly. I valued him highly, understood him very well, and with that combination of deep wisdom and romantic lightheartedness peculiar to him he had meant a great deal to me. His life had been over a long time before he died, but his death seems to have aroused in me memories of all the early days. I now feel quite uprooted. (Masson, 1985, p. 202)

Sigmund's reaction to this death contrasts with that to his mother's death, in 1930, when she was 95: "No pain, no grief, which is probably to be explained by the circumstances, the great age and the end of the pity we had felt at her helplessness. With that a feeling of liberation, of release. . . . I was not allowed to die as long as she was alive, and now I may" (Jones, 1955, pp. 152–53).

Her death, as he said, provided a relief that she was out of her pain, and, as Freud himself had been suffering from cancer for 7 years, he was spared the life-cycle reversal he dreaded: that he might die before she did. He did suggest there might have been other effects on him "in deeper layers" of his consciousness. We do know that he did not attend his mother's funeral, but sent his daughter, Anna, as "the family representative," suggesting avoidance of his feelings.

It is also significant that when his mother died, he was 75 and basically dying himself, whereas when his father died he was only 40, and around the time of the death he went through a major life crisis with symptoms of depression, "pseudo" cardiac problems, lethargy, migraines, and various other somatic and emotional concerns. He began his famous self-analysis and constructed the edifice of his new theory, which led to the publication of *The Interpretation of Dreams*. It was also at this time that he both formulated and then recanted his seduction theory (the theory that women's complaints of being sexually abused were generally valid). Many have viewed this recanting as a response to a sense of guilt over the thought that his theory of seduction could apply to his father's seduction of his sister.

Sigmund Freud provides an interesting example of the differences in reaction to loss depending on the life-cycle timing, the role of the person, and the nature of the death. Some deaths have more impact on a family than others. Particularly traumatic are untimely deaths, such as the early death of Sigmund's brother Julius. A similar example two generations later was the death of Sigmund's 4-year-old grandson, Heinz, who had been orphaned as an infant by the early death of Freud's daughter, Sophie. Freud wrote of him: "He was indeed an enchanting little fellow, and I myself was aware of never having loved a human being, certainly never a child, so much. . . . I find this loss very hard to bear. I don't think I have ever experienced such grief; perhaps my own sickness contributes to the shock. I work out of sheer necessity; fundamentally everything has lost its meaning for me" (Masson, 1985, p. 344). For more than 3 years he was apparently in a depression and unable to enjoy life. His strong reaction seems to be due partly to the death's coinciding with his own diagnosis of a cancer that was eventually fatal. He wrote to the child's father 3 years later: "I have spent some of the blackest days of my life in sorrowing about the child. At last I have taken hold of myself and can think of him quietly and talk of him without tears. But the comforts of reason have done nothing to help; the only consolation for me is that at my age I would not have seen much of him" (Clark, 1980, p. 441).

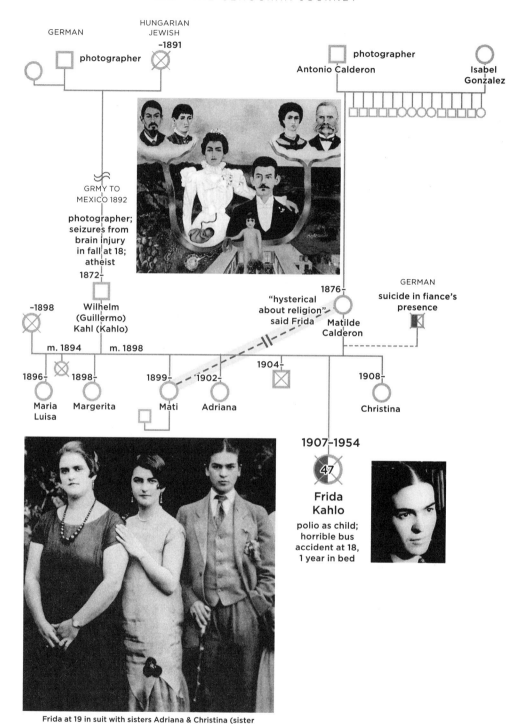

GERMAN

HUNGARIAN
JEWISH
–1891

photographer

photographer
Antonio Calderon

Isabel
Gonzalez

GRMY TO
MEXICO 1892

photographer;
seizures from
brain injury
in fall at 18;
atheist
1872–

Wilhelm
(Guillermo)
Kahl (Kahlo)

–1898

m. 1894   m. 1898

1896–

Maria
Luisa

1898–

Margerita

1899–

Mati

1902–

Adriana

1904–

1876–
"hysterical
about religion"-
said Frida
Matilde
Calderon

GERMAN
suicide in fiance's
presence

1908–

Christina

1907–1954

47

**Frida
Kahlo**

polio as child;
horrible bus
accident at 18,
1 year in bed

Frida at 19 in suit with sisters Adriana & Christina (sister
Mati had been cut off by mother for her marriage)

Genogram 5.5. The Kahlo Family.

Resilience in the Face of Loss

A family's resilience in the face of loss, trauma, and dysfunction enables it to survive (Walsh, 2006). It is important to explore such resourcefulness and to underline it. Mexican artist Frida Kahlo (Genogram 5.5) provides a remarkable example of such resilience through her amazing ability to transform cultural differences, disruption, loss, trauma, and physical disability into transcendent strength and creative energy. Her resilience and the resilience of her family are evident in many aspects of their history. She first became ill at age 6 with polio, which left her right leg weaker and smaller. At 18 she experienced a traumatic bus accident, in which she was impaled on a metal pipe, which went completely through her pelvis and fractured her spine. The accident left her with chronic pain for the rest of her life, in spite of numerous operations. Coincidentally, her father had suffered a fall at the same age, which left him with brain damage and seizures, changing the course of his life and dashing his hopes of university study. His accident and his mother's death the next year, compounded by his father's quick marriage to a woman with whom he didn't get along, influenced his resolve to immigrate to Mexico the following year (Herrera, 1984). In Mexico he changed his name from Wilhelm Kahl to Guillermo Kahlo. He became a noted photographer, although he suffered ongoing sequelae from his accident. Frida, who became his favorite child, also discovered an outlet in art following her accident. Like her father, she had held hopes of becoming a scholar and physician. Instead, she became an artist, like her father and her maternal grandfather before that.

Both of Kahlo's parents experienced severe traumas early in life. Her mother, Matilde Calderon, a brilliant and attractive woman of Spanish and Indian background, had been in love with a German, who committed suicide in front of her. All her life she kept a book of his letters. Frida's father and his first wife had three daughters, though the second died within a few days. Then his wife died tragically in childbirth with the third daughter, and he met his second wife, Matilde, the same night. She agreed to marry him only if he sent his two daughters away to a convent school. She also encouraged Kahlo to go into business as a photographer with her father. Unfortunately, he seems never to have come to terms with his earlier traumas. Over the years he became bitter and withdrawn in spite of his obvious abilities and early efforts to reinvent himself. It was his favorite daughter, Frida, who demonstrated the most remarkable ability to transform traumatic experiences into hope and art, in spite of much more severe disabilities.

Looking At Loss in Your Own Family

Given the anomie and disconnection of our society, the very experience of sharing a loss can help families to expand the context in which they see themselves—to experience continuity from past to future and see the connection to one another, to their culture, and to other human beings. Family rituals are excellent ways to promote healing and transformation. A toast made at a wedding or an anniversary party, or even a eulogy at another family member's death, may help to keep the dead person in the context of family relationships. One young man, making the family toast at Thanksgiving, gave thanks for the happy memories they all had of his brother's wife, who had died 2 years before in an automobile accident and whose loss had never yet been referred to. In another case a woman held a memorial service 25 years later for her brother, who had committed suicide on his birthday. She began a process of reconciliation around a loss that had gone unacknowledged for a quarter of a century. Such evocations to integrate loss may occur even long after the death. The healing process can benefit the family in profound ways.

Questions, again, are the most powerful tool for gaining a new understanding of losses.

- Are dates of death remembered or barely honored? How comfortable are family members in talking about the deceased and the circumstances of the death? Are both good and bad memories accessible?
- Consider the dealings with funeral directors, the rituals observed, who spoke at the service and who didn't—how did family members relate in the aftermath of loss, what did they appear to believe about the death, what did they fear, and what did they cherish about the lost person?
- How did various family members express their reactions to death? With tears? withdrawal? depression? affairs? frantic activity? Did they talk to each other about the loss?
- Who was present at the moment of death? Who was not present who "should have been"?
- How were family relationships at the time of death? Were there unresolved issues with the person who died?
- Who arranged the funeral? Who attended? Who didn't? Who gave the eulogy?
- Was the body cremated or buried? If cremated, what happened to the ashes? Is there a marker at the grave?
- Did family conflicts or cutoffs occur around the time of death?

- Was there a will? Who received what bequests? Were there family rifts because of provisions in the will?
- Do family members visit the grave and how often? Who mentions the dead and with what frequency? What happened to the belongings of the dead person?
- Was there secrecy about the cause or circumstances of the death? Were facts kept from anyone inside or outside the family?
- What mythology has been created in the family about the dead person? Has he or she been made into a saint?
- What would the history of the family have been like if the dead person had survived longer?
- Do family members feel stigmatized by the death (e.g., a suicide or death from AIDS)?
- How have the survivors' lives been influenced by their relationships with the person? What do they carry with them from this person?
- What are the family beliefs about afterlife and how have these beliefs influenced an understanding of the meaning of loss?
- What other beliefs do family members have that may help sustain them in the face of loss?

6 Where Do We Come From? Parents and Children

My mother. . . is monumental, really. . . Probably she is exactly like me; otherwise we wouldn't so hanker after one another whenever we are wise enough to keep apart. Her letters are things I dread, and she always asks for more of mine (I try to write monthly; but we haven't a subject we dare be intimate upon).

letter to Mrs. G. B. Shaw
—T. E. LAWRENCE

The Old Man. That's what Auma called our father. It sounded right to me, somehow, at once familiar and distant. An elemental force that isn't fully understood.

Dreams from My Father
—BARACK OBAMA

No one can ever replace our parents. They hopefully provided for us when we were infants and helpless, and throughout life we rely on them in one way or another. There is a debt we can never repay and at other times a pain we struggle to move beyond. Sadly, in the complex web of the family, many people feel little joy in the connection to parents. And few of us really get to know our parents as people. We may be too busy "fending off" what seem to be parental demands or the hurts of their absence, expectations, or abuse.

By seeing parents in the context of their lives—as children, as siblings, lovers, friends—and by exploring family patterns of parent-child relationships, one may come to a different understanding. The more fully we can relate to each parent's life, the more we will understand—and perhaps sympathize with—their position.

Without that empathy one is often left with a sense of mystification, and yet parents always matter. Barack Obama (Genogram 6.1) was haunted throughout his childhood by the absence of his father, who had left by the time he was 2:

There was only one problem: my father was missing. He had left paradise and nothing that my mother or grandparents told me could obviate that single unassailable fact. . . . My father became a prop in someone else's narrative. . . . I don't really blame my mother or grandparents for this. My father may have preferred the image they created for him—indeed, he may have been complicit in its creation. (Obama, 1995, p. 26)

Obama first met his half sister Auma as a young adult and he was shocked by what she told him about their father's life:

All my life I had carried a single image of my father, one that I had sometimes rebelled against but had never questioned, one that I later tried to take as my own. The brilliant scholar, the generous friend, the upstanding leader—my father had been all those things. I hadn't seen what perhaps most men see at some point in their lives: their father's body shrinking, their father's best hopes dashed, their father's face lined with grief and regret. . . . I'd seen weakness in other men— Gramps and his disappointments, [my step-father] Lolo and his compromise. But these men had become object lessons for me, men I might love but never emulate, white men and brown men whose fates didn't speak to my own. It was into my father's image, the black man, son of Africa, that I'd packed all the attributes I sought in myself, the attributes of Martin and Malcolm, DuBois and Mandela. . . . My father's voice had nevertheless remained untainted, inspiring, rebuking, granting or withholding approval. Now that image had suddenly vanished. Replaced by . . . what? A bitter drunk? An abusive husband? A defeated, lonely bureaucrat? To think all my life I had been wrestling with nothing more than a ghost. (Obama, 1995, p. 220)

Years later, after his father had died, Obama went to Kenya in a search to understand himself. He visited his father's third wife, Ruth, whom his father had divorced while her two sons were still children. She took out an album of pictures of the family when they were together years before. Obama wrote of it almost eerily:

They were happy scenes, all of them, and all strangely familiar, as if I were glimpsing some alternative universe that had played itself out behind my back. They were reflections, I realized, of my own long

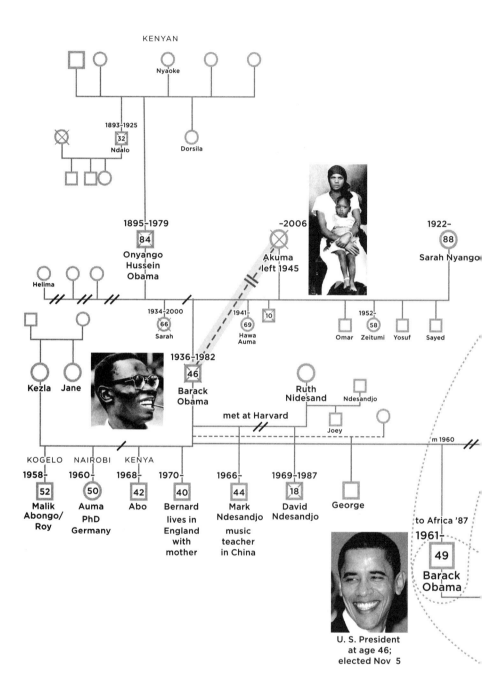

Genogram 6.1. The Obama Family. Dotted lines indicate 3-generation households.

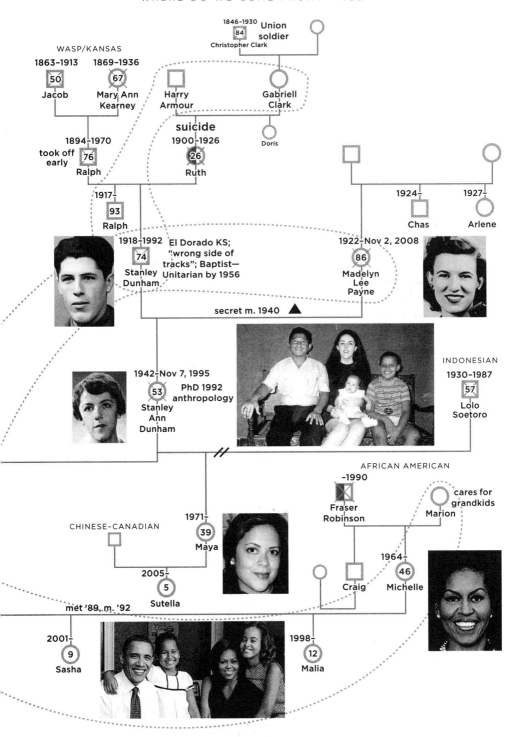

1846–1930
84
Christopher Clark
Union soldier

WASP/KANSAS

1863–1913
50
Jacob

1869–1936
67
Mary Ann Kearney

Harry Armour

Gabriell Clark

1894–1970
took off early
76
Ralph

1900–1926
26
Ruth

suicide

Doris

1917–
93
Ralph

1924–
Chas

1927–
Arlene

1918–1992
74
Stanley Dunham

El Dorado KS; "wrong side of tracks"; Baptist—Unitarian by 1956

1922–Nov 2, 2008
86
Madelyn Lee Payne

secret m. 1940 ▲

1942–Nov 7, 1995
53
Stanley Ann Dunham

PhD 1992 anthropology

INDONESIAN

1930–1987
57
Lolo Soetoro

AFRICAN AMERICAN

–1990
Fraser Robinson

cares for grandkids
Marion

CHINESE-CANADIAN

1971–
39
Maya

2005–
5
Sutella

1964–
46
Michelle

Craig

met '89, m. '92

2001–
9
Sasha

1998–
12
Malia

held fantasies, fantasies I'd kept secret even from myself. The fantasy of the Old Man's having taken my mother and me back to Kenya. The wish that my mother and father, sisters and brothers were all under one roof. . . . The recognition of how wrong it had all turned out, the harsh evidence of life as it had really been lived, made me so sad that after only a few minutes I had to look away. (Obama, 1995, pp. 342–343)

What is sad and touching and very common about this is that parents tend to live large in the hearts and fantasies of their children even if they have physically disappeared. In Obama's case it took until he was in his late twenties and his father had been dead several years to risk the journey to learn about him. He realized only when he was en route how strong his avoidance of this journey had been: "I began to suspect that my European stop was just one more means of delay, one more attempt to avoid coming to terms with the Old Man. . . . It wasn't that Europe wasn't beautiful; everything was just as I'd imagined it. It just wasn't mine. I felt as if I were living out someone else's romance; the incompleteness of my own history stood between me and the sites I saw like a hard pane of glass" (Obama, 1995, p. 301).

In fact, Obama spent much of his childhood living away from his mother as well, being raised by his maternal grandparents in Hawaii. So his search for his mother was also a part of his journey. He wrote of a visit she made to him while he was in college, when it became clear to him that she had never stopped loving his father: "She saw my father as everyone hopes at least one other person might see him; she had tried to help the child who never knew him see him the same way" (Obama, 1995, p. 137). But he was struggling to understand his mother as well:

In her smiling, slightly puzzled face I saw what all children must see at some point if they are to grow up—their parents' lives revealed to them as separate and apart, reaching out beyond the point of their union or the birth of a child, lives unfurling back to grandparents, great-grandparents, an infinite number of chance meetings, misunderstandings, projected hopes, limited circumstances. My mother was that girl with the movie of beautiful black people in her head, flattered by my father's attention, confused and alone, trying to break out of the grip of her own parents' lives. (Obama, 1995, p. 127)

Obama learned a great deal about himself as he thought about who his parents were, and who their parents were before them.

Many people who are unhappy with their own parents seek out others as replacements or try to find another more welcoming home. Such adaptive strategies may be necessary and extremely enriching, but they can never replace the real exploration of whom you really belong to.

This exploration can start simply by talking to parents about their lives. What were their dreams? Were those dreams realized? How did they feel about their own parents? What do they remember about their childhoods? One can also interview friends and other family members about parents—what were their impressions of them as children, as siblings, as friends, as workers, as lovers (though this may be touchy!)?

For some people the relationship with parents is the most difficult one they will know. Experiencing themselves as victims, they feel misunderstood, mistreated, abandoned in dangerous places, or required to perform adult tasks at too tender an age like Snow White, Cinderella, or Hansel and Gretel. They fantasize that they were adopted, once belonging to some other saner, kinder, more "normal" father and mother. And for some people it is impossible to mature beyond those childhood experiences of intimidation and powerlessness.

Later the parent/child roles may reverse: As parents age, they lean on their children more, become dependent, and the children's responsibility increases. This can be a gratifying time of human connectedness or, if earlier resentments persist, a time when problems intensify. It is often difficult for children, even as adults, to develop a clear sense of their parents, one that goes beyond early larger-than-life expectations of "mother" and "father." And it is also essential to realize that children have a tremendous power to hurt parents. When Maya Angelou's son chided her: "Mother, I know I'm your only child, but you must remember this is my life, not yours," her response was: "The thorn from the buds one has planted, nourished and pruned pricks most deeply and draws more blood" (Angelou, 1986, p. 7). We must remember that what we say to our parents taps into their profoundest feelings about themselves and about what we mean to them. Most of us grow up with very different feelings about mothers and fathers, because of the profoundly different roles each is "supposed" to play in our culture. A typical illustration of the different expectations is expressed by the son and daughter in Robert Anderson's play *I Never Sang for My Father*:

son: I just do not want to let my father die a stranger.
daughter: You're looking for something that isn't there, Gene. You're looking for a mother's love in a father. Mothers are soft and yielding. Fathers are hard and rough to teach us the ways of the world, which is rough, which is mean, which is selfish and prejudiced.

Son: What does it matter if I never loved him or he never loved me? And yet, when I hear the word "father," it matters. (Anderson, 1968, p. 113)

Perhaps we should consider the different problems and roles for daughters and for sons, for mothers and for fathers, even as we try to create a world with more flexibility in the roles fathers and mothers play in families. Traditionally, fathers have been more often unknown and unknowable, whereas mothers, more overtly present, get the brunt of our anger and more of our love. Mothers are often perceived as being overly present, offering too much advice and wanting too much intimacy. As one young woman has described it:

> Our fathers worked six days a week, twelve hours a day, and when they came home they were too tired for our exuberance and need. Or they were absent, or travelling, or dead. We remember them as people we hungered to know better, yet if they are with us now we refrain from asking the hard questions that make our hearts a battleground. These questions we keep for our mothers, with whom we seem locked in an unending arms-length minuet of impassioned love laced with fierce anger. (Kleiner, p. 3)

To fully understand parents, we need to question how the culture has often prescribed distance between fathers and children and between mothers and sons. We need to consider the constrictions traditional gender roles had on our families. This means expanding our view of men beyond the idea of the dominant male and the selfless female. We need to develop an appreciation of the men in our families who were able to admit doubts or to become nurturers, and the women who dared to defy conventions by expressing their strength directly.

The ideal for all of us would be to have a comfortable, trusting, person-to-person relationship with each parent. But this ideal is rarely achieved. Because it takes two adults to create a child, everyone starts out as part of a three-person system (at least), and this threesome generally becomes the central triangle in life. If everyone gets along, things are fine, but if there are conflicts, this triadic pattern develops problems. In fact, in "real" life the basic triad often fails to remain in place. Current estimates are that more than a third of today's children will live in a single-parent household before the age of 18; many others will be raised by grandparents, gay or lesbian couples, foster or adoptive families, or other types of caretakers.

The classic parent/child triangle involves the child or children siding with one parent while the other is the outsider. The children may feel close to their mother, who is seen as nurturing and reasonable, whereas the father is seen as withholding and unreasonable. Or they see their mother as intrusive and nagging and the father as "Mr. Nice Guy." It is hard to be equally friendly toward both parents if one of them is always angry with the other. Children will end up taking sides without even realizing what they are doing.

Such a classic good-guy/bad-guy triangle can be seen in Eleanor Roosevelt's family (Genogram 6.2). Both parents died when she was quite young, which probably locked her childhood view of the triangle in place, as there were no adult experiences to counteract the intense early memories. Had Eleanor's father lived, she might have developed a very different relationship with him, demanding a different kind of love—one with consistency and accountability. She might have become fed up with his erratic behavior. At best, Eleanor might have developed a more realistic view of both her father and mother, accepting both their flaws and virtues. As it was, she was a remarkable person who showed amazing fortitude in dealing with difficult circumstances and relationships. However, throughout her life she is said to have been initially enthusiastic in personal relationships but later disillusioned.

Eleanor's relationship to her father, Elliott, was very close. She was his first child, "a miracle from heaven," he had said (Lash, 1971), born 8 months after the double tragedy in the family, discussed earlier, when her uncle Theodore Roosevelt lost both mother and wife on the same night. Perhaps Eleanor was a consolation for her father's grief. He certainly identified with her, giving her the same nickname, Nell, that he had been called as a child. She, in turn, adored him. Though he died when Eleanor was only 10, she carried his letters around with her for the rest of her life. In her autobiography, completed when she was 74 years old, she wrote: "He dominated my life as long as he lived, and was the love of my life for many years after he died. With my father I was perfectly happy. . . . He was the center of my world. . . . With his death went for me all the realities of companionship which he had suggested for the future, but . . . he lived in my dreams and does to this day" (Roosevelt, 1984, p. 5). In contrast to the intense bond with her father, Eleanor's relationship with her mother was not close. She saw her mother as distant and unsympathetic. She saw herself as homely, and was sure that her mother concurred in this assessment. She recalled in her autobiography:

> My mother was one of the most beautiful women I have ever seen. I
> felt a curious barrier between myself and [my mother]. . . . I can still
> remember standing in the door, often with my finger in my mouth,

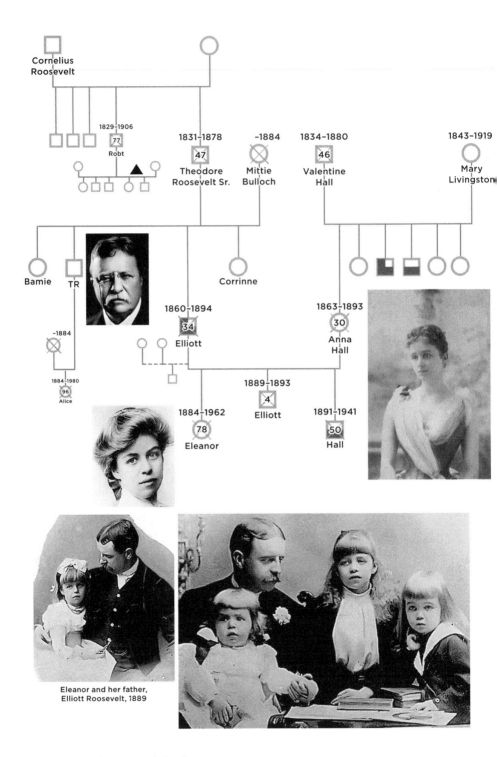

Genogram 6.2. The Roosevelt Family.

and I can see the look in her eyes and hear the tone of her voice as she said "Come in Granny." If a visitor was there she might turn and say, "She is such a funny child, so old-fashioned that we always call her 'Granny.'" I wanted to sink through the floor in shame. (Roosevelt, 1984, p. 3, 8–9)

Eleanor's world had begun to disintegrate before her father died. When she was 5, her father, a disturbed and erratic alcoholic, abruptly left the family. Although from a background of wealth and success, Elliott never lived up to his potential, dropping out of school in his teens. Despite his reputation as an adventurer, his amiability, good looks, and social position led to marriage with Anna Hall, a highly sought-after debutante. For the first few years of their marriage, his charm, intelligence, and inherited wealth stood him in good stead, although he did not himself provide much income for his family. Then, after a painful injury to his ankle, Elliott was transformed rather quickly into a depressed addict and alcoholic. Sometimes hostile and even suicidal, he would disappear, leaving his young wife and small children alone and unsure of his whereabouts. When he did finally reappear, there were drunken sprees and bouts of violence. Even then, however, Eleanor favored her father. In describing one of his returns, she remembered almost guiltily: "My father had come home . . . and I am sorry to say he was causing a great deal of anxiety, but he was the only person who did not treat me as a criminal" (Roosevelt, 1984, p. 7).

The family made various efforts to help their wayward son, persuading him to undergo several sanitarium stays. Finally, to protect his estate, they moved to have him judged insane and he was not allowed to live with his wife and children. For a time he made a partial recovery, working in a small southern factory town as part of his rehabilitation. During this time he lived with different women, and his family did not know where he was. (There is an interesting parallel in the previous generation of this family, where Elliott's uncle Robert maintained two separate families and two sets of children almost around the corner from one another. When his wife died he apparently moved his second family in with the first.)

In the midst of Elliott's problems, Eleanor's mother, Anna, took ill with diphtheria and died suddenly. Even here, Eleanor's first thoughts were of her father: "Death meant nothing to me, and one fact wiped out everything else— my father was back and I would see him very soon" (Roosevelt, 1984, p. 9).

There was, however, no storybook ending. Elliott continued to drink and could not care for his two small children, who ended up living with their kind but stern Grandmother Hall, who disapproved of their father. Elliott wrote Eleanor letters full of promise and hope but rarely visited. Once when he did visit, he took her to his club, but abandoned her in the vestibule. Hours later she had the humiliating experience of watching him carried out drunk. Despite such painful experiences, Eleanor continued to believe that one day he and she would go off blissfully together. She remembered his reassurances:

> He began . . . to explain to me that . . . he and I must keep close together. Some day I would make a home for him again; we would travel together and do many things. Somehow it was always he and I. I did not understand whether my brothers were to be our children or whether he felt that they would be at school and college and later independent. (Roosevelt, 1984, pp. 9–10)

The letters he wrote raised her hopes that he was coming home, only to disappoint her when he did not. Within a short time he moved back to New York under an assumed name and lived out of touch with the family. In 1894, only 2 years after his wife's death, he died of alcoholism. Later Eleanor wrote about her childhood:

> I acquired a strange and garbled idea of the troubles around me. Something was wrong with my father, but from my point of view nothing could be wrong with him. If people only realized what a war goes on in a child's mind and heart in a situation of this kind, I think they would try to explain more than they do, but nobody told me anything. (Roosevelt, 1984, p. 8)

Eleanor's love for her father remained unshaken even when, during an argument with an aunt when Eleanor was a teenager, the aunt told her the truth about her father's drinking and affairs. In fact, it seemed even to strengthen her belief that she and he had needed each other and that he was as vulnerable as she was.

Eleanor's one-sided loyalty provides a good example of how an unrealistic view of parents can be imprinted early and last throughout life if the need to preserve it is intense. In Eleanor's case, it was as if she allowed her imagination to fill in his absences with the father she wished she had. Of course, by doing that she never really knew the father she did have.

Nor did she ever gain a clear view of her mother. With the tremendous reservoir of affection she reserved for her father, there was little left for her mother. Her mother's judgmental attitude may have seemed to cause her father's problems. Young children often see things this way. Probably, the more she expressed her loyalty to her father, the more she felt rejected by her mother, who must have sensed Eleanor's preference. In turn, the more distant she was from her mother, the more she valued her special relationship with her father. In the end, she was not able to see either parent for who he or she really was.

For many years Eleanor's daughter Anna, named for her mother, was caught in a similar triangle in which she saw her father, Franklin, as the hero and her mother as the villain. She wrote: "It is no wonder that my Father was my childhood hero. . . . He talked about all sorts of things I liked to hear about—books I was reading, a cruise we might be going to take. . . . [Mother] felt a tremendous sense of duty to us . . . but she did not understand or satisfy the need of a child for primary closeness to a parent" (Asbell, 1982, p. 19).

Her son James wrote: "Having gained no useful knowledge on the subject from her own unhappy years as a child, mother was absolutely terrified to find herself a parent. . . . [Her] fear of failure as a mother in turn hurt her as a mother. For many years—until it was too late for her to become a real mother—she let our grandmother act as our mother" (Roosevelt, 1976, p. 24). Eleanor herself seems to have agreed about her difficulties as a mother, which was not surprising, given her own wretched childhood: "It did not come naturally to me to understand little children or to enjoy them . . . because play had not been an important part of my own childhood" (Asbell, 1982, p. 19). Anna's husband later reported that she used to tell him that her mother was unpredictable and inconsistent—sweet and lovely one hour, critical and demanding the next. Luckily for both mother and daughter, they lived long enough and worked hard enough to move past their conflicts and problems. Eleanor was to write later:

> Today no one could ask for a better friend than I have in Anna, or she has in me. Perhaps because it grew slowly, the bond between us is all the stronger. No one can tell either of us anything about the other, and though we might not always think alike or act alike, we always respect each other's motives, and there is a type of sympathetic understanding between us, which would make a real misunderstanding quite impossible. (Asbell, 1982, p. 31)

Many children never give up trying to mold their parents into the unconditionally loving caretakers they felt they never had. As adults, they may do this by continuing to seek parental approval or by continuing to act needy. In both cases, they are likely to be disappointed.

The Family of Franz Kafka

Some, like the Jewish Czech writer Franz Kafka (Genogram 6.3), never get past their preoccupation with whatever didn't work out in their relationships with their parents. Kafka was obsessed all his life by his problems in relating to his father. He made a well-known but failed attempt to reconcile with him, but also to change him, in a letter he never delivered. In this letter, he said: "My writing was all about you; all I did there, after all, was to bemoan what I could not bemoan upon your breast" (Kafka, 1953, p. 87). Not surprisingly, Kafka wrote about people caught up in terrifying situations where they were the victims of a senseless, impersonal, all-powerful, persecuting world.

Kafka saw his father as a loud, overpowering, hot-tempered man, self-centered, hypocritical, and incapable of providing emotional support yet sabotaging his children's efforts to break away. He believed his father intended to frighten him into being less timid and unmanly, a tactic that never worked. Always terrified of his father, Kafka blamed him for his own sense of guilt and lack of confidence.

Kafka viewed his mother as everything good: a peacemaker, kind and considerate, who buffered the tensions between him and his father. But in the end, he felt she failed to protect him and sided with his father, saying that she could not act as an independent spiritual force on her son's behalf because she loved her husband too much. Kafka's father was the villain and his mother the unwitting, if well-intentioned, accomplice. Kafka had a fleeting awareness of his own provocations in the pattern—always turning to his mother as intermediary and never dealing with his father directly.

In his letter to his father, written when he was 36, he tried to insist that no one was to blame for their relationship—from the beginning a mismatch of natures: "I too believe you are entirely blameless for our estrangement. But I am just as equally entirely blameless. If I could get you to acknowledge this, then what would be possible is—not a new life—for this we are both much too old—but still, a kind of peace, not a cessation, but still, a mitigation of your incessant reproaches" (Kafka, 1953, pp. 10–11).

Kafka proceeded to list incident after incident of his father's insensitivity. He blamed his stammering on his father for not allowing him to contradict. He said his father expected him to do poorly and sure enough, in his nervousness, he fumbled. The father expected him to marry, yet insisted that no one he wanted to marry was good enough. Kafka even predicted that his father would dismiss his letter with "Is that all you're so worked up about?"

Kafka's letter provides an astute analysis of the role played by the "good" parent, in this case his mother, in perpetuating a parental triangle:

Genogram 6.3. The Kafka Family.

Mother unconsciously played the role of a beater in a hunt. Even if in some unlikely event your upbringing could somehow have set me on my own feet by producing spite, aversion, or even hatred in me, mother balanced it out again by her kindness, her sensible talk (she was in the chaos of childhood the archetype of good sense!) by interceding for me, and I was again driven back into your orbit, from which I might otherwise have broken free, to both your advantage and mine. Or it was the case that no real reconciliation came about, that mother really protected me from you secretly. (Kafka, 1953, p. 31–32)

He realized his mother's efforts to keep the peace prevented him and his father from resolving their conflict. Her failure to confront the father made him feel justified. Kafka impeded his own efforts to come to terms with his father by relating only through his mother. He never managed to see his father as anything but a tyrant and a bully, failing to go beyond the surface behavior to understand his father's perspective.

Hermann Kafka had been the fourth of six surviving children in a family so poor they lived in a one-room shack. At 14 he left home to make his own way, which he did by determination and single-minded ambition. He married Julie Lowry, who came from better circumstances, but her mother had died when she was 3, leaving her with heavy responsibility for her younger siblings. Like her husband, Julie was vigorous and ambitious. They looked to each other for the love and caring they had missed in childhood. By all accounts they had a devoted marriage, working together in their dry-goods business and socializing in the evening.

Kafka, the oldest of four surviving children, thought he and his siblings were left out of this arrangement, raised by caretakers while the parents worked to establish the father's business. Probably Kafka felt powerless to make up for his parents' loss of their two other sons, who died of childhood diseases. No matter how successful he became, Herman Kafka continued to worry about his survival. He could not understand his children's complaints, especially those of his sensitive, ever-fretting son. His prime concern was to give them economic security and they failed to appreciate this.

Franz Kafka, who died at the age of 40, never could bring himself to marry. He feared that marriage and parenthood might make him more like his father. Even worse, he might have children who would resent him as much as he resented his father. In his letter Franz admitted that he was a difficult, obstinate son who tended to be oversensitive, and that there were times when he deliberately provoked his father by taking contrary opinions.

In a remarkable ending to the letter, Kafka offered a detailed rebuttal of all his arguments, anticipating his father's criticisms. He was sure his father would mistrust the letter, seeing it as full of veiled recriminations, and would chide him for continuing to accept money while criticizing him.

Despite the professed desire for reconciliation, the tone of the letter was bitter. By itself it probably would not have improved the relationship between father and son, though it would have been the most honest communication they had ever had.

However, true to the family triangle, instead of giving the letter to his father directly, Kafka gave it to his mother to deliver. She returned it to him, and he then kept it to himself. Family therapists often call this pattern the "two step"—a dance in which even an effort toward change is followed by a call back into line, which we accept. One wonders what might have happened if Kafka had then given the letter directly to his father.

The opposite side of the "parent as villain" is the "parent as saint." When the idealized image of one parent gives way to a disappointing reality, the previously excluded parent may then be seen as all good and the previously favored parent as all bad. This is an equally unrealistic view, again showing how triangles can distort relationships. Whether a parent is vilified or idealized, a transformative process is necessary to understand the parent's story in context, adding new perspectives that include other points of view.

The Dickens Marriage

When, after 22 years of marriage and 10 children, Charles Dickens decided to leave his wife, Catherine Hogarth Dickens, for his mistress, Ellen Ternan (Genogram 6.4), he justified his behavior by establishing his wife as the villain of the piece. Declaring he had never loved her, he blamed her for destroying their marriage, though the real precipitant of their separation was his affair with Ellen. In this context he reassessed the 20 years of their marriage: "I believe my marriage has been for years and years as miserable a one as ever was made. I believe that no two people were ever created with such an impossibility of interest, sympathy, confidence, sentiment, tender union of any kind between them, as there is between my wife and me" (Rose, 1984, p. 180). Catherine was, not surprisingly, depressed and lacking in confidence. Dickens's first direct act of separation was to wall up the connection between their bedroom and his dressing room, which he took as his own bedroom. He then set her up as the villain, saying that if her sister Georgina had not lived with them and become the energetic, intelligent, inventive, and attractive "mother" to the children, they would have had no mother. He said that his wife was the only human being he had ever known with whom he could not get along or find common interest—indeed, he said, no one could get along with her,

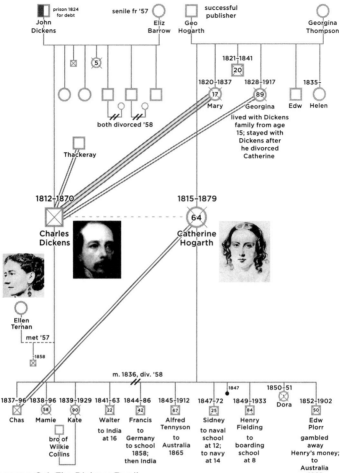

Genogram 6.4. The Dickens Family.

not even her own mother. Dickens's affair and sudden separation from his wife triggered disruptions with relatives, friends, and colleagues. He tried to blame everything on his wife and took elaborate efforts to protect the secrecy of his affair (never again having a single residence but always multiple abodes, so he could maintain the secrecy of his time with Ellen). His actions had a profound impact on his children, who ranged in age from 21 to 6 at the time of the separation. One son, Walter, left for India shortly before Dickens met Ellen and never returned. All but one of the Dickens children, who adored their father, sided with him. He was fun, magical, entertaining, famous, and funny. Their mother was passive, quiet, probably seriously depressed, and not very responsive. They blamed her for losing their father's love. Initially only the oldest son, Charlie, remained with the mother; he stopped talking to his father and defiantly announced his engagement to the daughter of Dickens's estranged publisher. Dickens was given custody of all the other children, moving them in with his wife's sister Georgina, who became the family caretaker. However, within a few months Dickens sent his son Henry, age 8, to join his three older brothers in boarding school, and for the first time left them there at the school for the Christmas holidays, which had always been the most festive of the Dickens family celebrations. Indeed, in his story "The Christmas Carol," one of the saddest memories evoked is of being left as a child in boarding school over the Christmas holidays. Dickens's oldest daughter, Mamie, ended up as his caretaker and never left him. The third child, Kate, helped her sister in caring for Dickens, but soon after married the younger brother of her father's closest friend, Wilkie Collins, who himself had a separate ménage with a young mistress. Years later, Catherine, hoping for some understanding of how wronged she had been as mother and wife, gave Kate the letters Dickens had written her as indication that he had indeed loved her, requesting that they be published. Kate consulted with George Bernard Shaw about the letters and he helped her to revise her view of her parents, particularly of her mother. Shaw said Katie's view of her parents' marriage as a case of "the man of genius tied to a commonplace wife" had been rudely upset by a writer named Ibsen. Shaw predicted that history would sympathize more with Catherine, who had sacrificed her life, to the extent of bearing Dickens ten children in 15 years, and that her only real sin was "that she was not a female Charles Dickens." Kate eventually cooperated in the publication of the story of the Dickenses' marital separation from her mother's point of view and dedicated it to her (Storey, 1939).

The Dickens marriage involved a triangle from the start, as Catherine's younger sister, Mary, immediately moved in with the couple. Dickens so idealized this sister-in-law that after her death the next year he wrote: "I have lost the dearest friend I ever had. . . . The very last words she whispered were of me. . . . I solemnly believe that so perfect a creature never breathed. . . . She had not a fault" (Mackenzie & Mackenzie, 1979, p. 59). He bought a double cemetery plot, hoping to be buried beside Mary, and celebrated the anniversary of her death all his life. Several years later, Catherine's younger sister Georgina, who bore a striking resemblance to Mary in both personality and physical appearance, joined the Dickens household. She was 15, the same age Mary had been when she moved in. Her resemblance to her dead sister was so strong that their mother said: "So much of Mary's spirit shines out in this sister, that the old time comes back again at some seasons, and I can hardly separate it from the present" (p. 133).

Over the years Dickens felt entitled to include other women in his marriage. Twice when Catherine suspected his affairs, he accused her of patho-logical jealousy and made her apologize to his mistress. As time went by he became increasingly convinced that his wife was boring and useless. As one of our most perceptive critics of marriage, Phyllis Rose, said in her book *Parallel Lives*: "Marriage and career, family and work, which so often pull a woman in different directions, are much more likely to reinforce one another for a man" (Rose, 1984, p. 150).

Dickens was a case in point. He, whose father lived in a debtors' prison, married "up." Catherine Hogarth Dickens was the daughter of a successful journalist. In the early years Dickens appears to have been extremely happy with her. He wrote of the early days of his marriage, "I shall never be so happy again . . . never if I roll in wealth and fame" (Rose, 1984, p. 149).

The Dilemma of Women's Roles in Families

As you consider your family tree, note the roles that women have played over the generations and note the prevailing cultural constraints of their times. Traditionally women have been evaluated primarily according to their beauty, their mothering, and their housekeeping skills. Their creative work has often had to be accomplished, as Catherine Bateson put it, "in scraps of rescued space and time in marginal roles that have to be invented again and again" (Bateson, 1990, p. 11).

Women who are not cut out to be good caretakers have never had an easy time. In the past a woman who wanted to have a life of her own, with its own adventures and quests, often developed an "eccentric story" in order to free herself from the strictures of marriage and family (Heilbrun, 1988). George Eliot, for example, removed herself from conventional expectations by her decision to live with a man who could not divorce his legal wife. By one act that was considered outrageous she escaped social demands and made up for her despair at being considered unattractive.

Illness, even to the point of invalidism, has sometimes been the only way women could see out of the "slavery" of traditional roles. We saw this with Elizabeth Barrett Browning, whose invalidism freed her from conventional expectations and allowed her a degree of flexibility to focus on her poetry— the tradeoff, of course, being confinement to her room.

Sonya Tolstoy provides another example of the "womanly" role. After 40 years of catering to her "genius" husband, Leo, she wrote: "Geniuses must create in peaceful, enjoyable, comfortable conditions; a genius must eat, wash, dress, he must rewrite his work countless times; one must love him, give him no cause for jealousy so that he has peace, one must raise and educate the innumerable children who are born to a genius, but for whom he has no time"

(Smoluchowski, 1987, p. 217). Providing such an atmosphere for genius was a constant struggle for Sonya Tolstoy; like her husband, she was brilliant, passionate, volatile, sensitive, easily jealous, and prone to self-analysis. She asked ironically: "But for what would I, an insignificant woman, need an intellectual and artistic life?" and replied: "To this question I can only answer, I do not know. But always suppressing my needs to care for the material needs of a genius is a great hardship" (p. 217). Sonya's questioning of her life and purpose will seem familiar to women even today.

Because women have been valued mainly for their caretaking roles, we must take care in rewriting the narratives of our families if we are to understand them in context. In the Tolstoy family it was many years before Sonya's son Sergei was able to appreciate her importance: "I understand better than I did then the importance of my mother in our family life and the great value of her care for us and for my father. At the time, it seemed to me that everything in our life went on of its own accord. We accepted Mother's care as a matter of course. I did not notice that beginning with our food and clothes to our studies and the copying for father, everything was managed by her" (Smoluchowski, 1987, pp. 124–125).

Finding Your Parents as You Lose Them

In the normal course of events, our parents will die within our lifetime, yet knowing this and fully realizing it are two different things. If the relationship with a parent has been estranged or stormy and much is left unsaid or unresolved, his or her loss will be even greater. But it is also possible that in the consciousness of a parent's dying, understanding between the generations may be achieved.

For most of her life Simone de Beauvoir (Genogram 6.5) devalued her mother as critical, unsophisticated, bourgeois, and guilt-inducing. She dealt with her by avoidance. But as her mother was dying, Simone came to reevaluate her, realizing that her mother had grown up to "live against herself." She recognized that a full-bodied, spirited woman lived inside her mother but was a stranger to her. Her mother had spent all her strength in repressing her desires, squeezing the armor of principles and prohibitions over her heart and mind, as she had been taught to pull the laces tight around her body.

De Beauvoir shows remarkable insight into the ways in which this constriction developed in her mother. Simone's father had studied law but spent much of his time as a dandy, improving his status through his marriage. Shortly after the marriage, however, Simone's maternal grandfather, who had been a wealthy banker, was sent to jail for fraud, and the family experienced a very public and humiliating bankruptcy.

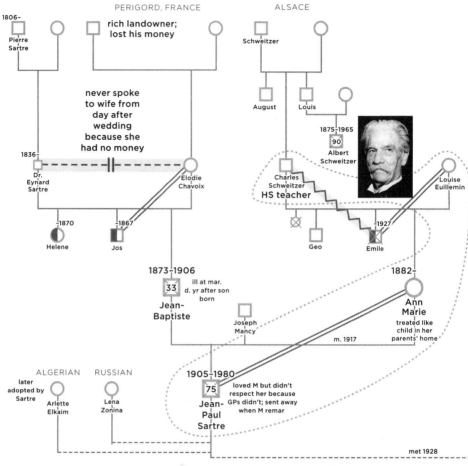

PERIGORD, FRANCE

ALSACE

1806–
Pierre
Sartre

rich landowner;
lost his money

Schweitzer

never spoke
to wife from
day after
wedding
because she
had no money

August

Louis

1875–1965
90
Albert
Schweitzer

1836–
Dr.
Eynard
Sartre

Élodie
Chavoix

Charles
Schweitzer
HS teacher

Louise
Euillemin

–1870

Helene

–1867

Jos

Geo

–1927
Emile

1873–1906
33   ill at mar.
      d. yr after son
      born
Jean-
Baptiste

Joseph
Mancy

m. 1917

1882–
Ann
Marie
treated like
child in her
parents' home

ALGERIAN

RUSSIAN

later
adopted by
Sartre

Arlette
Elkaim

Lena
Zonina

1905–1980
75
Jean-
Paul
Sartre

loved M but didn't
respect her because
GPs didn't; sent away
when M remar

met 1928

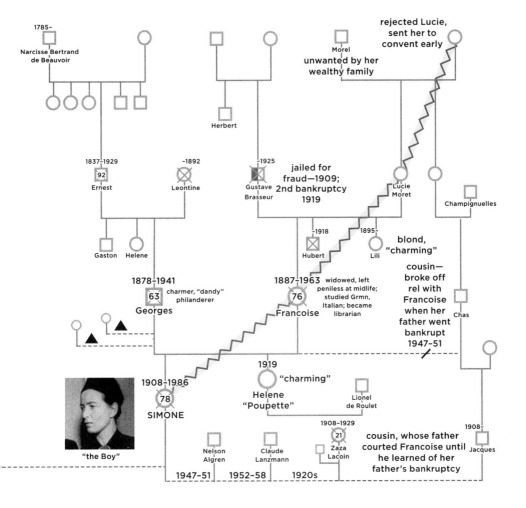

rejected Lucie,
sent her to
convent early

unwanted by her
wealthy family

1785–
Narcisse Bertrand
de Beauvoir

Herbert

Morel

1837–1929
92
Ernest

–1892
Leontine

–1925
Gustave
Brasseur

jailed for
fraud—1909;
2nd bankruptcy
1919

Lucie
Moret

Champignuelles

Gaston   Helene

–1918
Hubert

1895–
Lili

blond,
"charming"

1878–1941
63   charmer, "dandy"
        philanderer
Georges

1887–1963
76
Francoise

widowed, left
peniless at midlife;
studied Grmn,
Italian; became
librarian

cousin—
broke off
rel with
Francoise
when her
father went
bankrupt
1947–51

Chas

1908–1986
78
SIMONE

"the Boy"

1919
"charming"
Helene
"Poupette"

Lionel
de Roulet

Nelson
Algren

Claude
Lanzmann

1908–1929
21
Zaza
Lacoin

cousin, whose father
courted Francoise until
he learned of her
father's bankruptcy

1908–
Jacques

1947–51   1952–58   1920s

Genogram 6.5. The Sartre Family.

As Simone thought about her mother's life, she realized that her mother's concern for convention and her desire to please were compensation for the shame she felt about her father. She felt guilty all her life that her husband never received the dowry he expected. She saw her husband as noble for not blaming her for her family's poverty after the bankruptcy, though the husband was not much of a provider and the family struggled for many years just to survive. As Simone thought about her father's extramarital affairs, she began to appreciate just how difficult life had been for her mother and how strong her mother had been. Simone also developed an appreciation for the way her mother had recovered after her husband's death, which left her penniless at the age of 51. Francoise, apparently, did not let herself be trapped by her past, but had taken advantage of her late-life freedom to take courses and receive a certificate to work as a Red Cross librarian. She learned to ride a bicycle, studied German and Italian, reestablished ties with friends and relatives who had been driven away by her husband's surliness, and was able to satisfy one of her earliest longings—to travel.

As de Beauvoir reevaluated her mother, she perceived with touching clarity the tragedy of her mother's limited options:

> It is a pity that out of date ideas should have prevented her from adopting the solution that she came round to twenty years later—that of working away from home. . . . She would have risen in her own esteem instead of feeling that she was losing face. She would have had connections of her own. She would have escaped from a state of dependence that tradition made her think natural but that did not in the least agree with her nature. And no doubt she would then have been better equipped to bear the frustration that she had to put up with. (de Beauvoir, 1966, p. 25)

Although as a child Simone de Beauvoir had been very close to her mother, her adolescence became a stormy battle for independence, and the conflict continued in her adult life. When she learned that her mother had contracted terminal cancer, she was shocked. That her mother would die one day was a fact devoid of meaning for her—one of those things we all know but imagine will take place in some other "legendary" time. As she began to face the reality of her mother's impending death, she decided to attempt a reconciliation. But there, watching her mother in the hospital, she felt an intense desire to distance:

> The sight of my mother's nakedness jarred me. No body existed less for me: none existed more. As a child I had loved her dearly; as an

adolescent it had filled me with an uneasy repulsion, all this was perfectly in the ordinary course of things and it seemed reasonable to
me that her body should retain its dual nature, that it should be both
repugnant and holy—a taboo. But, for all that, I was astonished at the
violence of my distress. (de Beauvoir, 1966, pp. 19–20)

In time she achieved more perspective. She was no longer worried by her
mother's nakedness, yet had a fear of hurting her. More important, she began
to see her mother as a person:

She was capable of selfless devotion for my father and for us. But it is
impossible for anyone to say "I am sacrificing myself" without feeling
bitterness. . . . She was continually rebelling against the restraints and
the privations that she inflicted upon herself. . . . She flung herself into
the only other course that was available to her—that of feeding upon
the young lives that were in her care. "At least I have never been self-
centered; I have lived for others," she said to me later. Yes, but also by
means of others. She was possessive; she was overbearing; she would have
liked to have us completely in her power. (de Beauvoir, 1966, pp. 35, 38)

Gradually Simone saw her own part in her earlier alienation from her
mother, though it was difficult to overcome her negative reactions. She
would promise herself to find common ground with her mother, but then
she would be irritated by her mother's clumsy use of language. Even so, as
she sat with her mother in the hospital, she gradually developed the patience
to listen to her mother's story for the first time and to admire her courage:
"[Mother] said very firmly, 'I would not admit that I was old. But one must
face up to things; in a few days I shall be seventy-eight, and that is a great
age. I must arrange my life accordingly. I am going to start a fresh chapter.' I gazed at her with admiration" (de Beauvoir, 1966, p. 17). In absorbing
her mother's story, Simone realized she did not have the power to eradicate
the early unhappiness of her mother that had led her to make her children
unhappy and to suffer herself for having done so. She realized that if her
mother had embittered her childhood, she had more than paid her back.
Francoise had had an unhappy childhood herself. She was also the older sister in her family, and had grown up feeling that her mother was cold and
that her father favored the younger sister, Lili. Realizing that Francoise had
wanted from her children what she did not receive from her parents, Simone
began to comprehend the intensity of her mother's investment in her as the
intellectual older sister.

In the end, Simone managed to retrieve her relationship with her mother, which had been short-circuited so long before:

> I had grown very fond of this dying woman. As we talked in the half-darkness I assuaged an old unhappiness; I was renewing the old dialogue that had been broken off during my adolescence and that our differences and our likenesses had never allowed us to take up again. And the early tenderness that I had thought dead forever came to life again. (de Beauvoir, 1973, p. 76)

Unfortunately, too many people wait until it is too late before achieving such understanding. It is, of course, much easier to reconcile with your parents if they are still alive. But even if they are not, you can better understand yourself and your family by trying to discover as much as you can about them.

The goal of reconnecting is to share yourself with your parents, not just find out about their lives. Parents may resist one-way questions if they feel they are being "investigated." They are more likely to respond if you express interest in family stories. Self-disclosure, along with nonthreatening, specific questions, will encourage them to flesh out the details that will help you see them as human beings trying to get by as best they can.

In considering the idea of asking your parents questions, you may think, "Not my father, he's too intimidating" or "I could never talk to my mother—she's too domineering and intrusive." Whatever the parents' behavior, in these cases it is challenging to understand how they got to be that way. But parents who act controlling got that way somehow. Such behavior typically reflects a sense of insecurity or inadequacy rather than a willful attempt to harm a child. Once parents feel they still have something to offer, such as information about their own lives and experiences, the need to be so controlling may lessen.

Accepting parents means giving up efforts to change them. Lowering your expectations to zero will help you improve your relationship with a parent. This isn't to say that one does not keep working to understand parents and try to communicate more effectively. But instead of building the relationship on the basis of an expected "payback" from the parents, the emphasis is on how you relate to them.

Questions About Parents

- What kind of relationship did each of your parents have with each of their parents? their siblings? their grandparents? their aunts and uncles? How did they like school? Did they do well? Did they have friends? How did they spend their time? How did the family spend holidays and vacations?

- Were there critical life experiences that changed things for them—a death, an illness, a move, a change in financial circumstances? What do they remember of those experiences?

- What about their experiences growing up? How did they experience adolescence? Did their parents approve of their friends? What were their dreams?

- When your parents met each other, how did their parents react? Were there conflicts over the wedding? Did their parents disapprove of their childrearing practices?

- What was it like for them to become parents? What did they want to do differently from their own parents? What do they remember of your behavior as you grew up? Were you hard to discipline? What were the good memories? What did they find most difficult about parenting? What do they remember about times when you had problems?

- Were there times during parenting that were particularly difficult for them? your adolescence? early childhood? Were there hard times financially? Were there moves or migrations?

- Were there ways your mother or any other women in the family did not conform to the stereotypes of mother? Did your mother work outside the home? Did she want to? What about aunts and grandmothers? What were their dreams? How did they manage or react to the socially approved women's roles in their time? How did others react to them?

- Were there ways in which your father or other men in the family did not conform to the stereotypes of father? Were they affectionate? caretakers? talkers or storytellers? emotionally involved with other family members? Were these men able to show their vulnerabilities? How did they manage against the constrictions of men's roles in their time?

- What were the best models of parent-child relationships in the family? Why do you see them as good models? What were the typical patterns of parent-child relationships for each gender? What were the rules for parent-child relationships at each phase of the life cycle (infancy, childhood, adolescence, launching, young adulthood, maturity)? Are there clear expectations for how close your parents and you ideally ought to be in the family? Are you and your parents expected to spend leisure time together? holidays? to share intimate thoughts?

- Could you tell your parents what you appreciate about what they gave you and forgive them for what they were not able to give? What would you have to forgive?

7 Brothers and Sisters

I don't believe that the accident of birth makes people sisters and brothers.
It makes them siblings. Gives them mutuality of parentage. Sisterhood and
brotherhood is a condition people have to work at. It's a serious matter. You
compromise, you give, you take, you stand firm, and you're relentless. . . .
And it is an investment. Sisterhood means if you happen to be in Burma and
I happen to be in San Diego and I'm married to someone who's very jealous
and you're married to somebody who's very possessive, if you call me in the
middle of the night, I have to come.

—MAYA ANGELOU, 1991

You got to hold onto your brother and don't let him fall, no matter what . . .
you may not be able to stop nothing from happening, but you got to let him
know you's there.

—JAMES BALDWIN'S MOTHER IN "SONNY'S BLUES"

My dearest friend and bitterest rival, my mirror and opposite, my confidante
and betrayer, my student and teacher, my reference point and counterpoint,
my support and dependent, my daughter and mother, my subordinate, my
superior and scariest still, my equal.

—ELIZABETH FISHEL IN *Sisters*

Our sibling relationships are generally the longest relationships we have in
life and an incredible protection for well-being as we age. Although parents
are our first caretakers, from whom we learn about trust and independence, it
is our brothers and sisters with whom we first relate as partners and equals. In
some ways, we have more in common with our brothers and sisters—beginning with the fact that we shared our parents, our family history—than we
will ever have with others. In some families, siblings remain each other's most
important relationship. In others, their rivalry and conflict causes families to
break apart. Katharine Hepburn (see pagve 146 for genogram) said of her
sisters and brothers: "They are so much a part of me that I simply know I
could not have been me without them. They are my 'box'—my protection"

(Hepburn, 1991, p. 30). Siblings can become the models for future relationships with friends, lovers, and other contemporaries. In our modern world, spouses may come and go, parents die, children grow up and leave, but siblings, we hope, are always there.

Surprisingly, the importance of siblings has been overlooked in much of the psychological literature. Freud completely ignored sibling relationships. Although he had five sisters, a brother, and two half brothers, he wrote a whole autobiography without mentioning that he even had siblings! His early colleague and follower, Alfred Adler, did focus on sibling patterns in personality development, but when the two came to a parting of the ways it was Freud whose ideas became dominant. Freud, incidentally, viewed Adler's defection as the act of an ungrateful younger brother.

But the evidence is that sibling relationships matter a great deal. According to one important longitudinal study of successful, well-educated men (the Harvard classes of 1938–1944), the single best predictor of emotional health at age 65 was having had a close relationship with one's sibling in college. This factor was more predictive than childhood closeness to parents, emotional problems in childhood or parental divorce, or even having had a successful marriage or career (Valliant, 1977).

We've already taken a look at two celebrated siblings, Wilbur and Orville Wright (see page 112 for genogram), a duo so linked that one is never spoken of without the other. Obviously not all siblings are as close as they were. Childhood rivalries and hurts carry over into adulthood. At family get-togethers, everyone tries, at least at first, to be friendly and cordial. But beneath the surface, old conflicts may simmer. The oldest sister, once the responsible caretaker, may still resent her "bratty and irresponsible little brother," now a grown man, who teased her mercilessly throughout childhood. She may soon find herself falling into an old pattern of giving him advice. And he, though now a successful executive, may immediately go on the defensive because the old family script triggers memories of being bossed around and feeling impotent. A younger sister who felt dominated or abused by her older brother may feel uncomfortable even sitting at the same table with him. All the old, unpleasant memories flood back. Two brothers who spent their childhoods competing in sports, in school, and for parental attention may find themselves subtly competing in the holiday dinner-table conversation 30 years later. Even if there are no major flare-ups, family members may leave the dinner feeling bored or vaguely dissatisfied, glad that such occasions occur only a few times a year.

Unfortunately, parents sometimes make things worse. This is particularly true when siblings see one another only at the parental home or when adult siblings only hear about one another through the parents, especially the mother, who often becomes the family "switchboard." Whether deliberately or inadvertently, parents can perpetuate old sibling patterns. A mother may compare one child with another, perhaps chiding one for not calling as often as the other does. A father might talk repeatedly about how proud he is of his son, not realizing he is ignoring his daughter. A parent may elicit the support of one sibling in an effort to "shape up" another. Siblings themselves may even encourage this parental interference as this is the customary family pattern.

Sibling experiences vary greatly. An important factor is the amount of time brothers and sisters spend together when young. Two children who are close in age, particularly if they are of the same gender, generally spend a lot of time together; they must share their parents' attention, and they are usually raised under similar conditions. Siblings born farther apart obviously spend less time with each other and have fewer shared experiences; they grow up in the family at very different points in its evolution and in many ways are more comparable to only children.

In today's world of frequent divorce and remarriage, there may be a combination of siblings, step-siblings, and half siblings who live in different households and only come together on special occasions. There are also more only children, whose closest sibling-like relationships will be their playmates and cousins. And there are more two-child families as well, where the relationship between the two tends to be more intense because they only have each other. Clearly, the more time siblings have with one another, the more intense their relationships are likely to be.

Siblings who have little contact with outsiders grow to rely on each other, especially when parents are absent, unavailable, or inadequate. Charlie Chaplin and his half brother Sydney, 4 years older than he, are an example of an unusually close and life-long bond (Genogram 7.1). Sydney was less than 3 months old when his mother married Charles Chaplin, Sr., who became responsible for his support, though he did a very poor job of it. Chaplin, Sr., separated early from the boys' mother, became an alcoholic, and more or less abandoned them. Their mother suffered repeated bouts of insanity throughout their childhood and had to be institutionalized. Their aunt once said of the boys' relationship: "It seems strange to me that anyone can write about Charlie Chaplin without mentioning his brother Sydney. They have been inseparable all their lives, except when fate intervened at intervals. Syd, of quiet manner, clever brain and steady nerve, has been father and mother to Charlie. Charlie always looked up to Syd, and Sydney would suffer anything to spare Charlie" (Robinson, 1985, p. 2). At one point in childhood, when the brothers were separated, Sydney became concerned that Charlie was not responding to his letters, which was partly because he could not spell

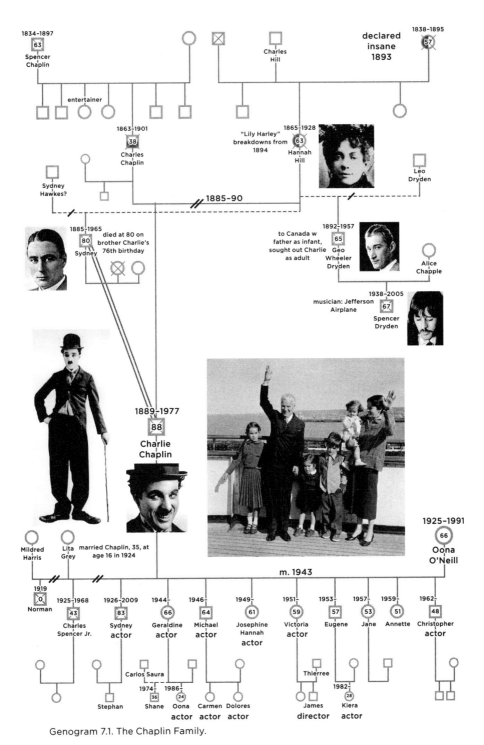

Genogram 7.1. The Chaplin Family.

well. Sydney reproached Charlie and touchingly recalled the misery they had endured together: "Since Mother's illness, all we have in the world is each other. So you must write regularly and let me know that I have a brother" (Chaplin, 1964, p. 82).

From early childhood they had to fend for themselves and move about from place to place—to the workhouse, to an orphanage, and to a series of apartments, having at times to help their mother receive care. Late in life Sydney, who had performed with his brother and then became his manager, wrote to Charlie: "It has always been my unfortunate predicament, or should I say fortunate predicament, to concern myself with your protection? This is the result of my fraternal or rather paternal instinct" (Robinson, 1985, p. 22).

Actually, Charlie Chaplin had another half brother, Wheeler Dryden. Three years younger than Chaplin, Dryden was never mentioned in either of Chaplin's autobiographies. Dryden's father abducted him away from his mother as an infant, and he didn't see Chaplin again until 1918, 26 years later, at which point Wheeler had to make many efforts to reconnect before Chaplin would even see or speak to him. Chaplin apparently got him to agree not to acknowledge their brotherhood, possibly to protect their mother's memory, as Chaplin does not mention that Sydney had a different father either. In later years Dryden worked for Chaplin and was a more than devoted follower. He seems to have totally revered his brother, following him around from a deferential distance, saving every scrap of memorabilia about him.

The extraordinary Bronte family (see page 62 for genogram), discussed in Chapter 3, also provides a touching illustration of the power of sibling relationships to compensate when other relationships are problematic in a family (Genogram 7.2). Charlotte Bronte once wrote: "The value of sisters' affections to each other: there is nothing like it in this world." The Brontes also showed an incredible creativity in the face of limitations in the roles allowed to women. The three sisters, Charlotte, Emily, and Anne, became one another's primary support. If they had not had each other in this way, the world might not have had the remarkable literature this sisterhood created.

Their mother died very early, leaving the children reliant on one another. When the two oldest sisters died, Charlotte, age 10, became leader and caretaker, the functional oldest. It was she who invented racy and dangerous games and who, in later years, became the primary spokesperson for the family, encouraging her sisters to write and publish and handling all family business with the outside world.

Branwell, the only son, was a year younger than Charlotte. The family "genius and prodigy," Branwell was the focus of parental energy, scheduled

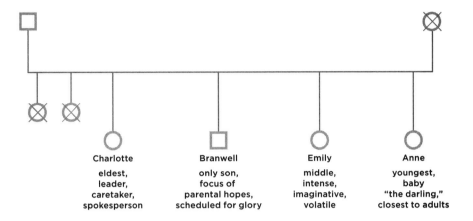

Genogram 7.2. The Bronte Family.

for glory but unable to live up to family expectations. The two younger sisters, Emily and Anne, although a year and a half apart in age, grew up almost like twins in closeness, though in personality they were very different. Emily was intense, athletic, often in a bad temper, and her imagination knew no restraint. Anne, the baby, was less drawn into her imagination than her older siblings, hiding a deep sadness behind a gentle exterior. The roles the Bronte sisters played are common sister roles: Charlotte, the director and social organizer, whose dramatic imagination directed the play of the other children; Emily, the isolationist, the stubborn, independent one; and Anne, the darling, the sweet one, an infant when the tragedy of the mother's death occurred and the one to grow up with the deepest attachment to an adult, her aunt Elizabeth, who came to care for them. It was said of the other siblings that they believed only in the reality of childhood, whereas Anne retained a skepticism about their romantic fantasies.

Twins

The ultimate shared sibling experience is between identical twins. They have a special relationship that is exclusive of the rest of the family. Twins have been known to develop their own language and maintain an uncanny, almost telepathic sense of each other. Even fraternal twins often have remarkable similarities because of their shared life experiences.

The major challenge for twins is to develop individual identities. Because they do not have their own unique sibling position, there is a tendency to lump twins together. This becomes a problem especially when, as adolescents, they are trying to develop their separate identities. Sometimes twins have to go to extremes to distinguish themselves from each other.

Esther Pauline Friedman and Pauline Esther Friedman, identical twins, better known as Ann Landers and "Dear Abby" (Genogram 7.3), were born 17 minutes apart on July 4, 1918 (see further discussion in Chapter 8, pages 299–300). With almost identical names, these famous twins demonstrate both the extremes of shared closeness and the intense, bitter competition of siblings. At times the bond between them was so strong that even their husbands felt like outsiders, but when the rivalry got too intense, they went for years without speaking. Despite these cutoffs, the sisters followed almost identical life paths in an uncanny way, each pursuing exactly the same course as housewife-turned-advice-columnist. When they came together again, it was in some ways as if they had never been apart.

The twins did not begin to separate until the question of marriage arose. Interestingly, both women were attracted to the same man. It was Abby who won out, and when she decided to marry, Ann found herself another groom so they could marry in a joint wedding. She even switched partners midway through the wedding plans when the first marital choice did not work out, and lined up a new mate in time for the double wedding with her twin sister. The two husbands were even connected, working in the same business organization for many years.

After the wedding the two couples left together for a double honeymoon. Unfortunately for Ann, her husband ran out of money midway through the trip, and the twins were forced to part. From this point on their lives began to diverge, although the closeness and the competition continued.

Some years later, bored with being a housewife and without work experience or a college degree to back her up (although both sisters had written for the same college newspaper!), Ann talked her way into becoming the writer of the Ann Landers advice column. Initially she called on her sister for help, but in less than 3 months Abby had moved to the West Coast and was involved with her very similar Dear Abby advice column. She had exactly the same lack of credentials. The competition now began in earnest, and an extraordinary rivalry soon developed, with questions even being raised about one plagiarizing the other—so similar was their work. Abby became widely syndicated, which rankled Ann, who had had the idea first. Over the years, including many years of total cutoff, the two sisters were both extraordinarily successful. Not surprisingly, their public did not always find it easy to distinguish them, as their opinions about real-life problems were so similar. In one

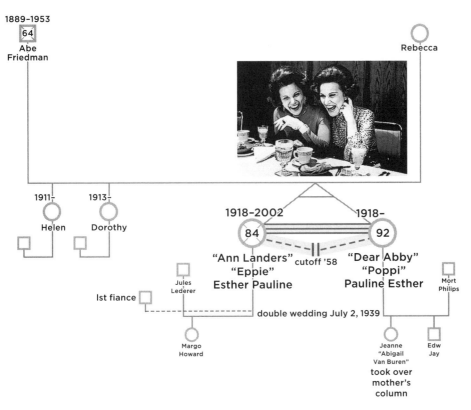

1889–1953
64
Abe
Friedman

Rebecca

1911   1913

Helen   Dorothy

1918–2002   1918–
84   92

"Ann Landers" cutoff '58   "Dear Abby"
"Eppie"   "Poppi"
Esther Pauline   Pauline Esther

Jules
Lederer

1st fiance

Mort
Philips

double wedding July 2, 1939

Margo
Howard

Jeanne
"Abigail
Van Buren"
took over
mother's
column

Edw
Jay

Both sisters loved Mort; Eppie met Jules while buying wedding dress for 1st fiance, but kept date for double wedding. Picture shows reconciliation meeting for 25th anniversary.

Genogram 7.3. The Landers Family.

area, they did disagree. Abby said she thought being a twin was marvelous. Ann said it was not easy.

Sisters

Sisters generally have been treated differently from brothers in families. The Wright brothers' father, Bishop Wright, for example, wrote to his youngest child and only daughter, then 15: "You have a good mind and good heart, and being my only daughter, you are my hope of love and care, if I live to be old. . . . But for you we should feel like we had no home" (Crouch, 1989, p. 87).

Katharine Wright was even called "Schwesterchen" (little sister), defining her primary role even in her nickname. Although both parents and all the children except Wilbur and Orville attended college, Katharine was the only one who went to Oberlin, where her work was outstanding. After college, however, she returned and obediently took on the role of caretaker for her father and brothers, devoting herself to them for the next 30 years. We can only wonder about the price the Wright family and other families have paid in the lost talents of their daughters.

There are many reasons for the complexity of sister relationships: the familial bonds, the length of these relationships, the caretaking responsibilities sisters share, and their competitiveness for male attention and approval. There is also a special intricacy and intimacy in sister relationships. It is almost as if women see in their sisters a reflection of aspects of themselves, while viewing men from a greater distance, often very great distance. Women are led by that distance and by the patriarchal power structure to romanticize and idealize men. On the other hand, women's response to women, and to sisters in particular, is often influenced by their closeness and by sharing the culture's general devaluation of female characteristics.

Much of our literature has denied the sharing of sister relationships. As Louise Bernikow (1980) pointed out, if we think of the most famous sisters in literature—Rachel and Leah in the Old Testament, Cordelia and her sisters in *King Lear*, Cinderella and her "wicked" stepsisters, or Chekhov's *Three Sisters*—a man always between the sisters, who are not supportive of each other. And mothers are hardly mentioned at all, unless divisively, as in *Cinderella*. Older sisters in literature are usually depicted as evil, whereas the youngest is "Daddy's girl," the infantilized baby and favorite, receiving Daddy's love and wealth in return for her loyalty and willingness to be his "love object." The price she pays of conflict with her mother and sisters and loss of their affection is overlooked. As Bernikow said:

They do each other no good, these female siblings, if the stories are to be believed. One would be better off without them. In this masculine vision, all women would be better off without other women, for the woman alone, motherless, sisterless, friendless—can fix her eyes solely on father, brother, lover, and therefore peace will reign in the universe. (Bernikow, 1980, p. 77)

Our parents usually die a generation before we do, and our children live on for a generation after us. It is rare that our spouses are closely acquainted with us during our first 20 or 30 years, or for friendships to last from earliest childhood until the end of our lives. Thus our siblings share more of our lives genetically and contextually than anyone else, and sisters even more, as sisters tend to be emotionally more connected and live longer than brothers. In fact, we can divorce a spouse much more finally than a sibling.

Luckily it is rare for siblings to break off their relationship or lose touch completely with each other. Sister pairs tend to have the closest relationships of all, often providing a basic feeling of emotional security in life. Sisters can provide role models for successful aging, widowhood, bereavement, and retirement. They act as caretakers and exert pressure on each other to maintain their values.

Sisters not only do more caretaking but also tend to share more intimacy and have more intense relationships, as well as more family responsibility, although they typically get less glory than brothers. From childhood on, most sibling caretaking is delegated to older sisters, with brothers freed for play or other tasks. In the classic story of childhood, *Peter Pan*, the only sister, Wendy, is immediately inducted into the role of mother, not only for her own brothers but also for Peter Pan and all the "lost boys."

As noted earlier, it is important in exploring the life choices of the women in a family to take into account the constraints of the particular time and culture in which these choices were made. A woman who wanted to avoid a move made necessary by her husband's job in order to remain near her sister was, until recently, considered strange indeed. She would probably be labeled "enmeshed" or "undifferentiated." And yet it is the sister who was there at the beginning, before the husband, and who will most likely be there at the end, after he is gone. In fact, a strong sense of sisterhood seems to strengthen a woman's sense of self.

Historically, the "weak" or "ill" roles sisters may have sometimes played have been a type of rebellion. Emily Bronte and Elizabeth Barrett Browning, for example, seem to have used their illness as a way to avoid conventional social behavior. Both had brothers for whom the father had extremely strong expectations, and both lost sisters and their mothers at an early age, which probably increased their conflict as strong women who by temperament could not accommodate the role prescribed for women.

In early childhood sisters are often caretakers of one another and of their brothers, as well as rivals and competitors for parental attention. Parents may, with the best of intentions, have conveyed very different messages to their sons than to their daughters. Here, for example, is a description by Jackie Robinson of his daughter, Sharon, the middle child between two brothers (Genogram 7.4), and of the role of his wife, who had had the same sibling constellation. Robinson himself was a youngest brother cared for by his next-older sister, Willa May, not by any of his three older brothers.

> She was just such an ideal and perfect child in our eyes and in the opinion of virtually everyone who came in touch with her that she sometimes seemed a little too good to be true. While fathers may be crazy about their sons, there is something extraordinarily special about a daughter. It's still the same—our relationship—perhaps even deeper. . . . Rachel had been brought up with the same family pattern—a girl in the middle of two boys. She was the busy, loving, but not necessarily always happy, mainstay of her family, who took care of her younger brother. With a kind of grim amusement, I recall our assumption that Sharon was strong enough to cope well with whatever she was confronted with. We took her development for granted for many years. She rarely signaled distress or called attention to her problems by being dramatic. (Robinson, 1972, p. 124)

In certain cultures, such as Italian and Latino, daughters are more likely to be raised to take care of others, including their brothers. Some cultural groups, such as Irish and African-American families, may, for various historical reasons, tend to overprotect sons and underprotect their daughters. Other cultural groups have less specific expectations. Anglos, for example, are more likely to believe in brothers and sisters having equal chores. But, in general, it is important to notice how gender roles influence sibling patterns in understanding a family.

Sisters of sisters tend to have very different sibling patterns than sisters of brothers because of our society's strong preference for sons. If the brother is older, he is often idolized and catered to. If the brother is younger, he may be envied and resented by the sister for his special status. Brothers and sisters can grow up in completely different cultures in the same households.

Because women tend to be so central in maintaining the emotional rela-

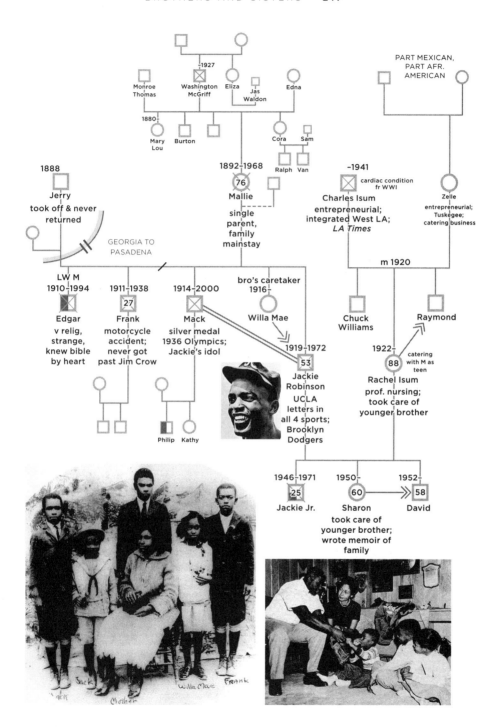

Genogram 7.4. The Robinson Family.

tionships in a family, sisters may focus their disappointments on each other or on their sisters-in-law, more than on their brothers, who are often treated as superior but not responsible for support when caretaking is required. Brothers may be expected to give financial support, but their work often provides an excuse for their lack of actual participation, whereas for sisters neither family commitments nor even work commitments are seen as an excuse for not taking responsibility for the needs of others.

Older women are especially likely to rely on their sisters, as well as their daughters and even their nieces, for support. Often they even live together. Sisters are the ones most often turned to by older widows, more often than are children, even when they live at a distance. Thus siblings, especially sisters, take on added significance for widows as confidantes, caretakers, and friends. Having a relationship with a sister stimulates elderly women to remain socially engaged with others as well. Although the relationships of sisters tend to be invisible in the value structure of the culture at large, sisters tend to sustain one another in time of need throughout life. In old age they may become indispensable. As Margaret Mead described it:

> Sisters draw closer together and often, in old age, they become each other's chosen and most happy companions. In addition to their shared memories of childhood and their relationships to each other's children, they share memories of the same house, the same homemaking style, and the same small prejudices about housekeeping. (Mead, 1972, p. 70)

Mead's comment is interesting in its focus on details. Especially as we grow older, it is the details—of our memories, of our housekeeping, or of our relationships with one another and with one another's families—that may hold us together.

The oldest sister can hardly avoid becoming the surrogate mother to her younger siblings. Margaret Mead herself (see page 318 for genogram), who was followed by a brother and then by three sisters, described having been enlisted by her grandmother (who lived with them) to take notes on her younger sisters' behavior:

> I learned to make these notes with love, carrying on what Mother had begun. I knew that she had filled thirteen notebooks on me and only four on Richard; now I was taking over for the younger children. In many ways I thought of the babies as my children, whom I could observe and teach and cultivate. I also wanted to give them everything I missed. (Mead, 1972, p. 64)

Unlike oldest sons, who typically have a clear feeling of entitlement, oldest daughters often have feelings of ambivalence and guilt about their responsibilities. Whatever they do, they feel it is not quite enough, and they can never let up in their efforts to caretake and make the family work right.

Birth Order

The oldest child's experience is very different from that of the youngest, and middle children have their own unique experience. Although birth order can profoundly influence later experiences with spouses, friends, and colleagues, a particular birth order does not guarantee a particular type of person. There are many other factors that influence sibling roles, such as temperament, disability, looks, intelligence, talent, gender, and the timing of each birth in relation to other family experiences—deaths, moves, illnesses, changes in financial status, and so on.

For these and other reasons, parents may have a particular agenda for a specific child, such as expecting him or her to be the responsible one or the "baby," regardless of that child's position in the family. Children who resemble a certain family member may be expected to be like that person or to take on that person's role. Children's temperaments may also be at odds with their sibling position. This may explain why some children struggle so valiantly against family expectations—the oldest who refuses to take on the responsibility of the caretaker or family standard bearer, or the youngest who strives to be a leader. In some families, it will be the child most comfortable with the responsibility—not necessarily the oldest child—who becomes the leader. Parents' own sibling experiences will affect their children as well. But certain typical patterns that reflect each child's birth order often occur.

Oldest Sons and Daughters

In general, oldest children are likely to be the overresponsible and conscientious ones in the family. They make good leaders, as they have experienced authority over and responsibility for younger siblings. Often serious, they may feel they have a mission in life. In identifying with their parents and being especially favored by them, they tend to be conservative even while leading others into new worlds, and although they may be self-critical, they do not necessarily handle criticism from others well.

We have already noted in Chapter 5 the specialness of Sigmund Freud's family position (see page 172 for genogram) in relation to the surrounding deaths of his paternal grandfather, two older half siblings, the infant brother who followed him, and a maternal uncle. Other factors influencing Freud's special position in his family include the fact that shortly after his birth the family developed financial problems, which forced them to migrate from their home in Bohemia to Vienna, after which time the father never seems to have had a secure financial base again. Sigmund's prerogative in relation to his five younger sisters and brother was astounding. The household was organized around his needs. He was the only one of the children who had a special space set aside for him to work. The family story goes that when his sister Anna wanted to play the piano, their mother bought one but immediately got rid of it because Sigmund complained that the noise bothered him. That was the end of the sister's music education! As in many cultures, the Freuds favored their son over their daughters. Sigmund's special position was further demonstrated when the family gave him the privilege at the age of 10 of naming his younger brother, whom he named after his hero Alexander the Great.

Sigmund apparently did not think much of his siblings, particularly his sisters. He once said to his younger brother Alexander: "Our family is like a book. You and I are the first and last of the children, so, we are like the strong covers that have to support and protect the weak girls who were born after me and before you" (Eissler, 1978, p. 59). More significantly, he did not mention his siblings once in his autobiographical writings about his own development. So it is not surprising that sibling patterns play no role in his psychological theories. He did, however, mention his nephew, John, 2 years older than he, who for the first few years of Sigmund's life was like a brother:

> Until the end of my third year we had been inseparable; we had loved each other and fought each other and . . . this childish relationship has determined all my later feelings of intercourse with persons my own age. My nephew, John, has since had many incarnations, which have revived first one and then another aspect of character and is ineradicably fixed in my conscious memory. At times he must have treated me very badly and I must have opposed my tyrant courageously. (Jones, 1953, p. 8)

Children often have more intense feelings about a slightly older sibling than a younger one. Sigmund Freud was never to have a true equal again. In later life he became a powerful leader, but, as is so often the case with firstborns, he had difficulty sharing the stage with colleagues who would not accept his leadership in every idea, bringing about a falling out with most of his followers (Adler, Jung, Stekel, Ferenczi, and others) as soon as they challenged him.

A major characteristic of the oldest is liking to lead others and assume responsibility for them, working hard to elevate the group to an elite position. George Washington, our first president (Genogram 7.5), is an outstanding

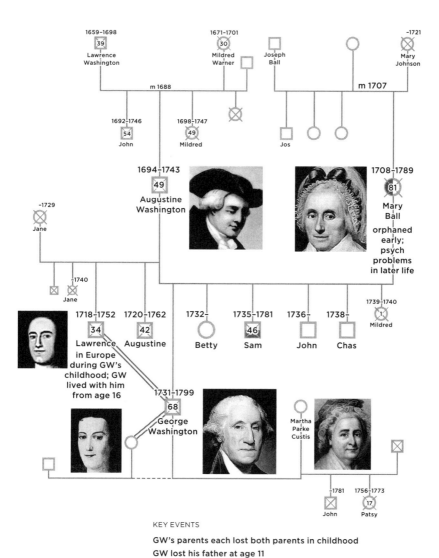

KEY EVENTS

GW's parents each lost both parents in childhood
GW lost his father at age 11
Then lost Lawrence, his "father replacement" at age 20

Genogram 7.5. The Washington Family.

example of this. Like Freud, Washington had two much older half brothers who were educated abroad and whom he did not get to know until adolescence, when Lawrence, the eldest, became his guardian after their father's death. Lawrence was in his mid-twenties and George was not yet in his teens. Washington's leadership ability was surely a major factor in the formation of the United States. At the age of 20 Washington joined the Virginia militia and quickly distinguished himself, becoming commander in chief of all Virginia forces by the age of 23. He had a seemingly miraculous ability to lead his men into battle and emerge unscathed. A brilliant leader, he kept a single-minded focus on his objectives and his obligation to duty, regardless of the sacrifices involved.

Washington's leadership skill, determination, and sense of responsibility were undoubtedly intensified by his father's sudden death when he was only 11, which left him responsible for his mother and four younger siblings. As just mentioned, George's older half brother, Lawrence, returned from abroad and became George's guardian and mentor. Unfortunately, Lawrence died just a few years later, when George was only 20, which left him even more alone in his role as family leader. Though he could never have children of his own, he became a devoted stepfather to his wife Martha's two children and to numerous other relatives, whom he supported, mentored, or even raised. As a brother, he was caring and responsible. He wrote of one of his own brothers late in life: "I have just buried a Brother [John] who was the intimate companion of my youth, and the friend of my ripened age" (Bourne, 1982, p. 111).

Being the firstborn can be a mixed blessing. As the answer to parents' dreams and as a beginning of a new family, the firstborn may receive an intensity of interest and devotion denied to the children that follow. But the burden may be heavy. Even when firstborns explicitly reject family expectations, uneasiness and guilt may plague them for not living up to their appointed role.

Another typical oldest was Che Guevara, the responsible oldest of five children (Genogram 7.6). Like George Washington, Che was a natural leader. It is, perhaps, no wonder that he became a hero of the guerilla revolutions in Cuba and South America. He was carrying out the role of the oldest, adhering to his parents' socialist and revolutionary values. They were exceptionally radical, dynamic, and open-minded, and in his radicalism Che was not rebelling against them but following in the family's footsteps. Che grew up surrounded by people emotionally involved with the Spanish Republican cause. He had a passion for justice and, as a classmate said of him, was mature for his age, "incredibly sure of himself and totally independent in his opinions" (Sinclair, 1970, p. 2). He took on difficulties as challenges, never complaining; though he had serious asthma all his life, he became an athlete and a tireless and daring traveler. He finished his 6-year medical program in 3 years. One biographer described him as seeming "to feel responsible for all the world's injustices." All these are typical characteristics of an oldest: mature for his age, super-responsible, uncomplaining, and a striver. In a way very similar to George Washington at the battle of Trenton, Che drew strength from his early failure in Guatemala to prepare and rise again for his next effort. This

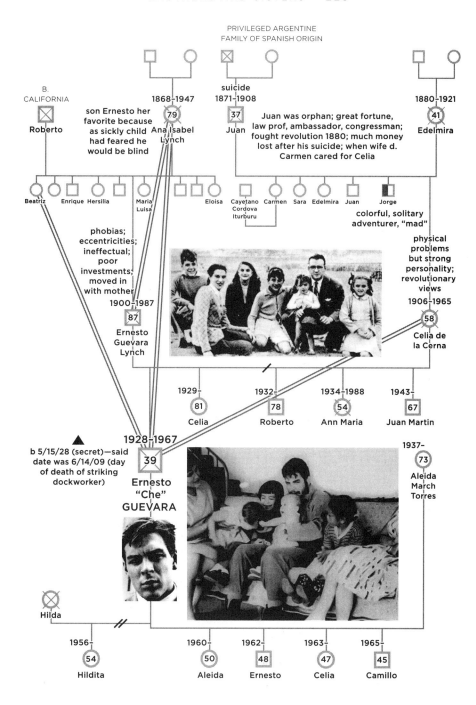

PRIVILEGED ARGENTINE
FAMILY OF SPANISH ORIGIN

B.
CALIFORNIA

Roberto

son Ernesto her
favorite because
as sickly child
had feared he
would be blind

1868–1947

79

Ana Isabel
Lynch

suicide
1871–1908

37

Juan

Juan was orphan; great fortune,
law prof, ambassador, congressman;
fought revolution 1880; much money
lost after his suicide; when wife d.
Carmen cared for Celia

1880–1921

41

Edelmira

Beatriz   Enrique   Hersilia   Maria
Luisa

Eloisa   Cayetano   Carmen   Sara   Edelmira   Juan   Jorge
Cordova
Iturburu

colorful, solitary
adventurer, "mad"

phobias;
eccentricities;
ineffectual;
poor
investments;
moved in
with mother

physical
problems
but strong
personality;
revolutionary
views

1900–1987

87

Ernesto
Guevara
Lynch

1906–1965

58

Celia de
la Cerna

1929–

81

Celia

1932–

78

Roberto

1934–1988

54

Ann Maria

1943–

67

Juan Martin

▲   1928–1967

b 5/15/28 (secret)—said
date was 6/14/09 (day
of death of striking
dockworker)

39

Ernesto
"Che"
GUEVARA

1937–

73

Aleida
March
Torres

Hilda

1956–

54

Hildita

1960–

50

Aleida

1962–

48

Ernesto

1963–

47

Celia

1965–

45

Camillo

Genogram 7.6. The Guevara Family.

confidence is also typical of an oldest, who can lead others against all odds, but with great and disciplined effort, not just bravado. He was also the beloved firstborn son of his talented mother, whose own brilliant and talented father had committed suicide after business losses, leaving her an orphan cared for by her oldest sister, but with a legacy of great thwarted hopes and possibilities, which she undoubtedly passed down to her firstborn son.

The oldest daughter often has the same sense of responsibility, conscientiousness, and ability to care for and lead others. However, daughters generally do not receive the same privileges, nor are there generally the same expectations to excel. Thus, they may be saddled with the responsibilities of the oldest child without receiving the privileges or enhanced self-esteem. When siblings are all female, oldest sisters may have certain privileges and expectations that would otherwise go to sons.

The Youngest Child

The youngest child often has a sense of specialness, which allows self-indulgence without the burdening sense of responsibility felt by the oldest. This pattern may be more intense the more siblings there are in a family. The younger of two probably has more a sense of "pairing" and twinship—unless there is a considerable age differential—than the youngest of ten. Freed from convention and determined to do things his or her own way, the youngest child can sometimes make remarkable creative leaps leading to inventions and innovations, as in the examples of Thomas Edison, Benjamin Franklin, Marie Curie, Jackie Robinson, and Paul Robeson.

Thomas Alva Edison, a youngest son (Genogram 7.7), invented the phonograph, the microphone, the motion picture camera and projector, the typewriter, and the light bulb, made the telephone practical, and devised more than 1100 other inventions. He very much followed his own path in life. Like another famous youngest, Benjamin Franklin, Edison left home in adolescence. Also like Franklin, Edison's special position may have been reinforced by the early childhood death of two older siblings, and a third at the age of 5. Besides being a youngest child, Edison came from a long line of independent, stubborn, ambitious, determined individualists. His great-grandfather, John Edison, was forced into exile at the time of the Revolutionary War because of his Tory allegiance. His grandfather was voted out of the Baptist church for ridiculing and refusing to obey its rules. His father had to flee back to the United States after participating in a rebellion against the Canadian government. Edison, too, was an individualist, and an amazing innovator as well, despite (or, some have argued, because of) only having 6 months of formal education.

In adult life Edison was eccentric. He dressed in baggy, shabby clothes,

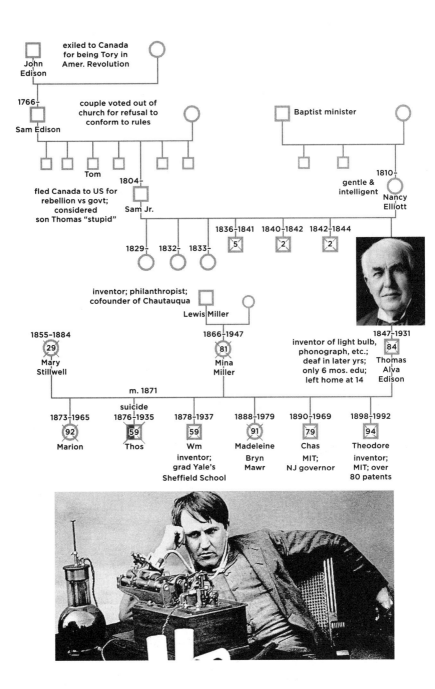

Genogram 7.7. The Edison Family.

although eventually he was a multimillionaire, he slept little and worked incessantly, and he was curious about everything. He developed into an extraordinarily good businessman, rewarding ingenuity and hard work but caring little for bureaucratic regularity. His concern about money was purely for the freedom it allowed him, a typical attitude among youngest sons.

Other general characteristics of youngest children are readily apparent. Because the youngest has older siblings who have often served as caretakers, he or she is more used to being a follower than a leader. The youngest may remain the "baby," a focus of attention for all who came before, expecting others to be helpful and supportive. Youngest children may feel freer to deviate from convention. Youngests may even feel compelled to escape from being the "baby," which may cause a rebellion, as with Edison and Franklin, who both ran away in adolescence.

Given their special position as the center of attention, youngest children may think they can accomplish anything. The youngest may feel more carefree, more content to have fun rather than achieve. Less plagued by selfdoubt, they are often extremely creative, willing to try what others would not even consider. They can also be spoiled and self-absorbed, and their sense of entitlement leads at times to frustration and disappointment. In addition, the youngest often has a period as an only child after the older siblings have left home. This can be an opportunity to enjoy the sole attention of parents, but can also lead to feelings of abandonment by the siblings.

Often the youngest child would rather be liked than right. John Adams, a good and typical oldest son, saw Benjamin Franklin (see page 36 for genogram), the youngest son of two youngests and the last of five generations of youngest sons, as too amused by frivolous pleasures and remaining noncommittal so that everyone would like him: "Although he has as determined a soul as any man, yet it is his constant policy never to say yes or no decidedly, but when he cannot avoid it" (Van Doren, 1938, p. 600). Franklin was indeed self-indulgent and rather underresponsible, particularly when it came to his family. He left his fiancée (who later became his wife) to go to England, writing to her only once in a whole year, and was later negligent of the feelings and needs of his wife and daughter, leaving them for years at a time for his social life of diplomacy abroad.

Like many youngest children, Benjamin Franklin was a rebel. He lived his life as an iconoclast, fighting the conventions that did not make sense to him. A major figure in the Revolutionary War, he was still a major force for change at the age of 81, when he became a primary framer and signer of the U.S. Constitution, a most remarkably unconventional document. He was not so much a leader of men as an indirect influencer of events, negotiating through diplomacy and guiding through his brilliance.

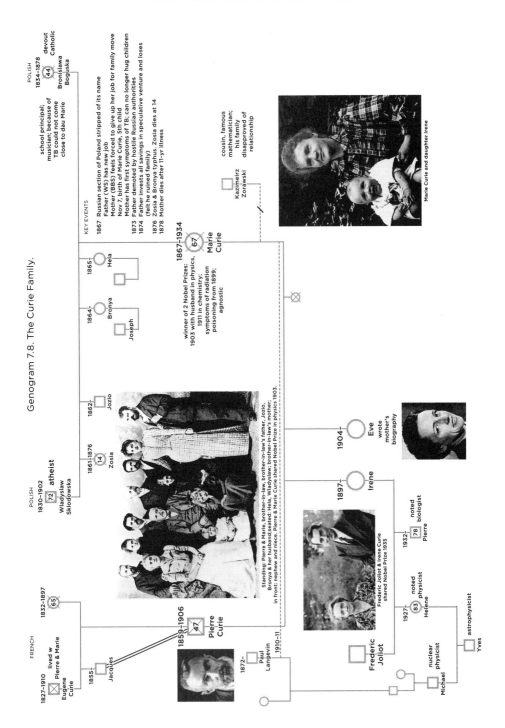

Genogram 7.8. The Curie Family.

KEY EVENTS

1867 Russian section of Poland stripped of its name
Father (WS) has new job
Mother (BBS) feels forced to give up her job for family move
Nov 7, birth of Marie Curie, 5th child
Mother has first symptoms of TB; can no longer hug children
1873 Father demoted by hostile Russian authorities
1874 Father invests all savings in speculative venture and loses
(felt he ruined family)
1876 Zosia & Bronya typhus. Zosia dies at 14
1878 Mother dies after 11-yr illness

POLISH
1834–1878
44
Bronisława
Boguska
devout
Catholic

school principal;
musician; because of
TB could not come
close to dau Marie

Kazimeirz
Zorawski
cousin, famous
mathematician;
his family
disapproved of
relationship

Marie Curie and daughter Irene

POLISH
1830–1902
72   atheist
Wladyslaw
Sklodowska

1861–1876
14
Zosia

1862–
Jozio

1864–
Bronya

Joseph

1865–
Hela

1867–1934
67
Marie
Curie

winner of 2 Nobel Prizes:
1903 with husband in physics.
1911 in chemistry;
symptoms of radiation
poisoning from 1899;
agnostic

FRENCH
1827–1910
Eugene
Curie
lived w
Pierre & Marie
Curie

1832–1897
65

Jacques
1855–

1859–1906
47
Pierre
Curie

Standing: Pierre & Marie, brother-in-law's father, Jozio,
Bronya & her husband; seated: Hela, Wladyslaw, brother-in-law's mother;
in front: nephew and niece. Pierre & Marie Curie shared Nobel Prize in physics 1903.

Paul
Langevin
1872–

1910–11

1897–
Irene

1904–
Eve

wrote
mother's
biography

Frederic
Joliot

Frederic Joliot & Irene Curie
shared Nobel Prize 1935

Helene
1927–
83   noted
physicist

Pierre
1932–
78   noted
biologist

Michael
nuclear
physicist

Yves
astrophysicist

A younger sister tends to be protected, showered with affection, and handed a blueprint for life. She may either be spoiled (more so if there are older brothers) and have special privileges or, if she is from a large family, be frustrated by always having to wait her turn. Her parents may have just run out of energy with her. She may feel resentful of being bossed around and never taken quite seriously. If she is the only girl, the youngest may be more like the princess, and yet the servant to elders, becoming, perhaps, the confidante to her brothers in adult life and the one to replace the parents in holding the family together.

Marie Curie (Genogram 7.8), the only person ever to receive two Nobel prizes (for her research on radiation), was another extraordinary youngest. Born Marie Sklodowska in Poland in 1867, the last of five children (with one brother and three sisters, the oldest of whom died in childhood), Marie showed an independence and lack of concern for convention from childhood onwards. Determined to follow her own path, she was perhaps the extreme noncaretaker, a common characteristic of youngest children. Like Edison, who paid no attention whatsoever to his clothing or surroundings, Marie Curie pursued her interest in science to the extreme. Shortly after she went to France to study, she was found unconscious on the street, weak from starvation, because she was too preoccupied with her work to bother with food.

What happens when two youngests get together is easy to imagine, as with Marie Curie and her husband Pierre, who was also a youngest. Neither Marie nor Pierre had any interest in housekeeping, what they ate, or how it was prepared. The story goes that when they were first married, Marie, in an effort to develop domestic skills, tried to learn to cook. One night after having made a great effort to prepare and serve a chop, she asked Pierre how he had liked it. He responded in absentminded astonishment, "But I haven't tasted it yet," before noticing he had just eaten the whole thing (Pflaum, 1989, p. 56). Neither spouse had any interest in their appearance, only in science. They could live a totally Spartan existence. Science filled every moment and Marie was oblivious to everything else. She pursued science with no interest in or ambition for success or honor, much less to lead others; her motivation instead was to answer her inner questions. Einstein once said of her that she was "of all celebrated beings, the only one whom fame has not corrupted" (Curie, 1939, p. xi). Her younger daughter, Eve, who wrote her biography, described her as remaining to her last day "just as gentle, stubborn, timid and curious about all things as in the days of her obscure beginnings" (Curie, 1939, p. xi).

Paul Robeson (Genogram 7.9), another brilliant and creative youngest, was the multitalented star in his African American family. An outstand-

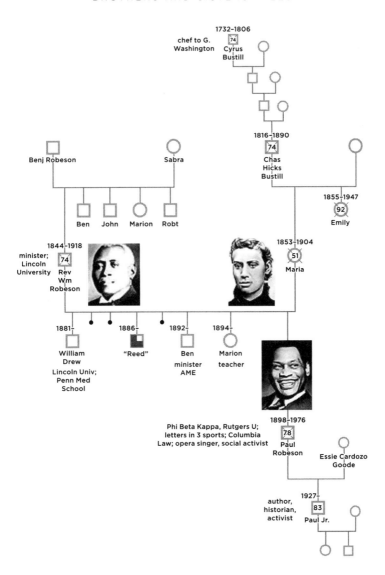

Genogram 7.9. The Robeson Family.

ing athlete in every sport, Phi Beta Kappa in college, lawyer turned world-famous singer and actor and then political speaker, Robeson was deeply aware of the importance to him of each of his siblings in his life. He said everyone lavished an extra measure of affection on him and saw him as some kind of "child of destiny . . . linked to the longed-for better days to come" (Robeson, 1988, p. 16). This is a common role for a youngest, especially when the family has experienced hard times. The oldest Robeson brother,

William Drew, was named for the father and followed in the father's footsteps, attending the same college, Lincoln, before going to medical school. According to Robeson, William was the most brilliant of the children and the one who taught him to study. William Drew never reached his potential, however, largely because of racism. Reed, the next brother, also brilliant but too overtly angry to survive easily as an African American in their community, became the "lost" middle child, though Paul felt he learned the quality of toughness from this brother. The third son, Ben, became an outstanding athlete and role model for Paul. He became a successful minister like the father. The fourth child and the only girl, Marion, became a teacher, like the mother, and was noted for her warm spirit. For Paul, Reed, Ben, and Marion—the three middle children and those closest to him in age—all played out variations of the middle-child role. Ben and Marion were "reserved in speech, strong in character, living up to their principles— and always selflessly devoted to their younger brother" (p. 13). This support was all the more important because their mother died tragically in a fire when Paul was only 5. Ben and Marion were willing to do without the limelight and to facilitate the relationships of others.

There were lessons also from Reed, who carried a little bag of stones for self-protection, should he encounter a dangerous situation. Robeson admired this "rough" older brother and learned from him a quick response to racial insults and abuse. Robeson had a special feeling for this middle brother, who did not live up to the father's high expectations for his children. Robeson later wrote:

> He won no honors in classroom, pulpit or platform. Yet I remember him with love. Restless, rebellious, scoffing at conventions, defiant of the white man's law. I've known many Negroes like Reed. I see them every day. Blindly, in their own reckless manner, they seek a way out for themselves; alone, they pound with their fists and fury against walls that only the shoulders of many can topple. . . . When . . . everything will be different . . . the fiery ones like Reed will be able to live out their lives in peace and no one will have cause to frown upon them. (Robeson, 1988, p. 14)

Although Reverend Robeson disapproved of Reed's carefree and undisciplined ways and eventually made him leave for his scrapes with the law, Reed, like many middle children, may have expressed feelings that others did not have the courage to express, in his case the rage against racism. Paul saw Reed as having taught him to stand up for himself. In the famous biographical play written about Robeson, he says there was one conversation he and his father could never finish. Remembering the night his father turned Reed out, fearing he would set a bad example for his younger brother, Paul imagines getting together with his father and brother Ben to go looking for Reed and bring him home. He imagines defending Reed to his father:

> Aw Pop, don't change the subject. . . . Reed was not a bad influence. Only horrible thing he said to me was, "Kid, you talk too much." All he ever told me to do was to stand up and be a man. "Don't take low from anybody, and if they hit you, hit 'em back harder." I know what the Bible says, Pop, but Reed was your son too! You always said you saw yourself in me. Pop, you were in all your sons. (Dean, 1989 p. 298)

This dramatization eloquently expresses the connectedness between siblings and how much it matters if one is cut off, even though others in the family may not realize it. It also conveys the way middle children may take rebel positions others in the family do not dare to express.

Middle Children

Follower to the oldest and leader to the youngest, middle children are less likely to show extremes. Without the rights and prerogatives of the oldest or the privileges and benefits of the youngest, they often feel somewhat lost and unappreciated, unless the middle child is the only girl or only boy. On the positive side, in intense, highly fused families, the somewhat removed middle child may become the negotiator, the one who avoids getting pulled into the family vortex.

The middle child in a family is "in between," having neither the position of the first as the standard bearer nor of the last as the "baby." Although they run the risk of getting lost in the family, especially if all the siblings are of the same sex, middle children may develop into the best negotiators, more even-tempered and mellow than their more driven older siblings and less self-indulgent than the youngest. They may even relish their invisibility, though they may also become the rebel, like Reed Robeson. Henry Adams (see page 71 for genogram) liked to say he had the good fortune to be born a fourth of seven children, which gave him a status so trifling he could fritter away his life and "never be missed" (O'Toole, 1990, pp. 3–4).

The middle sister is under less pressure to take responsibility, but she needs to try harder to make her mark in general, because she has no special role. She remembers running to catch up with the older sister from childhood, and running frantically from the younger one, who seemed to be gaining on her every minute (Fishel, 1979). The position of middle stimulates competitive feelings and leaves her vulnerable to maladjustment if she cannot find a place to stand.

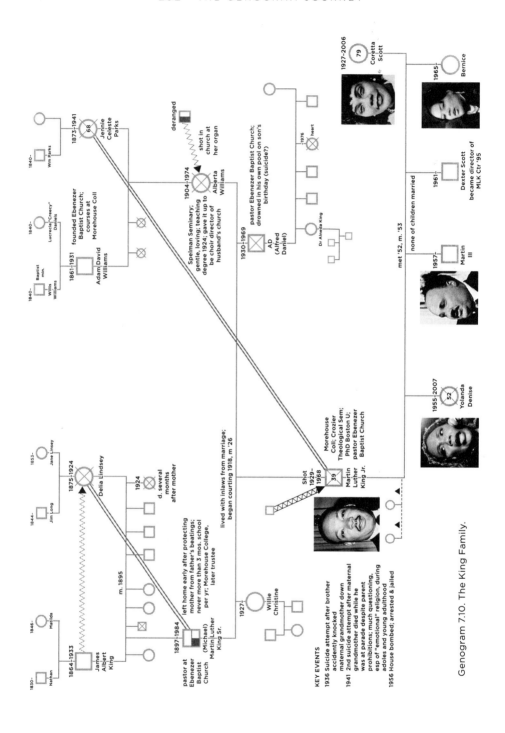

Genogram 7.10. The King Family.

KEY EVENTS

1936 Suicide attempt after brother accidentally knocked maternal grandmother down
1941 2nd suicide attempt after maternal grandmother died while he was at parade despite parent prohibitions; much questioning, esp of "emotional" religion, during adoles and young adulthood
1956 House bombed; arrested & jailed

She is the compromiser, the go-between, and tends to be gregarious and a good negotiator if she can define a middle path, a compromise between extremes.

Martin Luther King (Genogram 7.10) is an example of the best a middle child can be in terms of ability to play multiple roles and bring others together. His brilliant ideas of nonviolent group resistance are a good fit with his middle-sibling position, as siblings in the middle do not have might on their side and the power of joining forces comes naturally to them. Unlike the youngest, who is unlikely to make a good leader, middle children may become excellent leaders because they can draw together multiple factions through collaboration and mediation.

Not surprisingly, middle children may show characteristics typical of oldests or youngests, or both combined. Although the child may escape certain intensities directed at the oldest or the youngest, he or she may have to struggle to be noticed.

Mary Todd Lincoln (Genogram 7.11), the wife of Abraham Lincoln, was a middle child who sought recognition all her life. She was the third daughter in the large Todd family. Her father was the third son, "lost" among 12 children, who became a restless and often absent parent. Her mother was also a middle child, timid and unassertive. When Mary was 11 months old, she was abruptly weaned and lost her place as youngest to a first son. When she was 4, a second younger brother died. At 5 she lost her middle name, Ann, to a younger sister. At 6 her mother died, giving birth to a third brother. By the time she was 7 a new wife absorbed her father's attention.

Nine more children were born to the second family. All Mary's siblings may have felt disoriented in this family drama, but she seems to have been the most affected. Her two older sisters had already formed a strong alliance with each other. Ann, the youngest sister, was the namesake and favorite child of the aunt who took over the family after their mother died until the father remarried. And the two surviving sons held a special place in their father's and uncles' affections.

Thus Mary was the neglected middle child, whose response was a pervasive sense of insecurity. She was extremely vulnerable to slights, rejections, and the sense of being ignored. Not surprisingly, having felt invisible as a child, Mary developed a great determination to be recognized. She was a highly intelligent student, much better educated and socially sophisticated than Lincoln, a superb horsewoman, and an outstanding hostess. She was very ambitious for her husband and played the role of "the woman behind the man." Her husband referred to her as his "child wife" and "mother," suggesting, perhaps, that she vacillated between both roles. Lincoln's opponents criticized Mary for her extravagance, flamboyance, "interference" in

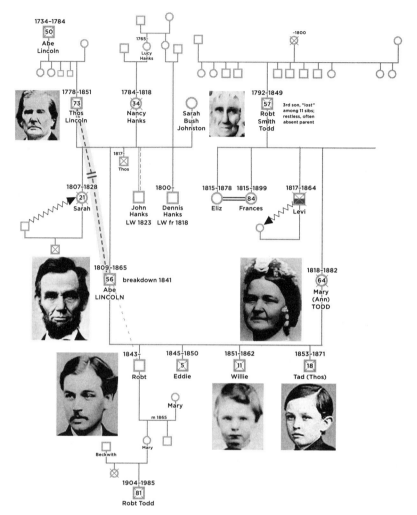

Genogram 7.11. The Lincoln Family.

politics, and unwillingness to accept the passive womanly role, all possible characteristics of a middle child who seeks attention. Later, when she was institutionalized in a mental hospital against her will, she managed to engineer her own release through great efforts to bring others to her cause. This was perhaps the supreme example of the resourcefulness of a middle child.

Only Children

Like middle children, only children show characteristics of both oldests and youngests. In fact, they may show the extremes of both at the same time. They

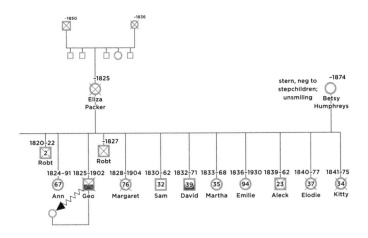

may have the seriousness and sense of responsibility of the oldest and the conviction of specialness and entitlement of the youngest. Not having siblings, only children tend to be more oriented toward adults, seeking their love and approval, and in return expecting their undivided attention. The major challenge for only children is to learn how to get along with others their own age. Only children often maintain very close attachments to their parents throughout their lives but find it more difficult to relate to friends and spouses.

Indira Gandhi (see page 122 for genogram), the second prime minister of India, is an example of an only child who grew up quite isolated and primarily in the presence of older people, becoming her father's confidante early in life. She clearly had the sense of mission and responsibility of an oldest, but as a leader she was autocratic and led a rather isolated existence, keeping her own counsel. Both her father and paternal grandfather were functional only children. Her father, Jawaharlal Nehru, was 11 years older than his next sibling, and the grandfather, Motilal Nehru, also a leader of India, was many years younger than his siblings. He was raised in the home of his adult brother because their father had died before Motilal was born. The illnesses of both Jawaharlal's mother and Indira's mother undoubtedly compounded their independent roles as only children and their connections to each other as father and daughter.

The French philosopher Jean-Paul Sartre (see page 200 for genogram) is another interesting example of an only child. His father died when he was just over a year old and he spent his early childhood with his mother and her parents. All the adult attention of this household became focused on him. By his own account, Sartre was a spoiled and pampered child: "My mother was mine; no one challenged my peaceful possession of her. I knew nothing of violence and hatred. Not having been bruised by its sharp angles, I knew reality only by its bright unsubstantiality. Against whom, against what, would I have rebelled? Never had someone else's whim claimed to be my law" (Sartre, 1964, p. 26).

Trouble began for Sartre at the age of 12, when his mother remarried and he was sent off to school. "He was an irascible, cantankerous, quarrelsome boy, most unpleasant toward his peers," remembered one of his classmates (Cohen-Solal, 1987, p. 45). Sartre's classmates felt only contempt for this pompous, affected child, who was always trying to be the center of attention. At times, he would try to buy friends or impress them by lying or with a spectacular misdeed. He was often beaten up and rarely asked to join the different teenage groups. He spent much of his time alone, creating his own world through his reading and writing. Eventually, Sartre did adapt to his new situation and found a kindred soul in a friend who was also an only child who liked literature and writing stories. He never did lose his sense of self-importance or confidence in his ability to do great things. It is perhaps not surprising that he was one of the founders of a philosophy that focuses on the importance of individual consciousness, the basic existential solitude of humanity, the absurdity of life, and the necessity for each individual to create his or her own reality.

Sibling Position and Marriage

Sibling relationships can often pave the way for good couple relationships—for sharing, interdependence, and mutuality—just as they can predispose partners to jealousy, power struggles, and rivalry. Because siblings are generally our earliest peer relationships, we are likely to be most comfortable in other relationships that reproduce the familiar sibling patterns of birth order and gender. And, generally speaking, marriage seems easiest when partners fit the original sibling pattern—for example, when an oldest marries a youngest, rather than two oldests marrying each other. If a wife has grown up as the oldest of many siblings and the caretaker, she might be attracted to a dominant oldest, who offers to take over management of responsibilities. But as time goes along, she may come to resent his assertion of authority, because by experience she is more comfortable making decisions for herself.

All things being equal (and they seldom are in life!), the ideal marriage based on sibling position would be a complementary one where the husband is the older brother of a younger sister and the wife is the younger sister of an older brother. However, the complementarity of caretaker and someone who needs caretaking, or leader and follower, does not guarantee intimacy or a happy marriage.

In addition to complementary birth order, it seems to help in marriage if one has had siblings of the opposite sex. Most difficult might be the youngest sister of many sisters who marries the youngest brother of many brothers, as neither would have much experience of the opposite sex in a close way, and they might both play "the spoiled child" waiting for a caretaker.

Eleanor Roosevelt, an oldest, and her cousin Franklin (Genogram 7.12), an only, are a good example of two strong-willed spouses whose marriage seems to have survived only because each evolved separate spheres. Leaders in their own separate worlds, they came to live apart except for holidays. Early in the marriage, Eleanor generally subordinated herself to Franklin and to his powerful mother, Sarah Delano, who played a major role in their lives. However, as she became more self-confident and developed interests of her own, she began to show the determination of an oldest. The crisis came when Eleanor discovered letters revealing Franklin's affair with Lucy Mercer. Apparently it was Franklin's mother who negotiated an agreement between them for Eleanor to return to the marriage by offering her son a deal he could not refuse: that if he left his family he would never receive another penny from her (Streitmatter, 1998). Because oldests and only children are oriented to parents, Sara may have been the only one who could have kept them from separating, and she did. The details of the contract she negotiated has been the only document at the Roosevelt archives not available to the public.

The Roosevelts remained married but began to live separate lives, with politics as their common ground. After Franklin's paralysis due to polio, Eleanor became essential to his political career. She nevertheless had her own political views and activities, her own living space in a separate house at Hyde Park, which she shared with her friends, and her own intimate relationships. With a creative ability to master the horrendous experiences of her childhood (discussed earlier), Eleanor managed to make the most of her life. But she did not fail to realize the price she was forced to pay. She later wrote about learning her husband had been elected president:

> I am sure that I was glad for my husband, but it never occurred to me to be much excited. . . . I felt detached and objective, as though I were looking at someone else's life. This seems to have remained with me down to the present day. I cannot quite describe it, but it is as though you lived two lives, one of your own and the other which belonged to the circumstances that surround you. (Asbell, 1982, p. 29)

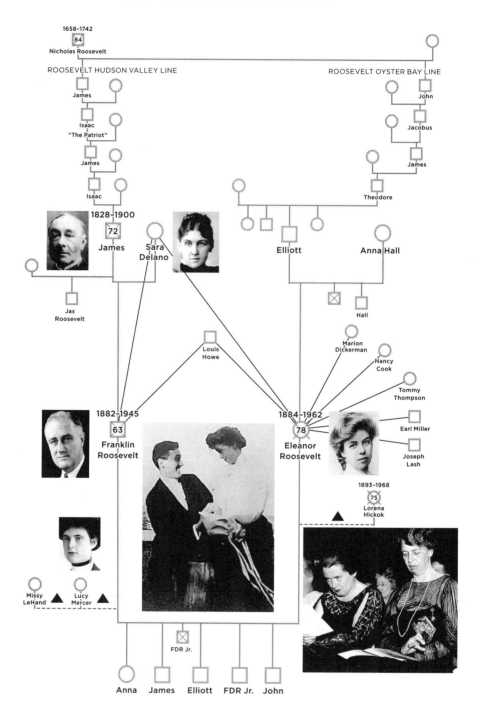

Genogram 7.12. The Roosevelt Family.

Eleanor's description of this experience not only reflects the gender bias, which has for so long required women to give up their own lives for their husbands, but also suggests the creative solution she and Franklin worked out with regard to their difficult dilemma in marriage, probably based in part on their childhood sibling roles. The remarkable thing about Eleanor is how effective she was in creating a life of her own. After Franklin Roosevelt's death in 1945, her career flourished even more, including her assignment as ambassador to the United Nations.

Richard Burton and Elizabeth Taylor, who married and divorced each other twice, provide a dramatic example of two youngest children who competed to be "junior," both seeking a caretaker. Burton was the second youngest of 13 children, but he was treated like a youngest, as he was raised apart from his younger brother. In very large families several of the younger children will often have the characteristics of a youngest. Elizabeth Taylor was the younger of two, with an older brother whose needs were often sacrificed to her stardom, which, of course, solidified her special position. Burton and Taylor were known for their histrionic love quarrels, each outdoing the other in their demanding and childish behavior.

There are, of course, many other possible sibling pairings in marriage. The marriage of two only children might be particularly difficult unless they have separate spheres like the Roosevelts did, as neither partner has the experience of intimate sharing that one does with a brother or sister. Middle children may be the most flexible, as they have experiences with a number of different roles.

When people who have struggled in their sibling position become parents, they may overidentify with a child of the same sex and sibling position as themselves. One father who was an oldest of five felt that he had been burdened with too much responsibility, while his younger brothers and sister "got away with murder." When his own children came along, he spoiled the oldest and tried to make the younger ones toe the line. A mother may find it difficult to sympathize with a youngest daughter if she always felt envious of her younger sister. This was how Simone de Beauvoir (see page 200 for genogram) described the relationship of her mother (the oldest of two sisters) with her and her younger sister:

> Until I began to reach adolescence Maman ascribed to me the loftiest intellectual and moral qualities: she identified herself with me and she humiliated and slighted my sister—Poupette was the younger sister, pink and fair, and without realizing it, Maman was taking her revenge upon her. (de Beauvoir, 1959, p. 33)

Parents may also identify with one particular child because of a resemblance to another family member. Whether these identifications are conscious or unconscious, they are normal. It is a myth that parents can feel the same toward all their children. Feelings depend on each child's characteristics and unique position in the whole family constellation.

Problems arise when the identification is so strong that parents perpetuate their old family patterns or when their own experience is so different that they misread their children. Two sisters may get along quite well, although their mother expects them to fight like cats and dogs the way she and her sister did. A parent who was an only child may tend to assume that normal sibling fights are an indication of serious problems.

Sibling Relationships in Adult Life

Sibling relationships can be a most important connection in adult life, especially in the later years. However, if negative feelings persist, the care of an aging parent may bring on particular difficulty. At such a time siblings may have been apart for years. They may have to work together in new and unfamiliar ways. The child who has remained closest to the parents, usually a daughter, often gets most of these caretaking responsibilities, which may cause long-buried jealousies and resentments to surface. Once both parents are no longer living, siblings are truly independent for the first time. From here on out, whether they see each other is their choice. This is the time when estrangement can become complete, particularly if old rivalries continue. The focus may be on concrete disagreements: Who should have helped in the care of an ailing parent? Who took all the responsibility? Who was more loved? Strong feelings can be fueled by all the old unresolved issues and conflicts. But the better relationship the siblings have, the less likely it is that this and other traumatic family events will lead to a parting of ways.

Questions About Sibling Patterns in Your Family

- Do members of the family conform to the generalized characteristics described for birth order (e.g., the oldest as leader, the youngest as rebel, the middle seeking recognition)? If not, are there mitigating circumstances that may have influenced sibling patterns, such as distance in age between siblings, a child with special needs or characteristics, other changes in the family around the birth of a child, and so forth?
- How were siblings in the family expected to behave—to be pals, "blood brothers," rivals, partners, opposites?
- Have family legacies influenced sibling roles and relationships?

- Are any siblings especially close in the family? Are any in business together? Are any estranged, and if so, what issues were involved? caretaking of a parent? rivalries about careers, money, spouses, who was the preferred child or whose children were more special? Do any specific sibling patterns run throughout the family?

- Did the parents tend to identify with the child of the same sex and sibling position as their own?

- Which sibling was the most "triangled" and do you have any hypotheses about why?

- Can you tell anything about the family values and patterns by the labels that different siblings had (the "star" and the "loser," the "angel" and the "villain," the "strong" one and the "weak" one, the "good seed" and the "bad seed")? Why might such labels have been given, beyond the obvious?

8 Couple Relationships

How soon the character of the race would change if pure and equal real marriages could take the place of the horrible relations that now bear that sacred name.

—LUCY STONE TO HENRY BLACKWELL, JULY 27, 1853

This fellow spirit has been so woven into mine that nothing could quite tear us asunder.

—ANTOINETTE BROWN
ABOUT HER MARRIAGE TO SAMUEL BLACKWELL, 1854

At the most only one bad woman exists in the world. It is unfortunate that each man considers his as being this unique one.

—GOTTHOLD GESSING (1729–1781) CIRCA 1780

Marriage is one of the most fascinating relationships to explore in learning about your family. What makes marriage work? How did your parents and grandparents do it? And how can anyone do it nowadays, especially with the profound complexities of divorce, remarriage, and the current pattern of two employed parents who must provide support both to children and aging family members in our highly mobile society?

Finding out how and when your parents, grandparents, and other couples in the family met, as well as the story of what attracted them to their spouses and how they decided to marry, will tell you something about how marriage takes place in a family.

Some cultures have no expectation that marriages will be intimate. Marriages are contracted between the fathers for the economic and social stability or betterment of the family. In our culture, marriage is thought to be a matter of individual choice of the partners for reasons of spiritual, emotional, and physical intimacy. This creates many problems, as the main need society has for marriage is for the production and nurturing of children. Thus we have many potentially conflicting goals at work in any particular family when it comes to the place of marriage in the family as a whole.

A particular problem in marriage is that it is the only family relationship in which exclusivity is expected. We can love more than one child, sibling, or parent. But we are not supposed to love more than one partner (at least not at one time!). Also, although marriage is the weakest relationship in the family, as our current divorce rate of 50% attests, it is the only one we swear is forever. Indeed it would probably be a good idea if we made that promise about our commitment to our parents, our siblings, and our children. Maybe the very fragility of the marriage bond is the reason we have to swear that our marriage vows are till death do us part. Indeed, the most powerful experiences human beings have of intimacy are probably in couple relationships, along with the most common sense of disillusionment. Being "in love" is more disorienting than any other relationship—and it is the most mysterious of emotions, as well as the one that most often fools us. It can make a blithering idiot out of the sanest person. Women have traditionally even lost their names, not to mention their identities, in this relationship. And both men and women have often been willing to give up everything for a love, who is presumably a hoped-for marriage partner, although many people are less willing to be generous to a long-term marital partner than to a new romantic partner. Our confusion between lust, love, companionship, loyalty, friendship, and sexual intimacy runs deep. And no other relationship is so linked to our very sense of who we are.

For these and other reasons some marriages are so full of intensity they seem intolerable. But marriages lacking in intensity also have their problems. Eugene O'Neill (see page 116 for genogram), whose difficulties with marriage and other relationships have already been discussed (see pp.115–119), had the following dream for the perfect marriage: "My wife and I will live on a barge. I'll live at one end and she'll live at the other, and we'll never see each other except when the urge strikes us" (Gelb & Gelb, 1987, p. 256).

But the conflicting goals, the intensity, and the difficulties of gender arrangements are not the only reasons marriage is so complex. It has often been said that what distinguishes human beings from other animals is the fact of having in-laws. Human beings are the only animals who tend to develop highly intense relationships with their in-laws. The joke that there are six in the marital bed is really an understatement. In the animal kingdom mating involves only the two partners, who usually mature, separate from their families, and mate on their own. But for us it is an entirely different proposition. Indeed, marriage places no small stress on a family to open itself to an in-law—an outsider who now becomes an official member of the family, often the first new member in years.

Naturally it is often hard to enter a family because of its long shared history of which the new spouse is not a part. And it is hard to include a new person who does not share the memories, private jokes, code words, and traditions you have in common as a family. Shortly after George Bernard Shaw married his wife, Charlotte, he described the problem of prior history for the new spouse in a letter to a woman friend:

> You do not understand the nature of Charlotte's objections to you; she has exactly the same objection to . . . everybody who forms the past in which she has no part. The moment you walk into the room where I am, you create a world in which you and I are at home and she is a stranger. It is just the same with me: the moment her old friends call I become a mere chance acquaintance. (Dunbar, 1963, p. 174)

Marriage shifts the relationship of a couple from a private twosome to a formal joining of two families. Issues that the partners have not resolved with their own families tend to be factors in marital choice and are very likely to interfere with establishing a workable marital connection in the context of the extended families. It may even be that much of the intensity of romantic love is determined by patterns in the families of origin. From this perspective Romeo and Juliet might have felt intensely attracted to each other precisely *because* their families hated each other. In idealizing the forbidden person, Romeo and Juliet, like many other romantic couples, including Tristan and Isolde, were spared any broader perspective on their relationship. In addition, their untimely deaths saved them from possible later conflicts over who would pick up the socks and how to handle the mother-in-law. In everyday life the outcome of such forbidden love affairs is not always so romantic. If couples marry expecting the other to solve their problems, they may soon be disappointed.

Marriage is indeed a difficult proposition. Yet the mythology of our culture portrays marriage—along with parenthood, to which it has long been the symbolic precursor—as the easiest and most joyous life-cycle transition. Our society's myths about marriage may add to its difficulty. Marriage, more than any other rite of passage, is viewed as the solution to loneliness or turmoil—the fairy-tale ending: "And they lived happily ever after." On the contrary, in the context of the multigenerational family life cycle, marriage comes in the middle of a complex process in the structure of two families, as they are transformed by new roles and relationships.

The following questions, developed with Betty Carter, can help couples understand the sociocultural context of any marriage.

- How much income does each spouse earn or have access to, and what effect does a large disparity in incomes have on the their overall decision-making process? Who manages the money, who has veto power, how are financial decisions arrived at, and whose name is on the assets?

- Is there an expectation that a wife should be supported financially for life by her husband? Any wife who plans to stay home with her children needs to be "economically viable" enough in money and skills to risk being a nonearner in a society with a 50% divorce rate.

- Does a husband give excuses that his work prevents greater involvement in the family? We need to question a wife's assumption that if she is not the primary parent it means she is not a "good mother."

- What are the wife's work and career plans? How does the husband view fathering and what parental roles does he take on?

- What is the ethnicity of each spouse? If they are of different races or ethnic backgrounds, what issues arise for them, their children, and their families of origin because of the difference? If you are in therapy, what race or ethnicity is your therapist? What impact do your and your therapist's racial and ethnic values have on attitudes about couple relationships and marriage?

- Gender, race, class, and sexual orientation connect people to a more powerful or less powerful place in all operating hierarchies. In what ways are racism, sexism, elitism, or homophobia played out in couple problems?

- Although progress has been made in civil rights for gays and lesbians, intense homophobia still exists in our society. If you or a family member is gay or lesbian, what have been the consequences of coming out in different contexts (work, family of origin, church or temple, etc.)? If you or the family member is closeted, what might the consequences be? Explore the impact of social stigma on all relationships in LGBT families.

- How has socioeconomic class affected the value systems held by you and your family members? How do you approach gender roles, education, religion, work, and so on? If you are a therapist, be aware of the influence of your own value system when discussing these value-laden issues with the couple.

- How much time does each parent spend with children? How much time do they spend alone together as a couple?

- How does the couple divide childcare and housework responsibilities? Are these tasks allocated according to traditional gender roles? Do both spouses find involvement with children and task allocation to be fair and satisfactory?

- How much time does each parent spend at work? How secure or satisfying is their work? Do they need to work as many hours as they do in order to support the family adequately? How do they define "adequately" in relation to their values?

■ What friendships and neighborhood or community connections do you and your family members have? How can these be better utilized?

■ What values make your life meaningful to you or your family members? Are there changes you could make that would help you live according to your values?

Courtship and weddings are fascinating nodal points to explore in learning how family process works. By examining marriages you can see how the family tends to deal with change, with outsiders, and with gender roles, and how successful people are at finding partners who complement them. It is also important to notice how power structures—gender, class, and race—influence couple relationships. In *Dreams from My Father*, Barack Obama described a discussion he had with his sister about marrying someone who was very different. He told her he dated someone white for almost a year. Alone together, he said, they could fall into their own private world, "Just two people hidden and warm, your own language, your own customs" (Obama, 1995, p. 210). But then one weekend she invited him to go with her to her family's country house:

> The house was very old, her grandfather's house. He had inherited it from his grandfather. The library was filled with old books and pictures of the grandfather with famous people he had known—presidents, diplomats, industrialists. There was this tremendous gravity to the room. Standing in that room, I realized that our two worlds, my friend's and mine, were as distant from each other as Kenya is from Germany. And I knew that if we stayed together I'd eventually live in hers. After all, I'd been doing it most of my life. Between the two of us, I was the one who knew how to live as an outsider. (Obama, 1995, pp. 210–211)

Obama's sister asked what happened and he told her that he began pushing the girlfriend away. When he thought about the future it pressed in on "our warm little world." He took her to see a play by a black playwright—an angry, funny play of "typical black American humor." Afterwards she asked why black people were so angry all the time and he responded that it was a matter of remembering and no one asks why Jews remember the Holocaust. She said that was different and that black anger was just a dead end. Though they had been close in their private relationship, in the larger context she could not understand his world and there was no solution possible other than to break up.

Even when couples get to the point of marriage, the tendency for relationships in a family to become polarized during the stress of a wedding can be intense. The new spouse may be subtly rejected as "not our class, darling," or of the "wrong" cultural or religious background. Parents may see their child's involvement with a partner who is "not our type" as a personal rejection. The tears that so frequently are shed on the wedding day may reflect the profound stress of the changes taking place in the family, rather than distress over the photographer's ineptitude, the guest list, the seating arrangements, the bridal gown, or the usher's cummerbund. Family conflicts around weddings can be fascinating indicators of underlying family values, alliances, and fears. And, of course, eloping or having a wedding without key family members may indicate family patterns just as clearly.

Given our culture's idealization of marriage, couples often define their problems primarily within the marital relationship, ignoring the need for other relationships—with parents, siblings, aunts, uncles, children, or friends. There is a tendency to put all our eggs in one basket. Spouses may overfocus on marital issues as the source of their happiness or dissatisfaction in life. If they feel dissatisfied, they may blame the partner—"He let me down; he doesn't love me"—or blame themselves—"If I were smarter, more attractive, etc., he would love me more." Once this personalizing process begins, it is very difficult to keep the relationship open.

The increasing interdependency of couples over time leads them to interpret more and more facets of their lives within the marriage. For example, if one partner becomes depressed during courtship, the other is not likely to take it personally, assuming instead that the depression probably has nothing to do with him or her. Such an assumption of not being responsible for the other's feelings permits a supportive response. After several years of marriage, however, this partner has a much greater tendency to view the other's emotional reactions as a reflection of his or her behavior and think: "It must mean I'm not a good spouse or I would have made my husband/wife happy by now."

Of course, the sense of responsibility for the other's well-being is more of a problem for women, as the culture also tends to hold them responsible for the happiness of others. But, once partners start taking responsibility for each other's feelings, more and more areas of the relationship may become tension-filled and therefore avoided. The wife may feel inadequate, guilty, and resentful. She may decide to avoid dealing with her husband because she does not want to arouse his irritability or blame, or she may become protective of him and stay silent to keep from making him upset. He may avoid raising issues that create tension out of fear of her annoyance. In either case, the more the reactions of each are a response to the other, the more communication will become constricted in emotionally charged areas and the less flexibility there will be in the relationship.

Married couples who find it threatening to have direct conflicts with each other may lower their anxiety by focusing their energy on their children, who oblige them by becoming the "problem," which allows the parents to form a united front.

The failure of partners to form a sense of identity before marriage leaves both spouses needing to build self-esteem in the marriage. Both may fear communicating with the other. He may think: "I must never let her know how worthless I am or I will lose her, because my parents never really loved me either, and I will never tell her that at times all her talk is boring." Meanwhile she is thinking: "I mustn't let him know how really worthless I feel or he will leave me, like my father did. And I mustn't let on that his endless silence watching sports and TV is boring. He has nothing to say."

In such couples, each partner puts the other in charge of his or her self-esteem: "I am worthwhile because you love me." Which means the converse would also be true: "If you don't love me, I am worthless." Thus couples may become bound in a web of evasiveness and ambiguity, because neither can dare to be straight, for fear of things turning out unhappily as they think happened in their families of origin. Messages between them become more and more disguised. They may end up doing things neither wants to do because each thinks the other wants it that way. As Groucho Marx put it:

> Lying has become one of the biggest industries in America. Let's take, for example, the relationship that exists between husband and wife. Even when they're celebrating their golden wedding anniversary and have said "I love you" a million times to each other, publicly and privately, you know as well as I do that they've never really told each other the truth—the real truth. I don't mean the superficial things like, "Your mother is a louse!" or "Why don't we get an expensive car instead of that tin can we're riding around in?" No, I mean the secret thoughts that run through their minds when they wake up in the middle of the night and see imaginary things on the wall. (Marx, 1989, p. 12–13)

To understand a family it is necessary to track the marital patterns over time. Look especially at periods of high marital tension, periods when partners became involved in affairs, periods of intense triangling with a child, a mother-in-law, or with other outsiders. See whether there are correlations between other family stresses and marital patterns in the family. Note also the messages that have been passed down in the family about marriage.

In the remarkable Blackwell family (Genogram 8.1), several unmarried aunts had a major role in raising a number of extraordinary children and apparently warned them repeatedly against marriage. In the grandparents' generation, one grandfather was a quarrelsome ne'er do well, who was said to have "crushed the life out of his wife." The other disgraced the family, first with his promiscuity, and then with his arrest and deportation for forgery. In the next generation the father died relatively young, leaving his wife and nine children unprovided for, as had his father and father-in-law. The family stories in the wake of such experiences may create powerful messages about the role and meaning of marriage. They do not, of course, doom the next generation to repeat the pattern. On the contrary, such marriages may become signals to the next generation for creativity in their life choices.

This was certainly the case for the Blackwells. All five of the Blackwell daughters chose to remain unmarried, though four of them adopted children. One, Elizabeth, became the first woman physician in the U.S.; another, Emily, followed her soon after; a third, Anna, became a journalist, and a fourth, Ellen, an artist. The fifth, Marion, was an invalid, though she, like three of her sisters, adopted a child to raise. The three sons were also amazing men in what they did with the family messages about marriage. Henry Blackwell fell in love with the famous suffragist Lucy Stone. He was attracted by her fiery speeches on the abolition of slavery and the rights of women. Indeed, her speeches were impassioned pleas against traditional marriage.

Henry Blackwell and Lucy Stone wrote their own marriage vows, which deliberately omitted the promise for the wife to obey, followed by an eloquent protest Henry had prepared against a woman's legal subservience to her husband in marriage: "I wish, as a husband, to renounce all the privileges which the law confers upon me, which are not strictly mutual" (Wheeler, 1961, pp. 276–277). Henry's protest became the model for generations of couples who wanted to transcend the traditional gender inequality of marriage. The couple kept separate names and bank accounts and he encouraged her wholeheartedly in her career as in everything else.

Lucy's family had also given her negative messages and stories about marriage. She had grown up anguishing over her mother's "bondage" and self-denial in relation to the father's abuse and dominance. Her father was "ugly" to his wife about money, and Lucy felt pained by the lack of freedom of her mother and all other women in marriage. She wrote a friend: "It will take more than my lifetime for the obstacles to be removed which are in the way of a married woman having any being of her own"(Wheeler, 1961, p. 277).

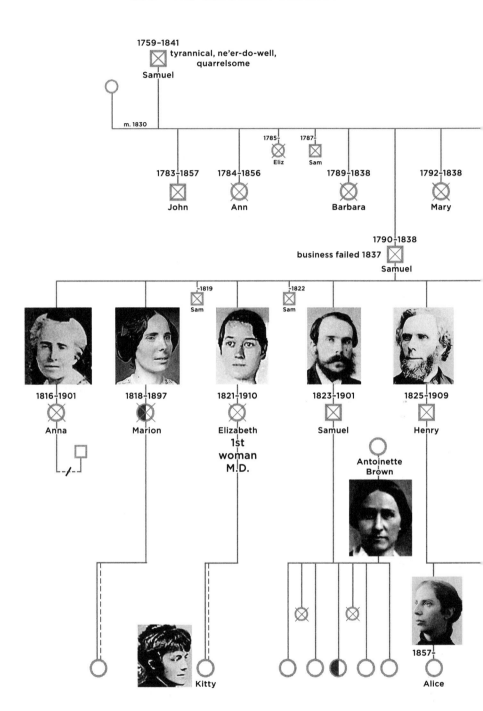

Genogram 8.1. The Blackwell Family.

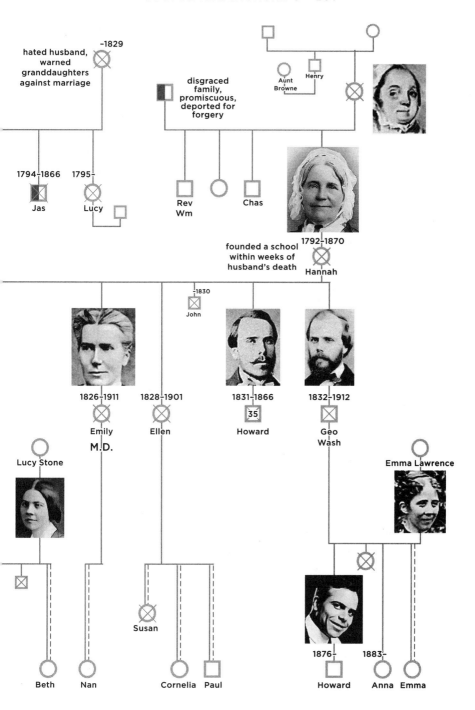

In fact, she had grown up determined never to marry, and changed her mind with great reluctance, becoming severely symptomatic with migraines and a near breakdown at the prospect. Her symptoms were so severe that her marriage to Henry Blackwell had to be postponed several times. Shortly before she "succumbed" she joked to her closest friend and future sister-in-law, Antoinette Brown, who soon after married Henry's brother Samuel: "If the ceremony is in New York, we want you to harden your heart enough to help in so cruel an operation as putting Lucy Stone to death. But it will be all according to law, so you need fear no punishment. I expect, however, to go to Cincinnati to have the ruin complete there" (Wheeler, 1961, p. 128). Henry himself wrote with similar humor to one of his good friends: "I have just entangled myself beyond the possibility of release. . . . I lose no time in conveying information of the frightful casualty." Despite Lucy's fears, the marriage was a long and happy one for both of them.

Soon after Henry and Lucy's marriage, Henry's older brother, Samuel Blackwell, met and wooed Lucy's friend, Antoinette Brown, the first woman minister in the United States. She also overcame her early reservations about marriage, just as Lucy had done.

In the long marriage that ensued, Samuel was most extraordinary for the untraditional caring role he played within his family. He readily shared in the work of the home and was viewed as a saint by the entire Blackwell family. Antoinette was also remarkable in her farsighted views about women's roles. She believed we needed to go further than just giving women more rights in a man's world. She made the revolutionary step of asserting that human knowledge would be enriched by adding to the traditions of logic and scientific inquiry the traditional "female" ways of knowing—intuition and personal experience. Antoinette and Lucy Stone had met years before at Oberlin College, where they formed a deep attachment and vowed never to marry. Both felt that marriage would be a severe hindrance to their work. Antoinette took the radical step of advocating that men's obligations should extend to family and home—a view that would take other feminists a full century to espouse. No other writer publicly proposed that men should share childcare and homemaking as well as the work for pay.

Supported by Samuel, who lived out his wife's ideas wholeheartedly, Antoinette had a full life as a minister, speaker, and author of poems, novels, and philosophical tracts until her death at age 96. She lived long enough to vote and receive an honorary doctorate of divinity from Oberlin, which had in her youth refused to grant her a ministerial degree, even after she had completed her studies there.

Of the marriages in the next generation, Antoinette said: "All of the sons-

COUPLE RELATIONSHIPS   **253**

in-law are good men and the marriages are more than usually satisfactory."
Samuel and Antoinette had five daughters, four successful and one an invalid,
just as in the previous generation there had been five daughters, four successful
and one invalid. And as in the previous generation, five unmarried aunts played
a critical formative role in the development of the children. It is interesting that
at least one of these daughters, Flo, rebelled against the prescription for women
in the family to have an independent career. She married a storekeeper, to the
family's great disapproval, though they eventually realized that he was an excellent choice for a husband, much in the model of Samuel. Moreover, Flo herself
eventually followed in her mother's footsteps, becoming a lay minister.

Although couples rarely notice the connection, it is surprising how often
people meet their spouses or make the decision to marry shortly after a critical family event. Antoinette Brown (Genogram 8.2), for example, had lost
five siblings in the years before she met Samuel Blackwell. She was perhaps
impelled toward Oberlin and the ministry out of a need to come to terms
with the early deaths of four of her siblings. The death of the fifth sister,
Augusta, who had followed Antoinette to Oberlin and who succumbed after
a 5-year struggle to tuberculosis, seems to have symbolized for Antoinette the
end of her family. This seemed to prepare the context in which she reversed
her decision never to marry after meeting Samuel the very next year.

The connections between extended family events and marital decisions
are often obscured. Families tell many stories about the reasons for marriage—love at first sight, the need for security, prospects of money and pres-
tige, anxiety about growing old alone, or the wish to have and raise children.
A systems thinker might see Romeo and Juliet as falling in love with each
other to lower their anxiety about conflicts between their warring families. It
is worth exploring your genogram for family events, particularly losses, that
may have influenced decisions to marry (as well as decisions to divorce).

There are, of course, gender differences in the way couples experience
their relationships. Women have traditionally been expected to give themselves up in a relationship, and men have been raised to see intimacy as a
threat to their autonomy. Thus men more often maintain a pseudo-indepen-
dent stance in marriage ("I am totally self-sufficient"), implicitly depending on their wives to take care of them while denying their dependence and
admitting no needs, doubts, or mistakes. Women, on the other hand, are generally expected to maintain a pseudo-intimacy ("I want to do whatever you
want to") while functioning almost entirely without spousal reassurance or
support for their needs.

Men's fear of admitting dependence and women's adaptiveness often work
together to inhibit an intimate marital relationship that permits differences

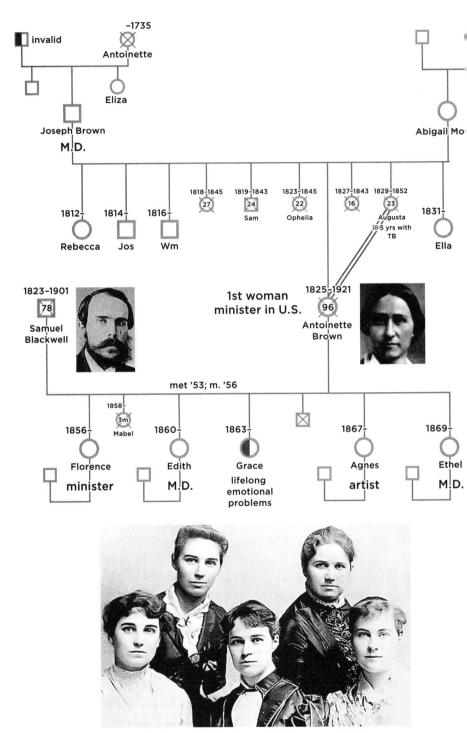

The five daughters: Agnes, Grace, Edith, Florence, and Ethel

Genogram 8.2. The Blackwell Family.

to exist. Generally speaking, we have socialized men so that they remain on the periphery of the family emotionally, while women have been constrained when they try to be anywhere else. In particular we have promoted the myth that marriage is like Cinderella being found by Prince Charming and then sacrificing her identity to his. As you think about the marriages in your family, explore how different family members have responded to this conundrum. This may expand your view of your "spinster" Aunt Mamie or give you a new appreciation of your granduncle who, though never a "success" in the business world, was the beloved nurturer of his children and grandchildren. You may see hidden strengths in these family members who overcame so many of society's gender-based rules.

A Complex Marriage: Gustav and Alma Mahler

In 1902 Gustav Mahler, age 42, one of the most gifted composers of the 20th century, married Alma Schindler, age 23, also a musical talent (Genogram 8.3). (Alma also eventually married two of the other major artistic geniuses of her time—the architect Walter Gropius and the writer Franz Werfel—and had love relationships with several others, including Oscar Kokoschka, Alexander Zemlinsky, Gustav Klimt, Gerhart Hauptmann, and Paul Kammerer.) For many years Gustav seems to have avoided marriage, perhaps because his parents' marriage was so unhappy. His mother, Marie, had suffered from unrequited love for someone else and married Gustav's father without loving him. She was a sweet, frail, quietly affectionate woman who was born lame. Gustav's irascible father brutalized his wife, beat his children, and ran after every servant. Gustav's love for his mother was as intense as was his dislike for his father. Marie bore 14 children in 21 years, losing eight sons in childhood. Gustav, the oldest surviving child, who had nursed his younger brother, Ernst, unceasingly until he died at 14, became the caretaker for the others. Until his marriage he lived with his sister Justine, who was his housekeeper, companion, and hostess for two decades. At 33 Justine had begun to think she was doomed to the fate of tending to her brother and would never have a life of her own. She loved him but felt like his servant. She was in love with Arnold Rose, the first violinist at the Vienna Opera, which Gustav conducted. Not surprisingly, perhaps, she married Rose the very day after her brother married Alma.

Gustav's attraction to Alma was immediate. She was beautiful, strong-minded, creative, and full of youth. The romance developed quickly, but trouble followed as soon as Alma let Gustav know her continuing ambitions to be a musician and composer. He responded harshly, calling her arrogant and reminding her of his view of a wife:

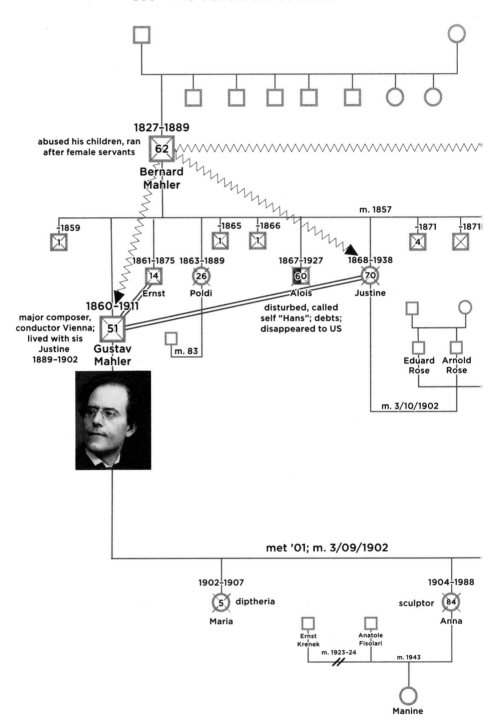

Genogram 8.3. The Mahler Family.

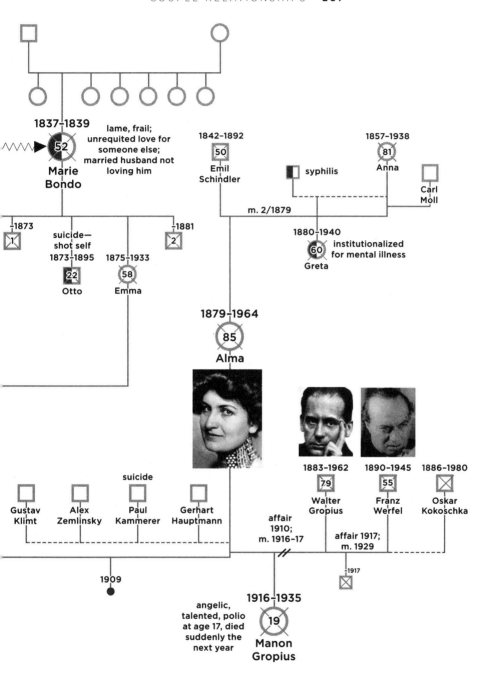

1837–1839

lame, frail; unrequited love for someone else; married husband not loving him

52

Marie Bondo

1842–1892

50

Emil Schindler

syphilis

1857–1938

81

Anna

Carl Moll

m. 2/1879

–1873

1

suicide— shot self

1873–1895

22

Otto

1875–1933

58

Emma

–1881

2

1880–1940

60

institutionalized for mental illness

Greta

1879–1964

85

Alma

1883–1962

79

Walter Gropius

1890–1945

55

Franz Werfel

1886–1980

Oskar Kokoschka

Gustav Klimt

Alex Zemlinsky

suicide

Paul Kammerer

Gerhart Hauptmann

affair 1910; m. 1916–17

affair 1917; m. 1929

1909

–1917

1916–1935

angelic, talented, polio at age 17, died suddenly the next year

19

Manon Gropius

You must become what I need, if we are to be happy together. . . . The role of "composer" falls to me—yours is that of loving companion and understanding partner. . . . You must give yourself to me unconditionally, shape your future life in every detail entirely in accordance with my needs and desire nothing in return save my love. (Monson, 1983, pp. 42–44)

Alma was shocked. He was asking her to give up her work and her self, and requiring her instead to dedicate herself to him and his music, which she didn't even like. Alma had grown up devoted to her father, who had died when she was 13. When she showed Gustav's letter to her mother, for whom she had always felt resentment, the mother urged her to end the relationship. But Alma, perhaps in defiance of her mother, chose to do the opposite. She soon paid heavily for her acquiescence!

As wedding plans proceeded, the tension between the couple continued. Gustav's friends found Alma rude and unappreciative of his work. His sister was jealous. In addition, as Alma soon realized, Gustav had completely neglected his finances and was heavily in debt. It would take her 5 years to remedy the situation. Although Gustav showed some flexibility during their brief courtship, as soon as the couple married he reverted to his rigid obsession with his work and acted more like her teacher than her lover.

In addition to copying his work for him, Alma's job was to keep everything running smoothly. She had become pregnant even before they married and, as the pregnancy developed, she felt her freedom disappearing: "Nothing has reached fruition for me, neither my beauty, nor my spirit, nor my talent. . . . I am living what only appears to be a life. I hold so much inside of me. I am not free—I suffer, but I don't know why or what for" (Monson, 1983, p. 65).

Like so many women, she was mystified by her problem, which her husband invalidated. One day when he found her crying he accused her of being unhappy because she didn't love him enough. She wrote in her diary: "There is such a silent struggle going on inside me! And such a dreadful longing for someone who thinks about ME—that helps me find MYSELF! I am drowning beneath the altar of family life. . . . It came over me that I had crossed that bridge once and for all—someone had taken me roughly by the arm and led me far away from my own self" (Keegan, 1992, pp. 110–111).

Even when she did find words for her frustration, complaining to Gustav the next year about his lack of acknowledgement of her and her work, his response was to blame her unhappiness on her: "Just because your budding dreams have not been fulfilled . . . that's entirely up to you" (Keegan, 1992,

p. 115). Over the next few years the couple grew further and further apart. Gustav was preoccupied with his work. Alma was depressed and frustrated. Their first daughter, Maria, named for Gustav's beloved but frail mother, died in 1907, at the age of 5. In his grief Gustav withdrew further. The same year he was diagnosed with a life-threatening heart condition; Alma herself was often physically ill as well as depressed. Neither of them had much energy left over for their younger daughter, Anna, born in 1904, who, left to her own devices, blamed herself for years afterwards for her sister's death, though it occurred when she was only 3. Gustav became preoccupied with fear that he would die himself. Having written eight symphonies, he feared that like Schubert, Beethoven, and Bruckner, he would not live past a ninth. He therefore chose to call his next work not his ninth symphony but *The Song of the Earth*, convincing himself that he would thus not tempt fate. He did later complete a ninth symphony, but he did not live to complete his tenth.

During this stormy period Alma became emotionally involved with one of Mahler's devotees, Ossip Gabrilovich (a common triangling pattern in situations of loss or threatened loss). Mahler was also preoccupied with his career struggles with the Vienna Opera, and with the anti-Semitism in the sociopolitical atmosphere of the era in Austria, which was limiting his opportunities. For a time they came to the United States, where he was much more appreciated but where Alma was all the more isolated. In addition, in 1909 she had a miscarriage, which revived the pain of the death of their first child.

In May 1910, Alma consulted a physician for what she called the "wear and tear of being driven on without respite by a spirit so intense as [Gustav's]" (Monson, 1983, p. 104). She feared she was on the brink of collapse. The doctor recommended a rest cure and she left for a spa. It is not surprising, in this context, that she became involved in a new romance, this time with Walter Gropius, a handsome, imaginative, talented German architect several years younger than she. Shortly afterwards, Gropius wrote to Mahler, as if Mahler were Alma's father, asking permission to marry her. Gustav went into a tailspin and became obsessed with fear of losing Alma. He vowed to change, and sought consultation with Freud. Freud's intervention is interesting from a family systems perspective. He zeroed in on the unresolved issues the couple had with their own parents, which had drawn Gustav and Alma to each other in the first place. He posed the challenge:

> How dared a man in your state ask a young woman to be tied to him? . . . I know your wife. She loved her father and she can only choose and love a man of his sort. Your age, of which you are so much afraid, is precisely what attracts her. You need not be anxious. You

loved your mother and you looked for her in every woman. She was careworn and ailing, and unconsciously you wish your wife to be the same. (Monson, 1983, p. 111)

Gustav began writing love letters to Alma, saying he must sound like a "schoolboy in love," but no longer hiding his feelings: "Freud is quite right—you were always the light and the central point for me! That inner light, I mean, which rose over all" (Monson, 1983, p. 113).

Here is the paradoxical aspect of so many marriages: Though men may have controlled and inhibited their wives' personal development, their own unarticulated dependence on their wives may be intense. This can leave the wife in a paradoxical situation: She is seen as vulnerable and emotionally dependent on her husband, yet expected to survive with almost no emotional support, validation, or understanding from him and made to feel crazy when she has trouble managing this Catch-22 situation.

In this case, the crisis led Gustav to begin playing for the first time the songs Alma had written years before, wanting her to return to the composing he had forced her to give up 9 years earlier. Instead of feeling support from him, Alma now felt he was invading her privacy. She never gained the courage to return to composing, though gradually the marriage mellowed. Gustav became more gentle. He had ignored her birthday and other holidays, never even giving her a wedding present, but he now bought her a diamond ring and made elaborate preparations for a Christmas celebration. He also became more expressive to his daughter Anna. Then, shortly after the Christmas of 1910, he contracted influenza and within a few months he died. Alma was 32.

As noted earlier, Alma went on to marry twice more and had relationships with a number of other men, including the dramatist Gerhart Hauptmann, the brilliant and controversial biologist Paul Kammerer, and the artist Oskar Kokoschka, whose demands were similar to those of Mahler: "You must force yourself to give up every thought of every production from your past and of every advisor prior to me. . . . I want you very much when you find your own being, your peace, and your freedom in my existence. . . . I warn you to decide whether you want to be free from me or in me" (Monson, 1983, pp. 145–146).

He actually took to signing his letters "Alma Oskar Kokoschka," as if to fuse their two identities. Though deeply drawn to Kokoschka, Alma had the wisdom, perhaps from hard experience, to resist his demands for fusion. She was deeply disturbed by the relationship, though she came to feel she could never be free of it: "I would like to break free from Oskar. . . . He makes me lose my momentum. . . . But now I know I will sing only in death. Then I'll be a slave to no man, because I will tend to my own well-being and to myself" (p. 164).

In an attempt to get away, Alma looked up Gropius again and convinced him within 2 weeks that they were in love with each other. It was not inconsequential to her that Gropius's birthday fell on May 18, Gustav's death day! She connected him with her loss in another way as well. Remembering her first meeting with him, she wrote:

> I believed that I was old and hateful . . . and suddenly there came a man into my life who was new to me and immediately taken by me. When he first told me that he loved me, I was happy as I had not been in years. This happened right after I had lost my beautiful child. I was destroyed and suffering. (Monson, 1983, p. 175)

Considering that this relationship was built on her previous losses, it is perhaps not surprising that she wanted to end the relationship soon after she and Gropius married and had another daughter in 1916. She tried to keep him from getting close to their new daughter, Manon, and turned her attention to the poet Franz Werfel, 11 years her junior. Soon she became pregnant by him. Gropius was led to believe the child was his, but when he realized it was not, he graciously let Alma go without reproach. The baby, born premature, died after a few months.

Over the next few years Alma struggled with herself about how to arrange her life. She could not marry Franz and she could not leave him. Several times a year the couple would part to do their own work and then they would reunite. Eventually, in 1929, they did marry. Their relationship was never really happy. Shortly before Werfel died in 1945, he wrote Alma a poem:

> *How very much I love you,*
> *I had not known . . .*
> *Why do we realize things*
> *Only after they have been taken from us?*

In Alma's last years Oskar Kokoschka turned up in New York, where Alma was living, and asked to visit her. They had corresponded over the years in fits and starts, in letters full of dreams of reuniting and unfulfilled possibilities. In the end Alma refused to see him. Perhaps she preferred to hold on to her dream of their love than to confront once again its complex reality.

Marital Complementarity

The saw that "opposites attract" is not entirely true: People generally choose partners who are similar to them in most important ways. Yet partners do tend to fall into reciprocal, complementary, and opposite roles in their couple relationships. It is almost as if they choose each other to express a hidden side of themselves.

Marriage involves so many levels of interdependence that outsiders may never really know the underlying contract that binds a couple together. And although differentness or complementarity may form the basis for the initial attraction, as things go along, these same differences can become the problem. For example, a wife who is one of eight children from a voluble working-class Italian family from Brooklyn may be extremely attracted to an upper-class Midwestern WASP who is an only child. Seeing him as the embodiment of the "American dream," she admires his quiet, stable strength, ambition, and ability to stay calm and rational, no matter how provoked. He finds her fun-loving, warm, and vivacious. He loves her family's spontaneity and open affection, not to mention the delicious rich food and joy in continuous celebration.

Everything is fine until they settle in after the wedding. At that point she begins to view his industriousness as "workaholism" and resents his stoic calm. Her liveliness and charm now seem full of histrionics and hysteria, and instead of "easy going" he calls her "careless." Her family, instead of being "fun-loving and colorful," is "boisterous, intrusive, and smothering." His family has gone from being "quietly charming and gracious" to "boring, vanilla, and uptight."

Maybe your mother played the martyr and stifled her own identity, while your father played the bully. Or maybe couple relationships in the family were characterized by power struggles, where neither partner could give in and fighting resulted in a stalemate. Perhaps wives ran the show, while their husbands sat quietly smoking and reading the newspaper in the corner. Whatever the patterns, you need to identify them and explore their meaning before you can be sure what your own role is and what you want it to be.

Exploring the patterns of complementarity in your family, particularly in marital relationships, will give you insights about patterns being passed down that you may want to change. As George Bernard Shaw's wife wrote:

> The conflict of temperaments is nature's way of avenging the race. Nature thrusts men and women into the arms of their opposites. . . . Ordinary, commonplace people are attracted by unlikeness: the strong by the weak, the passionate by the calm, the dark by the fair . . . marriage causes untold unhappiness . . . brought about by the clash. . . . We constantly blame only one, and probably the wrong one. For the troubles of my youth my mother seemed entirely to blame, but on mature reflection I see that this is a wrong view. (Dunbar, 1963, p. 252)

At the age of 42 George Bernard Shaw married Charlotte Payne-Townshend, who was then 41 (Genogram 8.4). Until that year Charlotte had been determined never to marry, and had turned down many proposals. Shaw was cynical about marriage, opposing it partly on political grounds, as a bourgeois institution and partly because of his experiences in his own family. Shaw's pattern of distancing from women who pursued him was longstanding. One admirer said of him: "The sight of a woman deeply in love with him annoyed him" (Holroyd, 1988, p. 428). Shaw's view of this woman was that: "I give her nothing; and I do not even take . . . anything, which makes her most miserable. When I tell her so, it only mortifies and tantalizes and attracts her and makes her worse" (p. 431).

This is the typical pattern of the pursuer/distancer relationship. The pursuer's pursuit distances the distancer, and his distancing attracts the pursuer more. What is most interesting about the pattern is that when either one changes role, the other seems to change as well. When Charlotte stopped pursuing, Shaw would begin to pursue her, and when he pursued her, she would tend to distance herself. Though Charlotte was in general the emotional pursuer, she also had the money and liked to travel, which enabled her to distance physically from Shaw and gave her a certain power over him.

She was herself the older of two sisters, and she perceived her own parents' marriage as a disaster. Her mother, who was English, hated Ireland and everything Irish. Her father, who was Irish, adored Ireland and was like a fish out of water anywhere else. Charlotte adored her sweet Irish father, whose gentleness provoked his wife to rage. Charlotte's mother longed for him to assert himself. Instead, he tried to deafen himself to his wife and make himself invisible (Holroyd, 1988, p. 433). He was a dreamer who hummed mildly under his breath and drummed his fingers on the arms of chairs. As Charlotte saw it, her mother extinguished his dreams and finally squeezed all the life out of him. Later Charlotte wondered whether her own hatred of her mother had killed her, as she thought her mother's hatred had killed her father.

Charlotte's mother pushed her relentlessly to marry, and Charlotte just as vehemently resisted. It wasn't until her mother died that Charlotte let herself fall in love for the first time. When this love ended in rejection, Charlotte wandered about for several years, trying to establish a meaning for her life. A friend who soon introduced her to Shaw described her thus:

> She found herself . . . alone in the world, without ties, without any definite creed, and with a large income. For . . . years she . . . drifted about—in India, in Italy, in Egypt, in London, seeking occupation and fellow spirits. . . . By temperament she is an anarchist—feeling any regulation or rule intolerable. . . . She is by nature a rebel. She has no snobbishness and no convention. (Dunbar, 1968, p. 98)

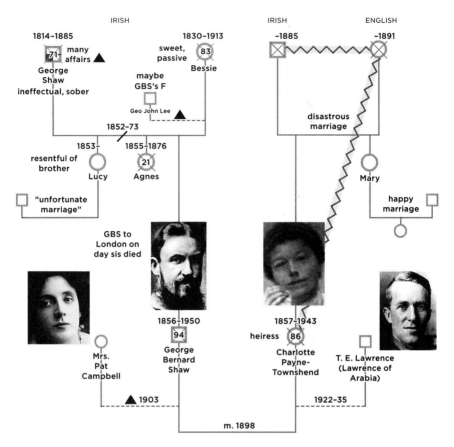

Genogram 8.4. The Shaw Family.

Then she met Shaw. He was 40; she was 39. They had a remarkable amount in common, not least their loathing of marriage. They were both rebels, radicals, and nonconformists who valued their independence. Shaw wrote of their early relationship:

> She also being Irish does not succumb to my arts . . . but we get on together all the better, repairing bicycles, talking philosophy and religion . . . or, when we are in a mischievous or sentimental hour, philandering shamelessly and outrageously. . . . She knows the value of her unencumbered independence, having suffered a good deal from family bonds and conventionality. . . . The idea of tying herself up again by a marriage . . . seems to her intellect to be unbearably foolish. Her theory is that she won't do it. (Holroyd, 1988, p. 435)

This makes their personalities sound ideally suited for each other. But, like most couples, they fell into complementary roles as their relationship evolved.

Charlotte began seeking more connection and when she did, Shaw retreated, warning: "From the moment that you can't do without me, you're lost" (Holroyd, 1988, p. 438). When she took his advice and tried to resist him by suddenly leaving for Ireland, he was nonplussed and complained: "Why do you choose this time of all others to desert me—just now when you are most wanted" (Holroyd, 1988, p. 436). He tried to distance himself into other relationships, but the greater the distance she kept, the more he found himself falling in love with her, though it petrified him. He wrote to her on the day before her return from Ireland:

> I will contrive to see you somehow, at all hazards. I must, and that "must" which "rather alarms" you, terrifies me. . . . If it were possible to run away—if it would do any good—I'd do it; so mortally afraid am I that my trifling and lying and ingrained treachery and levity with women are going to make you miserable, when my whole sane desire is to make you hap—I mean strong and self possessed and tranquil. . . . For there is something between us aside and apart from all my villainy. (Holroyd, 1988, p. 437)

He couldn't even admit that he cared enough to want to make her happy. That would imply too much dependence. Before seeing her, he instructed her on how she must keep her distance when they were alone together. But over the next few months their lives became more entwined. He ended his various relationships with other women and she gradually made herself indispensable to him, becoming his secretary and caretaker, as well as his companion. Shaw believed the status of marriage was almost essential for a woman's greatest possible freedom—but, of course, eschewed it for himself! When Charlotte finally tried to take his advice and proposed to him, he apparently responded "with shuddering horror & wildly asked the fare to Australia" (Holroyd, 1988, p. 442).

The couple soon reconciled, but Charlotte was, as usual, in the position of emotional pursuer. When Shaw rebuffed her, she backed off again: "I am in the rather unusual position of being perfectly free. . . . The personal happiness, which everyone puts first and which I had within my grasp was lost to me . . . and my life is a wreck; so I am free from the ordinary individual hopes, fears and despairs, which are so apt to become chains" (Dunbar, 1963,

p. 130). In her absence, Shaw began to realize how much he missed her: "It is so damnably inconvenient to have you out of my reach" (pp. 131–132). Shaw now began having accidents and physical symptoms. First he fell off his bicycle. Dramatist that he was, he played up his black eye and cut face to the hilt. But when Charlotte soon after invited him to go on a trip, he responded with sarcasm and avoidance: "No use in looking for human sympathy from me. I have turned the switch and am your very good friend, but as hard as nails" (p. 133). When she went off without him, his sarcastic humor intensified:

> What do you mean by this inconceivable conduct? Do you forsake all your duties—even those of secretary? Is it not enough that I have returned without a complaint to my stark and joyless life? . . . Are there no stamps? . . . Go then, ungrateful wretch: have your heart's desire: find a Master—one who will spend your money and rule your house. . . . Protect yourself for ever from freedom, independence, love, unfettered communion with the choice spirits of your day, a lofty path on which to go your own way and keep your own counsel, and all the other blessings which 999 women cry for and the thousandth cries to get away from. (Dunbar, 1963, p. 134)

The longer Charlotte was away, the more unstable he grew. Finally he wrote, describing himself as "detestably deserted," and pleading, "Oh Charlotte, Charlotte: is this a time to be gadding about in Rome?" (Holroyd, 1988, p. 455). Soon both of them were becoming symptomatic, he with headaches, toothaches, accidents, and finally gout, she with neuralgia, restlessness, and depression. As much as he missed her, he also feared her:

> But then I think of the other Charlotte, the terrible Charlotte, the lier-in-wait, the soul hypochondriac, always watching and dragging me into bondage, always planning nice, sensible, comfortable, selfish destruction for me, wincing at every accent of freedom in my voice, so that at last I get the trick of hiding myself from her, hating me and longing for me with the absorbing passion of the spider for the fly. (Holroyd, 1988, p. 455)

By the time she returned from Rome, he was desperate for her and in a disastrous situation, almost an invalid by virtue of an infected foot. Charlotte was appalled when she saw the circumstances in which he was living—filthy, wretched, malnourished, uncared for. His mother, with whom he lived, did nothing for him, if she even noticed his condition at all. Charlotte could never forgive her for her neglect of her son, though from the time of their marriage Charlotte provided an annuity for her. In fact both families had a lasting antagonism to the couple. Charlotte's sister never even wanted to meet Shaw, and his sister, who resented him in the first place, had even more resentment for Charlotte.

Exactly how the couple came to their final decision to marry will never be known. Charlotte never spoke of private things and Shaw always hid the deeply emotional events of his life in clownish descriptions. Something was changing with him. He had written: "I had always, from my boyhood had the impression that 38 to 40 was a dangerous age for men of genius and that I should possibly die like Mozart, Schiller, and Mendelsohn at that crisis" (Holroyd, 1988, p. 448).

He was, at the time, in constant pain and in need of a serious operation, which Charlotte finally arranged. His situation was somehow changed "by a change in my own consciousness. I found that my own objection to my own marriage had ceased with my objection to my own death" (Dunbar, 1963, p. 148). "Death did not come; but something which I had always objected to far worse: to wit, Marriage did" (Holroyd, 1988, p. 461).

George later told the story that he married because, being a wretch on crutches, stifled by chloroform and determined to die, "I proposed to make her my widow" (Holroyd, 1988, p. 461). Whether or not this humorous method was the one Shaw actually used, it is a remarkably Irish proposal, the joke being that the Irish ask a woman to marry by saying, "How'd you like to be buried with my folks?" (McGoldrick, 2005). Even years later Shaw insisted that he had made the decision from the point of view of a dying man, and said Charlotte had predicted he would otherwise become a permanent invalid. In fact, he wrote his own humorous announcement of the wedding for the newspapers, describing it as a totally chance event:

> As a lady and gentleman were out driving in . . . Covent Garden yesterday, a heavy shower drove them to take shelter in the office of the . . . Registrar there, and in the confusion of the moment married them. The lady was . . . Miss Payne Townshend and the gentleman was George Bernard Shaw. . . . Startling as was the liberty undertaken by the . . . official, it turns out well. Miss Payne Townshend is an Irish lady with an income many times the volume of that which "Corno di Bassetto" used to earn, but to that happy man, being a vegetarian, the circumstance is of no moment. (Dunbar, 1963, p. 151).

In ways the two "chance" partners were very different people. Like many oldests, Charlotte was responsible, accustomed to dominating and being the caretaker. Shaw, on the other hand, was the younger brother of two sisters. Like many younger brothers of older sisters, he was irreverent, creative, irresponsible, and used to having others take care of him. Charlotte may have married Shaw because she enjoyed his unpredictability and creative genius. Also, he was someone who seemed to need a caretaker. Though Shaw had finally achieved economic stability through the success of one of his plays a few months before he married, his decision may have been facilitated by Charlotte's wealth, which enabled him to provide for his mother, with whom he had lived until his marriage.

As is often the case, the complementary differences that brought them together were not enough to make for a successful marriage. Although the marriage lasted for 45 years and Shaw insisted to the end of his life that he could not have married anyone else, the two grew less intimate as the years went by. Charlotte loved to travel; he hated it. She, like her father, loved to be in Ireland; Shaw was ambivalent about ever returning to his homeland. Most important, Shaw came to believe that his wife was not a worthy discussant on one topic after another: religion, politics, and so forth, and he closed her out. Charlotte did handle Shaw's one major affair, with Mrs. Patrick Campbell, with great skill, continuing to socialize with him and refusing to be put off by the rumors of the affair. She was meanwhile preoccupied with her own spiritual search, which she did not share with her husband. From about 1922 she developed an intimate friendship with T. E. Lawrence (Lawrence of Arabia), 20 years her junior, and certainly one of the geniuses of the era, sharing with him the personal thoughts she could not share with her husband. This relationship lasted until Lawrence's death in 1935.

It was not until Charlotte's death in 1943 that Shaw, then in his eighties, read her correspondence with Lawrence and realized how he had misjudged her. He saw that he had missed out on the intellectual and emotional richness that she obviously had to share. He wrote:

> From a diary I discovered lately and some letters which she wrote to T. E. Lawrence, I realize that there were many parts of her character that even I did not know, for she poured out her soul to Lawrence. . . .
> I lived with Charlotte for forty years and I see now that there was a great deal about her that I didn't know. It has been a shock. (Dunbar, 1963, p. xi)

Shaw had expected someone to take care of him, not to be his intellectual companion. Unable to move beyond the expectations of his own unhappy family, he had not seen his wife for who she was. One might hypothesize that sibling complementarity (he a youngest, she an oldest), enabled them to remain married for 45 years, but the family legacy of marital unhappiness seems to have influenced their expectations of marriage, such that they were unable to be really intimate with each other.

Couple Triangles

When couples cannot resolve issues themselves, there are a number of common triangles that develop. They may come together around a mischievous or sick child and thus distract themselves from their problems with each other. Or they may focus on their in-laws as the source of the problem: "If it weren't for your mother's intrusiveness, we'd be all right." Men have traditionally moved outside the family when they have marital problems, concentrating on their work, seeking an affair outside the marriage, or focusing their energies on "male" activities—socializing with buddies at the pub, playing golf, and so on. Addictions are surely the most destructive of the common male responses to marital tension. Women, on the other hand, may turn their marital frustrations into anxiety, depression, social withdrawal, rigid housekeeping, or overinvestment in their children. Recently women are also turning more to addictions and affairs.

It has been said that the 21st century will be about the invention of the marriage-divorce cycle as the normal pattern of life for families, as this has become such a common process in family life. But generally families do not handle the breakdown of a marriage very well, and the unresolved relationships come back to haunt them later. Divorce most often leaves a legacy of dangling ends—the bric-a-brac of a lifetime, along with bitterness and cutoff that have to be gotten past. One young man summed up his resentment for his father's second wife by saying: "There she was redecorating my past with all her fake antiques."

When there are new or missing marital partners in a family brought on by separation, divorce, or early death, bridging the cutoffs in the family will open up another set of connections to people who belong—people with an investment in the person's past as well as in his or her future. Getting to know about every branch of the family may involve getting past some intense reactions of other family members and holding oneself steady in pursuit of the missing information on the family tree.

Divorce and Remarriage

It is important to explore the triangles that so often develop in divorced and remarried families to understand one's family patterns. It is extremely common for triangles to develop between children and their half siblings or stepsiblings and between the new spouse and the ex-spouse, and such patterns may continue even into the next generation, where the children on each side of the family perpetuate the negativity without even knowing each other or the reasons for the conflicts in the first place.

When Barack Obama visited his African relatives in 1987, 4 years after his father died, and met most of his extended family for the first time, he was immediately drawn into triangles set up by the conflicts between several different parts of his father's multiply divorced family (Genogram 8.5). His father's sister complained that Obama should have visited her first instead of connecting to his father's first wife, Kezia, and her family, which included Obama's half sister, Auma, the only one he had met before and the one with whom he had the most connection. All sorts of conflicts developed about whom he would spend more time with and to whom he would be more generous. There was also conflict in relation to the fact that during Obama's father's relationship with his third wife, Ruth, who was white, he had continued his relationship with Kezia as well, though she was also involved with someone else and over time had two younger sons, Abo and Bernard, there being question as to whether Bernard was actually Obama's father's son. Barack struggled with the question, wondering whether the truth should have an impact on his relationship with Bernard, whom he was just getting to know. The family reassured him that his father had been very accepting of Bernard and did not let it become an issue to him, accepting all the children as his own, though he had taken Kezia's two oldest children, Roy and Auma, away from the family home in Alego to live with him and Ruth in Nairobi, meaning that the two oldest were separated from their mother and had not known their youngest brothers.

During Obama's visit word came that the third wife, Ruth, was also resentful that he was in Africa and not coming to visit her. Obama was told that his father's third divorce was very bitter. Ruth had become involved with another man and tried to get her two sons by Obama's father, Mark and David, to change their name to that of her new husband. Mark did so, but the younger son, David, became rebellious and refused, actually moving back to live with his half brother Roy (Auma's brother), where he was when he tragically died at age 18 in 1983. This death occurred just a year after Obama's father died. The death left all the triangles and conflicts of the divorced and multiply remarried family in a very unresolved place. Luckily, through Obama's efforts to make connections to each part of the family and his willingness to visit each side and listen to them without choosing sides, he was able to learn a great deal more about his family and thus about himself. He even took an opportunity to question his half brother Mark about his

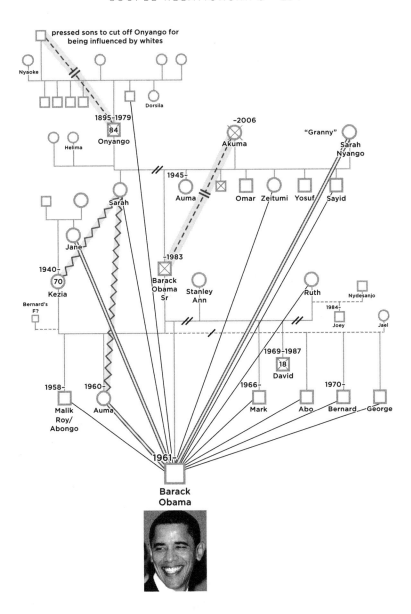

Genogram 8.5. The Obama Family.

lack of interest in their father, whom he had also hardly known because the parents divorced when he was still young and he rarely saw his father after the divorce. Mark's response is understandable: "I'm cut off from my roots. . . . At a certain point I made a decision not to think about who my real father was. He was dead to me even when he was still alive. I knew he was a drunk and showed no concern for his wife and children. That was enough. . . . Life's hard enough without all that excess baggage" (Obama, 1995, p. 344). Such responses are very common and understandable in the painful aftermath of losing a parent in a divorce. Obama had felt the same pain, but the effort to reconnect, even when the parent is gone, can make a tremendous difference, as Obama's memoir reveals.

Successful Couples

Some people continue to make and remake the same mistakes as they go through life. Others seem able to improve their situation, though the path is not necessarily straight. Agatha Christie (Genogram 8.6) perhaps the world's most famous mystery writer, demonstrates in her own history a transformation from her first to her second marriage, which probably had seeds in the struggles of her childhood. Agatha's parents, Fred and Clara Miller, had actually grown up in the same family, though her father was 8 years older than her mother. Agatha's mother was left a penniless widow with four small children at 27. She gave Clara, her oldest child, to her sister, "Aunt Grannie," who had just married Nathaniel Miller, an American businessman, with one teenage son from his previous marriage, Fred. Clara and Fred had two children and then 9 years later Agatha was born, the youngest, but in almost all ways an only child. She adored her father who never really made much of a living, and after his early death when she was only 11, she and her mother struggled increasingly to keep their home, making a home place one of the most important strivings of Agatha's life. The family had come from privilege but with her father's early loss, like that of her maternal grandfather's before, Agatha must have sensed how vulnerable a woman could be without her own resources. Agatha barely had any education and indeed her mother tried to prevent her learning to read too early, but she became a great reader and talented pianist as well.

As a young adult she became engaged to someone she had known since childhood with whom she was very compatible, but he was not sure she really loved him and gave her time to decide. When she met the charming Archie Christie, she decided with a few days to marry him instead. They married in 1914. It was wartime and in the first years and he was often away in the war. Once they were together after the war he seemed to lose interest in her and was preoccupied with his own interests, but not making much money. She began writing as a way to fill her time and hopefully to make some money so she would not have to rely on him. By 1926 he was spending almost no time with her and expected her to entertain herself. On the weekend of his daughter's 7th birthday, he told her he was in love with someone else and wanted

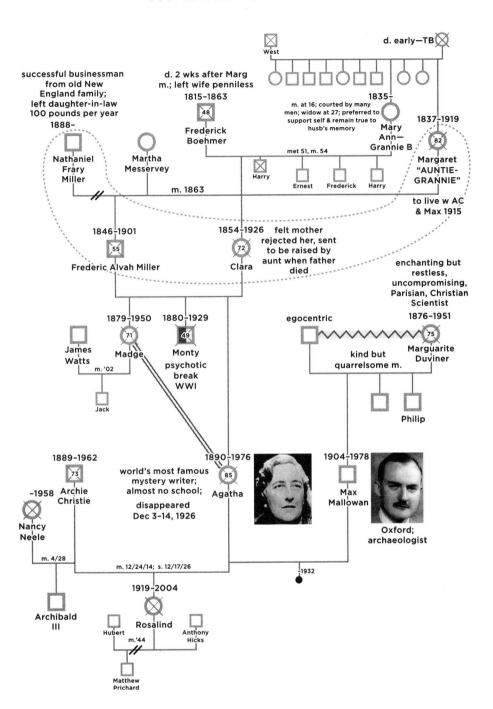

d. early—TB

West

successful businessman
from old New
England family;
left daughter-in-law
100 pounds per year
1888–

d. 2 wks after Marg
m.; left wife penniless
1815–1863

m. at 16; courted by many
men; widow at 27; preferred to
support self & remain true to
husb's memory

1835–
Mary
Ann—
Grannie B

1837–1919
82

Margaret
"AUNTIE-
GRANNIE"

Nathaniel
Frary
Miller

Martha
Messervey

Frederick
Boehmer
48

Harry

met 51, m. 54

Ernest   Frederick   Harry

m. 1863

to live w AC
& Max 1915

1846–1901
55

Frederic Alvah Miller

1854–1926
72

Clara

felt mother
rejected her, sent
to be raised by
aunt when father
died

enchanting but
restless,
uncompromising,
Parisian, Christian
Scientist

1879–1950
71

James
Watts

Madge

m. '02

1880–1929
49

Monty
psychotic
break
WWI

egocentric

kind but
quarrelsome m.

1876–1951
75

Marguarite
Duviner

Philip

Jack

1889–1962
73

Archie
Christie

–1958

Nancy
Neele

1890–1976
85

world's most famous
mystery writer;
almost no school;
disappeared
Dec 3–14, 1926

Agatha

1904–1978

Max
Mallowan

Oxford;
archaeologist

m. 4/28

m. 12/24/14; s. 12/17/26

–1932

Archibald
III

1919–2004

Hubert   Rosalind   Anthony
Hicks

m.'44

Matthew
Prichard

Genogram 8.6. The Christie Family.

a divorce. Agatha's mother, to whom she had become very attached over the years, had died a few months earlier, which compounded her distress. Shortly afterward, she disappeared for eleven days, which had all of Britain caught up in the search for her, an event that could have been right out of one of her mysteries, signing into a spa in another city using the name of his girl-friend. But once she was found, she acceded to the divorce, and he quickly remarried. A few years later, at the age of 40 she met a most unlikely partner: 26-year-old archeologist, Max Mallowan, oldest son of an impoverished Austrian immigrant and an artistic Parisian Christian Scientist, whose marriage had been "quarrelsome." Agatha, at 40, had by this time become a world famous mystery writer. She had had almost no formal education. Max, was an aspiring archaeologist who had attended Oxford University with Agatha's nephew, who was a researcher in the middle east. Agatha met Mallowan on a visit to some friends at the dig, and a series of mishaps turned into several long trips with him, during which the two realized they had a deep compatibility both physically and intellectually which lasted over the next thirty years. It was perhaps a factor in the success of their relationship that by the time they met they both had well-developed and independent personalities, interests, projects and sense of professional and cultural identity (Gill, 1990). Mallowan was not threatened by Christie's international fame as a mystery writer and was comfortable in her world of writers. For her part, she shared his passion for ancient cultures. Both were humorful, energetic, independent people and their compatibility lasted the rest of their lives. It is even interesting that while Christie's relationship with her daughter seems not to have been as close as she might have wished as Rosalind was growing up, in adulthood Rosalind's second marriage was to a man with whom she had a similar compatibility and who was very like her stepfather. The four of them shared a very close relationship.

Questions to Ask About Couple Relationships in One's Family

- What are the stories told in the family about how couples got together? What attracted spouses to each other? What made them decide to marry? What were the underlying dreams about marriage? the underlying fears? What messages got passed from one generation to another about marriage?
- Are there coincidences in timing between marriage decisions (when partners met, fell in love, decided to marry, or began to have marital problems) and other family events, particularly loss (deaths, moves, family traumas, other life cycle transitions)?

- What unresolved issues from their families of origin did members of the family bring into their marriages? Do spouses tend to be from the same ethnic, religious, and class background? If not, do they have issues about moving "up" in class or away from the family's religious or cultural traditions?
- How has immigration influenced couple relationships? Has it influenced language, power dynamics, partners' contact with extended family, or the extent to which certain cultural patterns are perpetuated?
- How did differences in ethnicity, class, race, religion, and sexual orientation influence couple relationships, and how did such differences influence how the larger family dealt with the partners over time?
- How did people's characterizations of each other change from the time of courtship through the marriage?
- What are the typical patterns of marriage in the family? Are there certain patterns of symmetry or complementarity: the tyrant/battleax and the doormat/mouse? fiery foes? Mutt and Jeff? Tweedledum and Tweedledee? the hand and the glove? the caretaker and the patient? the obsessive and the hysteric? the clam and the babbler?
- Did couples get into power struggles? Were they conflict avoiders? ships passing in the night?
- Are there typical triangling patterns in the marriages in the family? with a child? with an affair? with sports, TV, work, the Internet, the cell phone? a mother-in-law?
- Are there typical gender patterns in the marriages in the family? Do the men leave? Are the women long-suffering? Are the women frustrated impresarios? the men impulsive and frightening? Does either stay invisible?
- Are there any family messages or rules about marriage, such as that men are dangerous? that marriage takes away your freedom? that you can never be happy unless you're married?
- Have weddings in the family typically been traumatic affairs or happy gatherings? large and lavish? elopements? plain-clothes affairs with a justice of the peace? Did anyone not go to a wedding who should have been there? Have any cutoffs occurred around a wedding?
- Do marital partners tend to fight over money? sex? children? leisure activities? food? religion? politics? mothers-in-law?
- How did couples in the family negotiate the use of space, time, and money, where to go on vacation, which family traditions and rituals to retain from each family of origin and which ones to develop anew? How did they negotiate relationships with parents, siblings, friends, extended family, and coworkers?

▪ Are parts of the family tree missing or blurry because of divorce, early death, or in-law triangles? Can you see ways to gain access to the missing information? Who would be most upset if you connected with these sources? Can you gain the courage to deal with the loyalty conflicts, jealousy, or the sense of betrayal others may feel in order to reclaim your whole family?

▪ What are the norms in the family for marriage, and are they different from the dominant norms? Are there patterns of late marriage? divorce and remarriage? long marriage? happy marriage? not marrying? living together unmarried or in unconventional groupings? Are there lesbian or gay couples? marriages with an "extra" adult such as a mother-in-law or sibling who lives with the couple?

9 Culture: Ethnicity, Race, Class, Religion, and Historical Period

coauthored with Tracey Laszloffy

If the heart of Africa still remained elusive, my search for it had brought me closer to understanding myself and other human beings. The ache for home lives in all of us, the safe place where we can go as we are and not be questioned. It impels mighty ambitions and dangerous capers. . . . Hoping that by doing these things home will find us acceptable or, failing that, that we all forget our awful yearning for it.

All God's Children Need Traveling Shoes
—MAYA ANGELOU

A complex web of connections cushions us as we move through life: family, community, culture. And even though we may be moving toward becoming a larger, global community, we are still very much embedded in our local context. To understand our families, we must look deeply into their cultural context. When and where in history were family members born, and what life circumstances, migrations, and local or societal political and economic events circumscribed their lives? These are crucial questions to ask if we are to understand who we are as human beings. Genograms help us contextualize kinship networks in terms of culture, class, race, gender, religion, family process, and migration history. When we identify ourselves ethnically, we highlight themes of cultural continuity and cultural identity to make them more apparent. By its nature the process of learning cultural, religious, and class stories encourages us to recognize the multiple views of different family members. By scanning the family system culturally and historically and assessing previous life-cycle transitions, you can place your present issues in the context of your family's evolutionary cultural patterns of geography, migration, and family.

Families do not develop their rules, beliefs, and rituals in a vacuum. What we think, how we act, and even our language are all transmitted through the family from the wider cultural context. This context includes the culture in which we now live as well as that of our ancestors. A family's culture is influenced by its class, religion, patterns of migration, and geographic location, as well as by its racial and ethnic background and the historical period in which it exists. And culture itself is not a monologue, but a dialogue. No matter what a person's background is, it is, in effect, multicultural. In the same vein, all marriages are, to a degree, intermarriages. No two families share the exact same cultural roots. Thus the family in which we are born is made up of many cultural strands. For people to understand themselves, they need to understand their families, and to understand their families, they need to know about their families' cultural roots.

Families differ in the strength of the relationship they have with their cultural roots, but even when family members don't consciously connect with them, they still shape and influence the family's identity, patterns, and dynamics. Whether recognized or not, our cultures of origin are woven into the fabric of our families, influencing attitudes toward life, death, birth, sex, food, men, women, children, and the elderly. How much have family members conformed to what is expected of men and of women in their cultural group? How much closeness is expected or desired between family members? These patterns vary greatly from one cultural group to another. Italians, for example, tend to be close and enmeshed, sharing everything with each other and spending all holidays and much free time together. The Italian belief is that if you lose your family you might as well be dead. Scandinavian families generally maintain a greater distance and are much less likely to demonstrate anger or affection, even among close family members.

Every culture has its strengths and vulnerabilities. A family's xenophobia or open curiosity toward outsiders is probably a reflection of its cultural history. Were they poor, politically oppressed for centuries, or were they adventurers who moved about, gathering energy as they went? Were they members of the ruling class of the land, the dominant "tribe" in their cultural context, or the object of another group's colonizing or discriminatory efforts? If they are extremely nationalistic, they may have felt oppressed as a minority within a larger community. Sometimes there is an attempt to hold on tightly to cultural traditions, even if this means being closed to new experiences. Seeing attitudes about culture from a systemic perspective can help people understand their family origins and what led them to hold onto certain beliefs or shift to different beliefs. Under pressure from the dominant society, family members may try to "pass," renouncing their heritage, or they may cling to it unduly. For all of these reasons it is important to identify your family's cultural roots and examine how culturally based issues, themes, mores, and experiences shaped their growth and development over time.

Coming Home

Cultural critic and author bell hooks has written about the way that home is tied not only to our families of origin but also to place and space (geography), and to broader social factors such as race, gender, and class. If we remember home as a place where we experienced devaluation, either within our families or from external forces like poverty, racism, homophobia, or other kinds of devaluation and persecution, it can prevent us from making the journey home again. In her book *Belonging*, hooks (2009) explained that she left her family and her home state of Kentucky when she was 18 to escape the pain of a dysfunctional family and of the racism and classism she felt growing up in the South: "Since my native place was indeed the site and origin of the deep dysfunction that had damaged my spirit I did not believe I could be safe there. . . . My own deep wounds, the traumas of my Kentucky childhood are marked by the meeting place of family dysfunction and the disorder produced by dominator thinking and practice, combined with the effect of racism, sexism, and class elitism" (pp. 18, 52).

Within her family, her father was strongly patriarchal and her mother was subservient. Her father's sexism and her mother's acquiescence to it were wounding to hooks, but this was not the only source of childhood pain. When hooks was 8, her parents moved the family from the country to the city in their attempt to "move up" in the world. Her parents rejected the ways of the elders and traditions of ancestors they perceived as being "backwards." They wanted their children to be modern and sophisticated, which was all about trying to raise their class status and distance themselves from the shame they associated with being poor, rural, and black. But for hooks, the move to the city and the loss of connection with nature, the land, and the old ways were traumatizing. Moreover, in the city she experienced intensive and consistent racism that also inflicted deep wounds.

When she was 18, hooks left Kentucky and her family to attend college at Berkeley in California. She was trying to escape the pain that had haunted her as a child. Yet in leaving home, hooks became an exile, and that, too, hurt: "Living away from my native place I became more consciously Kentuckian than I was when I lived home. This is what the experience of exile can do, change your mind, utterly transform . . . [your] perception of the world of home" (hooks, 2009, p. 13). However, as exiled as she felt, for 30 years she did not feel that she could go home. "Like many writers, especially southerners, who have stayed away from their native place, who live in a state of mental exile, the condition of feeling split was damaging, and caused a breaking down of the spirit. Healing that spirit meant for me remembering myself, taking the bits and pieces of my life and putting them together again. In remembering my childhood and writing about my early life I was mapping the territory, discovering myself and finding homeplace" (p. 15).

In writing about belonging, hooks explained that it is common for people to try to distance themselves from their past, their families, and their cultural legacies in an effort to start anew. Yet these efforts to reinvent ourselves have a way of continually looping us back to our past. When we can finally stop fighting this and see our history as a resource that we can learn from, it will give us the power to find what we have been seeking all along—home.

How many of us have become exiles? How many of us have been trying to distance ourselves from home, both in terms of our family of origin and in terms of the experiences we had with respect to racial, ethnic, and religious background, class status, gender and sexual identities, and experiences with migration and geographic location? How many of us, like bell hooks, have been haunted by past pain related to dysfunction in our family or dysfunction tied to our cultural identities? In all likelihood, most of us have struggled with how to find our way home in ways that are honest yet healing, transparent, and transformative. What is vital to bear in mind is that the journey to go home again is not about regressing into sentimentalism. According to anthropologist Carol Stack, "No one, however nostalgic, is really seeking to turn back the clock. . . . What people are seeking is not so much the home they left behind as a place that they can change, a place in which their lives and strivings will make a difference—a place in which to create a home" (cited in hooks, 2009, p. 221).

Only by facing what she had left behind, and allowing herself to see the good and the bad, was bell hooks able to finally find herself: "I cannot live a grounded life without being grounded in a place" (hooks, 2009, p. 68). This grounding cannot occur unless and until we allow ourselves to go home again—to see, explore, investigate, expose, and ultimately understand and accept our families of origin and our cultural legacies, which for better and for worse are always a part of us.

Linda Burton and her colleagues have argued that it is essential for therapists to take into account the concept of homeplace in our work with clients (Burton, Winn, Stevenson, & Clark, 2004). They defined homeplace as: "the multilayered, nuanced individual and family processes that are anchored in a physical space that elicits feelings of empowerment, belonging, commitment, rootedness, ownership, safety, and renewal. This includes the ability to develop relationships that provide us with a solid sense of social and cultural identity" (p. 397). The notion of homeplace is relevant for people of all cultures throughout the life cycle. This is especially true for immigrant groups, who are away from the homes, networks, and communities that represent and celebrate their hometown rituals. Puerto Ricans on the mainland, for example, form social clubs with others from their hometown on the island as a way to stay connected to home. Homeplace also serves as the site of resistance against the oppressive forces of our society (Burton et al., 2004). Home provides security and safety to develop self-esteem, political consciousness, and resistance in the face of societal invalidation, racism, and other oppressive stereotypes. Those who are gay, lesbian, bisexual, or transgender may need special adaptive strategies to find a place they can feel at home, because the very place that others rely on fundamentally may become a place of great danger. This is often true as well for children whose families suffer from mental illness, violence, addictions, and other negative or disruptive forces.

We all need to experience a sense of belonging—to feel safe and secure— especially when living in a multicultural society where connecting with others who are different from us becomes particularly challenging. Indeed, the most challenging aspect of development involves our beliefs about, and interaction with, others who are different from ourselves: men and women, young and old, black and white, wealthy and poor, heterosexual and homosexual. Our level of maturity on this crucial dimension of tolerance and openness to difference is strongly influenced by how our families of origin, communities, cultures of origin, and society as a whole have dealt with difference. It is crucial to explore how one's sense of home may have been disrupted and to consider how discomfort with differences is related to these disruptions. Finding a way back home involves exploring and reconnecting with multicultural familial roots, which includes expanding one's capacity to embrace diversity.

In *Dreams from My Father* Barack Obama (1995) wondered to himself: "What is a family? Is it just a genetic chain, parents and offspring, people like me? Or is it a social construct, an economic unit, optimal for child rearing and divisions of labor? Or is it something else entirely: a store of shared memories, say? An ambit of love? A reach across the void?" (p. 327). In Africa Obama encountered a definition of family much broader than anything he had experienced in the U.S., underscoring the point that whereas family may or may not have a genetic component, it most certainly has a cultural component. How we understand what family is—who is included and excluded from this group— and the role it plays in our lives is shaped by our cultural contexts. The journey to go home again must therefore involve considering families within their cultural contexts and reconnecting in ways that are both narrow and wide, literal and symbolic, personal and cultural, and unique yet also connected to the broader story of our relations with one another and the world.

Ethnicity

Ethnicity refers to the group, clan, or tribe from which one's family comes. Groups share cultural customs and values, and usually language and national origins, but not always. Jewish groups, for example, come from two major sub-groups, Ashkenazic (Eastern European) and Sephardic (Spanish and Middle Eastern), and may have no common country of origin and no language in common; they may be Orthodox, Conservative, Reform, or nonreligious, but still they share cultural origins. National boundaries are often the result of political decisions by colonizing powers and frequently are a poor reflection of ethnic distinctions. The boundaries between countries in Africa and the Middle East, and between India and Pakistan, are recent creations and rarely reflect the ethnicities of the multiple ethnic groups in their boundaries. In the U.S. we have a tendency to define Native Americans as a monolithic group with little regard for the hundreds of different tribal groups that existed here long before white colonizers arrived and estabished arbitrary and imperial-ist boundaries between the U.S., Mexico, and Canada. So it is important to understand where family members come from and what their intergroup relationships were, going back as far as possible.

For African Americans the issue of ethnicity is complicated by the legacy of slavery, which forcibly transported Africans from their homes across the Atlantic and deprived them of any knowledge of their history and even of their names. This holocaust forever changed the lives of generations to come. Few have the opportunity to reach back and connect with the specific tribal groups from which their ancestors descended. Hence, there remains a deep cutoff from their ethnic roots; what stands in its place is a shared identity rooted in a multigenerational legacy of racial oppression. Although specific history is lost for most African Americans, one can often learn enough about a general cultural history to speculate about the influence on one's particular family. The cultural stories of others of the same background may give mean-ingful clues as well.

How Ethnicity Shapes Family Patterns

There are many ways that ethnicity shapes family patterns, which often remain invisible to the naked eye. Consider, for example, a family's attitude toward communication. Do family members believe that everything should get talked out? Do they dance around issues that might cause conflict, while talking a lot about politics or daily activities? Does one person do the talking for the whole family? Do family members express themselves in body language, music, food, or gifts rather than through verbal communication? The patterns that families develop are often influenced by ethnicity, even when this influence remains unrecognized.

In Jewish culture, for example, talk—articulating the meaning of experience—may be as important as the experience itself. Verbal communication—sharing one's ideas and perceptions—is deeply valued as a way of finding meaning in life. Among those of British ancestry, on the other hand, words seem valued primarily for their utilitarian, pragmatic value. As the son in the movie *Ordinary People* says about his brother's death: "What's the point of talking about it? It doesn't change anything." In Chinese culture, families may communicate about important issues through food rather than through words. Italians use both food and words—but words are used primarily for drama—to convey the emotional intensity of an experience. The Irish, who are perhaps the greatest poets in the world, often use words to buffer experience; for centuries they called on poetry or humorous language to make reality more tolerable. It has been suggested that they learned to use words more to cover up or embellish the truth than to express it. A different attitude is found in Sioux culture, where speech is actually proscribed in certain family relationships! A colleague of mine, married for many years to a Sioux, never exchanged a word with her father-in-law, and yet she felt a deep intimacy with him. Such a relationship is almost inconceivable in our digital, pragmatic world. She felt that the reduced emphasis on verbal expression seemed to free up Native American families for other kinds of experience—of each other, of nature, of the spiritual.

In contrast to the British, who value work, reason, truth, and above all individuality, the Irish have always preferred their dreams to the truth. A character in an Irish novel, when accused of being an inveterate liar, explains: "It's the poet's way of reaching for truth"(Flanagan, 1979, p. 166). The dream may serve as protection against reality. The father in Eugene O'Neill's *Long Day's Journey into Night* asserts:

edmund: Yes, facts don't mean a thing, do they? What you want to believe, that's the only truth! Shakespeare was an Irish Catholic, for example.
james: So he was. The proof is in his plays.
edmund: ... To hell with sense! ... Who wants to see life as it is, if they can help it?

How people relate to their illnesses also can be shaped by ethnicity. In Jewish families illness tends to be dealt with very actively and assertively.

Family members are generally knowledgeable about medicine and assertive in seeking doctors and treatments. For others, such as the Irish, nothing may be more embarrassing than talking about their bodies. There is a tendency among the Irish to believe that what goes wrong is a result of your sins, so if you become ill, it is God's punishment. Medical science may be almost irrelevant.

Some groups live primarily in the present whereas others pay more attention to the past and still others think mostly of the future. Indeed, in terms of the valuing of "time," the dominant U.S. ethnic groups, descendants of the British, generally value the present and the near future over either the past or the long-range future. Thus, the values espoused in this book regarding attention to both our history and the legacies we leave for our children's children are a challenge to mainstream ideas. For some groups, however, it is a most natural way of looking at things.

In families with mixed ethnic backgrounds it is important to explore how the values of each culture complement or clash with the other. Eugene O'Neill's wife, Carlotta, daughter of a Danish father and a mother of mixed German, Dutch, and Swiss background, recounted her scrambled parentage by saying:

> I have often wondered if the mixed blood of those different nationalities had much to do with it. It seems that I am always vacillating between extremes, and never choose a compromising and restful middle course. There are times when I feel within me a calling for the primitive, the wild and the elemental in nature and in art. . . . Then at times I crave the very reverse, the exquisite and the ultra-refined. . . . It is not pleasant to be like a living pendulum swinging between two natures. . . . Please do not think me morbid or abnormal . . . I enjoy too thoroughly to fight for my place in the world. (Sheaffer, 1973, p. 222)

It is important to be mindful of your ethnic background and how cultural patterns may be linked to your thoughts, feelings, behaviors, and interactions. Information about your ethnic background is a starting point for exploring how ethnic dynamics may be related to family patterns.

Ethnicity and Couple Relationships

Couples from different cultural groups may be drawn together by the very differences between them. Katherine Hepburn, with her Anglo ethnic identity, and Spencer Tracy, with his Irish-Catholic ethnic identity, illustrate the differences between these groups and how these differences may influence a couple's dynamics. Moreover, these differences are compounded if the Anglo is of the upper class and the Irish of working-class background, which has been the most common differential historically. Hepburn and Tracy differed dramatically in emotional expression. Hepburn, the upper-middle-class, liberal New England Protestant, preferred restraint, decorum, logic, and stoicism in all situations. Tracy, the ultra-conservative, urban, Midwestern, working-class Irish Catholic, was more erratic, less predictable, and less interested in logic. (In fact, Tracy's mother was Anglo as well, descended from the Browns who founded Brown University, but in her marriage to the hard-driving, hard-drinking Irish-Catholic truck salesman, son of immigrants in Milwaukee, she moved into his social context, as women so often have.) These contextual factors were probably compounded by Tracy and Hepburn's sibling positions: she a functional oldest and he a younger brother of a brother whom he seems to have loved and hated with equal intensity all his life.

Dorothy Parker once said of Katherine Hepburn: "She runs the gamut of emotion all the way from A to B" (Kanin, 1988, p. 17). Tracy, on the other hand, would go from violent drunken rages to merry times to sullen withdrawal in roller-coaster fashion. "With Spencer it was virtually impossible to know when he was pretending and when on the level" (p. 88). Whereas Hepburn was careful, thorough, methodical, and analytical in her acting and in her life, Tracy was an instinctive, intuitive actor who thought you went stale by overrehearsing and preferred to trust his intuition. Hepburn's values of propriety, cleanliness, frugality, hard work, and rugged individualism were legendary. She "created, with diligence and intention, a world of her own, and she lived in it happily ever after" (p. 11). Tracy, on the other hand, saw fun in everything, except his religion, but was full of unpredictable highs and lows. A hell-raiser from his youth, he attended 15 schools before finishing eighth grade, usually being expelled for truancy or fighting. He announced to his astonished family in adolescence that he wanted to become a priest, but soon changed his mind and joined the military instead. Garson Kanin, who knew both Tracy and Hepburn well and was one of the major promoters of the mythology around their couplehood, ascribed the different relationships to their ethnicity and class:

> When you enter her world you are expected to observe its strictness and you do without question. You eat a cooked fruit with every meat dish; you arrive on time and leave as early as possible (say, on her third yawn); you do not gossip; you agree with every one of her many opinions and approve each of her numerous plans; you do not get drunk

no matter how much you drink . . . you do not complain (you may, however, rail); you say nothing that may not be repeated; you refrain from lies, dissemblances, and exaggerations, you omit discussion of your physical state, symptoms, or ailments (unless preparatory to asking her advice); you take her advice; you do not use obscene, coarse, or lewd expressions. (Kanin, 1988, pp. 11–12)

Hepburn's approach to work was that it was never a chore to her, always a challenge. She did not settle for less. "She [took] endless showers, sometimes as many as seven or eight in the course of a day. Aside from her belief that cleanliness is next to Godliness, she used cold baths as a hairshirt sort of self-discipline, to strengthen character, intention and drive" (Kanin, 1988, p. 61).

Tracy was "a loner who flitted in and out of relationships from his youth, [who] could shift from charming merriment to weeklong alcoholic binges, becoming more cantankerous than usual, unshaven, not changing his smelly clothes for weeks, holing up in the dark in a heavy overcoat he wore even in summer" (Davidson, 1987, p. 7). Always a fighter and a rebel, he felt most comfortable in working-class contexts, dropping out of many schools even before he dropped out of college, whereas Hepburn set herself very clear goals and worked extremely hard to achieve them.

The couple even differed in what "home" meant to them. Kate was a "house person," viewing even an apartment as "an artificial and temporary abode." Spencer was perfectly content in a hotel room and told Kanin he always liked to live in small places "because I live a small life" (Kanin, 1988, p. 13).

Often the very ethnic differences that attract two people eventually become "the rub." For example, it has been common for Italians and Irish to marry each other. The two groups usually share the same religion, but they are otherwise almost complete opposites in style and values. Italians are often highly expressive, with a tendency toward intense, passionate relationships. The Irish may be more conflicted about expressing emotions, particularly those related to conflict or sexual feelings (even though they are, in general, highly articulate talkers, poets, jokesters, and storytellers). Although they are among the world's greatest fighters, when in a justifiable battle for a morally just cause (particularly involving politics or religion), for the Irish, leaving the scene is the primary response to upsetting family situations—to cool off, regain composure, and avoid saying or doing something you might regret later. Italians, on the other hand, are generally comfortable with any emotional expression, so long as the partner does *not* leave the scene. Thus, in a marital argument, an Italian wife might make outrageous, dramatic accusations or threats in order to convey the depth of her passion on a certain issue, and her Irish husband might perceive this outpouring as completely overwhelming. He might leave or be immobilized into stony silence, unable to formulate a response to the wife's "attack." This would devastate the Italian wife, who would feel certain her husband doesn't love her. For him such a response would merely be a way to stay sane and in control. He would see her "ranting" as a sign of loss of control, what he fears most.

Usually intermarried spouses personalize their differences and then try harder to do whatever they are accustomed to doing to cope with the problem. They may blame the other: "You don't love me. If you loved me you would never behave that way." Or they may blame themselves (Italian wife: "If I just try harder to make him understand how upset I am, he will stop." Irish husband: "If only I try harder to keep quiet and under control, this will blow over and she will stop acting so hysterical."). Such solutions naturally tend to intensify the problem.

What remains critical is to be attuned to the ways that couple dynamics may be linked to ethnic patterns, especially in interethnic relationships. Many white families tend to have a harder time identifying their ethnic roots, which is not to say these roots do not shape and influence relationships. But it may require a bit of probing to uncover the groups from which different family members have descended and to explore how these respective legacies may be tied to assumptions about how to express feelings, perceptions of time, how to handle conflict, how much contact to have with families of origin, and so on.

Race and Skin Color

Race and skin color are powerful organizing principles, especially in societies like the U.S., where there is a great deal of racial diversity. Racial minorities tend to recognize the significance of race and skin color, because society has a way of never letting them lose sight of this. They must be attuned to the realities of race and must teach their children how to survive in the face of experiences of racial discrimination and devaluation. Jackie Robinson's family struggled to survive in the face of relentless racism. In his autobiography, Robinson explained how his mother taught him how to handle encounters with discrimination: "My mother never lost her composure. She didn't allow us to go out of our way to antagonize whites, and still she made it perfectly clear to us and to them that she was not at all afraid of them and that she had no intention of allowing them to mistreat us" (Robinson, 1972, p. 6). Jackie's mother modeled never giving up or surrendering your dignity. It is little wonder that each time Jackie faced racism during his lifetime, he never backed down. He always held his ground, and his courage and determination, combined with his remarkable talents and capabilities, helped him to break a number of racial barriers during his lifetime.

At the same time that there is a need to cope with external racism and devaluation, many families of color also must cope with the ways that white supremacy infiltrates the psychosocial interior of families. This occurs through the color complex. In her book *Don't Play in the Sun: One Woman's Journey Through the Color Complex*, Marita Golden (2005) explained how, when she was 8 years old and playing with friends outside, her mother scolded her: "I've told you don't play in the sun. You're going to have to get a light-skinned husband for the sake of your children as it is" (p. 4). Her mother's words cut to the bone because she understood exactly what their full implication was: that she was too dark to ever be considered beautiful, good, valuable, and acceptable. It was a message she received over and over from family members and friends who "showered praise and compliments on lighter-hued, straighter-haired children for their beauty" (p. 8) while never extending similar praise to her or other brown to black children. Although Golden was clear about how wounded she felt as a result of her mother's admonition, she also realized in retrospect that her mother was merely trying to prepare her for the cruel realities of the world: "From the vantage point of the present, I know now that those words, so harsh, and so brutal, were offered to me not as the punishment I heard but as an act of love" (p. 11).

It is critical to be mindful of this phenomenon and the extent to which it shapes relationships among family members within families of color. In their book *The Color Complex*, Russell, Wilson, and Hall (1993) explained: "Even in families where color does not seem to be much of an issue, siblings learn to use their differences as ammunition in ordinary rivalries. Joni, a light-skinned woman, remembers that calling her still lighter-skinned sister 'a green-eyed bitch' inevitably sent her into a frenzy of rage. In healthy families, such sibling conflict may actually relieve pent-up feelings and make the whole issues seem less serious or threatening. It is when color remains an unspoken concern that children may suffer the most" (p. 96).

Most whites think of race as an issue only for people of color, failing to recognize the ways in which they too have a racial identity that shapes their lives. The privilege of whiteness makes it possible not to have to think about race, and, as a result, most whites do not consider the relevance of race until a family member dates or marries someone of color. As the United States becomes increasingly diverse, more and more people are marrying out of their ethnic and racial group. This is significant given that until the past generation, insidious laws prohibited people from marrying across racial lines. In fact, prohibitions against cross-racial unions have been the basis for a range of challenges and tensions within families for centuries. Remember the Barrett family, where Elizabeth Barrett Browning's father, Edward, strongly disapproved of her relationship with Robert Browning because he feared that Browning also had African and Jewish blood in his heritage. He worried that if any of his children married, the family's mixed-race heritage would be exposed in their progeny.

The point about white privilege is that it enables most white people to live without pondering how race influences their lives. Barack Obama (1995) exposed this dynamic in considering how his maternal grandparents, Stanley and Toot, came to allow their daughter, however grudgingly, to marry an African, a question that always puzzled him. He said: "When black people appear at all in the Kansas of my grandparents' memories, the images are fleeting . . . they are shadowy, silent presences that elicit neither passion nor fear" (p. 18). He said they probably never thought about race except when they observed someone else's racism: "Like most white Americans at the time, they had never really given black people much thought," because in their world, "the unspoken code that governed life among whites kept contact between the races to a minimum" (p. 18).

Several years after they were married, Obama's grandparents moved to Texas, and it was probably there that they first became aware of racism. Stanley was warned to not serve Mexican and black customers in the furniture store where he was a salesman, and Toot was accosted by a secretary in the bank where she worked for referring to the black janitor as "Mister Reed." Experiences like these shocked and offended them, but were probably the only times they thought about race overtly. Although Stanley insisted that they left Texas because they were disturbed by the racism there, Toot said they actually left in search of better work: "The word racism wasn't even in their vocabulary back then" (Obama, 1995, p. 21).

Obama hypothesized that his grandfather's receptivity to his daughter's marriage to a black man may have reflected his identification with outsider status as a child whose mother committed suicide and whose own father disappeared. Hence his daughter's interracial marriage was "at some deeply unexplored level . . . a window into his [grandfather's] own heart" (Obama, 1995, p. 22).

Once Barack was born, his grandparents were forever part of an interracial family. Of course, racial diversity in Hawaii was much more a part of the local culture than in the mainland U.S., which may have made things easier. Nevertheless, this once white family now had to deal with race overtly as an undeniable part of their everyday experience.

It is important to be curious about all the unions of different people within one's family—couples who came from different class backgrounds, religions, ethnic or racial groups—and to understand how family members thought about and responded to any interracial or other intergroup situation. Who was supportive of the relationship and who was against it? What reasons did they offer and how directly or indirectly were various opinions, beliefs, and reactions shared and communicated? How did triangles, alliances, or distance and cutoffs develop in response to racial issues?

Within families of color, how overtly are issues of race and skin color addressed among family members? What are the messages that different people convey? How have children been socialized with respect to racial awareness and coping with racism? How are some family members valued or devalued based on complexion? How have triangles, alliances, and cutoffs developed around issues of race or skin color? Overall, it is important to be curious about how families react to differences of all kinds, including those related to race and skin color.

Historical Context: A Family's Place in Time

It is vital to consider not only a family's cultural identity but also the broader sociopolitical context and historical forces that shaped family experiences. A compelling example of this can be observed in the case of famed painters Frida Kahlo and her husband, Diego Rivera (Genogram 9.1), who were typical of many families in their complex mixture of cultural heritages. It is impossible to understand Kahlo's family without considering the historical and cultural context in which they lived. Frida Kahlo, a revolutionary artist born in Coyoacán, Mexico, amidst political chaos, so identified herself with her political era that she used to say she had been born in 1910, the year of the Mexican Revolution, although in reality she was born 3 years earlier. Her life was fully caught up in the sociopolitical struggles of her culture and times, as her work reflects. Kahlo wrote in her diary later in life: "The clear and precise emotions of the 'Mexican Revolution' were the reason why, at the age of 13, I joined the Communist youth" (Fuentes, 1995, p. 282).

Kahlo grappled with the multiple cultural aspects of her identity—gender, ethnicity, and national identity—all her life, often depicting them in her art, with one foot located in the cultural ruins of ancient Mexico and the other in the industrial, imperialistic U.S. She was a complex mixture of competing and contrasting forces. On the one hand she was a young Mexican girl, and on the other a sophisticated woman of the world. Her works are a testament both to pre-Columbian and colonial cultural influences. Sometimes she depicted her husband inside her head, as if it was impossible to have an identity that he didn't in some way own; at other times her work radiated with her fierce independence. She was a vibrant, powerfully creative, and forceful woman, who was plagued with debilitating physical injuries and illness. She was openly bisexual, and although intensely jealous of Rivera's numerous infidelities, she too had affairs with many men and women. She was alternately hopeful and despairing and vacillated between periods of extreme isolation and wild bursts of exuberance and merrymaking.

Kahlo's life and work embodied a clash between forces that was a reflection of both the historical and cultural context of her times, as well as of the unique dynamics of her family's cultural legacy. Her father was a German-Hungarian Jew who immigrated to Mexico, where he deeply embraced the culture. Her mother was the daughter of a native Michoacán woman and a Spanish general—thus the literal embodiment of Mexican culture, forged through the clash between the conquering Spaniards and the conquered indigenous peoples. Kahlo intensely identified with her roots on both sides of her family system, finding ways to hold the tension between often conflicting aspects. This tension was something that was deeply entrenched within the Kahlo family system, beginning with her parents' marriage. Theirs was a tense and unhappy union, and one has to wonder to what extent their ethnic and religious differences contributed to the distance between them. Frida's mother was a devout Catholic and her conservative values often created distance between her and her daughters, as well as between her and her husband. Although Frida's father, "Herr" Kahlo, as she affectionately referred to him, was not a practicing Jew, he nevertheless transmitted this part of his heritage to Frida, who claimed her Jewish immigrant ancestry with pride.

Kahlo's strong ties to her mixed ethnic roots and the power that the historical context had on her life can be observed in a painting of her as a child with her parents and grandparents and in a later painting that adapts a genealogical chart of her 1936 family tree. In 1935 the Nazi government established the Nuremberg laws, which prohibited intermarriage and promoted "racial purity." Genealogical charts were one method the Nazis used to prove or disprove "racial purity." By 1936 Nazi-oriented manuals on how to conduct genealogical research were distributed in the German School of Mexico City, where many of the teachers joined the Nazi Party and encouraged their students to chart their family trees. Distressed by this, Kahlo adapted this device to emphasize her interracial origins, her subversive statement being a reflection of her identification with her Jewish and multiracial roots.

Kahlo's art also reflects both her passion for and attunement to the duality of Mexican culture in terms of the convergence of ancient Mezo-American and European Spanish roots. Her paintings routinely included religious symbols that were Jewish, Catholic, and indigenous, further

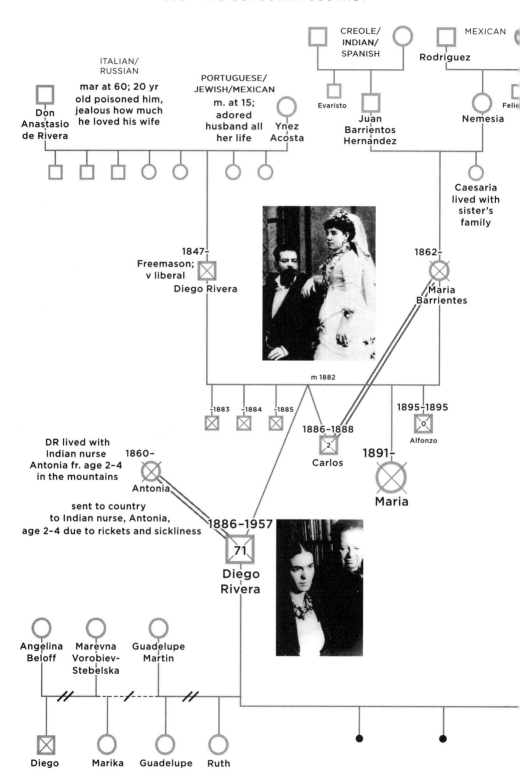

CREOLE/
INDIAN/
SPANISH

MEXICAN
Rodriguez

Evaristo

Juan
Barrientos
Hernandez

Nemesia

Feli

ITALIAN/
RUSSIAN

mar at 60; 20 yr
old poisoned him,
jealous how much
he loved his wife

Don
Anastasio
de Rivera

PORTUGUESE/
JEWISH/MEXICAN

m. at 15;
adored
husband all
her life

Ynez
Acosta

Caesaria
lived with
sister's
family

1847–
Freemason;
v liberal
Diego Rivera

1862–
Maria
Barrientes

m 1882

–1883   –1884   –1885

1886–1888
2
Carlos

1895–1895
0
Alfonzo

DR lived with
Indian nurse
Antonia fr. age 2-4
in the mountains

1860–
Antonia

1891–
Maria

sent to country
to Indian nurse, Antonia,
age 2-4 due to rickets and sickliness

1886–1957
71
Diego
Rivera

Angelina
Beloff

Marevna
Vorobiev-
Stebelska

Guadelupe
Martin

Diego

Marika   Guadelupe   Ruth

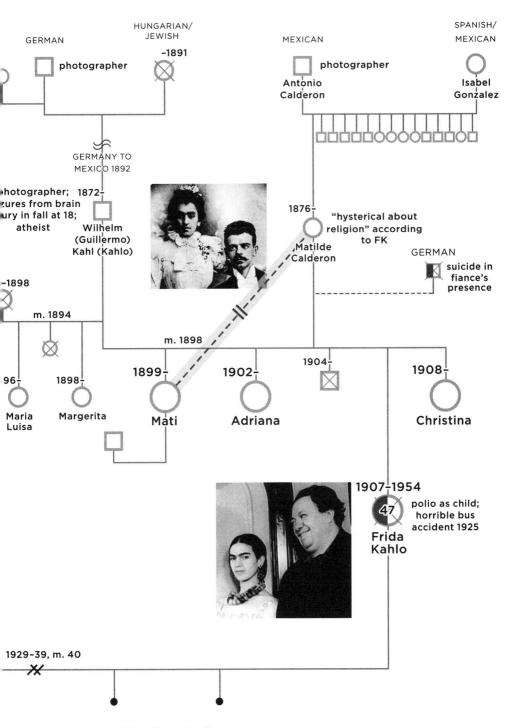

GERMAN

HUNGARIAN/
JEWISH

–1891

□ photographer

⊗

SPANISH/
MEXICAN

MEXICAN

□ photographer

Antonio
Calderon

○ Isabel
Gonzalez

GERMANY TO
MEXICO 1892

photographer; 1872–
zures from brain
ury in fall at 18;
atheist

□ Wilhelm
(Guillermo)
Kahl (Kahlo)

1876– ○ "hysterical about
religion" according
to FK

Matilde
Calderon

GERMAN

▣ suicide in
fiance's
presence

–1898

⊗

m. 1894

⊗

m. 1898

m. 1898

1904–

⊠

1908–

96– 1898–

Maria
Luisa

Margerita

1899– ○

Mati

1902– ○

Adriana

Christina ○

□

1907–1954

(47)

polio as child;
horrible bus
accident 1925

Frida
Kahlo

1929–39, m. 40

⊁

● ●

Genogram 9.1. The Rivera Family.

illustrating the impact of her family's mixed ethnic and religious roots on her life and her work.

When trying to understand a family from an intergenerational perspective, consider how the historical context shaped whatever behaviors occurred at a given point in time. The very same behaviors have different meanings and provoke different reactions depending on the historical period in which they occur. A woman who leaves an abusive relationship in the U.S. in the 21st century will be much better understood and protected than would have happened 100 years ago. As another example, consider societal and family reactions back in the 1950s to the decision to live with a partner of the same sex or the decision to have a cross-racial relationship. Living openly in congruence with one's sexual orientation would have been inconceivable just about any time prior to the latter 20th century. Similarly, for most of U.S. history interracial relationship have been legally and socially prohibited. Yet, as a result of profound social and legal changes, it is now possible for gay and lesbian couples to live together openly, and in some cases even to marry. Interracial marriages have been made legal in recent decades, following significant changes in social attitudes, normalizing and sanctioning such relationships. So it is important to assess any family pattern in its particular historical context.

Migration

Migration is another event that has great impact on a family. It is important to evaluate sibling relationships, for example, in the context of the timing of a family's migration. A family that migrates in the middle of the mother's child-bearing years may have two different sets of children: those born before and those born after the migration. The children born after the migration may have been raised in a much more hopeful context or, on the other hand, in a much more stressed family, struggling to acculturate and learn the language and missing their own culture.

A family's migration experience refers to the geographic routes that individuals and families have traveled. The experiences they had along the way shape family dynamics. The reasons why individuals or families migrate, and their relationship with the cultures they left behind, passed through, and resettled in, are essential factors in the family's character and developmental processes.

All too often, migration experiences are tied to stories of suffering and trauma, which leave an indelible impact on multiple generations of a family. As already mentioned, a traumatic case of migration was suffered by contemporary African Americans' ancestors, who were violently uprooted from their cultures and families of origin and relocated thousands of miles away as

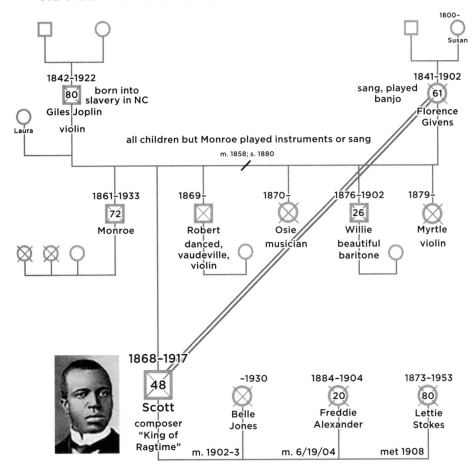

Genogram 9.2. The Joplin Family.

slaves. Not only did they endure a devastating physical separation from their homes, families, and communities, but they also had to endure the psychological and relational loss that resulted from being forbidden to maintain any overt association with their cultural tradition.

Other groups may also have histories of trauma associated with their migration. Jewish families, for example, were oppressed for hundreds of years. The Freud family (see page 172 for genogram) was forced to migrate twice, never again returning to their home in what is now the Czech Republic. Freud experienced continuous anti-Semitism, which limited his professional development. The Mahler family (see page 256 for genogram) experienced a very similar migration from the same region. Unlike Freud, however, Mahler left behind his Jewish identity, under the pressure of the times, so he could succeed musically in Vienna. One wonders what the Mahler family lost in the pain of migration and what price they paid emotionally and spiritually in giving up their religion and settling in a country that never would accept them for who they truly were. What does it cost a family in terms of a sense of belonging and identity to live in a place where their talents are not recognized? Even today the city of Vienna does not appear to acknowledge or celebrate Mahler's role in the history of music, although his music is played all over the world.

Scott Joplin (Genogram 9.2) was another gifted composer whose talent was not acknowledged as a result of the racist context in which he lived. His life, like that of all African Americans, was profoundly affected by his not being able to feel at home in his cultural context and the historical period in which he lived. The first African-American composer to fully develop his compositions into an American idiom, he was also the first child in his highly gifted musical family to be born after the end of slavery, and the only one who became a successful musician and composer. Although there is no doubt that Scott was extremely talented, family patterns linked to broader social conditions as an African-American family living in the South during the time of emancipation may have contributed to his special development and eventual success, as well as to the limitations on his musical accomplishments.

As mentioned, Joplin was forced to migrate several times (in an effort to improve his chances at success), first from Texarkana to St. Louis, then to Chicago, and then on to New York. His publishers refused to accept his operas, claiming that ragtime was the only acceptable music for a black man to compose. Had he been able to develop his talents fully without the rejections of those who felt he did not fit in, his musical innovations might have been even more amazing. He spent years trying to find a way to publish and produce his opera *Tremonisha*, finally exhausting his resources in the process. The opera was not fully performed until 1972, almost 60 years after Joplin's death! His situation is an illustration of both the opportunities made possible by the specific timing of his birth after emancipation, and the limitations of the repressive cultural context in which he lived.

Other groups have also suffered from traumatic migrations related to fleeing poverty, persecution, or war. Russian Jews fled from the pogroms and, later, the horrors of the holocaust; the Irish fled during the Irish famine in the mid-19th century; in the 1980s thousands attempted to escape the brutal Pol Pot regime in Cambodia; Mexicans and others in the Americas have risked their lives for decades to migrate to the U.S. in search of a livelihood.

Families' migration experiences often have many chapters, and the more they are understood, the more the family's ensuing patterns can be understood. For example, although most Latinos are keenly aware of their stories of migration from Central and South American countries and the Caribbean, there tends to be less awareness of the earlier migrations over many generations that culminated in the convergence of three incredibly diverse groups of people: the black Africans who were brought to the Americas as slaves, the indigenous Americans who originally migrated from Asia thousands of years ago, and the Spaniards who came as colonists and conquerors.

In addition to knowing the reasons and circumstances around why individuals and families have migrated, it also is important to consider the life-cycle stage at which families migrated and how different generations have adapted and acculturated to their new cultural contexts, which profoundly shape family dynamics. For example, if children in a family learn the language of the host culture before the parents do, which often happens, it undoubtedly influences family relationships, triangles, alliances, and cutoffs, which may develop later. If parents lose their status in the process of immigration, or if they increase their status by succeeding in ways they had hardly dreamed of when they came—it will influence family relationships for generations to come. Whatever a given family's unique migration story may be, it is essential to understand the reasons why movement occurred, what family members left behind, and what dreams or fears they brought with them to wherever they ended up going.

Social Class and Location

Social class is one of the most powerful organizing principles among human beings. In some societies, class is openly acknowledged as an overt way of structuring relationships among people. For centuries in India, explicit caste rules structured societal relationships and prevented different castes from marrying. In the United States, we tend to operate on the myth that we are a classless society, but, of course, this is not so. Social class shapes virtually every aspect of our lives, whether we realize it or not. Class values permeate all sorts of everyday activities, such as what car you drive (or even feel comfortable driving, and, of course, whether you even have a car!), or what music you listen to. Opera, for example, generally defines your class, unless you're Italian, as does a penchant for country-and-western music. Your leisure activities also reflect class attitudes: Golf and tennis tend to signify one class, bowling another. Symbols of class often show up in family rituals, especially weddings. For example, the upper class and working class may go all out for a wedding. The upper middle class, on the other hand, may see such display as "gauche."

Class, while difficult to define, is loosely based upon a complex interaction between variables such as education, occupation, income and wealth. In the U.S. education it is the most secure way we have of changing class. We seem to operate according to the notion that anyone can become anything through education, although we still have a remarkably stratified system of access to education, as well as of judging class according to the school attended, from the Ivy League and Seven Sisters colleges to state universities to community colleges and so forth. Occupation is another determinant of class right down to the fact that whether the work you do is defined as a job or a profession has class implications. An occupation at any class level may be a job but an occupation that is a profession implies a middle class status or higher. Moreover, while all occupations have specific class values associated with them, the class-based meaning associated with a given occupation may not be correlated with the actual income that the occupation renders. For example, comparatively speaking, an occupation as a mechanic does not engender as a high a social class rating as a being a college professor, and yet a mechanic may easily earn a substantially higher income than the professor. This leads to another key determinant of class: money.

Money can be sub-divided into two categories: income and wealth. Income refers to the money you earn for the work that you do. Wealth refers to the non-income based money and other assets (e.g., real estate, stocks, bonds, jewelry) that can be inherited by future generations.

Money, whether it is earned or inherited, is a symbolic clue to some of the most deeply held views about the meaning of life. It may represent love, security, happiness, success, power, shame, pride, fear, and many other things. Conflicts between the "tightwad" and the "spendthrift" may dominate family interactions, causing children to be in collusion with one parent against the other and disrupting or distorting family relationships. Moreover, conflicts and cutoffs in families are often linked to money issues. For example, when a family business or a will has left family money unequally divided among siblings, relationships are likely to be impaired or even cut off, often for generations. Sometimes family members may be held hostage by threats of being cut off and losing their inheritance if they contact a "forbidden" relative or marry someone from another race. In such cases, the only way to free one's self emotionally may be at times to "let go of the rope." Of course, if they are not prepared to lose the inheritance in order to keep the relationship, they will not be able to do the required emotional work.

While few of us think overtly about social class, nevertheless it is an integral aspect of how we experience reality. Each of us makes automatic and often unconscious class attributions on a minute by minute basis. And because we often do not know all of the relevant facts about a person's life (in terms of education, occupation, income and wealth), we tend to make class attributions based on a variety of social markers such as style of dress, mannerisms, speech, taste, particular behaviors, expressed attitudes, etc.

While we all make class attributions, often times the social markers we reference lead to inaccurate assumptions and conclusions. For example, we may attribute a higher class status to a person who shows up for a professional function wearing a crisply pressed designer suit, and assume the person who shows up wearing wrinkled slacks and a t-shirt is of a lower class status, but the reality may be exactly the opposite. This scenario underscores the dangers of making attributions based on simplistic assumptions that overlook the complexities of social class. In addition, there are the psychological effects of having or not having access to class privilege. Those who have it often feel a freedom that those who don't have do not feel. Hence, those without class privilege battle against the devaluation associated with "not having" and feeling judged to be "less than," which is likely to breed a vigilance about how they "present themselves." Conversely, those with class privilege, as a direct benefit of that privilege, do not feel the same pressure to "prove their worth" but feel greater freedom to show up in attire that may be judged as "lower class" with all the negative connotations this implies. Consequently, each of us would benefit from being more mindful of how we go about making class attributions. What markers do we reference that lead to certain conclusions and in what ways might our assumptions be overly simplistic or inattentive to some vital factor that could lead us to make a different conclusion?

The issue of the perception versus the reality of social class is further complicated by the fact that class is not a fixed dimension and can change over the course of our lifetimes. Whereas we cannot change our gender, our cultural background, or the facts of our history, most families have moved from one class to another over the past generation or two. And a great many of us are trying to move up in class all the time. Yet while the external reality of our social class may change over the course of our lives, psychologically our social class status tends to remain fixed, which is inevitably reflected in attitudes and behaviors. In other words, how we behave may not necessarily be congruent with the reality of our current social class location. As a colleague described it, "Consider the kin of an established upper-class family that, over the generations, has lost its wealth. The younger generations may still be highly educated and comfortable socializing in upper-class circles even though they have no inheritance and limited income. Conversely, the sons or daughters in a middle-class family who become wildly successful in business may be politically powerful but spend their money on ostentatious, cheaply built McMansions. The chameleon from "the sticks" in the South may manage to get to college, lose her accent, sneak her way into all the right social events, and marry into a wealthy family, but may continue to horde supplies bought in bulk at Costco that are warehoused in the basement" (C. Ruble, personal communication). These scenarios are examples of how our external social class locations may change dramatically, while our internal social class orientation remains far more fixed, continuing to reflect the class circumstance into which we were born and socialized.

An additional element of class is perception of class position, which may be based on many issues such as family circumstances, disability, or cultural background. Catherine Bateson grew up in the conservative 1950s, daughter of two very famous anthropologists. After her parents' divorce she lived with a family friend for several years, attending an elite school for girls in New York City while both parents were elsewhere doing their research. Catherine felt like a waif because of her family circumstances: "It was clear to me as it would have been to a lonely black or Jewish child in an alien school that the problem had to do with who we were—a different kind of people, a different kind of family. I lived in the wrong part of the city, came to school by subway, and shopped at Macy's. I was full of knowledge and experience that marked me as an oddity and yet I lacked the really important skills, particularly athletic skills that would have won acceptance" (Bateson, 1984, p. 72). In fact, when she finally confessed that she didn't even know the basics of the rules of baseball her mother suggested getting her a tutor! She was even more humiliated at the idea she would need a tutor to learn what everyone else grew up learning along the way.

Class issues have profound implications for family relationships and how family members perceive and relate to each other. The impact of class issues on family relationships tends to become especially pronounced when changes in class status occur within a family system. Though they are generally not talked about within a family, they are constantly played out in conflicts between couples, parents and children, in-laws and siblings. Consider famed advice columnists Ann Landers and Dear Abby (discussed in Chapter 7; see page 213 for genogram). The twins, along with their two older sisters, were the children of Jewish Russian immigrants who settled in Sioux City, Iowa. The parents came to the U.S. with almost nothing, and at first neither spoke English. They peddled chickens from a pushcart until they could buy a grocery store, enabling them to leave the poorer section of the city. Eventually the father became an entrepreneur who owned almost all the movie theaters in the area. The daughters were close growing up, attending high school and then college together. Yet class tensions related to their husbands' vastly different class backgrounds appear to have contributed to the falling out that occurred in their adulthood.

"Popo," Pauline Esther (later Dear Abby) met Mort Philips at a fraternity dance at the University of Minnesota, not realizing at first that he was heir to a Minnesota-based family fortune having gone from rags to riches just as hers did since their immigration. Eppie (Esther Pauline, who later became "Ann Landers"), was first engaged to a UCLA law student, Lewis Dreyer, but while shopping for her wedding dress she was picked up by a local hat salesman, Jules Lederer, son of a Romanian immigrant traveling salesman. She replaced Lewis with Jules in time to keep plans in place for a double wedding with Popo. After the truncated honeymoon, Eppie and Jules returned to a small apartment in Sioux City, where Jules worked. Popo and Mort moved into a luxurious home in Minneapolis with several servants and began the grooming process to take over the family business. Eventually Mort offered Jules a job selling pots and pans for one of his companies, and Jules's life circumstances moved upward as he became a successful business manager. Eppie eventually won a contest to replace the previous advice columnist Ann Landers and took over the name with which she became associated for the rest of her life (Pottker & Speziale, 1987). Shortly afterwards Popo began her own advice column as "Dear Abby" and the competition between them intensified. The twins' competition and the long cutoff in their relationship was undoubtedly fueled by tensions reflected in their divergent social class standing, tied to their husbands' vastly different socioeconomic status. Class differences such as these are a common source of conflict and resentment in families, where strong feelings may develop between siblings about who got more and who deserved more.

Parents and children may also have class differences. One way this commonly occurs is when a child is the first to have a college or professional education. While parents may be proud of their child's achievements, it is not uncommon for the resulting change in class status to become a source of tension. A chasm emerges between family members and the resulting loss created by social distance becomes more painful by virtue of the fact that it usually cannot be acknowledged. The same is true for the class distance created in a family by a child who is downwardly mobile through disability—retardation, mental illness, or other dysfunction. Families often feel shamed by their children's consequent loss of class status, especially because our society disallows families to deal directly with issues of class.

Family cutoffs in response to class issues often get played out in stereotypes about class difference: "They've gotten above themselves" or "They've got no manners." The inability to talk about the class distance makes it worse.

In addition, people may feel obliged in social situations to hide their origins—whether because of financial straits or because they were privileged—for fear of alienating others. And family members who are ashamed of their class background may cut off from the family as a result. The class shifts in a family can create or intensify distance, especially in parent-child relationships in adult life. Pressure on those whose class location differs from that of their family of origin may be intense. To better understand your cultural context, it can help to look at what circumstances in the family contributed to members changing class location. For example, were these changes related to education, financial success or failure, dysfunction of a family member, ability or disability, a family legacy or shifting social position through work or marriage? It is also helpful to examine how a change in one member's class status may have impacted relationships, especially between parents and children and between siblings, frequently privileging the one who rises in social status and marginalizing the one who has moved down in social class from the rest of the family.

While denying that class matters, families tend to be extremely conscious of class in their interactions, especially in relation to outsiders. Children tend to measure their family in relation to their age mates' families. For example, children might be embarrassed because their parents didn't speak "correctly." If a family's class experience was privileged, children might worry about their parents seeming snobbish or intimidating when introduced to school friends. Generally speaking, we tend to measure ourselves subconsciously in every interaction. We also tend to measure our families in relation to the rest of the community. In a letter that Ann Landers wrote to her daughter Margo, decades after she had to abandon her joint honeymoon because of her finances, she stated:

> I remember my own resentment against my parents . . . when I didn't do well in school one day, I came home and said to my father, "You failed your children. You didn't give us CULTURE. There is never anything to read in this damn house but Elks magazines." I can remember the hurt in his eyes. After all, what did [he] . . . know about "culture"? Nothing. I can assure you. But he knew an awful lot about how to love people and make them love him. He was a master at this. And he taught me a great deal that has made me able to do the work I am doing today. (Howard, 2003, p. 14)

Landers' poignant disclosure exposes how class dynamics affected her relationship with her parents. Her angry comment that Elks magazines were the only reading material in their home was a class reference. Moreover, although her awareness of their lower-class stature provoked anger toward her parents, undoubtedly the anger masked more vulnerable experiences of shame and inadequacy related to not feeling "good enough" in terms of the family's class status.

Couple choices are very much influenced by class aspirations, and in most families the acceptability of a marriage partner is probably determined more by class issues than by the new spouse's character. It may take years for family members to revise their initial perceptions of a spouse who marries in—if they ever do. As has been seen earlier, both of the families of Beethoven's parents (see page 126 for genogram) felt their children were marrying down—a common experience, and a common source of conflict and triangles in marital relationships ("your family looks down on my family; therefore you don't love me").

At times a family's prejudice against a marriage partner on the basis of class is hidden behind excuses that the partner is unacceptable because he or she is too "different." It is true, of course, that when children choose marriage partners from a radically different class background, families do have to work hard to bridge the distances the alliance creates.

It is also important to appreciate that various cultural groups view class differently: Anglos tend to take class stratification as a given—revealed in your first words and defining all social interactions. Puerto Ricans have also taken class stratification for granted. They are less likely to assume that people change class. On the other hand, Jewish families tend to encourage their children to rise in class, if at all possible. Others, notably Italian and Polish families, may feel ambivalent about their children rising in class, fearing the child will leave the family. African Americans have tended to believe that education offers the greatest likelihood of "making it," but may express concerns about "getting above yourself" or "putting on airs." A common tension among African Americans involves accusing upwardly mobile African Americans of being "bougie" (bourgeois) and having "sold out and forgotten where they came from." Those who have risen in class then distance themselves from poor and working-class relations, looking down on them and accusing them of being lazy and "ghetto." For the Irish, terms like "shanty Irish" and "lace curtain Irish" came to indicate class differences and carried a negative undertone; they feared being poor and they feared "getting above yourself." Polish families, like the Irish and African Americans, have good historical reasons for their ambivalence about rising in class, as traditionally the upper classes were identified with foreigners (especially the French). For them, remaining "salt of the earth" has been a strong value.

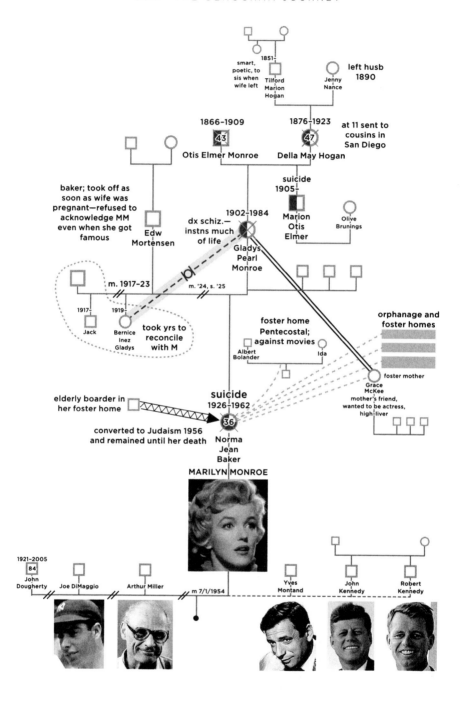

Genogram 9.3. The Monroe Family.

Religion and Spirituality

Whether or not a family defines their ethnicity in terms of a religious group, religion is a powerful dimension of culture that shapes family dynamics and patterns over time. The basic tenets and beliefs that particular religious groups espouse, the extent to which a family and its members adhere to or reject a given religious identification, and the extent to which that religion contributes to or is a basis for experiences with oppression and discrimination all affect family development.

A family's spiritual values are also part of the bedrock of understanding them. In adolescence and young adulthood especially, family members may be in conflict with the spiritual beliefs of their parents, rebelling against traditional practices and customs and seeking to coalesce their own religious and spiritual beliefs. This may create extreme strain on the family, as parents feel threatened on a personal level, and disrupt the whole continuity of the family. Part of understanding families involves pushing past the polemics of family arguments over religion and politics to understand the roots of each member's most cherished beliefs. Why has Uncle Joe become an atheist? Why does mom hold so tightly to saying the rosary every day? Why did one's grandparents sit shiva for their son when he married a "shiksa"? Unless you can imagine your way into the mindset of each family member, you will not really understand your family.

Often a person's experience with religion while growing up fosters an identification with and loyalty to that group. Conversely, it can provoke a reaction against and rejection of a given religious community of origin. The Kennedy family, where all members embraced their Catholic roots, is an example of the former, whereas Erik Erikson, who disavowed his Jewish roots, is an example of the latter.

The influence of religious experiences in childhood may also produce effects that are more complex than merely identifying with or disavowing one's religious community of origin. Marilyn Monroe (Genogram 9.3), born Norma Jean Baker in 1926, is someone who appeared to both connect with and disconnect from her primary religious community of origin. Monroe writes in her autobiography about the role God played in her life from earliest childhood: "Nearly everybody I knew talked to me about God. They always warned me not to offend Him. But when "Aunt" Grace (her mentally ill mother's best friend, who eventually adopted Marilyn) talked about God, she touched my cheek and said that He loved me and watched over me. Remembering what Grace had said I lay in bed at night crying to myself. The only One who loved me and watched over me was Someone I couldn't see or hear or touch. I used to draw pictures of God whenever I had time. In my pictures He looked a little like Aunt Grace and a little like Clark Gable" (Monroe, 1986, pp. 20–21).

Marilyn's mother had shown her pictures of Gable and tried to convince her that he was her father! In fact, it has never been confirmed who her father actually was. Her mother Gladys gave Marilyn's the last name of her ex-husband, Ed Mortensen, from whom she had separated the year before. Both Marilyn's mother and her grandmother were zealous Pentecostal evangelicals, but Norma Jean spent most of her childhood living in a series of foster homes. Her first and most consistent home was with Ida and Albert Bolender, whom she lived with from the time of her birth until the age of 7. They were Pentecostal and, like her mother, were fanatically religious. The Bolenders were extremely strict with Norma Jean, believing that a strong moral and religious background would benefit her throughout her life. Ironically, they condemned movies and warned about the sinfulness of sexuality; Norma Jean, meanwhile, grew up to become Marilyn Monroe, one of the world's most famous movie stars and sex symbols. It is as if her life became a reaction against the deeply restrictive and repressive religiosity she was subjected to in childhood. She lived at times with her aunt Grace and at other times with Grace's aunt Ana, a staunch Christian Science practitioner. Indeed, as much as Marilyn came to embody things that were condemned by her religious community of origin, she remained a Christian Scientist until the age of 30. At that point, Marilyn married Arthur Miller and converted to Judaism. Though neither he nor his family apparently cared about this issue, she insisted on the conversion and even after her divorce from Miller she maintained her Jewish identity until her death. It is perhaps also relevant that Miller and Monroe witnessed a traumatic fatal accident the day before their wedding, which precipitated their marriage and may have influenced Monroe's need for a spiritual home as well.

Marilyn went to a school with a very wide range of students from different social locations. One of Monroe's biographers described the social class mix of her school, making clear why she would have felt alone in the situation: Some (students) were chauffeured down from the gated mansions in the enclave known as Bel-Air, above Sunset Boulevard. Others were from the middle-class flatlands of West Los Angeles. And some—. . . (Monroe) among them—were within walking distance, from a poorer district known as Sawtelle. . . The area was a jumble of populations—Japanese immigrants, longtime California pioneers from the East and Midwest; recent Dust Bowl "Oakies" who had sought work and refuge in sunny California during the Depression; Hispanics and Mexican Indians; and older Los Angeles residents like Ana Lower (Aunt Grace's aunt, the Christian Science Practitioner with whom Marilyn was living)" (Spoto, 1993, pp. 73–74).

The makeup of her school contributed to her sense of alienation. One of Monroe's classmates described the school situation thus: "Los Angeles was a very divided, class-conscious society and this was unfortunately true of school life too. All the students were immediately, unofficially classified according to where they lived, and Sawtelle was simply not the place to be from. . . (Monroe) was from the wrong side of the tracks" (cited in Spoto, 1993, p. 74).

Marilyn experienced a sense of alienation and homelessness on many levels all her life. Her experience with religion in childhood was one of isolation, repression, and loneliness, despite the fact that religion could have provided her with a sense of community and connectedness. Her conversion to Judaism may have reflected a desire to become part of an extended family community, an attempt to find "homeplace." In Judaism she may have been seeking to fulfill her underlying spiritual and emotional hunger, her yearning to be a part of something bigger than herself—to be part of a community with a sense of historical continuity and connection (Zimroth, 2002), which were unfilled desires deeply rooted in an isolated childhood that haunted her throughout her life.

Families in which different religious and spiritual orientations are represented present both a challenge and an opportunity for children. On the one hand, being exposed to diverse ways of defining and experiencing religiosity and spirituality encourages the exploration of different perspectives and gives children the freedom to define their religion and spirituality for themselves. On the other hand, parents' different religious orientations can be a source of tension and conflict, and children may feel divided loyalties. When parents are of different faiths, how their children come to define themselves spiritually often hints at whom they feel closer to, or desire to be closer to, just as it may expose underlying family triangles or alliances.

Jawaharlal Nehru (see page 122 for genogram), the first prime minister of India, was the son of parents with very different orientations. Nehru's mother was a deeply devoted Hindu, whereas his father rejected religion in favor of secular humanism. Of these two dramatically different perspectives, Nehru eventually followed in his father's footsteps, proclaiming that all religion and spiritualism was absurd and defining himself as an agnostic. Nehru's identification with is father's perspective and disavowal of his mother's may say something about his relationship with each. Although, as discussed earlier, he felt closer to his mother, his father's approval was more important to him, leading him to model his own beliefs in concert with his father's. What is especially intriguing is that Nehru married a woman like his mother, a devout Hindu,

Kamala. Yet like his father had done with him, he openly expressed to his daughter, Indira, his ideas about the dangers of religion and the value of secularism. In a letter he wrote to her when she was 10 he explained:

> Religion first came as fear, and anything that is done because of fear is bad. Religion, as you know, tells us many beautiful things. When you grow up, you will read about the religions of the world and of the good things and the bad things that have been done in their name. It is interesting to notice here, however, how the idea of religion began. Later we shall see how it grew. But however much it may have grown, we see even today that people fight and break each other's heads in the name of religion. And for many people it is still something to be afraid of. They spend their time in trying to please some imaginary beings by making presents in temples and even sacrifices of animals. (Nehru, 2004, p. 72)

Indira seems to have experienced the same religious divide between her parents that Nehru experienced between his. And like Nehru, Indira followed in her father's footsteps, also rejecting religion. She married a non-Hindu man, Feroze Gandhi, who was Parsi. Moreover their two children married neither Hindus nor Parsis. Rajiv married Sonia, an Italian Catholic, and his brother Sanjay married Maneka, who is Sikh.

Culturally Based Secrets and Shame

Within many families, issues related to culture often form the basis for family secrets that are tied to feelings of guilt and shame. Family rules about who is valued, who is allowed to love and marry whom, who can have children and under what circumstances, and so on, are often tied to broader social beliefs and biases about race, ethnicity, religion, social class, gender, and sexual identity. In many cultural groups social divisions and inequalities are reinforced by strong prohibitions against romance and procreation that cross racial and social class boundaries and social conventions that strictly enforce compulsory heterosexuality and relationship patterns based on traditional gender roles. Secrets often develop when members violate these cultural norms. We have discussed how Katharine Hepburn, Margaret Mead, and Eleanor Roosevelt kept their bisexuality hidden, never disclosing it publicly or even to family members. The African-American poet Langston Hughes had a strained relationship with his father, influenced by the father's having abandoned him and his mother due to his own struggles with racism. Probably the tension between them was also heavily shaped by Langston's homosexuality, although, as far as we know, this remained an unnamed and unacknowledged truth between them. Hughes seemed to channel what he could not otherwise express into his writing. In his story "Blessed Assurance" he explored a father's anger over his son's effeminacy and homosexuality. Many of his poems used homosexual codes, a device often employed by one of his idols, Walt Whitman (McClatchy, 2002). Hughes often had to solicit support from sources that would never have accepted his homosexuality, beginning with his father and including organizations like the black churches that he often relied upon. His survival literally depended on his keeping his sexuality a secret.

Sometimes family secrets serve to hide how family members may have colluded with various kinds of prejudice and discrimination that are regarded as controversial or immoral by the broader society. The extremely painful secret of Charles Lindbergh's multiple families (see page 88 for genogram), which the children did not learn about until three decades after his death, was discussed earlier. Even before she learned about her father's secret families, Reeve Lindbergh's discovery of her father's racial prejudices forced her to painfully reexamine who her father was. The process of realizing parental limitations is something most children have to undergo in becoming adults, and shortcomings related to harboring prejudicial and oppressive views and activities can be especially disillusioning for them to reconcile. It was long after Charles Lindbergh's death that his daughter Reeve first heard a tape of a speech he made in 1941 telling the world that one of the greatest dangers to pre-World War II America was the influence of Jews in prominent positions. She had read the speech before, but somehow hearing it spoken by him for the first time brought his disturbing perspective home to her:

> I was again transfixed and horrified, again ablaze with shame and fury—"Not you!" I cried out silently to myself and to him—"No! You never said such things! You raised your children never to say, never even to think such things—this must be somebody else talking. It can't be you!" I felt a global anguish—the horror of the Holocaust, the words of my own father ignoring the horror, but surely not condoning the horror, surely not dismissing or diminishing it, surely not. But I also felt a piercingly personal rage, and if I could have written it down it would have looked something like this: "How could you do this to Mother? How could you leave her with this? . . . How could someone who spoke the words my father did in 1941, never repudiating or amending them for the rest of his life, how did such a person then raise children who, by his instruction and his example . . . had learned from him . . . that such words were repellent and unspeakable? How could that happen, and what did it mean not just for my

own family but for others?" And there are indeed many others who struggle as I do with the words spoken and written by past genera- tions, words left by the very people whom they have most loved and respected, words they cannot accept. (Lindbergh, 1998, pp. 201–203)

Lindbergh's daughter struggled, as many struggle, with who her father was, what he said and did, how to be accountable for it in the present, and how to understand the contradictions in the different messages given. In these kinds of situations, one of the hardest parts is having to make peace with such contradictions because those who have gone before have left a legacy of pain- ful and horrific thoughts and practices that must be modified if we are to cre- ate a just and fair world in the future. Understanding where our families are coming from culturally means understanding the pain reflected in the ways they were oppressed, as well as how they may have oppressed others through prejudiced attitudes and discriminatory behaviors.

Reconnecting to Home Through the Roots of Our Multiculturalism

Perhaps it is not surprising that Barack Obama (see pages 182 and 271 for genograms), having so many different cultures within himself, came to lead our nation at a time when the need to pull together our own diversity was becoming more apparent. Coming from a complex background, he struggled for much of his youth to find a sense of home. Ultimately his solution was to make home an inclusive community, built on "the promise that the larger American community, black, white, and brown, could somehow redefine itself" (Wolfe, 2009, p. 150). He concluded that what he himself represented in diversity would someday become the "American community."

Obama struggled for many years to come to terms with his father, whom he never knew, finally realizing on his trip back to Africa that his father had failed by holding himself apart from any home. Of course his mother did that as well, moving continuously and almost never returning to the mainland U.S. once she and her parents left when she was 18. Indeed, she was away from her son for years at a time. And Obama's father returned only once to see him after abandoning him at 2. Obama made tremendous efforts to understand what each of his relatives meant to him—to meet his African half siblings and a step-grandmother he had never known. His maternal grand- mother, who primarily raised him, died 2 days before his election as president. He has struggled over the years to understand the complexities of who he is racially and culturally. Given our complexities as a nation, his example may be a guide to building a broader home base, because his family reflects multiple ethnic and racial groups (white, African, African American, Indonesian, Chinese, Jewish) and multiple religious orientations. His paternal grandfather converted to Christianity and then back to Islam; his maternal grandparents came from different religious backgrounds.

For many years, Obama struggled with his multicultural roots. This was partly because he grew up without knowing his father except through the myths his mother and grandparents told about him. In part it was probably also because of the complexity of his family's roots, which, like so many families in the U.S., were shrouded in mystery and silence. After traveling to Africa, Obama recalled visiting his father's grave there and wrote to his dead father about what he now understood:

> If it weren't for that silence, your grandfather might have told your father that he could never escape himself. Or re-create himself alone. Your father might have taught those same lessons to you. And you, the son, might have taught your father that this new world that was beckoning all of you involved more than just railroads and indoor toilets and irrigation ditches and gramophones—lifeless instruments that could be absorbed into the old ways. You might have told him that these instruments carried with them a dangerous power, that they demanded a different way of seeing the world. That this power could be absorbed only alongside a faith born out of hardship, a faith that wasn't new, that wasn't black or white or Christian or Muslim, but that pulsed in the heart of the first African village and the first Kansas homestead—a faith in other people. The silence killed your faith. And for lack of faith you clung to both too much and too little of your past. (Obama, 1995, p. 428)

Obama continued by describing what the experience of finding his father meant for him:

> I felt the circle finally close. I realized that who I was . . .—the black life, the white life, the sense of abandonment I'd felt as a boy, the frustration and hope I'd witnessed in Chicago—all of it was connected with this small plot of earth an ocean away, connected by more than the accident of a name or the color of my skin. The pain I felt was my father's pain. My questions were my brothers' questions. Their struggle, my birthright. (Obama, 1995, pp. 428–429)

Obama's story beautifully illuminates the heart of what this chapter and this book are about. In him we see a person with a rich familial and cultural background. He personifies the complexities of identity that are emblematic of the increasingly diverse and multicultural world in which we live. His story reflects the complications, conflicts, cutoffs, and confusions that often arise in response to diversity. It also demonstrates so many of the core concepts presented in this book, including how families form triangles and alliances to manage anxiety and pain, how loss and secrets become intertwined and can organize multiple generations of a family system, and how issues of race, ethnicity, religion, gender, social class, migration, and geography intersect with the dynamics of power to shape family dynamics in complex ways. His story also highlights how a person can become exiled, both in familial and cultural terms, and how painful and dispiriting it is to live in exile. Most important, however, Obama's story provides a powerful example of how a person can take the journey home by probing to learn his history and by embracing the parts that reflect both pride and shame, joy and pain. It is an instructive illustration of how we can take similar journeys of courage by risking to wonder about the things we never dared to let ourselves wonder, risking to reach out to those we may never have talked to before or those we have not talked to for a long time, and to ask long withheld questions while daring to hear the answers. His is a cogent example of how we can find our ways back home, not in the sense of returning to the fantasy that never was, but in facing the truth of what was and building something meaningful from it. We can deepen our sense of self and of our groundedness by transforming our relationship with the past and with our familial and cultural legacies in terms of both the good and the bad, the pride and the shame.

Questions to Ask About Ethnicity, Race or Skin Color, Migration, Class, Money, and Religion

Ethnicity

- What are family members' ethnic backgrounds? Do their values and patterns seem consistent with the characteristics of the ethnic groups from which they come? If not, were they attempting to move away from their ethnic roots? And why might they not fit? Were family members proud or ashamed of their heritage? Where and how was cultural pride or shame manifested in the family system?
- Did intermarriages spark clashes of ethnic values or provoke cultural pride or shame? How did these clashes influence other family relationships? Did you grow up with certain ethnic stories, religious practices,

foods, music, or holiday rituals? Are you carrying these on with your own children?

Race or Skin Color

■ How does the family identify itself racially and what pride or shame is associated with this identity? What racial groups does your family of origin comprise?

■ What were the family messages about race and skin color when you were growing up?

■ How have those messages shaped racial self-identification and relationships?

■ Are there racial truths that no one talks about? Are there differences in complexion and skin tone within your family and, if so, how do they shape family dynamics?

Migration

■ What is the family's migration history? Where did they come from? Why did they immigrate? How many came together? What were their ages when they immigrated and how did that influence family patterns?

■ What was their experience as new immigrants and how did that influence your family's mythology—their hopes, dreams, and beliefs? Did they dream of returning to the country of origin? Did they try to leave their history behind?

■ How did family members deal with language differences? religious customs? the loss of those left behind?

Social Class

■ What were the family's values and rules about class? How were those values and rules transmitted? Have family members changed class by "marrying up" or "marrying down"?

■ Have siblings changed class and, if so, how did it affect their relationships?

■ Have class changes occurred through education, financial success or failure, marriage into another socioeconomic group, professional status, or disability? How did this affect sibling patterns? family holidays, gettogethers, and rituals?

Money

■ What were the attitudes in the family about money? Did they perceive it as the root of all evil? Did they always pay cash? save for a rainy day? always spend as if they had enough even if they didn't?

- What roles have family members played around money (the gambler, the tightwad, the compulsive shopper, the bargain hunter, the miser, the spendthrift, the hoarder)?
- Who handles the money? Who controls it?
- Have there been conflicts or cutoffs over wills?
- How do siblings in different financial positions deal with these differences?
- What are the family's beliefs about children's rights to support, help for education, inheritance, buying a home, and so on?
- How are financial arrangements made for the care of disabled family members and how does this intersect with emotional caretaking?
- Have there been gender differences regarding the control or management of money?

Religion and Spirituality

- What religions are represented in the family system and which orientations had the greatest influence in the family? What is the family's relation to organized religion? Are there informal beliefs in what is sacred—music, art, beneficence, spending time in nature? Social justice? What do family members believe about an afterlife?
- How are religious and spiritual differences negotiated?
- What kind of training did family members have in spiritual matters?
- Are there family secrets about religion or spirituality, such as an aunt's years in the convent or the father's aspirations to become a rabbi or minister, that explain later life choices?

10 The Genogram Journey: Reconnecting With Your Family

Shall I turn out to be the hero of my own life?

—DAVID COPPERFIELD

If you have a family gathering and a distant cousin comes who has been kept out of the family for a long time, it's a little uncomfortable. Let's bear the discomfort. It's worth it.

—PAUL ROBESON, JR.

Composing a life involves a continual reimagining of the future and reinterpretation of the past to give meaning to the present. . . . Storytelling is fundamental to the human search for meaning. Each [of us] is involved in inventing a new kind of story.

Composing a Life

—MARY CATHERINE BATESON

This chapter discusses the process of undertaking the genogram journey in an effort to change yourself in the context of your family systems. Although this process is one of the major modes of system change in family therapy, the actual approach is not widely understood. This chapter summarizes the efforts my colleague Betty Carter and I made over three decades to describe coaching individuals to go through this genogram journey (Carter & McGoldrick, 1976, 2001). This process is also often undertaken by therapists as part of their professional development.

The genogram journey toward mature relationships with your family begins with developing a state of self-knowledge and self-definition that involves being emotionally connected to others without needing to defend yourself, attack the other, or rely on the acceptance of others for your sense of self. Achieving maturity or differentiation means training ourselves to control our emotional reactivity so that we can think about how we want to respond rather than being at the mercy of our anger, fear, anxiety, compulsions, or sexual or aggressive impulses. This does not in any way mean suppressing emotional responsiveness. Grounding ourselves to connect emotionally with family members is the "blueprint" for all other emotional connections in our lives.

We would all like to be able to be ourselves with our families, to have them accept us for who we really are. But we may lose sight of the prerequisite—that we accept them for who they really are as well, getting past the anger, resentment, and regrets of not being a family like the Brady Bunch. Visits home, even for those who are highly successful in careers and other relationships, may mean reverting to childish responses. A daughter tenses up within a few minutes in reaction to her mother's implied criticism of her clothes, her haircut, or her boyfriend. A son returns for Thanksgiving with the image of those other families who have happy get-togethers—convivial, delicious, and full of good family feeling—while he experiences the subtle bitterness of his parents' ongoing war.

A part of us always longs to go back to the family—but to have it be different. This time, you tell yourself, you'll hold onto your adult perspective and not become defensive. You won't get caught up in your parents' battles or compete with your siblings for attention. Maturity, objectivity, humor, and serenity will carry the day, if only you can keep your distance.

Sometimes you can even manage to hold onto your sense of self for a little while. But then something seemingly trivial happens—perhaps your father makes a sarcastic joke at your mother's expense and she goes silent. This little scene may have occurred a hundred times in the past. In a second you fall into the role you played in childhood, jabbing back, moving in to protect your mother. In your frustration you gossip with your siblings about how impossible your parents are and you wonder how you managed to survive all the underlying hostility in your family for so long.

If you want to reconnect with your family, you will need to develop a kind of empathy, recognizing that you and your family belong to each other. This requires an acceptance of the almost mystical fundamental human connectedness we have as people. It means accepting that whatever terrible things another person might do, that person is human and we could be in his or her shoes. It means accepting parents with all their imperfections, which is not the same as accepting their imperfections themselves. For example, a person can acknowledge his or her father without needing to even the score for his emotional neglect or physical abuse or irrational demands and attempts at intimidation—without accepting the abuse itself—and while still holding him accountable for what he did. It is a matter of acknowledging that the relationship is about more than the abuse alone. The adult child who truly has an individual identity can be generous to a critical, distant father without becoming defensive, even when that father continues to be critical.

The work of understanding and reconnecting is a lifetime project. To create something new you will have to struggle against the definitions you are given so that you can define connectedness in ways that you find meaningful. As Edwin Markham (1932, p.1) once wrote:

He drew a circle that shut me out—
Heretic, rebel, a thing to flout.
But love and I had wit to win:
We drew a circle that took him in.

The genogram journey requires us to draw our own circles and transform our vision of our relationships, so you go home to a place different from the one you left. The aim is to find yourself as you find your family. This requires an approach that allows you to see the world from the perspective of each person in the family, to accept that the other person did not always meet your needs or understand your feelings. Too often, people try to change their families as a way of changing themselves, rather than changing themselves as a way of changing family patterns. There is a story of an old Hasidic rabbi who said that when he was young he set out to change the world, but as he got older he realized that was too ambitious and set out to change his state. Older still, he realized this was still grandiose and decided to change his town. Finally he realized he should limit himself to his family. As an old man he finally realized that he should have started with himself, and then maybe he could have succeeded in changing his family, his town, his state, and maybe even the whole world.

Change requires giving up wishing that family members had been different and had met your needs, understood your feelings, and always made you proud. This requires arriving at a new perspective from which it is possible to evaluate your own personal worth for yourself. It also means risking family disapproval, rejection, or inattention, without becoming disapproving, rejecting, or inattentive in return.

There are few pure saints or sinners in real families. Although we all need to protect ourselves from a relative who might actually hurt us—an active alcoholic or drug addict, for example—it is important not to write these people off as family members. You never know when they might change their ways, even after a lifetime of destructive behavior. Various events, especially aging and loss, can trigger a transformation.

This way of thinking about families was first articulated by Murray Bowen, who rocked the family therapy field and stunned his colleagues by presenting a daring analysis of his personal work on his own family relationships at

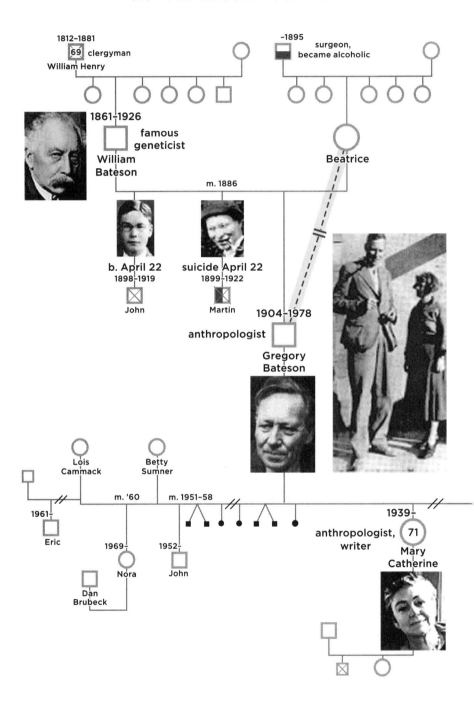

Genogram 10.1 The Mead Family.

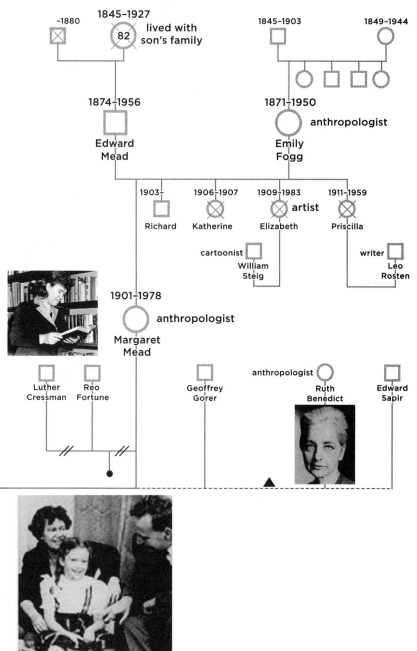

-1880

1845–1927
82   lived with
son's family

1845–1903   1849–1944

1874–1956
Edward
Mead

1871–1950   anthropologist
Emily
Fogg

1903–
Richard

1906–1907
Katherine

1909–1983   artist
Elizabeth

1911–1959
Priscilla

cartoonist
William
Steig

writer
Leo
Rosten

1901–1978   anthropologist
Margaret
Mead

Luther
Cressman

Reo
Fortune

Geoffrey
Gorer

anthropologist
Ruth
Benedict

Edward
Sapir

Margaret & Gregory with Catherine

a family research conference in 1967, where people expected another dry research paper (Bowen, 1978). Bowen's systems ideas were a revolutionary transformation of the notion that change should focus on the "sickest" or most dysfunctional family members. He proposed instead to focus on those who are most motivated. He developed a systems approach that did not work through the transference or doing supportive therapy in which the therapist "lends ego" to the client. This approach instead involves teaching or coaching people to apply systems thinking to their family relationships, focusing on understanding and then changing their own part in the system. This approach, as we have developed it over the years, requires that we also understand and address the powerful influences of culture, class, race, gender, religion, and sexual orientation on individual and family patterns both within the family and in the larger human community, as each person moves through his or her own individual and family developmental passage across the multigenerational family life cycle.

The fundamental guideline for going home again is: Don't attack, don't defend, don't placate, and don't shut down. Going home again means finding a way to be yourself and stay connected to your family without defending yourself or attacking others. The typical dysfunctional roles people get into in their families—where one becomes the caretaker and the other the caretakee, or one always pursues and the other distances—develop because family members have not evolved a sufficient sense of self to function for themselves. One plays wounded daughter to the arrogant and uncaring father, or dutiful brother to a prodigal sibling.

Defining your actual responsibility toward your family is a very personal matter—only you can know what obligations you have to be generous, loving, or thoughtful toward others, no matter what hurt they have caused you. The experience of many adult children of alcoholics stands as an example. If a father chooses to be a depressed and withdrawn alcoholic, the adult child may decide to treat him with compassion and to do whatever is possible to change his self-destructive behavior, realizing also that the father's destiny is beyond anyone's control. At the same time, the adult child must learn to appreciate his or her own limitations. The Alcoholics Anonymous serenity prayer can be very helpful to anyone facing difficult family circumstances: "May I have the serenity to accept the things I cannot change, the courage to change the things I can, and the wisdom to know the difference."

Mary Catherine Bateson (Genogram 10.1), the only daughter of two world-renowned anthropologists, Margaret Mead and Gregory Bateson, did not have an easy childhood. The relationship between her parents was not harmonious. Her father left her mother when Catherine was 7 and they divorced when she was 11. Her mother often left her with other caretakers for long periods. Both parents were often preoccupied with their own concerns and attended to her needs only partially and intermittently. As an infant, she was mostly cared for by a nurse. After her parents separated, she would periodically visit her father, who soon remarried and fathered another child, a son. On at least two occasions her father made inappropriate sexual advances to her. However, she was able to maintain emotionally important, if sometimes physically distant, relationships with both her parents. She is a stirring example of a person who, as an adult, was able to go home again.

Catherine was surprised that, in Margaret Mead's autobiographical writings, her mother described herself and Gregory Bateson as nurturing personalities. Mead and Bateson believed that Catherine was a perfectly contented child. Catherine herself admitted that she never complained because she had to be a "good girl" so that her parents would want to be with her as much as possible. If she was unpleasant to be with, she would lose them to other activities. Throughout her own memoir, Catherine Bateson shows an astute perception of the need to remain her own self—not a replica of her parents: "I have not read or reread all the published works of Mead and Bateson, neither of which I know completely, for to do so would be to remake myself as an expert instead of a daughter" (Bateson, 1984, p. 227).

Bateson's story is one of acceptance of her parents as they were—with their faults and limitations—and of looking for the value in her relationship with each of them: "The voices of my parents are still very much with me, for I hear their echo in so much that I see and encounter. . . . Their voices are blended now into the complex skein. It was difficult for me sometimes, as a child, to decode the differences and similarities and to pitch my own voice in harmony but yet distinct" (Bateson, 1984, p. 220).

Finally, Bateson remembered more what she received than what she did not receive from her parents. She felt that she got a sense of basic trust, self-confidence, faith, strength, and resiliency from her mother. As a professional anthropologist and mother herself, Bateson came to appreciate how well organized and masterful Mead had been, always keeping Catherine well cared for in the "extended family" of professional colleagues she had created. As she described it, Catherine made her own synthesis from the models offered by her parents and others around her. Like her mother, she had to juggle multiple commitments and to adapt and improvise in a culture in which she could be only partly at home. As for her father, although she spent less time with him, she was grateful for their long walks and talks where he taught her about nature and science and answered her difficult questions about the way the world works.

Having struggled greatly with her parents' separation and divorce, Catherine came to fear that she would follow in her parents' footsteps of numerous failed marriages. She spent a lot of time trying to understand her parents' marriages and their differences.

Bateson's memoir demonstrates in a most touching way her effort to see her parents from many perspectives: as children in their own families, as lovers and marital partners, as siblings, as professionals. In many ways Mead and Bateson were opposites. She was American, practical, effusive, poetic. He was British, impractical, detached, scientific. Margaret thought that problems usually have a solution, whereas Gregory thought that most people's efforts to improve things usually made them worse. Margaret appreciated the various conventions and rules of different societies; Gregory lived his life as unconventionally as possible. Margaret loved religious ritual; Gregory was an atheist. She loved people; he preferred animals. Her moral concerns focused on the development of societies; his focused on ecology or the world as a whole. She loved to be the organizer. He eventually came to see her organizing abilities as controlling. He was more abstract, more interested in finding the patterns of life than in controlling the particulars. She paid attention to the details. "In the marriage she was the one who set the patterns, for Gregory lacked this fascination with pervasive elaboration," Bateson wrote. "His life was full of loose ends and unstitched edges, while for Margaret each thread became an occasion for embroidery" (Bateson, 1984, p. 27).

Catherine was forced to wonder how two such different people ever married. She speculated that her mother was most attracted to Bateson's cultural differentness, and noted that she herself had also married a man from a different culture (Iran).

In trying to understand her parents' differences for herself, she noted their different sibling positions and roles in their families. Margaret was the oldest of five, all but one girls; Gregory was the youngest of three—all boys. She said of her parents dissimilar approaches to solving problems:

> Margaret's approach must have been based on early success in dealing with problems, perhaps related to the experience of being an older child and amplified by years of successfully organizing the younger ones. Gregory's experience was that of a younger child with relatively little capacity for changing what went on around him. Instead, he would seek understanding. (Bateson, 1984, p. 176)

She speculated further on the influence of early family events on her father's approach to life: "It may be that the suicide of his brother Martin in 1922, which followed on heavy-handed parental attempts at guidance and led to a period of increasing efforts to shape Gregory's choices as well, was an ingredient in his anxiety about problem solving and indeed about any effort to act in the world" (Bateson, 1984, p. 176).

Sickly in childhood and not an outstanding student, Gregory Bateson was considered the least promising of the three brothers. Their father, a famous British geneticist, expected the oldest son, John, to be the leader. John and the middle brother, Martin, 2 years apart in age, were extremely close. Gregory was 4 years younger and grew up somewhat separately. At age 20 John was killed in World War I. A few days later his mother wrote to Martin: "You and Gregory are left to me still and you must help me back to some of the braveness that John has taken away" (Lipset, 1980, p. 71).

Following John's death, a rift developed between Martin and his father, whose mother had coincidentally died 2 months before John. The father, perhaps now doubly bereft, began to pressure Martin, who was a poet, to become a zoologist. Relations between father and son deteriorated. When, in addition, Martin felt rebuffed by a young woman he admired, he took a gun and shot himself in Trafalgar Square on his brother John's birthday, April 22, 1922, in what was described as "probably the most dramatic and deliberate suicide ever witnessed in London" (Lipset, 1980, p. 93).

This was the legacy for Gregory, "the runt," as he called himself. All the family's expectations that their oldest son would become a great scientist, following in the father's footsteps, now came down upon him. Gregory's solution was to study anthropology, a science different from his father's field, biology, which also allowed him to escape from the family pressure by way of fieldwork. All his life, Gregory would resist the expectations of others. The shift in Gregory's sibling position in early adult life may indeed have contributed to the incompatibility between him and Margaret, even though their birth positions were complementary.

There is some similarity between Gregory, whose role as the only surviving child intensified his relationship with his mother to the point of toxicity, and Margaret Mead's father, who was an only child, doted on by his mother after his father's death when he was only 6. Whereas Bateson cut off his mother to avoid the pressure of the legacy, his future father-in-law, Edward Mead, had brought his widowed mother with him into his marriage and she lived in the Mead household for the rest of her life. Catherine traced her father's relationship with his parents to the eventual difficulties between her parents:

Gregory felt that to move ahead with his own life he would have to leave Margaret, bringing into his conflicts with her a store of hoarded hostility to his mother. He brought to the marriage the experience of being the youngest child of his own famiy, whereas . . . (Margaret) went through life acting and feeling like a responsible oldest child.. . . . It was Gregory, more than anyone else, who lashed back at her for trying to manage his life. . . . [He] began with his rebellion against Margaret, a rebellion shot through with resentment against his family and especially against his mother (Bateson, 1984, pp. 46, 111, 160).

Tracing marital relationships in the Bateson family back reveals problematic issues even in the previous generation. Gregory's parents, Beatrice and William, had a prolonged courtship, which would lead one to suspect possible difficulties in the family relationships. In fact, Gregory's maternal grandmother called off her daughter's engagement to William because he got drunk. She was trying to protect her daughter from her own fate, as her husband (the maternal grandfather) had been an alcoholic. However, Beatrice recontacted William through an ad shortly after her father died and married him soon afterwards.

In the next generation, Gregory happened to meet and fall in love with Margaret just after becoming estranged from his mother, Beatrice. Margaret and her second husband were doing anthropological work in a remote area of the world at that time. One might speculate that the children in the Bateson family could only connect to their spouses after disconnecting, through death or cutoff, from a parent.

Catherine Bateson made an enormous effort to understand her parents through an exploration of their lives. She worked to see them as people with their own sets of problems. Most important, she tried to see them as children in the multigenerational context of their families, struggling to come to terms with their parents in much the same way she struggled to come to terms with them. She was able to accept their differences without blaming either of them. Although it was her father who left her mother, she tried not to judge him, only to understand him. Throughout their lives, she maintained connections with both parents. Gregory always sought to interest his daughter in what *he* considered "important matters," but never paid attention to hers. She did not reject her father for not validating her interests. Nor did she try to change him. When, toward the end of his life, he became interested in ecology, he elicited and got her help in organizing his project.

Catherine maintained both personal and professional contact with her mother as well. They did presentations together. They planned a conference on rituals together. Particularly important, Catherine was able to appreciate her mother's efforts not to dominate her life. She said of her:

> The thing she was most afraid of as a parent was that her capacity to think herself into the lives of others, imagining possible futures, would lead her to guide me in a way I would later repudiate. In any quarrel between us, the thing that would have hurt her most, because it had been said to her so many times, would have been to accuse her of dominating me or interfering with my life. (Bateson, 1984, p. 110–111).

We can see here that Margaret herself was concerned about differentiation and not intruding on her daughter's personhood, which probably was important modeling for Catherine. It may also reflect an Anglo sensibility to privacy and not intruding on anyone else's space, which might be viewed very differently in other cultures. Mother and daughter both worked at their separateness:

> This was a point of vulnerability so deep that we conspired to protect the relationship, she by refraining from advice and indeed by trying to restrain her imagination about me, I by carefully monitoring the kinds of indecision or uncertainty I shared with her. I learned to show my imagined futures to her only when they already had a degree of vividness that I could continue to acknowledge as my own, unable to say, this is your plan I have been living, your fantasy projected onto me. She had the capacity to live many lives, participating richly, reaching out in complex empathy, grasping hold of possibilities that had so far eluded the imagination of others, and so she had to monitor the dreams she dreamed for others. (Bateson, 1984, p. 111)

Through these efforts not to have a relationship of control, mother and daughter were able to avoid the power struggle that so plagued the parents' marriage.

One of the most touching issues Bateson explored was her mother's secret and what her secrecy cost both of them. Margaret's sexual liaisons and particularly her bisexuality were discovered by her daughter only after her death in 1978, when a close family friend gave Catherine a letter that Margaret had written many years earlier, intended for those she loved in the event of her death. The letter seemed to Catherine to be an expression of her mother's concern that details of her life might be revealed under circumstances of scandal or notoriety, without her being able to provide explanation or reassurance. Margaret apparently became increasingly grieved that many aspects of her life could not be shared and troubled about the pain that the revelation of her secret might cause to others:

> I have become increasingly conscious of the extent to which my life is becoming segmented, each piece shared with a separate person, even where within the time and space of that segment I feel that I am being myself, and my whole self in that particular relationship.... It has not been my choice of concealment that any one of you have been left in ignorance of some part of my life which would seem, I know, of great importance. Nor has it been from lack of trust—in any person—on my part, but only from the exigencies of the mid-twentieth century when each one of us—at least those of us who are my age—seems fated for a life, which is no longer sharable. (Bateson, 1984, p. 115)

Catherine, who was only 15 when her mother wrote this letter, was one of the ones to whom it would have been sent. She said:

> I knew little until after her death of the pattern of relationships to male and female lovers that she had developed, so that trying to look back on who she was as a person and as my mother has been complicated by the need to revise my picture of her in important ways and by the need to deal with the fact of concealment. I have been at times angered at the sense of being deliberately deceived and at having been without doubt a collaborator in my own deception, limiting my perceptions to the images she was willing to have me see. I have sometimes felt myself doubly bereaved as well, having radically to reconsider my convictions about who she was and therefore, in relationship to her, about who I was and am, surprised at last by the sense of continuing recognition. (Bateson, 1984, p. 119)

Margaret's concern about the possible negative impact of the secrets in her life is impressive, as is her effort to counteract their negative potential by her letter. But what is most impressive about Catherine's commentary is her recognition of the part she played in her mother's secrecy and her willingness to explore her own complicity.

In the end, Catherine Bateson was able to accept both her mother and her father in herself. Margaret and Gregory were far from perfect as parents, but their daughter's ability to take what they had to offer her and transform it into a significant part of her own self is most impressive. She used this acceptance to deal with their deaths:

The contained world of early childhood no longer exists, but my concerns remain similar to theirs and the analogies that bridge from the microcosm to the wider world continue. . . . I have wanted to write a small book. . . . I have tried to weave my own ambivalence into this book, letting love and grief, longing and anger, lie close to the surface, and making it clear that there is no perfection to enshrine and no orthodoxy to defend, but much to use and much of value. (Bateson, 1984, p. 227)

Bateson said she started with a view of her life as a sort of desperate improvisation in which she was constantly trying to make some coherence from conflicting elements to fit rapidly changing settings:

When we speak to our children about our own lives, we tend to reshape our pasts to give them an illusory look of purpose. But our children are unlikely to be able to define their goals and then live happily ever after. Instead, they will need to reinvent themselves again and again in response to changing environment. . . . Life [is] an improvisatory art, about the ways we combine familiar and unfamiliar components in response to new situations. . . . I believe that [we have] overfocused on the stubborn struggle toward a single goal rather than on the fluid, the protean. . . . Women have always lived discontinuous and contingent lives, but men today are newly vulnerable, which turns women's traditional adaptations into a resource. (Bateson, 1989, pp. 12, 3–4, 17)

We and our families are always struggling to reinvent ourselves and transform our difficult and painful experiences into something creative and positive. As Bateson said:

Part of the task of composing a life is the artist's need to find a way to take what is simply ugly and instead of trying to deny it, to use it in the broader design. There is a famous story about a Chinese master painting a landscape. Just as he is nearly finished, a drop of ink falls on the white scroll, and the disciples standing around him gasp, believing the scroll is ruined. Without hesitating, the master takes the finest of hair brushes and, using the tiny glob of ink already fallen, paints a fly hovering in the foreground of the landscape. . . . The purpose here is to discover grace and meaning in a picture larger still. (Bateson, 1989, p. 211)

The idea of reconnecting with family is to strive to make "hope and history rhyme"—that is, to forge connections to one's history that will open up the future. This requires creating a sense of family and "home"—in which no one's experience has to be outside history, whether because of race, class, gender, shame, or secrecy—a place where the complex and ambiguous connections that entwine your family can be validated.

An important place to reconnect with family is at the celebrations that mark family holidays and transitions—weddings, funerals, and reunions. Family rituals are important experiences, incorporating familiar and often symbolic meanings. Such occasions involve intentional repetition of words, music, food, drink, smells, sights, ceremony, and behavior that suggests continuity. Although this can be stifling if the rituals are hollow, it can be healing and enriching if the person makes the rituals personally meaningful. Family gatherings also offer a good opportunity to hear family stories, observe family relationships in action, and practice changing one's own part in the family drama.

Consider what family stories might be like from the angle of a different participant, the so-called villains, for example. Imagine what Cinderella's stepmother's perspective might be on her spoiled, goody-two-shoes stepdaughter to whom everything comes naturally and whom everyone adores (Friedman, 1990). Consider the dilemma her stepsisters were in, not conforming to the culture's requirements of a woman—that she be small, beautiful, gentle, long suffering, and unassertive!

People can also think about what would happen if they changed their own part in family relationships. If you always lock horns with your father, you could change your tune and begin to say: "You've got a point there, Dad. . . ." If a person has had a poor relationship with a parent for a long time it is important to proceed slowly. One must not expect too much too soon. A relationship can't be forced.

Letters can be useful in efforts to reconnect. They can be an effective method of reconnecting with an estranged or difficult parent, for example. Letters allow you to prepare exactly what to say and say it carefully, without accusation or defense. Most important, letters allow you to convey the whole message before having to respond to the other person's reactions. With luck, the letter will be a first step that leads to more personal communications.

Pictures are also wonderful triggers for memories and help family members feel they are being given to, even as they share difficult memories. By enlarging old family photographs and distributing them to the family, new messages can be conveyed about continuity.

The first step in this process is to define one's own beliefs and life goals rather than just accepting the family or the culture's values unthinkingly or reacting to them. The process often entails hiring a therapist who takes the role of coach or consultant in helping people to become observers of their own roles and behavior in their families, training them to become researchers of family patterns, and then to bring their behavior more in line with their deepest values. The process begins with examining one's genogram and exploring the patterns in the social system and translating complaints about others in the family—and in larger systems as well—into personal empowerment and to work on changing negative aspects of one's own role and behavior where possible.

The genogram journey entails exploring individual symptoms and problems in terms of the entire spectrum of functioning and relationships. The focus is on overall patterns in the network of relationships rather than primarily on the individual's intrapsychic processes. The emphasis is on the "who, what, when, where, and how" of family patterns and themes, rather than on the "why" of individual motivation. This can be surprisingly difficult, even for systems thinkers. The main work takes place in the relationships with actual family members, although thinking and careful planning are essential prior to embarking on the journey. Feelings are connected back to family emotional patterns and relationships, the aim being to develop the most connection possible with each person in the family.

This approach assumes that it is relevant to understand both the historical processes in the family and the larger social context in order to transform family relationships in the present. This does not discount the impact of the internal psychological or physiological system on a person's functioning. Rather, the internal and external systems are seen as having significant reciprocal influence on each other. Obviously where there is the potential for emotional, physical, or sexual abuse, it is essential for the person to protect him or herself. But even in situations where face-to-face contact is not advisable or appropriate, there may be other avenues of approach, through e-mail, letters, or other forms of contact that keep the lines open. The assumption is that external systems frequently determine internal feeling states.

If one employs a therapist for the process, the role of the therapist or coach is very different from the role traditional therapists have taken in therapy. In this method, the "natural" system is given clear priority over the therapeutic system. Bowen used to say that he spent only 50% of his energy coaching his clients and the other 50% trying to stay out of the person's family process. The coach tries to steer emotional issues and expression of feelings toward the evolving family relationships—where they belong—rather than focusing on how they may become displaced into the therapy relationship. Because this approach does not view change as brought about through a corrective relationship with a therapist, transference phenomena are actively discouraged, and therapists attempt to stand on the sidelines of the natural system, serving as consultants and trying to avoid being pulled into the family emotional field, while developing a reality-oriented, open, and, hopefully, warm and respectful relationship with the person who is seeking consultation.

An important part of the genogram analysis is to conceptualize current problems in terms of triangles, looking for the family forces that maintain the dysfunctional relationships or exacerbate stress. A family with a seriously dysfunctional member, for example, will probably have an overburdened caretaker (usually female), perhaps another giving advice on how to handle the situation better, and other family members trying to escape the emotional turmoil by distancing. The person needs to analyze how triangles are operating in the family and think how their input into the triangles may become a way of untying the knot that distresses them. Once this initial work has produced some relief, the person can look for ways his or her emotional reactivity may be connected to triangles and issues in the family of origin or the larger social context and consider possible work on these.

A key part of this work will focus on detriangulation, which is the process whereby people free themselves from the enmeshment of a triangle and develop separate person-to-person relationships with each of the other members of the triangle and of the family. As illustrated throughout this book, involvement in triangles and interlocking triangles is one of the key mechanisms through which patterns of relating and functioning are transmitted over the generations in a family.

A person may become enmeshed in many intense triangles in the family of origin, the immediate family, the work system, with friends, or in the community. We believe that all intense emotional triangles interlock with parental triangles. Motivated people can often change their behavior in other current triangles even without any particular effort with the family of origin.

But the basic assumption of systems thinking is that if you change your emotional functioning in your family, the system will eventually change. From this perspective family relationships are forever, and it never makes sense to write off a family member, even though, in cases of abuse, serious addiction, or mental illness it may be necessary to maintain a safe distance.

The one exception is couple relationships, the only "optional" relationships in a family—the only ones that we choose and that we may decide to end. (Even here, however, a person cannot end ongoing connections to a former partner if they have had children together. In other words, one can be an ex-spouse but not an ex-coparent, an ex-father, ex-mother, or ex-child.) If one partner really changes and the other remains inaccessible or unchanging, the couple system is not viable, and the first partner has little option but to move on. Thus, if the wife of an alcoholic differentiates, it may precipitate her husband's recovery, or she may learn that her husband is too caught up in his addiction to respond, no matter what she does. If he chooses his addiction over the marriage, her only real choice may eventually be to leave.

The difference between this and a relationship with an alcoholic parent or sibling is that in those relationships, the mature family member remains open to the possibility of a transformation of the relationship, however unlikely. In general, the systemic assumption is that if one person changes her or his role, the system will be altered, and the person will be able to function more freely in current and future relationships, whether family-, social-, or job-related. The goal here is, however, to free oneself from triangulated relationships and reactive behaviors, to relate in a caring, non-defensive, non-attacking way— not to change the other members of one's family.

People's ability to change their emotional functioning will depend, of course, on a number of factors. Children and people of any age who are not financially independent will have limited ability to take a position of emotional independence in a family. Furthermore, as indicated earlier, there are situations in which family members are so locked into their addiction or other dysfunctional patterns that a differentiating move may clarify that the immediate system is too rigid, disengaged, or immature to move beyond its reactivity. In such cases the person's efforts to differentiate may still bring forth positive results in the broader system, changing the legacy for the next generation even though there is no change in the immediate family. This perspective requires one to think about change in very broad and long-range terms, as is necessary in changing larger societal patterns of injustice and oppression. As the adage attributed to Margaret Mead goes: "Never doubt that a small group of thoughtful, committed people can change the world. Indeed, it's the only thing that ever has." The same might be said about the efforts of a thoughtful, committed family member in changing a system.

Gaining a systemic perspective on one's problems means shifting from a view of "the self *or* others" to a view of "self *with* others." Whereas other psychological models focus on the internal experience of an individual who is experiencing problems, this orientation focuses on "knowing the system, the structure and how it works, and moving self into the structure in order to rework one's place in it, thereby changing one's internal experience" (Gilles-Donovan, 1991, p. 9). While you may initially view yourself as victim or rescuer, with judgmental reports on the emotional reactions and behaviors of other family members, with effort you may be able to look beyond your own experience to view your family as a system in which each person plays a part and observing the circular processes in family interactions.

The genogram journey begins with taking a broad perspective on any current problems and the central relationships and inquiring about similar issues at other levels of the system. You inquire about other members' views of central issues, and gradually explore triangles and automatic reactive processes. We have also found it helpful to read the stories of others who have done similar family research to help hold onto a family systems perspective.

The journey involves, of course, developing your own genogram, including the biological, legal, and other relationships with godparents, foster parents, and family friends, as well as mapping the sociocultural, religious, and migration history of the family. Mapping family history through discussion of the genogram helps you view issues from a family perspective.

Developing a family chronology to show in chronological order the major family events and stresses is also essential; this is especially useful for tracking the motion of family patterns over time and understanding the intersection of any symptoms with larger system patterns. This is important because the connections among major family events tend to be obscured by the anxiety that these events create, as I have tried to illustrate throughout this book.

During the initial phase of engaging your family, it is important to take a calm, matter-of-fact approach to help defuse the intensity of emotion that is often aroused when family patterns are explored. Once this process has begun, it helps to keep notes or a journal record of your thoughts about emotional patterns of interaction, reciprocity in family relationships between overfunctioners and underfunctioners, triangles, effects of sibling position on relationships, and the transmission of relationship patterns from one generation to the next. Hopefully, the questions and themes outlined in this book will be a helpful guide in this process.

Planning: Learning About the System and Your Role in It

Once your anxiety is low enough to discuss how your personal thoughts and feelings fit into family patterns, it is time to consider possible changes and their effects and to begin planning change. You may ask, "How might I go about trying to get to know my father better, and how would that help me with my current problem?" It is important to think through such questions to be sure you are ready to embark on the journey before you begin. It is more important to think of the overall relationships than to begin by trying to think of how to structure a particular conversation. The specifics are a result of being clear on what you want to accomplish in the relationships, not a gimmick or trick of saying something unexpected. As you begin to observe and listen at family gatherings, instead of participating in your usual role, you may experience shifts in thinking or relating; these should be carefully incorporated into your planning for further change.

Gaps in the genogram or family chronology are obvious places to start. The assumption is that the more information you have, the better position you are in to evaluate what has happened in your family and to understand your position and change it if you wish. One might look, for example, at the similarity between the central triangles with parents and siblings over three generations and the family stress at crucial points in the family history, such as at times of loss, marriage, or the birth of each child. Other patterns to explore include the reciprocity in the marriages in the family: Who is the pursuer and who is the distancer? Who overfunctions and who underfunctions? Who tends to move in and who tends to move out? What toxic issues tend to be avoided? All of these issues are of primary importance. If you feel too caught up emotionally in the immediate situation in your family, try to slow yourself down to to sit still for "history." It can be useful to examine the crisis theme and the red-hot triangle in which it is embedded and track them through the extended family and through past generations. For example, if you have a child who is acting out, you might want to to look at disruptions and stresses in parent-child relationships in previous generations and through the extended family. This will give you access to the relevant historical information through which you can gain perspective on the current situation.

We favor holding off on concrete moves until you get a general notion of how the emotional system operates, what the central issues are, and what your own agenda and motivations are. If you want to make someone else happy, save someone, change someone, tell someone off, get someone's approval, or justify and explain yourself, the effort is likely to fail.

The genogram journey involves developing personal and authentic emotionally engaged relationships with family members and changing your part in repetitious, dysfunctional emotional patterns. It involves learning to see your parents as the human beings they are or were, and relating to them with respect and generosity. This sounds so simple that it is difficult to convey the anxiety it can arouse at each step of the way, even for people who are committed to the work. The first moves to make will depend on what kinds of relationships you currently maintain with family members and what objectives you have for changing these relationships. A relationship that has been intense and conflictual will require a gentler re-approach than that used in moving toward someone who has been distant.

For example, Cheryl, a 30-year-old African-American social worker who had not seen her father for many years, spent several sessions with a coach describing her current marital and in-law conflicts, which had led her to seek help. She had not corresponded with her father since he left the family to live with a girlfriend years before. She had had a distant relationship with her mother since she left home at 17 to live with an aunt and attend college. She considered her mother "hopeless" for having stayed so long with her father, who was cold and critical, and then with a boyfriend, whom she was still supporting. She saw both parents as irrelevant to her current life and problems. After discussing the striking patterns of marital conflict, in-law problems, and emotional cutoffs on her genogram, she began to look at these issues in light of her family's struggle as African Americans, a story that involved, among other things, her grandparents' migration from North Carolina and Arkansas to New Jersey in the 1940s under incredibly difficult circumstances. She was encouraged to explore her role in her family of origin as a way to gain more flexibility for her marriage and to think about how that might relate to her parents' earlier struggles. She and her unmarried aunt with whom she had lived were the first ones in her family to accomplish the goal of attending college, and she was the first to attend graduate school, though education had been a long-held family value. She had never thought about her mother's efforts to contribute to her school expenses, even while she had lived with her aunt. As she explored with the coach the cutoff with her parents, she became aware that her issue with her mother was much less intense than the one with her father. As her first move of reentry, she decided to write a letter to her father in which she referred briefly and regretfully to their cutoff, having come to acknowledge that he had, in fact, made several efforts to reconnect, which she had rebuffed over the years. She expressed interest in his life, his wife, and his young son, whom she had never met. She said she wanted to bring him up to date on her life, especially because of all the years they had missed. To her mother, for whom she realized she had fewer conflictual feelings, she wrote in more depth about her life and proposed to visit her in the near future. Both parents responded promptly and Cheryl began her journey to learn more about their struggles, which helped her to understand her own.

If you are involved in a conflictual relationship with a parent and the issue has been displaced onto some specific concrete explosion, such as a falling out over a long-past insult, or onto some ritual argument over religion or politics, we frequently recommend "letting go of the rope"—that is, to let go of the argument to allow the buried emotional issues to emerge. The following case is an example of this.

> Kathy came from an Irish Catholic family. She was the only member who had left the Church and married a Protestant. Since her marriage, she had had little except superficial contact with her mother because, she said, the religious issue always stood in the middle of their relationship. After some discussion, Kathy became interested in the idea of trying a "reversal," which became increasingly true as she carried it out. She wrote to her mother that she was coming to appreciate her mother's strong faith, and wished that she could share it, although she found she could not. She said that she admired her mother's inner peace, which seemed to be related to her faith, and that she felt somewhat lonely and cut off from her family as a result of not being able to share their faith. To her great surprise, her mother responded warmly, saying that she had been very touched by the letter and was surprised that Kathy thought she had such inner peace because at times she herself felt isolated. Hearing this, Kathy felt she could move toward her own more important personal relationship issues with her mother.

Even when family members do not respond warmly, it is enormously helpful to give up fruitless arguments. The very pause that "letting go of the rope" can create often gives one a peacefulness in being with the family member while not needing to respond, and the relationship may eventually move on to other more emotionally important issues.

If you have been maintaining routine, "dutiful" contact with the family through general letters addressed to both parents or phone conversations with only the mother, who acts as the central switchboard, you may want to establish direct contact with your father and other family members, even though this may be awkward at first. This shift alone may bring long-buried issues to the surface, as it did for another Joe, a 40-year-old, working-class, Italian garage mechanic, who initially described his family as "friendly and close." He saw no connection between the state of his family relationships and the problem for which he was referred by his wife's doctor: dealing with the effects of his wife's serious physical illness. Joe reported that he called his mother weekly for an exchange of general family news. He saw his father, brother, and sister at holiday get-togethers a few times a year. Initially he maintained that he would have no difficulty talking directly with each family member, but that it would make no real difference. However, once he started to do it, he found that he became intensely nervous after a few minutes with his father because he could find nothing to say; his brothers quickly turned the phone over to their wives; and his sister responded to a call from him with an angry attack about his having left responsibility for their aging parents entirely to her. These responses enabled him to recognize that he had been emotionally pulling away from his wife in her illness as he had pulled away from his family and their concerns. He embarked on restoring his family relationships with the initial motivation that they could offer one another support.

If you have a routinized relationship with one or both parents that is not overtly hostile, a first step might be to break off routine patterns such as daily phone calls or weekly visits on a certain day, making contacts less ritualized and more unpredictable. Such initial contacts are usually followed with brief visits, during which the main task is to observe and listen to family interaction in a new way. This information is then incorporated into the further planning, during which you develop tentative hypotheses concerning your role in the family process, what role you would like to have, and what predictions you can make about the reactions of others to any changes you may make. Once you have begun to think about yourself and your family in systems terms and to make initial shifts in your position, you may begin to put thought and effort into the endeavor, focusing first on the family themes that seem most relevant to your current life.

At this point, pay very careful attention to the details of relationship interaction so you can figure out what changes you can make in word and deed to promote positive change. It is very important to get a grasp here of the family's cultural norms, which are influenced by their race, ethnicity, religion, education, income, gender attitudes, and life stage. "Too involved" is a totally different concept in Jewish, Scandinavian, and African-American families. Reactions can never be understood or addressed apart from their socioeconomic context, whether they concern in-laws, addictions, abuse, or mental illness. All are experienced and construed differently in different cultures and you can't push the system too far beyond its comfort zone or there will be problematic backlash. All of this becomes particularly intricate when family members are from different cultures.

Guidelines

The following guidelines may help you in working on relationships with your family.

- Keep your own counsel. Do not try to share efforts with others in the family. At times there is a strong pull to "differentiate together"—with a spouse, for example, or a favorite sibling—but working out your family relationships is an individual process and talking about it with others in the family may raise their anxiety and lead them to try to influence or undermine the process.

- Change must be undertaken because *you* want to change the relationships—it should not be undertaken for the sake of your coach, a partner, or anyone else. Also, it must never be an effort to change others in the family, tempting as that ambition may be.

- Never underestimate the family's reaction to the process. Be prepared for it. Reactivity is likely to be intense and you must beware of being taken off guard.

- The main guidelines for relating are: *Don't attack, don't defend, don't placate, and don't shut down.* It helps to have a plan including how to deal with others' reactions so you don't get caught up in the family's emotional reactivity.

- Strong feelings of anger or hurt are important signals about family process. When you start to see the family as made up of villains or victims, or feel victimized yourself, it is essential to rethink the situation and come back with a revised plan that acknowledges the circular processes of the system.

- Distance from an intense emotional field is important in order to gain objectivity. But this move should be intentional and based on flexibility, so you are ready to respond when another family member begins moving toward you.

- When anxiety is high, it helps to expand the context, exploring patterns in the larger family system to increase the context in which problems can be dealt with or absorbed.

- Never stay with the family longer than you can afford to be generous. Once you are feeling grouchy it's better not to try to engage. Family visits should be limited to maintain focus.

- Serious issues should be addressed individually rather than in large, ritualized family gatherings.

■ If someone is blocking the way to a family member, it is futile to try to get around such interference. The obvious solution is to develop a relationship with the blocking person, even when he or she seems peripheral. If, for instance, a sister-in-law monitors all a brother's contacts, it is essential to develop a relationship with her in order to get connected to him.

■ Letters that are not attacking or defensive can help to open difficult emotional issues without having to deal with the immediacy of system reactivity. Predicting responses in the letter itself can even deflect some intensity, although you must be careful not to inflame the other with underlying accusations. In general, writing individual letters, and taking up only one emotional issue at a time, may help to keep focus.

Dealing with Structural Issues of Oppression

We all have specific emotional issues and triangles related to our stage of the family life cycle and to the particular history and circumstances of our families of origin. In addition, many problematic issues and triangles in the families of people of color and and those in the LGBT communities are directly related to their lack of power and stigmatized status in the larger society. The most important point is to find a way to get on the same side to overcome obstacles rather than letting social problems divide you and your family members.

Janella and Joyce, a young, middle-class, lesbian couple, sought coaching because of the intense conflict in their relationship. "She's totally hyper," said Joyce, a graphic artist of Polish-German background. "Every time we get settled, she decides that the neighbors don't approve of our relationship and we've got to move. We've moved four times in 4 years and now she wants to move again." Careful exploration of the situation by the therapist revealed the fact that Janella, whose parents had emigrated from Cuba, was a schoolteacher and feared, realistically, that she would be fired if her sexual orientation were known. Subsequent coaching sessions led to Joyce's understanding of the possible consequences for Janella, which in turn led to their decision to move one last time to a community that supported racial diversity as well as same-sex couples. Once Janella was in a more comfortable cultural context, the couple could move on to dealing with the complex and acrimonious reactions to their sexual orientation in both families of origin.

It is essential to evaluate carefully the consequences of changing your roles in any system, emotional or social, and to incorporate these caveats in the planning. It is also essential to acknowledge that disadvantaged social status reduces the options available for personal change. The difficulties of changing in the face of social obstacles and stigma should not be attributed to one's lack of motivation or maturity, but rather appreciated as social structures into one's context.

Focus and Duration of the Genogram Journey

Because the genogram journey is about changing relationships, which in turn affects the themes and patterns that will be transmitted to the next generation, it is important to be aware of the typical triangles and issues at each stage of family life. For example, a stepfather's work on how to position himself with an adolescent stepson (as a benign and casual friend and mentor) in relation to the son's biological mother (who is the only one in a position to set limits) is completely different from coaching a biological father about how to deal with his teenage son (as a caring but limit-setting parent) in relation to his wife, who is the coparent. Dealing with children who have left home and become self-supporting is yet another completely different endeavor.

Once you have decided to embark on the genogram journey, there may be a period of enthusiasm for the work around some central focus—the relationship with a parent or a spouse, a significant family secret, or a cutoff. But it is essential to plan ahead for the system's reactivity, which may be intense, especially if the system is rigid.

Most people tend to do this work in phases, with occasional periods of inactivity. People may also vary in their ability to work at certain levels. For example, some work very well for a time in the nuclear family but have great difficulty moving into the extended family. Others work well and hard in the parental generation but have great difficulty understanding how symptoms are related to a spouse or an ex-spouse. At times, it helps to shift work to another level as a way around an impasse at the immediate level. If you work at this over time you may have relief of immediate stress as well as an increased ability to deal differently with future stress.

The hopeful and expansive orientation of this approach in its focus on the connectedness of all systems tends to encourage you to find the strengths and resources in your history and in your present that will empower you for the future. The basic idea of the genogram journey is this: If you can change the part you play in your family—and hold it despite the family's reaction and while keeping in emotional contact with family members—you maximize the likelihood that your family will eventually change to accommodate your change, though this is not a guarantee! Any change involves a minimum of three steps:

1. the change itself
2. the family's reaction to the change
3. dealing with the family's reactions to the change

These three steps can, of course, take years. Most of us do what Bowen called "the two-step" much of the time: We attempt to change, but when someone says, "change back," we do it. Successful change involves going beyond this and planning how to deal with the predictable reaction to the initial effort.

The ideal of the genogram journey is to develop a person-to-person relationship with each living person in your family. The process of working out personal relationships occurs at different levels, starting with the immediate household—usually the most intimate level and often the most intense because of the high level of ongoing involvement. However, for most people it is also the area linked to the highest motivation. The next level is that of the family of origin. The most difficult relationships to work out here are also the most important: the triangle with your parents and then relationships with your siblings. Aunts, uncles, or grandparents are usually at somewhat greater distance. These relationships may, however, prove extremely fruitful for an understanding of some of the closer relationships and for stopping repetitive patterns. At a still greater distance are cousins and research on the family history and genealogy. The payoff for work at these levels is least immediate, but it can give a rich perspective on one's origins and on certain highly significant family patterns that may flow over many generations.

Once you have clarified your role in the family and have an understanding of some of the basic themes or triangles, it is essential to track what role you usually take in the family. Anywhere that the role has become stuck, it can help to change a habitual pattern of relating by saying or doing the opposite of what you usually say or do in response to someone else. Although you may at first think of this as "lying," the reversal of the process actually expresses the unspoken and unacknowledged other side of a stuck issue and tends to break up rigid, predictable, repetitive communication patterns. For example, a wife who ordinarily gets angry when her husband gets sick and calls him a hypochondriac can reverse her pattern and play Florence Nightingale; a man who usually cannot talk to his father because he is so dictatorial can ask for advice and try to listen attentively to his input. If you are usually the one with advice and ideas, you can be helpless and out of ideas. The key to such reversals is that you have to carry them out in an openhearted way, without sarcasm or resentment, so you must be ready before you start the process.

When triangles have become apparent, detriangling is the major task.

Detriangling entails shifting the motion of a triangle and unlocking the compulsory loyalties so that three dyadic relationships can emerge from an enmeshed threesome. Using a reversal to detriangle places you in a different position in the recurring patterns of a triangle. For example, a son who has an overly close relationship with his mother and a distant relationship with his father might begin to detriangle by going to his father with the confidences his mother has inappropriately shared with him and saying, "Mom seems terribly upset, and I'm sure you will be able to help her out. I don't know why, but she came to me with her worries and said . . . ."

To prevent a two-step, the original plan would have to include a way to deal with the mother's anger and sense of betrayal when the father confronts her with the son's report. The son might handle this by telling his mother, if she confronts him, that he was so upset by her distress that he felt he had to share it with his father to get him to help her out.

It is important to realize that strategies such as reversals should not be undertaken lightly. They succeed only when the person doing them has the emotional control to edit his or her feelings of hurt, anger, sarcasm, and vengeance, and when the reversal conveys a respect for the other. Such techniques are not a substitute for person-to-person intimacy. In disciplined hands, they can substitute for the destructive emotional games and repetitive interchanges that often make relationships dysfunctional and thus reduce some of the distance or repetitious conflict that stands in the way of intimacy.

Opening Up a Closed System

Sometimes, merely contacting family members who have been cut off from the family can begin the process of opening the loaded issues in a family. Bowen believed that in some situations, setting up "a tempest in a teapot"— magnifying small emotional issues in such a way that old, dormant triangles are activated—can open the family in a new manner. Tactics that stir up an emotional system may be necessary when patterns have become obscured in a quiescent system. Triangles are likely to be reactivated in the next family crisis, unless the underlying pattern can be modified.

It might be necessary to activate a dormant triangle, for example, if a person cannot move directly toward his father without the father's withdrawing. In such a case it may be necessary to move toward those people with whom the father has relationships, perhaps the father's siblings or his parents. Such moves, sometimes referred to as "wagon training" because they involve activating connections with all the people the distant person is connected to, not only can provide a wealth of information and perspective on the father, but might also activate the triangle between the father, his brother, and their mother. Once the father realizes that his brother is giving family information, he may want to share his side of the story. If the father felt like the outsider in the relationship with his mother and brother, he is likely to fear being the outsider again if his own child moves toward his brother. If the direct contact with the uncle is not enough to create a shift, the son may want to mention a toxic family issue to the uncle, on the assumption that the uncle might then take a different move with the father and thus open the system. If the system is very closed, the son may have to magnify a small issue with the uncle in order to push the system to react. It is important to distinguish such an effort from destructive and hurtful threats or unleashing secrets in a family without consideration for the people involved in the emotional process.

Women are typically the carriers of family heritage in certain ways. They often feel more responsible for the family, for those in need, for dealing with the pain of family secrets, and for injustices done to family members. Men may disconnect more easily, given society's support for the "independent" male. Older sisters may be particularly accessible and helpful in promoting family reconnections because they are likely to feel so responsible for family well-being. However, as with race or any other issue of injustice in relationships, a sister will have to come to terms with the unfairness of gender roles before she will become free to move toward a new equilibrium and attempt to change oppressive family rules of overresponsibility for daughters and glory for sons. Because of our society's rules for male and female socialization, men may fit into the stereotypes of being less accessible, less willing to acknowledge their vulnerability, and less aware of the emotional process in the family. However, if you keep a life cycle perspective you may find situations where men in your family can become more open, especially during times of transition and loss.

Being able to clearly state one's thoughts or feelings on a subject without being attacking or defensive is, of course, the ultimate goal. But there are many times when other ways of communicating must be established first in order to open up a system. This is especially true in tight triangles in which taking a clear position may create a negative reaction and tend to close down relationships.

Consider the situation of the newly married couple, Cindy and Mike. Mike's mother, Susan, had told her son negative things about Cindy, which Mike then repeated to Cindy, who became very upset. How might Cindy deal with this situation? One option would be for Cindy to directly tell her mother-in-law what she thought of such criticism, but this would undoubtedly intensify Susan's negativity toward her. Another option would be for Cindy to say to Mike: "I wish you could stand up to your mother. I don't think I deserve her dislike of me." She might then say to the mother-in-law, "Mike told me what you said about me, and I was upset and hurt by what you are saying to him. In the future, I wish you would tell me directly what you think of me."

Hopefully one does arrive at a point where thoughts and feelings can be expressed this directly, but it is usually possible only in a cultural context in which emotional directness between a mother-in-law and a daughter-in-law is acceptable and in which the system is relatively open and anxiety-free. When it is not, "I positions," where one clearly states one's opinion, may raise the tension further. The mother's negativity might increase, though becoming subtler, out of anxiety that her son will again tell his wife of her feelings if she speaks to him too directly. In this case Cindy decided to detrianglulate by use of a reversal. She found time alone with her new mother-in-law and said, "Mike has been telling me some of the things you've been saying about me, and I'm so relieved to know, because I was so worried that you would not like me and would wish your son hadn't married me." When Cindy said this, she felt a sense of immediate relief. And as she told her mother-in-law of her real anxiety about not being accepted, the mother-in-law looked very surprised, probably fearing that her son really had told Cindy the negative things she had been saying, but seeming to be relieved that Cindy didn't appear to know of her hostile comments. She began reassuring Cindy about her positive feelings. Subsequently, Mike noted with surprise that his mother had completely stopped her negative comments. Cindy smiled to herself, relieved that things had eased and feeling more empowered to work out more of a personal relationship with her mother-in-law.

Humor

The intense and automatic reaction of the system to resist change has led to the development of various direct and indirect strategies, including the ability to laugh at ourselves and gain a certain lightness with regard to our own emotional reactivity. Humor is one of the most effective ways to detoxify and reframe a situation. Part of the power of triangles, ruts, labels, and rigid patterns is that they make us feel stuck, take the situation too seriously, and lose our sense of humor. A surprising and gently humorous redefinition of a situation, always without sarcasm, may jostle that inflexibility in such a way that the challenge is softened by an element of sharing. Of course the difference between humor and sarcasm can be a sharp edge and one must be very careful to carry it out with love and kindness. After a mother's long story about her husband's neglect, a son might smile and say, tongue-in-cheek: "It sounds like you're having a hard time appreciating the space he leaves you to create your own life."

Carrying a situation to the point of absurdity often helps people gain perspective on their overly intense involvement in a rigid position and reduces what was threatening and serious to triviality. After long complaints about a wife's conversational style at a party, the son might say jokingly to his father: "It sounds like you shouldn't take her anywhere until she learns how to behave."

The very act of sharing a laugh can help to reduce the tension and restore some of the commonality that has been cut off by bitterness. By suddenly disorganizing the established social situation, humor creates a surprising new arrangement and opens new possibilities. "Just think," one daughter remarked, "of the wonderful opportunity that impossible man is giving you to learn patience." (This would obviously be inappropriate, if the wife were being intimidated or abused by a bullying husband.) Humor relabels a situation and may allow us to gain power over a system in which we have previously been caught. It is essential to understand the difference between the playfulness of genuine humor and the anger and bitterness of sarcasm. In order to avoid the latter, one has to move emotionally away from anger and become aware of the absurdity of the struggle. It may enable you to concentrate on your own values and wishes, rather than remaining stuck and helpless about another person's behavior or point of view.

A Personal Note

I myself began coaching after hearing Murray Bowen give a presentation on family systems theory in which he said that if you haven't worked out your relationship with your own mother to the point where you can sit comfortably in the same room with her, you have not really learned how to work systemically. I could hardly hear his presentation because I was so sure he had never met anyone like my mother and didn't know what he was talking about. But in the back of my mind I was awed to think that somehow I could possibly get to the point of having a relationship with my mother. I had struggled with her all my life. At my wedding luncheon a couple of years earlier, a friend had said how delighted he was to know her daughters. Her response, spoken loud enough for me to hear: "When you have a child like Monica, it's not worth having children." She had been critical and emotionally withholding all my life, and even my friends preferred not to come over if they knew she'd be home.

I had had a lot of therapy by that time, which had confirmed my hypotheses about how difficult she was and provided me with all kinds of psychological labels that reassured me that the problem was hers and not mine. I had "realized" that my mother was a woman with her own problems, limited in what she could give us, and that the best thing to do was to keep things calm and not get too involved, focusing instead on my marriage and my friends.

After I heard Bowen's talk I arranged to begin coaching with one of his followers, Phil Guerin. Though my relationship with my mother had been stormy and negative as I grew up, it had become more distant and tenuously calm after my years of individual therapy, in which I learned to be less reactive but not to actually try to develop a personal relationship with her. I realized that I missed having a more positive relationship with my mother, even though the relationship was better than it had once been—because I kept a cool distance and focused my energy on friends and my marriage. In coaching I was encouraged to look at this relationship in a larger context—first in relation to my very close attachment to my father and to Margaret, the African-American caretaker who had raised us. Margaret had come to work for my family the week I was born and stayed until her death the year after I left home for college. I felt in a triangle with my husband and my mother as well, as he was the only one in the family who refused to placate her, and she didn't appreciate it, which put a strain on all our relationships.

I tried to gather genogram information, though my mother was very uncooperative, saying that nothing in her miserable childhood had been carried over into our family. When I kept pursuing the family history, she accused me of trying to destroy her by bringing up painful subjects. I began to sense dimly that her withholding behavior was not personal, but I couldn't think how to proceed. My coach suggested I stop pursuing her entirely and explore who else on my genogram might be able to teach me about my family. I thought that was ridiculous. It was a known fact that most of my relatives were "boring." But when I began to question this assumption, it was quite obvious I was grossly mistaken. My mother had been the youngest of three sisters by 7 years. Her oldest sister would thus know much more family history than she. And there was her middle sister, 4 years older than she, who had been closest to my mother's hated mother. I hadn't seen her in years, but she would probably have a lot of different information, if I could get her to share it.

My oldest aunt responded positively from my first phone call. I hadn't seen her since my wedding 2 years earlier, but she quickly invited me to visit her in her new home. The visit was a revelation. What I most remember was her telling me she remembered the night my mother was born! I actually couldn't believe my mother had ever been born, thinking of her as arising full grown from Zeus's head or something! My aunt shared many memories of my mother as bratty and often crying as a little girl, once humiliating their mother by managing to find her way to church and walking all the way up the center aisle in her little dirty clothes looking for her mother. My aunt had gotten in big trouble because she was supposed to be babysitting for my mother. She went on to tell me that my grandmother didn't have an easy life, with a policeman for a husband and never knowing if he'd come home or be killed on the job; she added, "And don't let anybody tell you different." Of course there was only one person who would tell me different. That would be my own mother, who used to describe her mother as "the vainest woman who ever walked the earth," and told me how she had had an affair with the local priest right under the nose of my grandfather and used to tell my mother not to come home after school because Father Egan would be there; my mother had thus become a "street kid" and started smoking in third grade. She felt her mother had ruined her childhood by seeing her as a nuisance and ranting at everyone.

When I returned from visiting my aunt, my mother called immediately to say she heard I had been invited to her sister's new house, which even she hadn't been to yet. The triangle was activated! The following weekend I went to visit my parents, and my mother had a whole box of family memorabilia on the table for me. She said she was going through things and found these and thought, as I had such an interest in the family history, that I might want it. How many times before I had asked my mother for family memorabilia and she had said there was none! Suddenly out it came, with the stories to go with it. Once I had another source of information and had stopped quizzing her, it seemed, she wanted to offer me her perspective.

Some time later I arranged to visit my middle aunt in Chicago. I had asked her to bring any family pictures she had but she said she could only find three. None had any family members—one was of the house they grew up in, one was of my grandmother's piano, a result of a settlement when my grandmother was in a ferry accident, and one was of the very priest my mother felt had ruined her life. My aunt described how amazing my grandmother was at finding the one magnificent item in any junk shop and her love of beautiful things. I laughed to myself because my mother was exactly the same and had become a successful antique dealer in later life. She wondered what had happened to the piano and I had to sheepishly admit that I had inherited it! When she showed the picture of Father Egan I was stupefied and pretended I didn't know who it was. "Oh," she replied, "That was my mother's greatest friend, don't you know him?!" Later in the ladies' room I dared to raise the priest issue with my cousin, who had come along. I said that the story that came down our side of the family was that he had ruined our mother's childhood and humiliated our grandfather. She responded she hadn't heard they had an affair, but, she said, "You know, our grandmother was one of the early liberated women on Staten Island, the first to drive a car. She was very daring, so an affair wouldn't surprise me." The circuits were being blown on my

THE GENOGRAM JOURNEY: RECONNECTING WITH YOUR FAMILY **347**

perspectives on my family history. From here I proceeded very carefully, trying never to get ahead of my mother's willingness to share what she felt comfortable with. In fits and starts and over the many more years I was lucky to have her, our relationship grew stronger and stronger and more honest until the very day of her death—just as the first edition of this book, which she had read and commented on in earlier versions, was almost ready for press. I had originally published the story of my coaching in a slightly disguised form without discussing it with my family. Finally a friend of my mother recognized it and told her about it. By that time I was no longer fearful of what she would think; I was concerned mostly that she would be upset by what I said about my father, who had slightly come off his pedestal in my efforts to understand him. But she said she didn't want to read it. By that time I was able to accept that, where on an earlier day I would have been very judgmental about her fear of knowing and dealing with issues forthrightly. I had come to be a much less judgmental daughter, as she had come to be a much less judgmental mother. It is for these transformative changes, which have meant so much in my life, that I have dedicated this book to her. She taught me a great deal about courage even as I learned many fears and insecurities from her, and I hope I can, as she did, keep growing until my last day.

References

Anderson, R. (1968). *I never sang for my father.* New York: Random House.

Baldwin, J. (1991). Sonny's blues. In Minnesota Humanities Commission (Ed.), *Braided lives: An anthology of multicultural American writing.* St. Paul, Minnesota: Minnesota Humanities Commission.

Bernikow, L. (1980). *Among women.* New York: Harper & Row.

Bowen, M. (1978). *Family therapy in clinical practice.* New York: Jason Aronson.

Burton, L., Winn, D. M., Stevenson, H., & Clark, S. L. (2004). Working with African American clients: Considering the "homeplace" in marriage and family therapy practices. *Journal of Marital and Family Therapy, 30*(4), 113–129.

Carter, B., & Peters, J. K. (1996). *Love honor and negotiate: Making your marriage work.* New York: Pocket Books.

Carter, B., & McGoldrick, M. (2001). Family therapy with one person and the family therapist's own family. *Journal of Marital and Family Therapy,* 27(3), pp. 281–300.

Carter, E. A., & McGoldrick Orfanidis, M. (1976). Family therapy with one person and the family therapist's own family. In P. J. Guerin (Ed.), *Family therapy* (pp. 193–219). New York: Gardner.

Conroy, P. (1988). *The prince of tides.* New York: Houghton Mifflin.

Fishel, E. (1979). *Sisters: Love and rivalry inside the family and beyond.* New York: William Morrow.

Flanagan, T. (1979). *The year of the French.* New York: Holt, Rinehart & Winston.

Friedman, E. (1990). *Friedman's fables.* New York: Guilford.

Giamatti, A. B. (1989). *Take time for paradise: Americans and their games.* New York: Summit.

Gilles-Donovan, J. (1991, Summer). Common misunderstandings. *American Family Therapy Academy Newsletter,* 7–14.

Golden, M. (2005). *Don't play in the sun: One woman's journey through the color complex.* Garden City, NY: Anchor Press.

Griffin, S. (1992). *A chorus of stones.* New York: Doubleday.

Haley, A. (1976). *Roots: The saga of an American family.* New York: Doubleday.

Haskell, M. (1990). *Love and other infectious diseases.* New York: William Morrow.

Heilbrun, C. G. (1988). *Writing a woman's life.* New York: Norton.

Kleiner, P. *Good mother; good daughter.* Unpublished manuscript.

Kotre, J., & Hall, E. (1990). *Seasons of life.* Boston: Little, Brown.

Markham, E. (1932). *The shoes of happiness and other poems.* New York: Doubleday.

McCullough, D. (2001). *John Adams.* New York: Simon & Schuster.

McGoldrick, M. (2005). Irish Families. In M. McGoldrick, J. Giordano, & N. Garcia-Preto (Eds.). *Ethnicity and family therapy.* New York: Guilford.

McGoldrick, M., Carter, B., & Garcia Preto, N. (Eds.). (2010). *The changing family life cycle* (4th ed.). Boston: Allyn & Bacon.

McGoldrick, M., Gerson, R., & Petry, S. (2008). *Genograms: Assessment and intervention.* New York: Norton.

McGoldrick, M., Giordano, J., & Garcia Preto, N. (2005). *Ethnicity and family therapy* (3rd ed.). New York: Guilford.

Nabokov, V. (1992). *The real life of Sebastian Knight.* New York: Vintage.

Rose, P. (1984). *Parallel lives: Five Victorian marriages.* New York: Vintage.

Russell, K., Wilson, M., & Hall, R. (1993). *The color complex: The politics of skin color among African Americans.* Garden City, NY: Anchor Press.

Valliant, G. E. (1977). *Adaption to life.* Boston: Little, Brown.

Walmsley, J. (2003). *Brit-think, Ameri-think.* New York: Penguin.

Walsh, F., & McGoldrick, M. (Eds.). (2004). *Living beyond loss: Death and the family* (2nd ed.). New York: Norton.

Witchel, A. (1989, November 12). Laughter, tears and the perfect martini. *New York Times Magazine,* 102–105.

ADAMS FAMILY SOURCES

Adams, J. T. (1976). *The Adams family.* New York: Signet.

McCullough, D. (2001). *John Adams.* New York: Simon & Schuster.

Musto, D. (1981). The Adams family. *Proceedings of Massachusetts Historical Society, 93,* 40–58.

Nagel, P. C. (1983). *Descent from glory: Four generations of the John Adams family.* New York: Oxford University Press.

Nagel, P. C. (1987). *The Adams women.* New York: Oxford University Press.

Nagel, P. C. (1997). *John Quincy Adams: A public life.* New York: Knopf.

O'Toole, P. (1990). *The five of hearts: An intimate portrait of Henry Adams and his friends 1880–1918.* New York: Ballantine.

Shepherd, J. (1975). *The Adams chronicles: Four generations of greatness.* Boston: Little, Brown.

ANGELOU SOURCES

Angelou, M. (1970). *I know why the caged bird sings.* New York: Random House.

Angelou, M. (1974). *Gather together in my name.* New York: Bantam.

Angelou, M. (1981). *The heart of a woman.* New York: Bantam.

Angelou, M. (1986). *All God's children need traveling shoes.* New York: Vintage.

Angelou, M. (1993). *Wouldn't take nothing for my journey now.* New York: Random House.

Angelou, M. (2007). *Letter to my daughter.* New York: Random House.

Kite, L. P. (1999). *Maya Angelou.* Minneapolis, MN: Lerner.

McPherson, D. A. (1999). *Order out of chaos: The autobiographical works of Maya Angelou.* New York: Peter Lang.

Oliver, S. S. (1989). Maya Angelou: The heart of a woman. In J. M. Elliott (Ed.), *Conversations with Maya Angelou* (pp. 135–139). Jackson, MS: University Press of Mississippi.

Shuker, N. (1990). *Maya Angelou.* Englewood Cliffs, NJ: Silver Burdett Press.

BARRETT AND BROWNING SOURCES

Browning, V. (1979). *My Browning family album.* London: Springwood.

Forster, M. (1988). *Elizabeth Barrett Browning: A biography.* New York: Doubleday.

Karlin, D. (1987). *The courtship of Robert Browning and Elizabeth Barrett.* New York: Oxford University Press.

Marks, J. (1938). *The family of the Barrett.* New York: Macmillan.

Markus, J. (1995). *Dared and done: The marriage of Elizabeth Barrett and Robert Browning.* New York: Knopf.

Maynard, J. (1977). *Browning's youth.* Cambridge, MA: Harvard University Press.

Ryals, C. de L. (1993). *The life of Robert Browning.* Cambridge, MA: Blackwell.

BATESON AND MEAD SOURCES

Bateson, M. C. (1984). *With a daughter's eye.* New York: William Morrow.

Bateson, M. C. (1990). *Composing a life.* New York: Atlantic Monthly Press.

Bateson, M. C. (1994). *Peripheral visions.* New York: William Morrow.

Cassidy, R. (1982). *Margaret Mead: A voice for the century.* New York: Universe Books.

Grosskurth, P. (1988). *Margaret Mead: A life of controversy.* London: Penguin.

Howard, J. (1984). *Margaret Mead: A life.* New York: Ballantine.

Lipset, D. (1980). *Gregory Bateson: The legacy of a scientist.* Englewood Cliffs, NJ: Prentice.

Mead, M. (1972). *Blackberry winter, my earlier years.* New York: Simon & Schuster.

Rice, E. (1979). *Margaret Mead: A portrait.* New York: Harper & Row.

BEETHOVEN SOURCES

Forbes, E. (Ed.). (1969). *Thayer's life of Beethoven.* Princeton: Princeton University Press.

Matthews, D. (1988). *Beethoven*. New York: Vintage.

Solomon, M. (1977). *Beethoven*. New York: Schirmer.

Solomon, M. (1988). *Beethoven essays*. Cambridge: Harvard University Press.

BLACKWELL, STONE, AND BROWN SOURCES

Binns, T. B. (2005). *Elizabeth Blackwell*. New York: Franklin Watts.

Cazden, E. (1983). *Antoinette Brown Blackwell: A biography*. Old Westbury, NY: Feminist Press.

Hays, E. R. (1967). *Those extraordinary Blackwells*. New York: Harcourt Brace.

Horn, M. (1980). *Family ties: The Blackwells, a study of the dynamics of family life in nineteenth century America*. Unpublished doctoral dissertation, Tufts University.

Horn, M. (1983). Sisters worthy of respect: Family dynamics and women's roles in the Blackwell family. *Journal of Family History, 8*(4), 367–382.

Kerr, A. M. (1992). *Lucy Stone: Speaking out*. New Brunswick, NJ: Rutgers University Press.

Lasser, C., & Merrill, M. D. (1987). *Friends & sisters: Letters between Lucy Stone and Antoinette Brown Blackwell 1846–93*. Chicago: University of Illinois.

Wheeler, L. (1961). *Loving worriers: Selected letters of Lucy Stone and Henry B. Blackwell, 1853 to 1893*. New York: Dial.

BRONTE SOURCES

Barker, J. (1994). *The Brontës*. London: Weidenfeldt & Nicolson.

Barker, J. (1998). *The Brontës: A Life in Letters*. New York: The Overlook Press

Bentley, P. (1969). *The Brontes and their world*. New York: Viking.

Bronte, C. (1922-2004). *Villette*. New York: E. P. Dutton.

Cannon, J. (1980). *The road to Haworth: The story of the Brontes' Irish ancestry*. London: Weidenfeld and Nicolson.

Chitham, E. (1986). *The Brontes' Irish background*. New York: St. Martin's Press.

Chitham, E. (1988). *A life of Emily Bronte*. New York: Basil Blackwell.

Chitham, E., & Winnifrith, T. (1983). *Bronte facts and Bronte problems*. London: Macmillan.

du Maurier, D. (1961). *The infernal world of Branwell Bronte*. Garden City, NY: Doubleday.

Frank, K. (1990). *A Chainless Soul: A life of Emily Bronte*. New York: Ballantine.

Frazer, R. (1988). *The Brontes: Charlotte Bronte and her family*. New York: Crown.

Gaskell, E. (1975). *The life of Charlotte Bronte*. London: Penguin.

Gerin, W. (1961). *Branwell Bronte*. London: Thomas Nelson & Sons.

Gerin, W. (1971). *Emily Bronte: A biography*. London: Oxford University Press.

Hannah, B. (1988). *Striving toward wholeness*. Boston: Signpress.

Lane, M. (1969). *The Bronte story*. London: Fontana.

Lock, J., & Dixon, W. T. (1965). *A man of sorrow: The life, letters, and times of Reverend Patrick Bronte.* Westport, CT: Meckler Books.

Moglen, H. (1984). *Charlotte Bronte: The self conceived.* Madison, WI: University of Wisconsin Press.

Peters, M. (1974). *An enigma of Brontes.* New York: St. Martins Press.

Peters, M. (1975). *Unquiet soul: A biography of Charlotte Bronte.* New York: Atheneum.

Spark, M., & Derek, S. (1960). *Emily Bronte: Her life and work.* London: Arrow Books.

Wilks, B. (1986). *The Brontes: An illustrated biography.* New York: Peter Bedrick Books.

Wilks, B. (1986). *The illustrated Brontes of Haworth.* New York: Facts on File Publications.

Winnifith, T. Z. (1977). *The Brontes and their background: Romance and reality.* New York: Collier.

Wright, W. (1893). *The Brontes in Ireland.* New York: D. Appleton & Company.

CHAPLIN SOURCES

Bessy, M. (1983). *Charlie Chaplin.* New York: Harper & Row.

Chaplin, C. (1964). *My autobiography.* New York: Simon & Schuster.

Chaplin, C., Jr., Rau, N., & Rau, M. (1960). *My father, Charlie Chaplin.* New York: Random House.

Chaplin, L. G., & Cooper, M. (1966). *My life with Chaplin: An intimate memoir.* Brattleboro, VT: Book Press.

Epstein, J. (1989). *Remembering Charlie.* New York: Doubleday.

Robinson, D. (1983). *Chaplin: The mirror of opinion.* Bloomington, IN: Indiana University Press.

Robinson, D. (1985). *Chaplin: His life and art.* New York: McGraw-Hill.

CURIE SOURCES

Curie, E. (1939). *Marie Curie: A biography.* New York: Doubleday.

Giroud, F. (1986). *Marie Curie: A life.* New York: Holmes & Meier.

Pflaum, R. (1989). *Grand obsession: Madame Curie and her world.* New York: Doubleday.

Reid, R. (1974). *Marie Curie.* New York: E. P. Dutton.

Steinke, A. E. (1987). *Marie Curie.* New York: Barrons.

DE BEAUVOIR SOURCES

Appignanesi, L. (1988). *Simone de Beauvoir.* New York: Viking Penguin.

Ascher, C. (1981). *Simone de Beauvoir: A life of freedom.* Boston: Beacon.

Bair, D. (1990). *Simone de Beauvoir: A biography.* New York: Summit.

de Beauvoir, S. (1959). *Memoirs of a dutiful daughter.* New York: Harper & Row.

de Beauvoir, S. (1966). *A very easy death*. New York: Warner Paperback Library.

de Beauvoir, S. (1974). *The second sex*. New York: Vintage.

Francis, C., & Gontier, F. (1987). *Simone de Beauvoir: A life, a love story*. New York: St. Martin's Press.

Fullbrook, K. & Fullbrook, E. (1994) *Simone de Beauvoir and Jean Paul Sartre*. New York: Basic Books.

Rowley, H. *Tête-à-tête: Simone de Beauvoir and Jean-Paul Sartre*. New York: HarperCollins.

DICKENS SOURCES

Johnson, E. (1980). *Charles Dickens: His tragedy and triumph*. New York: Penguin.

Kaplan, F. (1988). *Dickens: A biography*. New York: William Morrow.

Mackenzie, N., & Mackenzie, J. (1979). *Dickens: A life*. New York: Oxford.

Storey, G. (1939). *Dickens and daughter*. London: Frederick Muller Ltd.

Tomalin, C. (1991). *The invisible woman: The story of Nelly Ternan and Charles Dickens*. New York: Knopf.

EDISON SOURCES

Conot, R. (1979). *Thomas A. Edison: A streak of luck*. New York: Plenum.

Frost, L. A. (1984). *The Edison album: A pictorial biography of Thomas Alva Edison*. Mattituck, NY: Amereon House.

Josephson, M. (1959). *Edison: A biography*. New York: McGraw-Hill.

Venable, J. D. (1961). *Mina Miller Edison: Daughter, wife and mother of inventors*. East Orange, NJ: Charles Edison Fund.

Wachhorst, W. (1984). *Thomas Alva Edison: An American myth*. Cambridge, MA: MIT Press.

FONDA SOURCES

Collier, P. (1992). *The Fondas*. New York: Putnam.

Fonda, A. (1986). *Never before dawn: An autobiography*. New York: Weindenfeld & Nicolson.

Fonda, J. (2006). *My life so far*. New York: Random House.

Fonda, P. (1998). *Don't tell dad*. New York: Hyperion.

Guiles, F. L. (1981). *Jane Fonda: The actress in her time*. New York: Pinnacle.

Hayward, B. (1977). *Haywire*. New York: Knopf.

Teichman, H. (1981). *Fonda: My life*. New York: New American Library.

FRANKLIN SOURCES

Bowen, C. D. (1974). *The most dangerous man in America: Scenes from the life of Benjamin Franklin*. Boston: Little, Brown.

Clark, R. W. (1983). *Benjamin Franklin: A biography.* New York: Random House.

Fay, B. (1969). *The two Franklins: Fathers of American democracy.* New York: AMS Press.

Franklin, B. (1968). *The autobiography of Benjamin Franklin.* New Haven, CT: Yale University Press.

Labaree, L. W., Ketcham, R. L., Boarfield, H. C., & Fineman, H. H. (Eds.). (1964). *The autobiography of Benjamin Franklin.* New Haven, CT: Yale University Press.

Lopez, C. A., & Herbert, E. W. (1975). *The private Franklin: The man and his family.* New York: Norton.

Middlekauf, R. (1996). *Benjamin Franklin and his enemies.* Berkeley, CA: University of California Press.

Osborne, M. P. (1990). *The many lives of Benjamin Franklin.* New York: Dial.

Randall, W. (1984). *A little revenge: Benjamin Franklin and his son.* Boston: Little, Brown.

Seavey, O. (1988). *Becoming Benjamin Franklin: The autobiography and the life.* University Park, PA: Pennsylvania State University Press.

Skemp, S. L. (1990). *William Franklin, son of a patriot, servant of a king.* New York: Oxford University Press.

Stevenson, A. (1987). *The real Benjamin Franklin: The true story of America's greatest diplomat.* Washington, DC: National Center for Constitutional Studies.

Van Doren, C. (1991). *Benjamin Franklin.* New York: Viking.

Wright, E. (1988). *Franklin of Philadelphia.* Cambridge, MA: Harvard University Press.

Wright, E. (1990). *Benjamin Franklin: His life as he wrote it.* Cambridge, MA: Harvard University Press.

FREUD SOURCES

Anzieu, D. (1986). *Freud's self analysis.* Madison, CT: International Universities Press.

Appignanesi, L., & Forrester, J. (1992). *Freud's women.* New York: Basic.

Burlingham, M. J. (2002). *Behind glass: A biography of Dorothy Tiffany Burlingham.* New York: Other Press.

Carotenuto, A. (1982). *A secret symmetry: Sabina Spielrein between Jung and Freud.* New York: Pantheon.

Clark, R. W. (1980). *Freud: The man and the cause.* New York: Random House.

Eissler, K. R. (1978). *Sigmund Freud: His life in pictures and words.* New York: Helen & Kurt Wolff Books, Harcourt Brace, Jovanovich.

Freud, E. L. (1975). *The letters of Sigmund Freud.* New York: Basic.

Freud, M. (1982). *Sigmund Freud: Man and father.* New York: Jason Aronson.

Freud, S. (1988). *My three mothers and other passions.* New York: New York University Press.

Gay, P. (1988). *Freud: A life for our time.* New York: Norton.

Gay, P. (1990). *Reading Freud.* New Haven, CT: Yale University Press.

Gicklhorn, R. (1979) The Freiberg period of the Freud family. *Journal of the History of Medicine, 24*, 37–43.

Jones, E. (1953, 1954, 1955). *The life and work of Sigmund Freud.* (Vols. 1–3). New York: Basic.

Jones, E. (Ed.). (1975). *Letters of Sigmund Freud.* London: Cambridge University Press.

Krüll, M. (1986). *Freud and his father.* New York: Norton.

Mannoni, O. (1974). *Freud.* New York: Vintage.

Margolis, D. P. (1996). *Freud and his mother.* Northvale, NJ: Jason Aronson.

Masson, J. (Ed.). (1985). *The complete letters of Sigmund Freud to Wilhelm Fleiss: 1887– 1904.* Cambridge, MA: Belnap Press.

Masson, J. (1992). *The assault on truth.* New York: Harper Collins

Peters, U. H. (1985). *Anna Freud: A life dedicated to children.* New York: Shocken.

Roazen, P. (1993). *Meeting Freud's family.* Amherst, MA: University of Massachusetts Press.

Schur, M. (1972). *Freud: Living and dying.* New York: International Universities Press.

Swales, P. (1982). Freud, Minna Bernays, and the conquest of Rome: New light on the origins of psychoanalysis. *The New American Review, 1*(2/3), 1–23.

Swales, P. (1986, November 15). *Freud, his origins and family history.* Presentation at UMDNJ Robert Wood Johnson Medical School, Piscataway, NJ.

Swales, P. (1987, May 15). *What Freud didn't say.* Presentation at UMDNJ Robert Wood Johnson Medical School, Piscataway, NJ.

Young-Bruel, E. (1988). *Anna Freud: A biography.* New York: Summit.

GANDHI SOURCES

Chadha, Y. (1997). *Gandhi: A life.* New York: John Wiley.

Easwaran, E. (1972). *Gandhi the man* (2nd ed.). New York: Nilgiri/Random House.

Erikson, E. H. (1969). *Gandhi's truth: On the origins of militant nonviolence.* New York: Norton.

Gandhi, M. K. (2008). *An autobiography: On my experiments with truth.* Ahmedabad, India: Navajivan Publishing House.

Gold, G., & Attenborough, R. (1983). *Gandhi: A pictorial biography.* New York: Newmarket.

Kripalani, K. (1999). *Gandhi.* New Delhi, India: Interprint.

Woodcock, G. (1971). *Mohandas Gandhi.* New York: Viking.

GUEVARA SOURCES

Anderson, J. L. (1997). *Che Guevara: A revolutionary life.* New York: Grove.

Deutschmann, D. (Ed.). (2006). *Che: A memoir by Fidel Castro.* Melbourne, Australia: Ocean Press.

James, D. (2001). *Che Guevara: A biography.* New York: Cooper Square Press.

Ortiz, V. (1968). *Che Guevara: Reminiscences of a Cuban revolutionary war.* New York: Monthly Review Press.

Sinclair, A. (1970). *Che Guevara.* New York: Viking.

HAWTHORNE SOURCES

Cowley, M. (Ed.). (1983). *The Hawthorne reader.* New York: Viking.

Crews, F. (1966), *The sins of the fathers: Hawthorne's Psychological Themes.* Berkeley: Univ. of California Press.

Erlich, G. (1986). *Family themes and Hawthorne's fiction: The tenacious web.* New Brunswick, NJ: Rutgers University Press.

Hawthorne, J. (1888) *Nathaniel Hawthorne and his wife: A biography* (Vols. 1–2). Grosse Pointe, MI: Scholarly Press.

Hawthorne, N. (1882–1883). *The complete works of Nathaniel Hawthorne.* (Ed. G. Lathrop). New York: Riverside.

Hawthorne, N. (1969). *The portable Hawthorne.* New York: Viking.

Miller, E. H. (1991). *Salem is my dwelling place: A life of Nathaniel Hawthorne.* Iowa City: University of Iowa Press.

Wagenknecht, E. (1961). *Nathaniel Hawthorne: Man and writer.* New York: Oxford University Press.

Wineapple, B. (2004). *Hawthorne: A life.* New York: Random House.

Young, P. (1984). *Hawthorne's secret: An untold tale.* Boston: David R. Godine.

HEPBURN AND TRACY SOURCES

Anderson, C. (1988). *Young Kate.* New York: Henry Holt.

Anderson, C. (1997). *An affair to remember.* New York: Morrow.

Davidson, B. (1987). *Spencer Tracy: Tragic idol.* New York: E. P. Dutton.

Edwards, A. (1985). *A remarkable woman: A biography of Katherine Hepburn.* New York: Simon & Schuster.

Hepburn, K. (1991). *Me.* New York: Knopf.

Higham, C. (1981). *Kate: The life of Katharine Hepburn.* New York: Signet.

Kanin, G. (1988). *Tracy and Hepburn: An intimate memoir.* New York: Donald I. Fine.

Leaming, B. (1995). *Katharine Hepburn.* New York: Crown.

Mann, W. J. (2006). *Kate: The woman who was Hepburn.* New York: Henry Holt.

Parish, J. R. (2005). *Katherine Hepburn: The untold story.* New York: Advocate Books.

Porter, D., (2004). *Katharine the great.* New York: Blood Moon Productions.

HOOKS SOURCES

hooks, b. (1990). *Yearning: Race, gender and cultural politics.* Boston: South End Press.

hooks, b. (1996). *Bone black: Memories of girlhood,* New York: Henry Holt.

hooks, b. (1997). *Wounds of passion: A writing life*. New York: Henry Holt.

hooks, b. (1999). *Remembered rapture: The writer at work*. New York: Henry Holt.

hooks, b. (2009). *Belonging: A culture of place*. New York: Taylor & Francis.

HUGHES SOURCES

Hughes, L. (1945). *The big sea: An autobiography*. New York: Knopf.

McClatchy, J. D. (2002). *Langston Hughes: Voice of the poet*. New York: Random House.

Rampesad, A., & Roessel, D. (2002). *The collected poems of Langston Hughes*.

JOPLIN SOURCES

Berlin, E. A. (1994). *King of ragtime: Scott Joplin and his era*. New York: Oxford University Press.

Curtis, S. (2004). Dancing to a black man's tune: The life of Scott Joplin. Columbia, MO: University of Missouri Press.

Gammond, P. (1975). *Scott Joplin and the ragtime era*. New York: St. Martin's Press.

Haskins, J. (1978). *Scott Joplin: The man who made ragtime*. Briarcliff Manor, NY: Scarborough.

Preston, K. (1988). *Scott Joplin: Composer*. New York: Chelsea House.

Websites:

www.personal.psu.edu/users/j/n/jnm144/scott%20joplin.htm

www.scottjoplin.org/biography.htm

KAFKA SOURCES

Citati, P. (1989). *Kafka*. New York: Knopf.

Glazer, N. N. (1986). *The loves of Franz Kafka*. New York: Schocken Books.

Heller, E. (1974). *Franz Kafka*. Princeton, NJ: Princeton University Press.

Kafka, F. (1953). *Letter to his father*. New York: Schocken Books.

Kafka, F. (1982). *Letters to Ottla and the family* (R. Winston & C. Winston, Trans.). New York: Schocken Books.

Pawel, E. (1984). *The nightmare of reason: A life of Franz Kafka*. New York: Vintage.

Robert, M. (1986). *As lonely as Franz Kafka: A psychological biography*. New York: Schocken Books.

Wagenbach, K. (1984). *Franz Kafka: Pictures of a life*. New York: Random House.

KAHLO AND RIVERA SOURCES

Alcantara, I., & Egnolff, S. (1999). *Frida Kahlo and Diego Rivera*. New York: Prestel Verlag.

Drucker, M. (1991). *Frida Kahlo*. Albuquerque, NM: University of New Mexico Press.

Grimberg, S. (2002). *Frida Kahlo*. North Digton, MA: World Publications Group.

Herrera, H. (1984). *Frida.* New York: Harper Collins.

Herrera, H. (1991). *Frida Kahlo: The paintings.* New York: Harper Collins.

Fuentes, C. (Ed.) (1996). The diary of Frida Kahlo: An intimate self-portrait. New York: Harry N. Abrams.

Kahlo, F. (1995). *The letters of Frida Kahlo: Cartas apasionadas.* San Francisco: Chronicle Books.

Kahlo, F. (2001). *The diary of Frida Kahlo: An intimate self-portrait.* Toledo, Spain: Abradale Press.

Kettenmann, A. (2002). *Frida Kahlo, 1907–1954: Pain and passion.* New York: Barnes & Noble Books. (Original publication 1992, Cologne, Germany: Benedikt Taschen Verlag GmbH.)

Marnham, P. (1998). *Dreaming with his eyes open: A life of Diego Rivera.* New York: Knopf.

Monasterio, P. O. (Ed.). *Frida Kahlo sus fotos.* Mexico: Banguo de Mexico.

Rivera, D. (1991). *My art, my life: An autobiography.* New York: Dover.

KENNEDY FAMILY SOURCES

Andrews, J. D. (1998). *Young Kennedys: The new generation.* New York: Avon.

Collier, P., & Horowitz, D. (1984). *The Kennedys.* New York: Summit Books.

Davis, J. (1969). *The Bouviers: Portrait of an American family.* New York: Farrar, Straus, Giroux.

Davis, J. (1984). *The Kennedys: Dynasty & disaster.* New York: McGraw-Hill.

Davis, J. (1993). *The Bouviers: From Waterloo to the Kennedys and beyond.* Washington, DC: National Press Books.

DuBois, D. (1995). *In her sister's shadow: The bitter legacy of Lee Radziwell.* New York: St. Martin's Press.

Gibson, B., & Schwarz, T. (1993). *The Kennedys: The third generation.* New York: Thunder Mouth's Press.

Gibson, B., & Schwarz, T. (1995). *Rose Kennedy and her family.* New York: Birch Lane Press.

Hamilton, N. (1992). *JFK: Reckless youth.* New York: Random House.

Heymann, C. D. (1989). *A woman named Jackie.* New York: New American Library.

James, A. (1991). *The Kennedy scandals and tragedies.* Lincolnwood, IL: Publications Internations Limited.

Kearns Goodwin, D. (1987). *The Fitzgeralds and the Kennedys.* New York: Simon & Schuster.

Kelley, K. (1978). *Jackie Oh!* Secaucus, NJ: Lyle Stuart.

Kennedy, R. (1974). *Times to remember.* New York: Bantam.

Klein, E. (1998). *Just Jackie: Her private years.* New York: Ballantine.

Klein, E. (2003). *The Kennedy curse.* New York: St. Martin's Press.

Latham, C., & Sakol, J. (1989). *Kennedy encyclopedia.* New York: New American Library.

Leamer, L. (2001). *The Kennedy men: 1901–1963.* New York: Harper Collins.

Maier, T. (2003). *The Kennedys: America's emerald kings.* New York: Basic.

McTaggart, L. (1983) *Kathleen Kennedy: Her life and times.* New York: Dial.

Moutsatos, K. F. (1998). *The Onassis women.* New York: Putnam.

Rachlin, H. (1986). *The Kennedys: A chronological history 1823–present.* New York: World Almanac.

Rainie, H., & Quinn, J. (1983) *Growing up Kennedy: The third wave comes of age.* New York: G.P. Putnam's Sons.

Saunders, F. (1982). *Torn lace curtain: Life with the Kennedys.* New York: Pinnade Books.

KING FAMILY SOURCES

Carson, C. (Ed.). (2001). *The autobiography of Martin Luther King.* New York: Warner Books.

Franklin, V. P. (1998). *Martin Luther King, Jr. biography.* New York: Park Lane Press.

King, M. L., Sr., & Riely, C. (1980). *Daddy King, an autobiography.* New York: Morrow.

Lewis, D. L. (1978). *King: A biography* (2nd ed). Chicago: University of Illinois Press.

Oates, S. B. (1982). *Let the trumpet sound: The life of Martin Luther King, Jr.* New York: New American Library.

ANN LANDERS AND ABBY SOURCES

Howard, M. (2003). *Ann Landers in her own words.* New York: Warner.

Kogan, R. (2003). *America's mom.* New York: HarperCollins.

Pottker, J., & Speziale, B. (1987). *Dear Ann, Dear Abby: The unauthorized biography of Ann Landers and Abigail Van Buren.* New York: Dodd, Mead & Company.

LINCOLN AND TODD SOURCES

Baker, J. (1987). *Mary Todd Lincoln: A biography.* New York: Norton.

Eliot, A. (1985). *Abraham Lincoln: An illustrated biography.* New York: W. H. Smith.

Neely, M. E., & McMurtry, R. G. (1986). *The insanity file: The case of Mary Todd Lincoln.* Carbondale, IL: Southern Illinois University Press.

Oates, S. B. (1977). *With malice toward none: The life of Abraham Lincoln.* New York: New American Library.

Oates, S. B. (1984). *Abraham Lincoln: The man behind the myths.* New York: Harper & Row.

Sandburg, C. (1926). *Abraham Lincoln: The prairie years* (Vols. I–II). New York: Harcourt, Brace & Company.

Schreiner, S. A. (1987). *The trials of Mrs. Lincoln.* New York: Donald I. Fine.

LINDBERGH SOURCES

Lindbergh, R. (1998). *Under a wing: A memoir*. New York: Dell/Random House.

Lindbergh, R. (2003). *Forward from here*. New York: Simon & Schuster.

MAHLER SOURCES

Blaukopf, K. (1985). *Gustav Mahler*. New York: Limelight Editions.

De La Grange, H. (1976). *Mahler*. London: Victor Gollancz Ltd.

De La Grange, H. (1995). *Gustav Mahler: Letters to his wife*. Ithaca, NY: Cornell University Press.

Keegan, S. (1992). *The bride of the wind: The life of Alma Mahler*. New York: Viking.

Lebrecht, N. (2010). *Why Mahler?* New York: Pantheon.

Mahler, A. (1971). *Gustav Mahler: Memories and letters*. Seattle, WA: University of Washington Press.

Martner, K. (Ed.). (1979). *Selected letters of Gustav Mahler*. New York: Farrar, Straus, Giroux.

Monson, K. (1983). *Alma Mahler: Muse to genius*. Boston: Houghton Mifflin.

Secherson, E. (1982). *Mahler*. New York: Omnibus Press.

MARX BROTHERS SOURCES

Adamson, J. (1973). *Groucho, Harpo, Chico, and sometimes Zeppo*. New York: Simon & Schuster.

Arce, H. (1979). *Groucho*. New York: G. P. Putnam's Sons.

Bergan, R. (1992). *The life and times of the Marx Brothers*. London: Green Wood Publishing.

Chandler, C. (1978). *Hello, I must be going: Groucho and his friends*. Garden City, NY: Doubleday.

Crichton, K. (1950). *The Marx brothers*. Garden City, NY: Doubleday.

Marx, A. (1972). *Son of Groucho*. New York: David McKay Co.

Marx, A. (1988). *My life with Groucho*. Fort Lee, NJ: Barricade Books.

Marx, G. (1989). *Groucho and me*. New York: Simon & Schuster.

Marx, G. (1963). *Memoirs of a lover*. New York: Simon & Schuster.

Marx, G. (1967). *The Groucho letters*. New York: Simon & Schuster.

Marx, H., & Barber, R. (1985). *Harpo speaks*. New York: Limelight Editions.

Marx, M. (1986). *Growing up with Chico*. New York: Limelight Editions.

Stables, K. (1992). *The Marx bros*. Greenwich, CN: Brompton Books.

MONROE SOURCES

Barris, G. (1995). *Marilyn: Her life in her own words: Marilyn Monroe's revealing last words and photograph*. New York: Citadel Press.

Leaming, B. (1998). *Marilyn Monroe*. New York: Three Rivers Press.

McDonough, Y. Z. (Ed.). (2005). *All the available light: A Marilyn Monroe reader.* New York: Simon & Schuster.

Monroe, M. (1986). *My story.* Briarcliff Manor, NY: Stein & Day.

Monroe, M. (2001). *My story: Marilyn Monroe.* New York: Cooper Square Press.

Morgan, M. (2007). *Marilyn Monroe: Private and undisclosed.* New York: Carroll & Graf Publishers.

Spoto, D. (2001). *Marilyn Monroe: The biography.* New York: Cooper Square Press.

Summers, A. (2000). *Goddess: The secret lives of Marilyn Monroe.* London: Phoenix Press.

Zimroth, E. (2002). Marilyn at the Mikvah. In Y. Z. McDonough. (Ed.), *All the available light: A Marilyn Monroe reader.* New York: Simon & Schuster.

NEHRU-GANDHI FAMILY SOURCES

Ali, T. (1985). *An Indian dynasty.* New York: Putnam.

Frank, K. (2002). *Indira: The life of Indira Nehru Gandhi.* New York: Houghton-Mifflin.

Nehru, J. (1958). *Autobiography: Toward freedom.* Boston: Beacon.

Gopal, S., & Iyengar, U. (Eds.). (2003). *The essential writings of Jawaharlal Nehru.* Oxford, UK: Oxford University Press.

Nehru, J. (2004). *Letters from a father to his daughter.* New York: Viking Press.

Wolpert, S. (1996). *Nehru.* New York: Oxford University Press.

OBAMA SOURCES

Firstbrook, P. (2010). *The Obamas: The untold story of an African family.* London: Preface Publishing.

Dunham. S. A. (2009). *Surviving against the odds. Durham*, NC: Duke Unviersity Press.

Remnick, D. (2010). The bridge: The life and rise of Barack Obama. New York: Knopf.

Grimes, N., & Collier, B. (2008). *Barack Obama: Son of promise, child of hope.* New York: Simon & Schuster.

Obama, B. (1995). *Dreams from my father: A story of race and inheritance.* New York: Three Rivers Press.

Obama, B. (2008). *The audacity of hope: Thoughts on reclaiming the American dream* (Reprinted ed.). New York: Vintage.

Wolfe, R. (2009). *Renegade: The making of a president.* New York: Crown.

O'NEILL FAMILY SOURCES

Black, S. (1999). *Eugene O'Neill: Beyond mourning and tragedy.* New Haven, CT: Yale University Press.

Bowen, C. (1959). *The curse of the misbegotten.* New York: McGraw-Hill.

Gelb, A., & Gelb, B. (1987). *O'Neill.* New York: Harper & Row.

Scovell, J. (1999) *Oona: Living in the shadows: A biography of Oona O'Neill Chaplin*. New York: Grand Central Publishing.

Sheaffer, L. (1968). *O'Neill: Son and playwright*. Boston: Little, Brown.

Sheaffer, L. (1973). *O'Neill: Son and artist: Volume II*. Boston: Little, Brown.

ROBESON SOURCES

Dean, P. H. (1989). Paul Robeson. In E. Hill (Ed.), *Black heroes: Seven plays* (pp. 27–353). New York: Applause Theatre Book Publishers.

Duberman, M. B. (1988). *Paul Robeson*. New York: Knopf.

Ehrlich, S. (1988). *Paul Robeson: Singer and actor*. New York: Chelsea House Publishers.

Larsen, R. (1989). *Paul Robeson: Hero before his time*. New York: Franklin Watts.

Ramdin, R. (1987). *Paul Robeson: The man and his mission*. London: Peter Owen.

Robeson, P. (1988). *Here I stand*. Boston: Beacon.

ROBINSON SOURCES

Falkner, D. (1995). *Great time coming: The life of Jackie Robinson from baseball to Birmingham*. New York: Simon & Schuster.

Rampersad, A. (1997). *Jackie Robinson: A biography*. New York: Knopf.

Robinson, J. (1972). *I never had it made: An autobiography of Jackie Robinson*. New York: Putnam.

Robinson, R. (1996). *Jackie Robinson: An intimate portrait*. New York: Abrams.

Robinson, S. (1996). *Stealing home*. New York: HarperCollins.

Tygiel, J. (1997). *Baseball's great experiment: Jackie Robinson and his legacy*. New York: Oxford University Press.

ROOSEVELT FAMILY SOURCES

Asbell, B. (Ed.). (1982). *Mother and daughter: The letters of Eleanor and Anna Roosevelt*. New York: Coward McCann & Geoghegan.

Bishop, J. B. (Ed.). (1919). *Theodore Roosevelt's letters to his children*. New York: Charles Scribner's Sons.

Brough, J. (1975). *Princess Alice: A biography of Alice Roosevelt Longworth*. Boston: Little, Brown.

Collier, P., & Horowitz, D. (1994). *The Roosevelts*. New York: Simon & Schuster.

Cook, B. W. (1992). *Eleanor Roosevelt 1884–1933: A life: Mysteries of the heart, Vol. 1*. New York: Viking Penguin.

Cordery, S. A. (2007). *Alice*. New York: Viking.

Donn, L. (2001). *The Roosevelt cousins*. New York: Knopf.

Felsenthal, C. (1988). *Alice Roosevelt Longworth*. New York: G. P. Putnam's Sons.

Fleming, C. (2005). *Our Eleanor*. New York: Simon & Schuster.

Fritz, J. (1991). *Bully for you, Teddy Roosevelt*. New York: G.P. Putnam's Sons.

Hagedorn, H. (1954). *The Roosevelt family of Sagamore Hill*. New York: Macmillan.

Kearns Goodwin, D. (1994). *No ordinary time. Franklin and Eleanor Roosevelt: The home front in World War II*. New York: Simon & Schuster.

Lash, J. P. (1971). *Eleanor and Franklin*. New York: Norton.

McCullough, D. (1981). *Mornings on horseback*. New York: Simon & Schuster.

Miller, N. (1979). *The Roosevelt chronicles*. Garden City, NY: Doubleday.

Miller, N. (1983). *FDR: An intimate biography*. Garden City, NY: Doubleday.

Miller, N. (1994). *Theodore Roosevelt: A life*. New York: Morrow.

Morgan, T. (1985). *FDR: A biography*. New York: Simon & Schuster.

Morris, E. (1979). *The rise of Theodore Roosevelt*. New York: Ballantine.

Pringle, H. F. (1931). *Theodore Roosevelt*. New York: Harcourt, Brace, Jovanovich.

Roosevelt, E. (1984). *The autobiography of Eleanor Roosevelt*. Boston: G. K. Hall.

Roosevelt, E., & Brough, J. (1973). *The Roosevelts of Hyde Park: An untold story*. New York: Putnam.

Roosevelt, E., & Brough, J. (1975). *A rendezvous with destiny: The Roosevelts of the White House*. New York: Dell.

Roosevelt, J. (1976). *My parents: A differing view*. Chicago: The Playboy Press.

Roosevelt, T. (1925). *An autobiography*. New York: Charles Scribner's Sons.

Rowley, H. (2010). *Franklin and Eleanor: An extraordinary marriage*. New York: Farrar, Straus, Giroux.

Streitmatter, R. (Ed.). (1998). *Empty without you: The intimate letters of Eleanor Roosevelt and Lorena Hickok*. New York: Da Capo Press.

Teichman, H. (1979). *Alice: The life and times of Alice Roosevelt*. Englewood Cliffs, NJ: Prentice-Hall.

Youngs, W. T. (1985). *Eleanor Roosevelt: A personal and public life*. Boston: Little, Brown.

SARTRE SOURCES

Cohen-Solal, A. (1987). *Sartre, a life*. New York: Pantheon.

Sartre, J. P. (1964). *The words*. Greenwich, CN: Fawcett.

Madsen, A. (1979). *Hearts and minds: The common journey of Simone de Beauvoir and Jean Paul Sartre*. New York: Morrow Quill Paperback.

SHAW AND PAYNE-TOWNSHEND SOURCES

Brown, M. (2005). *Lawrence of Arabia: The life, the legend*. London: Thames & Hudson.

Dunbar, J. (1963). *Mrs. G.B.S.: A portrait*. New York: Harper & Row.

Holroyd, M. (1988). *Bernard Shaw, Vol. I: The search for love, 1856–1898*. New York: Random House.

Holroyd, M. (1989). *Bernard Shaw, Vol. II: The pursuit of power, 1989–1918*. New York: Random House.

Holroyd, M. (1991). *Bernard Shaw, Vol. III: The lure of fantasy, 1918–1951*. New York: Random House.

TOLSTOY SOURCES

de Courcel, M. (1980). *Tolstoy: The ultimate reconciliation*. New York: Charles Scribner's Sons.

Edwards, A. (1981). *Sonya: The life of countess Tolstoy*. New York: Simon & Schuster.

Maude, A. (1987). *The life of Tolstoy* (Vols. I and II). New York: Oxford University Press.

Simmons, E. J. (1960). *Leo Tolstoy* (Vols. I and II). New York: Vintage.

Smoluchowski, L. (1987). *Lev & Sonya: The story of the Tolstoy marriage*. New York: G. P. Putnam's Sons.

Stilman, L. (Ed.). (1960). *Leo Tolstoy: Last diaries*. New York: G. P. Putnam's Sons.

Tolstoy, L. (1964). *Childhood, boyhood, youth*. Baltimore: Penguin.

Tolstoy, N. (1983). *The Tolstoys: Twenty-four generations of Russian history*. New York: William Morrow.

Troyat, H. (1967). *Tolstoy*. New York: Dell.

Wilson, A. N. (1988). *Tolstoy*. New York: Norton.

QUEEN VICTORIA SOURCES

Auchincloss, L. (1979). *Persons of consequence: Queen Victoria and her circle*. New York: Random House.

Benson, E. F. (1987). *Queen Victoria*. London: Chatto & Windus.

Ferguson, S., & Stoney, B. (1991). *Victoria and Albert: Family life at Osborne House*. New York: Prentice-Hall.

Hibbert, C. (1984). *Queen Victoria in her letters and journals*. London: Penguin.

James, R. R. (1983). *Prince Albert*. New York: Knopf.

Strachey, L. (1921). *Queen Victoria*. New York: Harcourt, Brace, Jovanovich.

Weintraub, S. (1987). *Victoria*. New York: E. P. Dutton.

Wilson, E. (1990). *Emminent victorians*. New York: Norton.

Woodham-Smith, C. (1972). *Queen Victoria*. New York: Donald Fine, Inc.

WASHINGTON SOURCES

Bourne, M. A. (1982). *First family: George Washington and his intimate relations*. New York: Norton.

Ellis, J. J. (2004). *His excellency: George Washington*. New York: Knopf.

Furstenberg, F. (2006). *In the name of the father: Washington's legacy, slavery and the making of a nation*. New York: Penguin.

Johnson, P. (2005). *George Washington: The founding father.* New York: Harper Collins.

Randall, W. S. (1997). *George Washington: A life.* New York: Henry Holt.

Wiencek, H. (2003). *An imperfect god: George Washington, his slaves and the creation of America.* New York: Farrar, Strauss & Giroux.

WRIGHT FAMILY SOURCES

Crouch, T. D. (1989) *The Bishop's boys: A life of Wilbur and Orville Wright.* New York: Norton.

Howard, F. (1987). *Wilbur and Orville: A biography of the Wright brothers.* New York: Knopf.

Kelly, F. C. (1989). *The Wright brothers: A biography.* New York: Dover.

Kinnane, A. (1982). *The crucible of flight.* Unpublished manuscript.

Kinnane, A. (1988, Spring). A house united: Morality and invention in the Wright brothers' home. *Psychohistory Review, 367–397.*

Mackersey, I. (2003). *The Wright brothers: The remarkable story of the aviation pioneers who changed the world.* New York: Time/Warner.

Maurer, R. (2003). *The Wright sister.* Brookfield, CT: Millbrook Press.

Miller, I. W. (1978). *Wright reminiscences.* Dayton, OH: Privately printed.

Renstrom, A. G. (1975). *Wilbur and Orville Wright: A chronology commemorating the one hundredth anniversary of the birth of Orville Wright.* Washington, DC: Library of Congress.

Walsh, J. E. (1975). *One day at Kitty Hawk: The untold story of the Wright brothers and the airplane.* New York: Crowell.

Wright, M. (1999). *Diaries: 1857–1917.* Dayton, OH: Wright State University.

Index

Note: Italicized page locators indicate a figure or photo.

Eleanor Roosevelt's intense bond with, 187, 189, 190, 191

Franz Kafka's relationship with, 192, 194, 195

gender-related roles and child's expectations of, 185–86

Mary Catherine Bateson's relationship with, 317, 320–25

Simone de Beauvoir's relationship with, 199, 202

female socialization, opening up closed family system and, 341

Ferenczi, Sándor, 220

fighting, distance maintained with, 107, 108, 109

finances, secrets around, 79, 82

firstborns, characteristics of, 219–22, 224

Fishel, Elizabeth, 206

Fitzgerald, John Francis ("Honey Fitz"), 161, 164, 165

Fitzgerald, Josie Hannon (Mrs. John Francis Fitzgerald), 164, 165

Fitzwilliam, Peter, 168

Fleiss, Wilhelm, 174

Fonda, Henry, 79

Fonda, Jane, 79

Fonda, Peter, 79

Fonda, Susan (Mrs. Henry Fonda), 79

Fonda family

genogram for, *80–81*

suicide in, 79

forbidden love, patterns in families of origin and, 244

foster parents, children raised by, 186

founding fathers (U.S.), problematic relationships with mothers and, 53

Franklin, Benjamin

ambivalent relationship between father and, 50–51

biographers of, on omissions in writings of, 50

contradictory impressions of, 34–35, 38

excerpt of letter to son William, 48–49

family "program" and name chosen for, 41

genogram of, *37–38*

identification with his Uncle Tom by, 39–40

lack of information about mother of, 53

looking at from family systems perspective, 51–52

multigenerational pattern of cutoffs in family of, 28–29

pivotal role of deaths in family of, 38, 39, 137

questions arising from genogram of, 51

repetition of illegitimacy in family of, 49–50

secrecy surrounding birth and parentage of son William, 49–50

as youngest child in family, 224, 226

Franklin, Benjamin, Sr., 39, 41, 44, 50–51, 52

Franklin, Deborah (Mrs. Benjamin Franklin), 49

Franklin, Ebenezer, 38

Franklin, Ellen, 44, 49

Franklin, James, 28, 39

Franklin, John, 39

Franklin, Josiah, Jr., 38, 39, 44

Franklin, Josiah, Sr., 38, 44, 45

Franklin, Temple, 44, 49

Franklin, Thomas, 38, 52

Franklin, Tom, 39, 52

Franklin, William, 28, 44, 50, 51

excerpt from Benjamin Franklin's letter to, 48–49

secrecy surrounding birth and parentage of, 49–50

fraternal twins, 211

Frazer, Rebecca, 66

French families, class and, 302

Freud, Alexander, 41, 220

Freud, Amalia, 171, 175

Freud, Anna (daughter), 174, 175

Freud, Anna (sister), 171, 220

Freud, Jacob, 171, 174, 175

Freud, Julius, 41, 171, 175

Freud, Martin, 174

Freud, Minna, 174

Freud, Sigmund, 171, 259

anti-Semitism and lifework of, 294

family secrets of, 24

name chosen for, 41

sibling relationships ignored in writings of, 207, 220

special family position for, 219–20

Freud, Sophie, 175

Freud family, 137

genogram for, *172–73*

migration, trauma and, 294

pattern repetitions and legacy of loss in, 171, 174–75

Friedman, Esther Pauline ("Ann Landers"), 212, *213,* 299, 300, 301

Friedman, Margo, 301

Friedman, Pauline Esther ("Dear Abby"), 212, *213,* 299, 300

friendships, marriage and, 246

friends of family, as sources of family information, 58

funerals

reconnecting with family at, 327

rituals around, 139

fusion

in Bronte family, tragic losses and, 61

cutoff and, 111, 115, 117

in O'Neill family, 115, 117–18

triangulation and tracking patterns of, 134